A RHETORIC FOR
WRITING TEACHERS

A RHETORIC FOR WRITING TEACHERS

FOURTH EDITION

Erika Lindemann

with Daniel Anderson

New York   Oxford
OXFORD UNIVERSITY PRESS
2001

Oxford University Press

Oxford   New York
Athens   Auckland   Bangkok   Bogotá   Buenos Aires   Calcutta
Cape Town   Chennai   Dar es Salaam   Delhi   Florence   Hong Kong   Istanbul
Karachi   Kuala Lumpur   Madrid   Melbourne   Mexico City   Mumbai
Nairobi   Paris   São Paulo   Shanghai   Singapore   Taipei   Tokyo   Toronto Warsaw

and associated companies in
Berlin   Ibadan

Copyright © 1982, 1987, 1995, 2001 by Erika Lindemann

Published by Oxford University Press, Inc.
198 Madison Avenue, New York, New York 10016
http://www.oup-usa.org

Oxford is a registered trademark of Oxford University Press.

Library of Congress Cataloging-in-Publication Data
Lindemann, Erika.
  A rhetoric for writing teachers / by Erika Lindemann.—4th ed.
    p. cm.
  ISBN 0-19-513045-6 (pbk.)
    1. English language—Rhetoric—Study and teaching.   2. Report writing—Study and
  teaching (Higher)   I. Title.

  PE1404.L53 2001
  808'.042'071—dc21   00-046515

Since this page cannot legibly accommodate all the copyright notices,
pages xiii–xv constitute an extension of the copyright page.

Printing (last digit): 9 8 7 6 5

Printed in the United States of America
on acid-free paper

For my nieces and nephews

Contents

Preface

All teachers stand on the shoulders of others. Writing teachers are especially generous about sharing what works well in their classrooms. They
routinely exchange writing assignments, ideas for in-class activities,
handouts, and lesson plans. Their conversations, even those tinged with
frustration, demonstrate a confidence in their students' abilities and a
conviction that good writing and good teaching matter. Profoundly
grateful to be in such company, I have tried in this book to explain
some of the lessons that these good colleagues have taught me—about
students, about writing, and about teaching.

The fourth edition of *A Rhetoric for Writing Teachers* appears almost
twenty years after the first edition was published. During that time, the
field of composition studies has grown tremendously, so much so that
one book cannot embrace all that we have learned about helping students
become confident writers. The view that composing is a social as well
as an individual act, shaped by and shaping our interactions with others,
has become commonplace. It has prompted teachers to design meaningful assignments that accomplish real communication, to guide students
toward becoming effective collaborators in the classroom, and to respond
to students' writing by attending to the message and not just to the
surface features of a text.

In some ways, teaching writing also has become more difficult than
it was when this book first appeared. In many places, writing classes
are still too large. Many writing teachers are undervalued, especially in
institutions that exploit part-time labor or that assign teachers trained
in other fields to English language arts classes. Today's classrooms also
present challenges for teachers who applaud but may not know how to
capitalize on the astonishing diversity of backgrounds, abilities, and first
languages that their students bring to school. And for all teachers, new
technologies present both problems and possibilities that we could not
even have imagined a generation ago.

In preparing this edition, I have tried to keep in mind an audience of
prospective classroom teachers, readers who want an introduction to
their important work with students. Their interests have prompted my
selection of materials and just as often restrained me from going into

too much detail. Chapters have been updated, and "Some Important Dates in the History of Composition and Rhetoric" now includes significant developments in the field from 1969 to 1987. The "List of Works Consulted" has been expanded to include videocassettes and Internet sites as well as traditional forms of scholarship. It also has been reorganized into twelve categories to make finding materials on particular topics less frustrating. My colleague, Daniel Anderson, has contributed a valuable chapter on teaching writing with computers. I am grateful not only for his generosity in sharing his expertise but also for the many ways in which he daily, patiently encourages the mouse-challenged to rethink their teaching.

I owe special thanks to those readers who suggested ways to improve this book: the students in Robert Parham's composition classes at Armstrong Atlantic State University, Stephanie Almagno, and Richard Leahy. D. Anthony English of Oxford University Press offered generous encouragement and experienced advice, and Justin Collins deserves my gratitude for his professionalism and significant help in seeing the manuscript through production.

I hope that this book will raise as many questions as it answers. Because you have lived in classrooms most of your life and experienced firsthand both the pleasures and frustrations of writing, be assured that you already know a great deal about teaching composition. That knowledge-born-of-experience will serve you well. But other kinds of knowing can be just as important. You also can learn much about teaching writing from talking with yourself, with other teachers, with students, and with this and other books. The theories, teaching practices, and conventional wisdom set forth here originate in just such conversations, in the talk of people who persistently reflect on what it means to teach well. Welcome to that conversation. And best wishes for every success in your teaching.

Chapel Hill   E. L.
1 August 2000

Acknowledgments

Theron Alexander, "The Individual and Social Change." Reprinted from *Intellect*, December 1974. Copyright 1974 by the Society for the Advancement of Education.

Robert Bain, "Reading Student Papers," *College Composition and Communication* 25 (October 1974), 307–09. Reprinted by permission of the National Council of Teachers of English and the author.

David Bartholomae, "Teaching Basic Writing: An Alternative to Basic Skills," *Journal of Basic Writing* 2 (Spring/Summer 1979), 85–109. Copyright 1979 by the *Journal of Basic Writing*.

Roy Blount, Jr., *Crackers* (Alfred A. Knopf, 1980). Copyright © 1980 by Roy Blount, Jr. Reprinted by permission of Random House, Inc.

James Britton et al., *The Development of Writing Abilities, 11-18* (Schools Council Research Studies, Macmillan Education, 1975).

James Britton, *Language and Learning* (Boynton/Cook, 1993). Copyright © James Britton, 1970. Reprinted by permission of Heinemann.

The Common Sense of Science by Jacob Bronowski, Cambridge, Massachusetts, Harvard University Press, Copyright © 1953. Reprinted by permission of Harvard University Press and Heinemann.

Kenneth Burke, *A Grammar of Motives*. Copyright © 1969 by The Regents of the University of California. Reprinted by permission of the Regents of the University of California and the University of California Press.

Kenneth Burke, "Rhetoric—Old and New," *Journal of General Education* 5 (April 1951), 203–09.

Forrest Burt, ed., *The Effective Writer: A Freshman English Manual*. Copyright © 1978 by Forrest Burt. Reprinted by permission.

Francis Christensen and Bonniejean Christensen, *Notes toward a New Rhetoric*, 2d ed. Copyright © 1978 by Bonniejean Christensen. Reprinted by permission of HarperCollins Publishers, Inc.

Richard Coe, *Process, Form, and Substance: A Rhetoric for Advanced Writers*, 2d ed. Copyright 1990 by Prentice Hall.

Conference on College Composition and Communication, "Resolution on Testing and Writing" (1978). Reprinted by permission of the National Council of Teachers of English.

Charles Cooper, "An Outline for Writing Sentence- Combining Problems," *English Journal* 62 (January 1973), 96–102, 108. Reprinted by permission of the National Council of Teachers of English.

Charles Cooper, "Responding to Student Writing," in *The Writing Processes of Students* (1975). Reprinted by permission of the author.

Charles Cooper and Lee Odell, eds., *Evaluating Writing: Describing, Measuring, Judging.* Copyright © 1977 by the National Council of Teachers of English. Reprinted by permission of the publisher.

Marilyn M. Cooper and Michael Holzman, *Writing as Social Action* (Boynton/ Cook, 1989). Reprinted by permission of Heinemann.

Edward P. J. Corbett, *The Little Rhetoric and Handbook,* 2d ed. Copyright © 1982 by Scott, Foresman and Company. Reprinted by permission of Addison-Wesley Educational Publishers, Inc.

Frank J. D'Angelo, *A Conceptual Theory of Rhetoric.* Copyright © 1975. Reprinted by permission of the author.

Frank J. D'Angelo, "A Generative Rhetoric of the Essay," *College Composition and Communication* 25 (December 1974), 388–89. Reprinted by permission of the National Council of Teachers of English.

Frank J. D'Angelo, *Process and Thought in Composition,* 3d ed. Copyright © 1985 by Frank J. D'Angelo. Reprinted by permission of the author.

Lisa Ede and Andrea Lunsford, "Audience Addressed/Audience Invoked: The Role of Audience in Composition Theory and Pedagogy," *College Composition and Communication* 35 (May 1984), 155–71. Reprinted by permission of the National Council of Teachers of English.

Peter Elbow, *Writing without Teachers.* Copyright © 1973. Reprinted by permission of Oxford University Press, Inc.

Linda S. Flower and John R. Hayes, "The Dynamics of Composing: Making Plans and Juggling Constraints," and John R. Hayes and Linda S. Flower, "Identifying the Organization of Writing Processes," in *Cognitive Processes in Writing,* ed. Lee W. Gregg and Erwin R. Steinberg. Copyright © 1980 by Lawrence Erlbaum Associates, Inc. Reprinted by permission of the publisher and authors.

Diana Hacker and Betty Renshaw, *Writing with a Voice: A Rhetoric and Handbook.* Copyright © 1989 Diana Hacker and Betty Renshaw. Reprinted by permission of HarperCollins College Publishers.

Edward B. Jenkinson and Donald A. Seybold, "Prologue," from *Writing as a Process of Discovery.* Copyright © 1970. Reprinted by permission.

James L. Kinneavy, *A Theory of Discourse.* Copyright © 1980 by W. W. Norton, Inc. Reprinted by permission of the author.

Ann Landers, letter from "Eyes Opened" appeared in the *Miami Herald,* July 1979. Permission granted by Ann Landers and Creators Syndicate.

Richard A. Lanham, *Revising Prose,* 4th ed. Copyright © 2000 by Allyn and Bacon. Reprinted by permission.

Guy R. Lefrancois, *Of Children: An Introduction to Child Development,* 8th ed. Copyright © 1995. Reprinted with permission of Wadsworth, an imprint of the Wadsworth Group, a division of Thomson Learning. Fax: 800 730-2215.

Marcia B. Baxter Magolda, *Knowing and Reasoning in College: Gender-Related Patterns in Students' Intellectual Development*. Copyright © 1992 by Jossey-Bass, Inc., Publishers. Reprinted by permission of John Wiley and Sons, Inc.

William E. Mahaney, *Workbook of Current English*. Copyright © 1978 by McGraw-Hill Book Company.

Donald M. Murray, "Internal Revision: A Process of Discovery," in *Research on Composing*, ed. Charles Cooper and Lee Odell. Copyright © 1978 by the National Council of Teachers of English. Reprinted by permission of the publisher.

NCTE Commission on Composition, "Teaching Composition: A Position Statement," *College English* 46 (October 1984), 612–14. Reprinted by permission of the National Council of Teachers of English.

Elizabeth Cowan Neeld, *Writing*, 3d ed. Copyright © 1990, 1986, 1980 by Scott, Foresman and Company. Reprinted by permission of HarperCollins College Publishers.

Talcott Parsons, *The Social System*, new ed. (1991). Reprinted by permission of Routledge.

William T. Reilly, memorandum, 1 October 1976. Reprinted with permission.

Joseph Ryan, "The Function and Format of a Course Syllabus" and "Checklist for a Course Syllabus." Reprinted by permission of the author.

Mina P. Shaughnessy, *Errors and Expectations*. Copyright © 1977 by Mina P. Shaughnessy. Reprinted by permission of Oxford University Press, Inc.

Nancy Sommers, "Revision Strategies of Student Writers and Experienced Writers," *College Composition and Communication* 31 (December 1980), 378–88. Reprinted by permission of the National Council of Teachers of English.

Karl Wallace, "*Topoi* and the Problem of Invention," *Quarterly Journal of Speech* 58 (December 1972), 387–95. Used by permission of the Speech Communication Association.

Constance Weaver, *Grammar for Teachers: Perspectives and Definitions*. Copyright © 1979 by the National Council of Teachers of English. Reprinted by permission of the publisher.

Glenn R. Williston, *Understanding the Main Idea, Middle Level*. Copyright 1976 by Jamestown Publishers, Providence, Rhode Island. Reprinted by permission.

W. Ross Winterowd, *The Contemporary Writer*, 2d ed. Copyright © 1981 by Harcourt Brace Jovanovich, Inc. Reprinted by permission.

part one

THE COMPOSING PROCESS

one

Why Teach Writing?

> Read not to contradict and confute; nor to believe and take for granted; nor to find talk and discourse; but to weigh and consider.
>
> FRANCIS BACON

Teaching writing can be enormously rewarding. We may value our work for different reasons, but to give our teaching purpose, to justify our energies, we must believe that our efforts make a difference. Unfortunately, our self-esteem may be assaulted by parents, legislators, business and professional people, even other teachers, who charge that we are not doing an especially effective job. If we become preoccupied with reacting to what we perceive as criticism, we may neglect to assert the validity, even the necessity, of our work. Experienced teachers know that writing can be taught, that it has become increasingly important to teach it well. They observe growth in their students and know how to adapt their teaching to individual learning styles. They read books and articles to improve their work. They try different teaching methods, searching for and refining those that work best. Dedicated teachers know failure as well as the quiet sense of accomplishment that results from a student's victory over a persistent writing problem.

Most beginning teachers, however, have not had the opportunity to develop a philosophy of teaching. They remember how they were taught; they read; they listen to others suggest what writing courses ought to do—but evaluating the information is difficult. Until they develop a conceptual framework to help them sort out what they read and hear, they must teach by trial and error. They must adopt someone else's assumptions until they formulate their own.

This book should help facilitate that process. Although you will find in it unmistakable evidence of my assumptions about teaching writing, I do not suppose you will agree with all of them. Examine them against your own experiences as a writer, a student, and a teacher. You may want to reject some ideas, modify others, and use the rest to shape your own philosophy of teaching. By such a process of discovery, each of us defines for ourselves what it means to teach well.

WRITING AS ECONOMIC POWER

Presumably teaching writing has value because using written English well is a form of power. Yet is that assumption still true in our telephone, television, multiple-choice-test society? In grade eight we tell students that they will need to write well for high school classes, when in fact some students complete high school without writing much at all. In high school we tell students that they will need to write term papers and essays in college, when in fact students who eventually go to college may never write term papers and essays, except perhaps in first-year composition classes. We tell college students that they must write well to realize their professional goals after graduation, when in fact some of our students will become members of highly paid professions without learning to write well. Lawyers, for instance, often consult books of sample letters and briefs rather than write their own. Politicians outline their speeches along certain lines but leave the actual drafting to paid staff writers. Members of other professions do not compose their own letters, memos, or reports; they dictate them or fill out preprinted forms to request parts and services and complete other business transactions. Although our students cannot escape all writing, many of them (more than writing teachers want to think about) do get diplomas, degrees, and jobs without needing to write much or well.

The argument that writing well opens doors to many satisfying, lucrative professions no longer holds up as well as it used to. However, even though many entry-level jobs do not demand exceptional writing skills, students applying for these positions are instantly branded as illiterates if their resumes or letters contain misspelled words. Employees create similarly adverse impressions on the job if responses to memos, notes left for secretaries, and brief reports written for supervisors are confusing. The ability to write well still creates economic power. If we will examine, together with our students, the kinds of writing required in jobs that interest them, they will discover important work-related reasons to improve their skills. Students who need college degrees to enter their chosen fields must write well enough to satisfy professors in their major, faculty members who regard effective communication an essential professional skill:[1]

> An engineer, without the tools of communication, is unable to sell his [or her] ideas, no matter how good those ideas are. (C. L. Gilmore, Industrial Engineering)

1. The quotations from faculty members and employers appear in Forrest Burt, ed., *The Effective Writer: A Freshman English Manual* (Boston: American Press, 1978), back cover.

Proficiency in written English is a must for a public school teacher who nourishes any hope at all of establishing credibility as a professional. (David G. Armstrong, Educational Curriculum & Instruction)

Most students consider English a waste of time. Yet, I get letters from former students thanking me for the strict approach I took toward writing. (D. Saylak, Civil Engineering)

Once students enter a profession, they will find important correlations between writing well and professional advancement. Although writing well may not guarantee promotion, writing poorly jeopardizes success. Employers expect written communications to be clear and concise:

Inadequate communication skills will have a direct bearing on a college graduate's promotion opportunities. (A. K. Butler, Associate Director of Personnel, Continental Oil Company [CONOCO])

My major criticism of the written communications of our newly hired graduates is that they write too much or too little. The knack of effective communication is to give all that is needed for complete understanding, but no more. (Paul J. Wolfe, Executive Vice President, Mobil Oil Corporation)

WRITING AS SOCIAL NECESSITY

The ability to write well is also important because language is indispensable to living in society. Human beings are social animals who use language to make sense of the world. We write grocery lists to help us remember what to buy at the supermarket. We take notes at meetings, during telephone conversations, as we read, to remind ourselves of significant details. Travelogues, diaries, and other first-person documents also represent ways of talking to the self, of making sense out of countless experiences we must integrate if our daily lives are to have meaning. Even though this kind of writing may appear to be private, intended only for ourselves, we find the "sense" of what we write in a context shaped by others. We write to remember and to organize our lives, necessary functions of living in societies.

Writing is also an established form of social commitment. Hotel reservations and cancellations, consumer complaints, contracts, warranties, changes of address, most financial and legal transactions do not become official until the parties receive notice in writing. We establish orderly, formal relationships between people with pen and paper, not by telephone or through informal conversation. Ask politicians, administrators, or bureaucrats to commit spoken statements to paper, and they become decidedly uncomfortable. In our society, "putting it in writing" has greater force than speaking.

WRITING AS KNOWING

Writing also helps us solve problems. The "problem" may be personal, as it is in the following letter to Ann Landers:

Dear Ann: I'm a 26-year-old woman and I feel like a fool asking you this question, but—should I marry the guy or not? Jerry is 30, but sometimes he acts like 14. We have gone together nearly a year. He was married for three years but never talks about it. My parents haven't said anything either for or against him, but I know deep down they don't like him much.

Jerry is a salesman and makes good money but he has lost his wallet three times since I've known him and I've had to help him meet the payments on his car.

The thing that bothers me most, I think, is that I have the feeling he doesn't trust me. After every date he telephones. He says it's to "say an extra goodnight" but I'm sure he is checking to see if I had a late date with someone else.

One night I was in the shower and didn't hear the phone. He came over and sat on the porch all night. I found him asleep on the swing when I went to get the paper the next morning at 6:30 A.M. I had a hard time convincing him I had been in the house the whole time. Now on the plus side: Jerry is very good-looking and appeals to me physically. Well—that does it. I have been sitting here with this pen in my hand for 15 minutes trying to think of something else good to say about him and nothing comes to mind. Don't bother to answer this. You have helped me more than you will ever know.—Eyes Opened (*The Miami Herald*, July 22, 1978)

The real audience for this letter is not Ann Landers but "Eyes Opened," who debates with herself the merits of marrying Jerry. Most of us have had similar experiences. Writing may have helped us sort out a misunderstanding with a friend, plan a vacation, or make an important decision.

The problems writing helps us solve are not necessarily personal. Although investigators sometimes begin research projects because some personal experience has roused their curiosity, eventually they must explain the subject objectively. They must record their attempts to find logic in experience. Books, articles, technical reports, laws, and creeds represent solutions to problems, answers to questions human beings must ask because they are aware of their surroundings. Their need to know eventually becomes a need to share their knowledge with others. In one sense, then, all writing solves a problem: How can I communicate my understanding of this subject to my reader?

Writing permits us to understand not only the world but also the self. We discover who we are by writing. College students, for example, write to acquire particular ways of communicating ideas *as* historians, economists, educators, engineers. They learn the professional dialect that their discipline sanctions and the forms of written discourse appropriate for communication among its members. In the humanities and in some academic settings (but not all), the essay remains the sanctioned form for expressing our professional selves. Rarely, however, does the essay satisfy the formal demands of writing tasks that doctors, social workers, hotel managers, and pharmacists encounter. Those professions have their own special jargons and characteristic forms. Mastering them enables students to *be* doctors or social workers or managers, enables them to understand what they read and how to communicate in writing with their colleagues.

THE HUMANISTIC PERSPECTIVE

Writing teachers confront paradoxes. Because we acknowledge a world dominated by mass media and sometimes narrow definitions of "professionalism," we help students develop those writing skills that will advance their careers. At the same time, we also recognize that writing does not serve merely a utilitarian function. That is why we encourage students to appreciate writing that discovers meaning, form, and self. Writers write because they have to; they must explore their experiences and locate themselves in relation to a complex society. *Because* other media threaten to re-create us as plastic people, Disney delusions, and Madison Avenue stereotypes, we want students to write honestly, with a kind of tough sensitivity, about subjects that matter to them.

Learning to write well, then, has value far beyond any power to bring in a paycheck or pass a course. Students will not underestimate the importance of a good salary or a passing grade, but they also can come to appreciate a skill that helps them relate ideas, solve problems, make sense of their experiences, and manipulate a complex symbol system to influence others. The uniquely human ability to use language, to create meaning, enables us to share experiences and transfer knowledge. It also can separate us, especially when our use of language creates misunderstanding or deceives. Writing teachers must place themselves at the center of this paradox, encouraging their students to use language effectively for a variety of purposes and audiences.

Obviously, then, we teach more than comma rules and topic sentences. We teach students how writing discovers the self and shares it with others. In "Imagination and Discipline in the Writing Class," Richard Gebhardt suggests that "it makes little sense for English teachers to square off in defense of either 'lock-step instruction in prose mechanics' or 'freedom that comes from avoiding the rules.' Instead, writing teachers should realize that, in spite of differences in emphasis, the teaching of writing involves both discipline and imagination" (p. 28). We must resist any inclination to define our work too narrowly. Students who know what conjunctions are but cannot use them in a sentence need our help as much as students who have "good ideas" but present them in hopelessly written form. Both the ideas and their presentation, both the product and the process that generates it, should concern us.

The significance of this broader perspective is not so much *what* it includes, but *that* it includes everything. An effective writing teacher needs to know much more than can be found in most composition guides and grammar handbooks. The "discipline" to which we belong is housed not only in English departments but also in linguistics, psychology, sociology, education, and other fields that contribute to our understanding of how human beings communicate. We are members of an interdisciplinary profession, rooted in the humanities, certainly, but borrowing important insights from the sciences and social sciences too.

AN OVERVIEW OF THIS BOOK

What, then, must we know to teach writing well? We must know both the practical and the theoretical, two senses of "knowing" that Gilbert Ryle calls knowing *how* and knowing *that*:

> In ordinary life . . . as well as in the special business of teaching, we are much more concerned with people's competences than with their cognitive repertoires, with the operations [knowing how] than with the truths [knowing that] that they learn. Indeed even when we are concerned with their intellectual excellences and deficiencies, we are interested less in the stock of truths that they acquire and retain than in their capacities to find out truths for themselves and their ability to organise and exploit them, when discovered. (*The Concept of Mind*, p. 28; bracketed material is my addition)

Most of the chapters in this book discuss the practice of teaching writing. They describe *how* we can guide students through the composing process. The pedagogical emphasis is especially evident in Chapter 7 (Prewriting Techniques), Chapter 8 (Shaping Discourse), Chapter 9 (Teaching Paragraphing), Chapter 10 (Teaching about Sentences), Chapter 11 (Teaching about Words), and Chapter 12 (Teaching Rewriting), where our performance as teachers most crucially affects our students' performance as writers. Chapter 13 (Developing Writing Assignments), Chapter 14 (Responding to Student Writing), Chapter 15 (Designing Writing Courses), and Chapter 16 (Teaching Writing with Computers) also emphasize practice, suggesting strategies for making our performance as teachers more effective.

Although *how*-knowledge may seem most useful to a writing teacher, *that*-knowledge is equally important. Understandably, we find the day-to-day practice of teaching so time-consuming that we tend to disregard theoretical concerns. Reading students' papers, not theory, occupies our evenings at home. Nevertheless a theoretical understanding of what writing involves is crucial to our work. In the first place, that-knowledge explains why particular practices seem more appropriate than others. When we command a theoretical framework that explains our activities, we are better able to evaluate student performance, revise courses, and justify our work to interested parents and administrators.

Second, that-knowledge helps us solve teaching problems. Suppose, for example, that you have been teaching average college students. Next semester, however, you plan to teach advanced composition or to tutor students in a writing center. If you command a sufficiently broad theoretical understanding of your work, you can apply your knowledge to the new context and avoid wasting a semester in hit-and-miss experimentation. Or, suppose a student who has been working faithfully on sentence-combining exercises suddenly begins writing sentence fragments. With a knowledge of linguistic theory, you can diagnose the problem and help the student overcome it.

Three chapters in this book are essentially theoretical: Chapter 4 (What Do Teachers Need to Know about Rhetoric?), Chapter 5 (What Do Teachers Need to Know about Linguistics?), and Chapter 6 (What Do Teachers Need to Know about Cognition?). These chapters are not meant to be comprehensive or detailed discussions. Of necessity, they can only summarize important rhetorical, linguistic, and psychological scholarship that bears on our teaching. They describe principles and methodologies in other fields so that you may understand why certain teaching practices are successful given what we know, theoretically, about how human beings communicate. Chapters 4, 5, and 6 cannot substitute for primary sources. If a particular work or point of view piques your curiosity, your next step is to consult the original texts. If those texts lead you to others, so much the better.

As you will discover in reading Chapter 2 (What Is Writing?) and Chapter 3 (What Does the Process Involve?), distinctions between theory and practice are not always clean. The theories discussed in these chapters evolved from observing how people write. When we apply these theories to our teaching, they guide our daily practice in the classroom. But when our teaching raises questions theories cannot answer, we must revise them to incorporate what we have observed in the practice of teaching. Theory suggests practice; practice tests theory and may spawn new theories. Both that-knowledge and how-knowledge are indispensable to writing teachers. Although theories in and of themselves make fascinating study for some people, you may be tempted to slight them to get to more practical matters discussed in other chapters. Resist the temptation if you can, for theories give coherence and direction to the practical. They demonstrate the complexities of the writing process and the importance of teaching it well.

two
_____

What Is Writing?

Writing is just work—there's no secret. If you dictate or use a pen or type or write with your toes—it is still just work.

SINCLAIR LEWIS

Writing is a process of communication that uses a conventional graphic system to convey a message to a reader. Let's examine this working definition in detail. Writing is

- a process of communication
- that uses a conventional graphic system
- to convey a message
- to a reader.

All processes of communication have elements in common. "Who says what to whom" characterizes written messages as well as spoken ones. This chapter describes those elements, the ingredients we combine in varying proportions to compose written and spoken messages. How we combine them, "the *process* of communication," is the subject of Chapter 3. Although this chapter concerns itself primarily with the rhetorical context that shapes students' papers, keep in mind that teaching is a process of communication too. Classroom talk, student-teacher conferences, and comments written on students' papers also represent contexts in which teachers convey messages to students.

The working definition of writing given at the beginning of this chapter specifically names three elements present in any rhetorical context: a conventional graphic system, a message, and a reader. The statement "who says what to whom" introduces a fourth element, a "who" or writer. The so-called "communication triangle" (which does not include the graphic system) introduces the subject, the larger reality (topic) from which writers draw the more narrow, specific message (thesis).

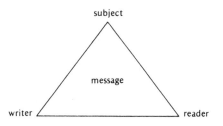

The communication triangle offers students a useful model for defining rhetorical problems such as those framed by most writing assignments. The terms are relatively simple, and the diagram establishes relationships between terms. In formulating questions about those relationships, we can help students plan their response to the assignment:

> What do I know about my subject? (writer–subject relationship)
>
> Who is my audience? (writer–reader relationship)
>
> What does my audience need to know to understand the subject? (reader–subject relationship)

Roman Jakobson's diagram represents a more elaborate version of the communication triangle ("Linguistics and Poetics," p. 353). Because his model contains six terms, it offers a more complex view of the rhetorical context in which writing occurs. As teachers, we need a more detailed understanding of that context than we might expect of our students.

context
message

addresser   addressee

contact
code

Because Jakobson intended the diagram primarily to explain "factors inalienably involved in verbal communication," some of his terms differ from those used in other models. Let's examine each term as it applies specifically to writing.

THE ADDRESSER

The addresser or writer composes the message. In our classes the most important addresser is the student writer, a complicated human being whose experiences, perspectives, and unique language shape every feature of written discourse. Teachers who assume that they are instructing "beginning writers" are mistaken. Most of our students have been writing for many years; they have been immersed in language from birth. Although they may lack confidence with the conventions of written English expected in school, they bring to our classes considerable experience with language. To teach them well we must know as much about them as we have time to learn and patience to discover. Otherwise, we can't determine whether our teaching enhances or interferes with their ability to write effectively.

Today's classrooms are complex places that bring together students of extraordinarily diverse backgrounds. They may be older students returning to school after years of working or caring for families. They may be immigrants or children who grew up in households in which languages other than English were spoken. In Los Angeles, for example, more than 100 languages are represented among students attending public schools, and in other parts of the country, Asian and Hispanic students are no longer a minority. Many classrooms also are more hospitable than they once were toward students with physical, emotional, and learning problems. Even in classrooms that seem relatively homogeneous, we need to be aware that all writers compose messages from unique frames of reference. Most teachers respond to this diversity by individualizing instruction as much as possible. If we also remember that every addresser is an expert, certainly about his or her own experiences, diversity in a classroom becomes invaluable. It enables teachers and students to learn from one other.

Students, however, are not the only addressers in a classroom. Teachers too express messages, both spoken and written, and act as models for students. If we write as frequently as we ask our students to, we will be better able to discuss with them the strategies and habits of experienced writers. If we respect our rhetorical skills, we also can shape messages for students that will make our class discussions, conferences, and responses to their writing effective.

THE ADDRESSEE

The addressee is the receiver of the message, the reader. The meaning of the term *reader* is complicated by another term, *audience*, sometimes used as a synonym for *reader*. Although *reader* obviously refers to those who decode written messages, *audience* sometimes means "the people I have in mind as I write." In other words, *audience* is a term often used in discussing the *relationship* between the writer and the reader. Because scholars regard the reader–writer relationship differently, they are likely to define the terms *reader* and *audience* variously. Lisa Ede and Andrea Lunsford contrast two perspectives on audience in "Audience Addressed/Audience Invoked: The Role of Audience in Composition Theory and Pedagogy." One view regards the writer as dealing with an "audience addressed," a "real" reader existing outside the text. The writer can determine this reader's values, beliefs, and knowledge about a subject by analyzing them. Given this view, the writer's analysis of the audience and its expectations significantly shapes the presentation of material. The writing is successful if the real reader responds to it in ways the writer intended.

An "audience invoked," on the other hand, is a reader "constructed" by the writer, a fiction, not a real person. "The central task of the writer, then, is not to analyze an audience and adapt discourse to meet its needs. Rather, the writer uses the semantic and syntactic resources of language to provide cues for the reader—cues which help to define the role or roles the writer wishes the reader to adopt in responding to the text" (p. 160). Given this view, writers can never completely "know" their readers but have many options for defining the roles an audience may assume in reading a text.

Ede and Lunsford argue that both views of audience oversimplify the relationships between writers and readers. Writers can become their own readers, as they do when they review a draft, or they may invite a real reader's comments to help them revise what they want to say. Readers as well as writers can be creative, accepting and changing their roles as they engage a text. And writers can shift their understanding of an audience, depending on the demands of the rhetorical situation. Ede and Lunsford urge us to respect the "integrated, interdependent nature of reading and writing" (p. 169): "because of the complex reality to which the term audience refers and because of its fluid, shifting role in the composing process, any discussion of audience which isolates it from the rest of the rhetorical situation or which radically overemphasizes or underemphasizes its function in relation to other rhetorical constraints is likely to oversimplify" (p. 169).

Students who have not had much experience writing for audiences often have difficulty addressing even an audience of peers. Their "What do you want?" and "How long does it have to be?" reveal that they expect The Teacher to be the only reader for any writing they do. For most academic writing, the teacher really is the only audience, but students also need practice writing for themselves, for each other, for audiences outside the classroom. Helping students write for increasingly diverse and complex audiences enables them to establish larger networks of social relationships. For this reason, the investigators in Britain's Schools Council Project urge writing teachers to give greater attention to the addressee:

> We want to suggest that one important dimension of development in writing ability is the growth of a sense of audience, the growth of the ability to make adjustments and choices in writing which take account of the audience for whom the writing is intended. This accommodation may be coarse or fine, highly calculated or totally intuitive, diffused through the text or explicit at particular points in it; but, whatever the form of its realization, a highly developed sense of audience must be one of the marks of the competent mature writer, for it is concerned with nothing less than the implementation of his concern to maintain or establish an appropriate relationship with his reader in order to achieve his full intent. (James Britton et al., *The Development of Writing Abilities, 11–18*, p. 58)

CONTEXT

All messages come from somewhere. *Context* refers to all of those experiences, beliefs, and forms of knowing that serve as potential subjects for our writing. "To be operative," says Jakobson, "the message requires a context referred to, seizable by the addressee, and either verbal or capable of being verbalized" (p. 353). In practice, context represents a complicated configuration of knowledge, language, and thinking that shapes every message. We encounter its importance every time we talk with people in professions different from our own. Although my brother is a librarian by profession, he has renovated several houses and knows how to talk with contractors. They understand each other's messages about PVC pipe, the r-values of insulation, and using a dead man to support a heavy load. The context of their conversations is shaped not only by a shared, specialized vocabulary but also by conventional procedures for building houses, accepted strategies for solving problems, and ways of knowing that outsiders can scarcely appreciate. Successful conversations with contractors, then, require that both parties speak from a shared context.

The same is true of written communication. Writing that is not "seizable by the addressee" miscommunicates. Writing shaped by a context that an addresser and addressee share has a reasonable chance of being comprehended. As we will see in Chapter 6, interpreting and sharing "reality" is a complicated process, but for now, we can define *context* to mean an entire world of subject matters or topics that writers develop into messages. For all writers, such worlds are culturally and socially constructed. The academic world, for example, is made up of many communities of knowledgeable peers, people who experience their disciplines by means of shared assumptions about what the field encompasses, how it investigates problems, what it regards as evidence, and how it publishes its findings to those inside and outside the community. Because these assumptions are lived in language, many writing teachers believe that they can help students succeed in school by broadening their understanding of how these academic discourse communities function. Writing-across-the-curriculum programs attempt to give students such an understanding. They assign a high priority to context.

MESSAGE

Message refers to what is being said *about* the topic or subject, about the context. In a writing course the term *thesis* refers to message, to experience that is filtered, narrowed, and interpreted by the writer. When we ask students "What is the point of this essay; what is being said here?" we are asking them to restate the thesis or message. We also are discussing message whenever we talk about the organization of written discourse; its structure reflects the order we impose on our experiences in shaping what we want to say.

CONTACT

For communication to occur, the addresser and the addressee must somehow be in contact with each other. A physical as well as psychological connection must exist between them. In speech, contact is generally visual and auditory. Because speaker and listener occupy the same space and time, the speaker can observe signs of recognition or confusion in the listener's stance and facial expressions, revising the message to make it clearer.

In writing, contact is achieved through ink on paper. Whether taken from a printer or a typewriter, or written on with pen or pencil, paper represents for most people a medium less comfortable than the human voice. Writer and reader are separated in time and space. Our readers cannot offer us reassuring feedback as the words appear on the page, and we cannot look over their shoulders as they read, elaborating on our meaning or correcting misunderstandings. Although we may value our word processors, most of us also can remember how awkward we felt confronting a computer keyboard for the first time. Ink on paper can be a forbidding channel for bringing writer and reader together.

For some students, contact creates serious "writer's block"; they freeze at the prospect of putting words on paper.[1] Sometimes this unreasonable fear results from the perception that writing represents failure. "Teachers have always found fault with my writing; you will too, so why bother?" To protect themselves from defeat, such students may become perfectionists, or they may tell you, "I can't do English." They simply may refuse to write. Some may have developed poor handwriting as a defense mechanism. Realizing that they *must* write, they hope we will interpret their scrawling in their favor, reducing the number of errors they must confront when the paper is returned. Red ink, the conventional medium for comments on school assignments, also creates a strong psychological channel between student and teacher. Some students can attend to it, responding to what has become a "color of authority," while other students view it as a "color of defeat." Overwhelmed by copious red marks, students cannot comprehend the teacher's advice because the medium has created a psychological barrier to communication.

CODE

Code refers to the language of the message, a subject we will examine again in Chapter 5. Mathematics, braille, computer programming languages, semaphore, the International Phonetic Alphabet, Morse code,

---

1. For a helpful discussion of "writer's block," see Mike Rose, ed., *When a Writer Can't Write: Studies in Writer's Block and Other Composing Process Problems* (New York: Guilford Press, 1985).

and the linguistic features of speech are all examples of codes. The code that most concerns writers is the English graphic system, which consists of three types of signals:

1. Alphabet letters and conventions for arranging them into words, sentences, and paragraphs;
2. A system of punctuation marks that separate the structural units of a communication: commas, periods, exclamation points, question marks, dashes, hyphens, semicolons, colons, single and double quotation marks, slash marks, apostrophes, parentheses, ellipses, brackets [ ], and braces { };
3. Mechanical customs. Most textbooks define *mechanics* inadequately, but the term generally refers to matters of manuscript form rather than to conventions that express meaning. That is, mechanics determine what the text looks like rather than what it says. The writer's use of margins, indentation, italics, boldface, numerals, symbols such as @, $, %, &, and *, capital letters, abbreviations, even the convention of writing from left to right—all these belong to mechanics.

The English graphic system has a long history and, like the language itself, has changed over time. We have gained and lost alphabet letters and redefined formal conventions. Medieval monks, for example, rarely indented their writing; parchment was simply too expensive to waste. Instead, they indicated "paragraph" by writing in a different color, adding a decorative (illuminated) letter, or changing the script. The practice of indenting paragraphs or separating them by a line of white space developed relatively recently. Conventions governing paragraph length also have changed. Nowadays, paragraphs tend to be shorter than they were 100 years ago, perhaps because we are accustomed to seeing over-differentiated paragraphs in magazines, newspapers, and advertisements.

Any code is both systematic and arbitrary. The alphabet letters, punctuation marks, and mechanical customs of written English function together in predictable patterns, but the patterns are conventional. That is, we agree to use the symbols in certain ways. There is (now) nothing especially sacred about the system. Children often make up their own secret codes to communicate with their friends, leaving adults to wonder what they are telling one another. Other people in other times and places also have communicated effectively by consenting to use graphic systems we cannot understand without special training: the Cyrillic alphabet, the Germanic runic system, the ogham, the Cherokee syllabary, Hebrew script, Egyptian hieroglyphs, Sumerian cuneiform, and the Greek alphabet. As writers and writing teachers, we have a special interest in the code. Although it permits many options for making meaning, inexperienced writers sometimes find it a frustrating system to use, one that threatens to shut them out of meaning making altogether. An important

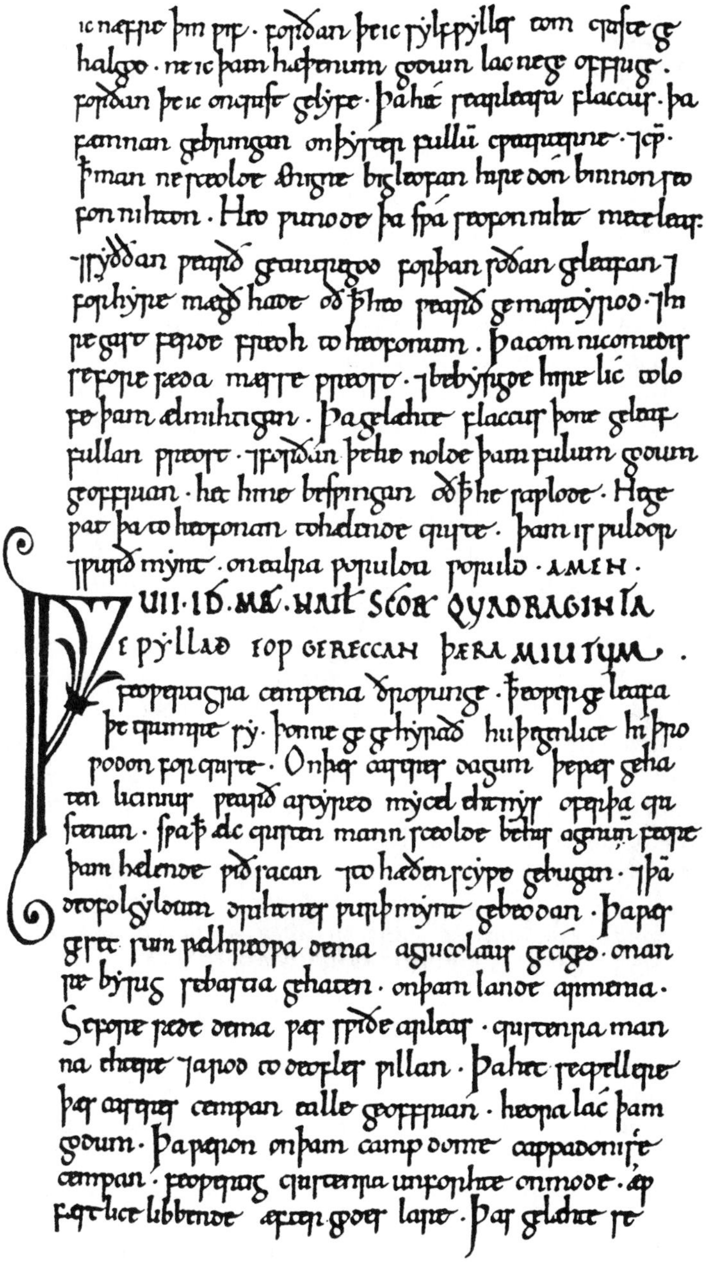

FIGURE 2.1 A page of Old English written in the early eleventh century in Insular hand (Cotton Julius E vii f 59)
Reprinted by permission of the British Library.

goal of any writing teacher is to help students gain confidence in their ability to use the code effectively, perhaps even to find pleasure in manipulating the symbols.

SUMMARY AND APPLICATIONS

Clearly our working definition, "Writing is a process of communication that uses a conventional graphic system to convey a message to a reader," is not as simple as it appears. Every term, viewed in isolation, introduces a complex element to the process. The process requires a writer (addresser), a reader (addressee), a subject matter (context), one or more propositions (message) drawn from the subject matter, a channel that brings writer and reader together (contact), and a conventional system of visible marks (code). Viewing the terms in isolation, however, is unwise. Every rhetorical situation represents a different configuration of Jakobson's terms. All of the elements are present in all acts of writing. Before we examine how writers use these elements to create written discourse, the subject of Chapter 3, let me offer some suggestions for using Jakobson's diagram (or the simpler communication triangle) in the classroom.

As we have already seen, the diagram can help students plan their papers. Embedding each element of the diagram in a question encourages writers to consider carefully all the dimensions of the assignment, to define a rich rhetorical problem to solve. Second, the diagram explains why writing well, balancing all of the elements effectively, is difficult. Every paper requires a slightly different balancing act. As Wayne Booth's "The Rhetorical Stance" describes, "unbalanced" stances result from a speaker's or writer's failure to adjust the subject to the needs of an audience. Once students appreciate that every assignment presents several options for treating the subject matter, audience, and so on, they also may understand why there is no One Way, no Magic Pill, no single principle that solves all writing problems for all time. Third, the diagram implies that students (and teachers) must attend to all of the elements rather than focus exclusively on the code or on "good ideas." Mechanically clean papers that say nothing are as ineffective as brilliant discussions that ignore the reader's expectations about conventional punctuation.

Jakobson's diagram offers a useful framework not only for explaining principles to students but also for guiding our performance as teachers. Keeping the diagram in mind, we can draft better writing assignments, specifying more than just a topic. We can enlarge the scope of our comments on papers to address how well the student has defined a purpose and audience for the message. The diagram also may help us correct misunderstandings that occur when we communicate with students in the classroom or in conferences. Did they fail to grasp a lesson because I taught it poorly? Because they were inattentive or unprepared for class? Because the subject matter itself was difficult? Or because the code I used contained ill-defined or abstract terms?

Finally, the diagram helps us describe what Jakobson calls the "basic functions of verbal communication," which are known in traditional rhetoric as "the modes of discourse": narration, description, exposition, and argumentation. When we classify examples of writing by modes, we are describing, in effect, the writer's purpose in combining the elements Jakobson diagrammed. Although none of the elements is ignored, one may receive greater emphasis. For example, if the writer's purpose is to persuade the reader, the discourse will tend to emphasize "addressee." The traditional label for discourse that focuses primarily on the reader is *argumentation*. Jakobson claims that discourse oriented toward the addressee has a *conative* "function"; James Kinneavy in *A Theory of Discourse* says that such discourse has a *persuasive* "aim."

Regardless of the label—and we have amassed a host of them over the years—we can classify kinds of writing by describing which element receives the primary focus. Table 2.1 may help you organize such a discussion. The left-hand column lists each of the rhetorical elements we have examined in this chapter. The sentence written across the top establishes six ways of classifying writing. We can identify which element of Jakobson's diagram seems most prominent; we can describe the purpose or aim of the writing; we can label it by using Jakobson's terms, Kinneavy's, or those of other writers and teachers; and we can group it with similar examples. To understand how the six classification systems relate to each other, read the chart from left to right and supply the appropriate term from each column: "When the focus is primarily on the *reader/addressee*, the purpose or aim is to *persuade the reader*, which Jakobson calls the *conative function* (of discourse), which Kinneavy calls the *persuasive aim* (of discourse), which also may be called *persuasion, argument, rhetoric (narrowly defined)*, and which has examples in *propaganda, debates, editorials, and sermons*."

A word of caution. Most classification systems have limited usefulness. Although the chart attempts to organize the many terms we use to discuss writing, it also oversimplifies matters. Most writing does not belong exclusively to any one category. A good dictionary may concern itself primarily with the code, but it also anticipates the needs of its readers by arranging entries in alphabetical order. An emphasis on one element doesn't deny the presence of others.

Furthermore, although the communication triangle and Jakobson's diagram conveniently list some of the *elements* present in spoken and written communication, neither diagram is a model of the *process* whereby writers make meaning.[2] Both diagrams reduce a complicated process to a few terms and ignore crucial interrelationships among the

2. See especially the objections to "positivist models" that Ann E. Berthoff raises in "I. A. Richards and the Philosophy of Rhetoric," *Rhetoric Society Quarterly* 10 (Fall 1980), 195–207.

TABLE 2.1

When the focus is primarily on the →	→ the purpose or aim is to →	→ which Jakobson calls the →	→ which Kinneavy calls the →	→ which may also be known as →	which has examples in →
writer/ addressee	express the self (individual or group)	emotive function	expressive aim	"creative" writing	diaries creeds manifestos
reader/ addressee	persuade the reader	conative function	persuasive aim	persuasion argument rhetoric (narrowly defined)	propaganda debates editorials sermons
reality/context	explain the world	referential function	referential aim	exposition scientific or technical writing	lab reports textbooks directions manuals
message	create a text which can be appreciated in its own right	poetic function	literary aim	narration description "imaginative" literature	movies jokes songs literary genres
contact	keep lines of communication open	phatic function			"In this paper I..."
code	use language to discuss language	metalingual function		metalanguage	dictionaries grammars usage guides underlining words for emphasis*

*I am indebted to William Irmscher for pointing out that underlining words calls attention to them *as code*.

terms. They say nothing, for example, about the writer's purpose, meaning, or intention. So, although the diagrams may be helpful, they are also seductive; they can mislead us into assuming that writers translate ideas into words simply by combining "elements," like shaking together so many chemicals in a test tube. In truth, the composing process is much more complicated than that. It involves making choices, posing questions, recording and reviewing possible solutions to a writing problem, and eventually, after many tentative formulations, creating the meaning we intended to convey to a reader about our subject.

three

What Does the
Process Involve?

There is no royal path to good writing; and such paths as exist . . . lead
through . . . the jungles of the self, the world, and of craft.

JESSAMYN WEST

WHAT EXPERIENCE TELLS US

Writing involves not just one process but several. Most of them seem
to be mental and consequently difficult for researchers to reconstruct.
Also, the processes change depending on our age, our experiences as
writers, and the kind of writing we do. Indeed, they seem as complex
and varied as the people who use them. Although we are a long way
from understanding completely how writers create even the simplest
kinds of discourse, we can observe many activities by examining our
own writing habits.

Think about the most recent significant writing you did—a letter, an
article, a report, or something that required more elaborate preparation
than putting together a grocery list. Try to reconstruct what you did,
from beginning to end, to create the piece. What prompted you to do
the writing? Why did writing serve your purposes better than speech?
How much time elapsed between the "need" to write and drafting the
first words? What mental processes were going on during that time?

This book, for example, evolved from my teaching. Unlike many writing tasks, the need to write it was self-imposed, prompted by reassuring
comments from fellow teachers that, yes, they would find such a book
helpful. But the project also gave me the chance to examine my own
teaching and to read books and articles I had wanted to study. In publishing the book, I hoped to reach a large audience, many more teachers
than I could speak to in a class or workshop. In the three years after I
began work on the project, I digested a great deal of reading, redesigned
my courses to try out new teaching methods, and talked to many writing
teachers. In the process, I became a different kind of teacher, unable
now to identify specifically all of the experiences and influences that
shaped the ideas you are reading.

Drafting and revising the book took two years, but the procedure involved habits similar to your own. Do you complete "starting rituals"? Do you customarily begin drafting a piece in a particular place or at a particular time? Do you compose with a pen or pencil or at the typewriter or word processor? Straight through or with frequent breaks? What changes do you make as you are drafting? What revisions do you save for later? How do you determine when the piece is finished?

Most writers develop starting rituals to help them confront the blank page: cleaning house, raiding the refrigerator, sharpening pencils, tidying the desk or arranging writing materials just so, carefully copying a title onto the page. Before I begin, I must clear off the kitchen table, spread out books and notes I plan to use, and pour myself something to drink (in the mornings, coffee; in the afternoons, a diet soft drink).

Although I can compose informal letters at the word processor, I must draft significant material in pencil on long, yellow legal tablets, pausing frequently in midsentence to discover where the words are taking me. Like most writers, regardless of the medium, I rarely construct a formal outline, although each chapter of this book grew out of a detailed one-page list of phrases that identified the order of topics I planned to discuss. Also, like most writers, I revise as I draft, reworking sentences, substituting a word for one that doesn't quite fit, but postponing major revisions by writing marginal notes to myself. As a rule, my first draft represents agonizing effort, painstaking word-for-word labor that only here and there satisfactorily expresses what I want to say.

Then, I must leave the piece for a while, returning to it hours or days later to evaluate it and plan further revisions. Often, it helps to discuss the draft with someone else. However critical another's response may be, it nevertheless suggests sources of confusion, undeveloped ideas, vague language, and alternatives for improving the piece. In the process of talking out the draft or evaluating someone else's written comments, I find my real message. If my deadline permits, I revise the piece at least twice, the first time on paper and the second time as I type the text into the word processor. My attention focuses on getting the words to express what I want to say and responding to questions or objections that my audience might raise. Then I edit, proofreading for grammatical and punctuation problems. At this stage I also check spelling and make minor revisions in word choice. When I read my "finished" work, immediately or weeks later, I always discover something else I could have attended to but didn't.

Clearly, writing is a messy business, rarely in real life as tidy as textbooks describe it. We don't begin at step one, "find a topic," and follow an orderly sequence of events to "proofread the paper." Certainly, we plan what we want to say before we begin drafting, but the act of writing generates new ideas and shapes new plans. In other words, prewriting and writing can occur simultaneously. So can drafting and rewriting, for we never commit words to paper without changing at least one or two here and there, in our minds as well as on the page. Unfortunately, this chapter must examine these processes sequentially, beginning from a fixed point and discussing in turn three stages of composing: prewriting, writing, and rewriting. However, as you read each section, recall your own writing experiences. They should tell you that the process isn't linear. It is recursive, like the forward motion of a wheel, its leading edge breaking new ground but then doubling back on itself.

PUBLISHED ACCOUNTS OF THE PROCESS

Many published sources offer information, impressions, and theories about composing. Accounts of actual writers at work—biographies, letters, writers' journals, and manuscript studies—reveal what their authors have to say about their craft.[1] Theoretical discussions such as those cited in Chapters 4, 5, and 6 also attempt to explain creativity and language use. As teachers, however, we probably will find the most valuable information in studies that record and explain observations of student writers. Such accounts obviously have limitations. Most students can't verbalize accurately or completely what they're doing when they write; consequently, investigators can only infer from overt behavior the feelings, attitudes, and thoughts occupying the student's mind. Even the best research design can't control or explain all of the variables, and researchers must examine considerable complex data to derive valid, reliable conclusions, often discovering that an answer to one research question raises additional problems to investigate.

Nevertheless, several studies tell us a great deal more about the composing processes of students than we've ever known before. The discussion that follows derives primarily from the work of James Britton and his colleagues in Britain's Schools Council Project, *The Development of Writing Abilities, 11–18*; from Janet Emig's *The Composing Processes of Twelfth Graders*; and from John R. Hayes and Linda S. Flower's analyses of "thinking aloud" protocols, verbal descriptions of what writers report they think and do while they compose.[2] These investigations employ different methods, terminology, and numbers of subjects, but they substantially agree on what the process entails.

---

1. See especially Malcolm Cowley, ed., *Writers at Work* (New York: Viking, 1958). Donald Murray, *A Writer Teaches Writing*, 2d ed. (Boston: Houghton Mifflin, 1985), pp. 253–59, contains an extensive bibliography of discussions by writers about writing.
2. See John R. Hayes and Linda S. Flower, "Identifying the Organization of Writing Processes" and "The Dynamics of Composing: Making Plans and Juggling Constraints," in *Cognitive Processes in Writing*, ed. Lee W. Gregg and Erwin R. Steinberg (Hillsdale, NJ: Lawrence Erlbaum Associates, 1980), pp. 3–50. See also Sharon Pianko, "A Description of the Composing Processes of College Freshman Writers," *Research in the Teaching of English* 13 (February 1979), 5–22; and Sondra Perl, "The Composing Processes of Unskilled College Writers," *Research in the Teaching of English* 13 (December 1979), 317–36.

PREWRITING

According to Britton, "Writing is a deliberate act; one has to make up one's mind to do it" (p. 22). The urge to write may come from within or be imposed from outside, as it is when students confront a school assignment. Nevertheless, we choose or refuse to write, either decision implying its own consequences. Deciding whether or not to write depends on the nature of the stimulus and the context. For example, students must make a greater effort to accept a restrictive teacher-made assignment than one that permits choices. Once aware of the need to write, we begin prewriting.

Prewriting or invention, to borrow the term used in classical rhetoric, enables us to understand and begin to solve the problem the stimulus creates for us. "In every kind of writing," maintains Britton, "defining the nature of the operation, devising ways of tackling it, and explaining its meaning and implications to oneself are essential states that the mind engages" (p. 90). Prewriting helps us examine what we know. We recall ideas, relate old and new information, assess the reader's expectations, and generally explore the problem from many angles. We work out provisional answers to such questions as "What is this for?" (purpose), "Who is this for?" (audience), "What do I want to say?" (point of view on the subject), and "How can I best say it?" (code).

Though this process may appear to occur within the individual writer's mind, in isolation from other people, it rarely happens that way. Karen Burke LeFevre, in *Invention as a Social Act*, draws on the work of social theorists and on the practices of writers in many walks of life to develop a theoretical framework for invention. She arranges four perspectives on invention—Platonic, internal dialogic, collaborative, and collective—along a continuum that accounts for the range of ways we explore the knowledge and attitudes we bring to bear on a writing problem. The Platonic view argues that invention is the private act of an individual writer drawing on inner resources to develop ideas and feelings about the subject of a piece of writing. In this view, inspiration comes from within, from a private sense of reality or truth. Lefevre argues, however, that this view abstracts the writer from society and fails to acknowledge that invention is usually a collaborative process.

Internal dialogic, collaborative, and collective views of invention involve an "other" in the creative process. The internal dialogic perspective regards the writer as an individual engaged in dialogue with another "self," an internal partner who serves as censor, monitor, or guide. This guide is the "oneself" Britton claims we must talk with to understand the nature and implications of the task. The collaborative perspective holds that actual people interact with us to create a constructive environment for prewriting, that we negotiate a text in conversation with others (including the authors of books and other texts), who may suggest ideas, who respond to what we are thinking and writing, and without whom composing cannot move forward. The collective perspective "is based on an assumption that invention is neither a purely individual nor an interpersonal act or process; rather, it is encouraged or constrained by social collectives whose views are transmitted through such things as institutions, societal prohibitions, and cultural expectations" (p. 50). We encounter collective invention whenever we guide our work by responding to sociocultural forces, including assumptions about what we should and should not say, about topics that seem risky or safe, and about who we are as writers. According to Lefevre, even when writers are acting alone, they are pervasively affected by their relationships to others.

Because Hayes and Flower studied the composing processes of individuals, their model focuses primarily on the actions of the isolated writer. Even so, the model suggests that writing occurs in a context shaped by information and experiences stored in our long-term memory, by generalized goals and strategies that we have used in the past, and by the "task environment," which includes such external influences as the writing assignment and an evolving draft. For Hayes and Flower, prewriting (they call it *planning*) includes three subprocesses: generating, organizing, and goal setting. Generating involves retrieving relevant information from long-term memory. Though generating material sometimes produces notes and typically characterizes early segments of the protocols Hayes and Flower examined, the generating process also can appear later on, when we sense a need to close gaps in our material or decide to elaborate an idea initially sketched out too hastily. Organizing entails selecting the most useful material and developing a writing plan that "may be structured either temporally (e.g., 'First, I'll say A, then B.') or hierarchically (e.g., 'Under topic number one, I should discuss A, B, and C.') or both" ("Identifying the Organization of Writing Processes," p. 14). Goal setting allows us to develop criteria by which to judge the text we will write: "Better keep it simple"; "I'll need a transition here."

In Hayes and Flower's model, these subprocesses are not employed in some linear fashion; rather, writers continually move back and forth among them, guided by a "monitor" that helps us identify and solve rhetorical problems. In planning, as in every phase of composing, we constantly interrupt ourselves, first generating material stored in long-term memory, then perhaps writing out a brainstormed list, then organizing the list by drawing circles around items we judge appropriate, then going back to the assignment to discover requirements that we might have missed. We continually create and re-create hierarchies of goals, our internal monitor determining what issue we will take up next and how much attention we will devote to it.

All of our planning serves at least two functions. First, we begin to develop our message so that it corresponds to what we know. Second, we assess our feelings about the message, making a commitment to it that seems right for us. As we explain things to ourselves, we also are aided and constrained by our past experiences with writing. Many inexperienced writers, for example, are unable to move confidently back and forth among the subprocesses of invention or prewriting. They believe that they must attend to everything at once, including spelling and mechanical correctness. Unlike experienced writers, who feel comfortable about putting their subject matter on hold in order to focus on a concern with audience, many student writers exhaust themselves trying to manage everything simultaneously. They are unable to develop effective hierarchies of goals, which will allow them temporarily to postpone one problem to solve another. For this reason alone, students need time to attend to prewriting—in every assignment they undertake. They also need help identifying how writers juggle planning tasks. We can provide such guidance by encouraging students to become conscious of what they do as they plan a writing project, by modeling or discussing with students the kinds of goal-based plans we might develop in responding to an assignment, and by allowing time for students to discuss their plans with classmates.

Prewriting may take from a few moments to many years and can be postponed now and then, sometimes quite constructively. We have all had the experience of concentrating on something else when suddenly a piece of the writing puzzle that had stumped us earlier pops into our heads. That sudden insight, the "Eureka moment" or point of illumination, often occurs after we stop attending consciously to the problem and mull it over subconsciously for a while. Sometimes, what we are *not* doing during prewriting can be as significant as our conscious deliberations.

WRITING

Sooner or later we begin the physical act of drafting, a relatively painless decision for most people. For some, however, making a few tentative scrawls on the page is a torturous affair. The pencil-holding hand slowly, deliberately shapes each letter until a certain warm-up period gets underway. Other writers complete starting rituals, such as putting down a title or asking the teacher a question that may be a request for reassurance: "Can I write whatever I want?" "Does it have to be neat?" Translation: "Getting started is tough, so please let me know that I don't have to worry about your accepting my ideas on top of everything else I'm going through just now."

> After making a start, children sometimes decide that it won't do and begin again. The strength of their conviction that a new start must be made, even though the teacher may have no complaints about what has been written, is sometimes remarkable. They are not easily persuaded to reconsider a decision to reject what they have done. Some seem to make a habit of rejecting their beginning, and rarely complete anything. These may be timid children for whom committing themselves to paper at all—"finding a tone to talk with" and "being oneself in talking"—imposes a severe strain. (*The Development of Writing Abilities, 11–18*, p. 34)

Once students make a "good start," they seem to resent interruptions from outside and concentrate intensely on their work. However, they frequently interrupt themselves, pausing for periods of three to thirty seconds on the average. During this time, facial expressions and gestures reveal frustration or pleasure with what is appearing on the page. The pauses that punctuate the act of writing serve several functions. First, they enable us to scan the text so that we can make minor alterations or write notes about major changes to make later. Second, pausing helps us look forward to plan the next idea or rephrase a thought we've begun to express. In "Hand, Eye, Brain: Some 'Basics' in the Writing Process," Emig notes that many experienced writers prefer to write drafts in long-hand. Writing by hand, she suggests, constructively slows down the process, permitting half-formed or unexpected ideas to develop. Writing by hand also may be aesthetically important to some writers: "We may be able to make personal statements initially or steadily only in our own personalized script, with all of its individualities, even idiosyncrasies" (p. 61).

Hayes and Flower also have observed interruptions during the process of drafting, which they call *translating*. "The function of the *translating* process is to take material from memory under the guidance of the writing plan and to transform it into acceptable written English sentences" (p. 15). In composing aloud, writers often punctuate the translating process with questions—"Rousseau did what?" "How do I want to put this?"—as if searching for the next part of the sentence they are writing. Translating, like all of the processes that go into composing, also can be interrupted by editing.

One of the constraints on composing is how much information we can hold in our short-term memory. Five to seven items, what we have written and what we intend to write, can be suspended until we have determined what meaning they will take:

> The fluent writer . . . can hold not only whole words and phrases, but meanings as well, and possibly even general intentions (which can scarcely be thought of as items), so that it is much easier for what is written to have coherence. If, on the other hand, the teasing out of the thought becomes particularly difficult, all the resources of the short-term memory may have to be concentrated on a few words. That is when a writer may lose the track of his thoughts, omit or repeat words, misconnect or blunder in some way. (*The Development of Writing Abilities*, 11–18, p. 45)

Writers in the act of drafting are incredibly busy solving problems. We are calling up strategies we have used before to see if they will work for us this time. But because each writing task presents us with a new set of demands, past experience sometimes offers little help. Then, we must devise other ways to deal with the problem. Writing is problem-solving. As Flower and Hayes explain in "The Dynamics of Composing," the problems we are trying to solve may be one of three kinds. Sometimes we confront a "knowledge problem" that forces us to "move from a rich array of unorganized, perhaps even contradictory perceptions, memories, and propositions to an integrated notion of just what it is [we] think about a topic" (p. 34). Sometimes we encounter a "language problem." We may know what we want to say, but we can't make the words work. Or, we may find ourselves grappling with a "rhetorical problem," a persistent uncertainty about our purpose, our sense of audience, or our projected self, which may cripple our ability to generate both ideas and language (p. 40). Experienced writers develop strategies for addressing all three types of problems, flexible ad hoc plans or hierarchically organized moves that reduce or postpone the constraints we face. Good writers spend considerable time planning ways to reduce "cognitive strain," and they "appear to have more flexible, high-level plans and more self-conscious control of their planning than poor writers" (p. 44). Consequently, Flower and Hayes conclude that "one way to improve people's writing is to improve the planning process they go through *as they write*" (p. 44).

REWRITING

Having drafted the piece (or a substantial section of it), most writers begin what Emig calls *reformulation*, a process that includes everything from correcting minor mechanical errors to changing the work substantially. The term *rewriting* incorporates both *revising* and *editing* (or proofreading). When we ask students to correct errors in a paper, check spellings, solve subject–verb agreement problems, and straighten out punctuation, we are asking them to edit, not revise, their work. True revision involves reseeing, rethinking, and reshaping the piece, resolving a tension between what we intended to say and what the discourse actually says. In revising we assess the "fit" among the elements of Jakobson's diagram, and where we notice incongruities, we stop to untangle them. Both revising and editing, then, are necessary to rewriting a draft.

Hayes and Flower call these two activities *editing* and *reviewing*. "The *editing* process examines any material that the writer puts into words. . . . Its purpose is to detect and correct violations in writing conventions and inaccuracies of meaning and to evaluate materials with respect to writing goals" (p. 16). In other words, editing is triggered automatically and may briefly interrupt any of the processes that go into composing, including generating, organizing, or translating material into written English. "*Reviewing*, on the other hand, is not a spur-of-the-moment activity but rather one in which the writer decides to devote a period of time to systematic examination and improvement of the text. It occurs typically when the writer has finished a translation process [drafting] rather than as an interruption to that process" (p. 19).

Rewriting requires us to shift perspective, which up to this point has focused on generating material and shaping a text. Now we become alternatively a detached reader, substituting for our intended audience, and an involved reader, discovering how well we said what we hoped to. Donald Murray calls these activities *external* and *internal revision*. External revision requires us to become an outsider, to be concerned with the exterior appearance of the discourse, its language, punctuation, and style, its overall effectiveness on the intended audience. Internal revision, the kind writers spend the most time on, requires us to please ourselves, to discover what we intended to say and where our subject, language, and voice have led us.

> During the process of internal revision, writers are not concerned with correctness in any exterior sense. They read what they have written so that they can deal with the questions of subject, of adequate information, of structure, of form, of language. They move from a revision of the entire piece down to the page, the paragraph, the sentence, the line, the phrase, the word. And then, because each word may give off an explosion of meaning, they move out from the word to the phrase, the line, the sentence, the paragraph, the page, the piece. Writers move in close and then move out to visualize the entire piece. Again and again and again. ("Internal Revision: A Process of Discovery," p. 92)

As we shuttle back and forth between our two roles as readers, we change the text both to satisfy our audience and ourselves. In "Writer-Based Prose: A Cognitive Basis for Problems in Writing," Flower notes that writers in the process of drafting sometimes are too busy translating their own thoughts into language to consider a reader. Consequently, early drafts may be writer-based, their primary goal being to satisfy ourselves that we have said what we meant. Later, we focus greater attention on the needs and expectations of our audience, transforming writer-based prose into reader-based prose. If we are unable to step back from our struggles with a topic to consider the perspective of a reader, the draft may remain writer-based. Teachers see this problem when a student's thesis or argument appears at the end of a paper, not at the beginning, where readers expect to find it. Such students have turned in a "discovery draft," a text that reflects the "associative, narrative path of the writer's own confrontation with her subject" (p. 20). Discovery drafts are important because they help writers find their messages, but because they leave readers in the dark about what the message is, they need revision.

Most students have little experience with rewriting as we have defined it broadly here. They know to correct errors but rarely concern themselves with more than the paper's exterior appearance. For them, rewriting is punishment, a process of correcting errors *after* the paper receives a grade. Unfortunately, writing teachers encourage this view. If we insist that all writing be neat, we unintentionally discourage students from performing the messy draftwork essential to rewriting. If our comments on students' papers address only spelling, punctuation, and sentence errors, we are saying that they matter most, students inferring our real priorities from what we mark. If we offer students few opportunities to discuss one another's drafts, we also limit their ability to anticipate what readers expect. If we fail to give students specific instruction in rewriting or class time to work on drafts *before* they're due, we shouldn't be surprised to receive final papers that are really only first drafts. When what we say is inconsistent with what we do, students develop mistaken notions about the importance of rewriting.

The composing process ends when we have finished rewriting. We stop because a deadline is at hand or because we've worked out all the possibilities that interest us in the piece. Sometimes we contemplate our work with considerable satisfaction and pride. Many of our students, however, do not. Emig notes that, for her twelfth-grade subjects, stopping "is a mundane moment devoid of any emotion but indifference and the mildest of satisfactions that a task is over" (p. 87). No matter how students may have viewed their achievements in the past, they seem to have learned that school-sponsored writing always "fails." It's always returned with at least one defeating comment. Lynn, one of the students in Emig's study, may be typical of others who find little pleasure in contemplating the finished work: "She seems to mean first that her teachers, on the whole, write evaluative comments that do not deal with what she is really trying to say; and that they are not really interested in reading and evaluating any reformulation she might attempt" (p. 68). Students like Lynn accuse us, perhaps justifiably, of failing to keep our readers in mind as we comment on their papers.

Most researchers who study composing explicitly warn against oversimplifying what writers do. Composing is not one process, but many. Some activities interrupt others or become subprocesses of other processes. Some writers may not use all of the processes all of the time. Though writing teachers have long regarded composing as an activity that occurs in "stages," most stage models are too simplistic. They do not account for individual differences among writers. They do not appreciate the complex intermingling of activities, decisions, constraints, and goals writers juggle. Even a model like the one presented in this chapter is misleading. We can *talk* about prewriting, writing, and rewriting separately, but in real life these processes all interact with one another and are extremely difficult to distinguish.

Although we still have much to learn about composing, Flower and Hayes construct a useful simile to describe the writer at work, networking ideas in the switchboard of the mind:

> A writer caught in the act looks . . . like a very busy switchboard operator trying to juggle a number of demands on her attention and constraints on what she can do:
>
> She has two important calls on hold. (Don't forget that idea.)
>
> Four lights just started flashing. (They demand immediate attention or they'll be lost.)
>
> A party of five wants to be hooked up together. (They need to be connected somehow.)

A party of two thinks they've been incorrectly connected. (Where do they go?)

And throughout this complicated process of remembering, retrieving, and connecting, the operator's voice must project calmness, confidence, and complete control. ("The Dynamics of Composing," p. 33)

For better or worse, teachers exert a significant influence on students' abilities to "project calmness, confidence, and complete control" when they write. Because classrooms are busy places, we lack the time to observe carefully how individual students create written messages. That is why in this chapter we've examined the process in some detail. But before we leave the busy switchboard operator, we need reminding about the larger context in which "this complicated process of remembering, retrieving, and connecting" takes place.

WRITING AS SOCIAL INTERACTION

Researchers who helped us understand what writers do broke important ground in the 1970s and 1980s. They moved us from a preoccupation with the written product toward a responsible understanding of the processes writers engage. They required us to question what happens in the writing class and to develop strategies for supporting writing-as-process. They helped us create student-centered classrooms that directed attention not only to *what* students write but also to *how* they manage prewriting, writing, and rewriting.

In the 1980s, scholars began questioning the process model described in this chapter, not so much because it was wrong but because it was incomplete. Flower herself notes, "Early work in cognition, like most other work at the time, focused on the individual (Emig, Flower and Hayes). The Flower/Hayes cognitive process model is a case in point. Although this model suggests *key places* where social and contextual knowledge operate within a cognitive framework, that early research did little more than specify that the 'task environment' was an important element in the process; it failed to account for *how* the situation in which the writer operates might shape composing . . . " ("Cognition, Context, and Theory Building," p. 283). Most process models depict the writer in isolation, a solitary figure separated from the world of ideas and people that language is intended to bridge. In the scene above, the switchboard operator, networking calls that represent her own ideas, is the only human being present. How does she know, we might ask, which ideas to "connect somehow"? How did she learn which flashing lights merit attention?

She knows these things because she is not, in fact, working in isolation. She lives, as all writers do, in a culture shaped by language. Writing is not merely a process of networking ideas or of bringing an isolated writer together with isolated readers. Writing is a way of living in social groups, of interacting with others and having them interact with us. "Writing is a form of social action. It is part of the way in which some people live in the world. Thus, when thinking about writing, we also must think about the way that people live in the world" (*Writing as Social Action*, p. xii).

In an important essay first appearing in 1986, Marilyn Cooper responded to the process-centered view, with its images of the solitary author, by proposing instead an ecological model for writing. Just as natural environments comprise dynamic interlocking systems in which organisms both respond to and alter their surroundings, writers are "continually engaged with a variety of socially constituted systems" ("The Ecology of Writing," p. 367). Cooper identifies at least five systems that every writer is necessarily involved in:

- The system of ideas is the means by which writers comprehend their world, to turn individual experiences and observations into knowledge.
- The system of purposes is the means by which writers coordinate their actions.
- The system of interpersonal interactions is the means by which writers regulate their access to one another.
- The system of cultural norms is the means by which writers structure the larger groups of which they are members.
- The system of textual forms is, obviously, the means by which writers communicate. (pp. 369–70)

The ecological model usefully complicates the learning and teaching of writing because it reminds us of the social context in which all writers work. Let's consider how these systems might influence the work of a student writer encountering a new "ecosystem"—graduate school.

Put yourself in the place of a first-year graduate student in English, a successful writer who graduated last spring with an English major. Schooling has already given you considerable experience writing book reports, academic essays, perhaps even a senior thesis. Nevertheless, as a first-year master's candidate, graduate school will challenge you in new ways. You will be unfamiliar with textual forms such as comprehensive or qualifying examinations. You may have no idea what a master's thesis should be or what to make of the scholarly articles your professors assign. Perhaps the roles or voices you may assume in your writing have changed too. The papers you write for some professors may encourage you to adopt a more collegial stance. Initially, you may be uncomfortable with the system of interpersonal interactions that permits you to address teachers and other graduate students as colleagues in a scholarly community. Although you still write for some of the same purposes you did when you were an undergraduate student, new purposes for writing emerge: to gain professional respect, to advance scholarship, to overturn received knowledge. Even what you write about, the system of ideas, may differ from the topics and ways of addressing them that characterized your undergraduate work.

To say that the first year of graduate school can be confusing is to state the obvious. Less obviously, the first year of graduate school also will alter your attitudes and behavior as a writer. In your interactions with others you will learn not only new facts and interpretations but also what "counts" as a fact or an interpretation. Members of the community also will teach you what is worth knowing as you prepare for examinations or consider topics for your master's thesis. You will gain a sense of what is worth writing about, what relationships are possible among members of the community, and what conventions govern genres such as comprehensive examinations, theses, and scholarly articles.

Joining a new discourse community not only transforms the writer; the writer also participates in transforming the community. First-year graduate students learn how the members of the community expect them to make meaning but then use that knowledge to make new meanings. They begin to use language in new ways, to talk about new facts and interpretations, to adopt new reasons for writing. Over time, they also may change the conventions governing the texts they write. The relationship among people using language in any discourse community is reciprocal, dynamic. The processes of any individual writer shape and are shaped by the processes of all the other writers within the community.

To regard writing as social interaction is not new. Even so, most writing classes are not places that encourage community. Students work on their assignments alone. They rarely write for one another or discuss their work with classmates. Teachers expect the class to be quiet and fill up most of the hour with their own voices. Schools virtually ignore the notion that all uses of language are essentially social.

In "Writing and Knowing: Toward Redefining the Writing Process," James A. Reither concludes that "writing and what writers do during writing cannot be artificially separated from the social-rhetorical situations in which writing gets done, from the conditions that enable writers to do what they do, and from the motives writers have for doing what they do" (p. 621). That is why we must reexamine what goes on in writing classes, what textbooks recommend, even what our own experiences as writers suggest, so that we can appreciate the complex relationships writers enjoy with other writers and readers. For it is also true that a growing number of writing classes encourage students to use writing to interact with one another. They engage in collaborative projects and groupwork. They discuss work in progress with classmates. Their writing emerges from their own interests and accomplishes goals they have defined for themselves. Such classes enable students to see themselves as real writers and readers, engaged with others in using language to shape communities.

part two

RHETORICAL THEORY AND PRACTICE

four

What Do Teachers Need to Know about Rhetoric?

[Rhetoric] is rooted in an essential function of language itself, a function that is wholly realistic, and is continually born anew; the use of language as a symbolic means of inducing cooperation in beings that by nature use symbols.

KENNETH BURKE

PRELIMINARY QUESTIONS

The history of rhetoric covers almost 2500 years, beginning with the work of Corax of Syracuse in the fifth century B.C.E. and extending to present-day discussions of language "as a symbolic means of inducing cooperation." Throughout its history, the discipline has accumulated principles that reflect the changing needs of those who practice it. It has experienced countless shifts of emphasis. For most of its history, rhetoric also has been associated with education. A prominent discipline in the schools for centuries, rhetoric embraces the work of teachers who studied the tradition and taught others to practice it. As writing teachers, we are part of that tradition and ought to understand its broader currents and crosscurrents.

We also need to know about rhetoric for other reasons. It is, first of all, a compelling subject to study. While we certainly can teach writing well without ever having read Aristotle, knowing what he said is useful nevertheless. Studying rhetoric for its own sake introduces us to some of the most influential thinkers of Western culture. Second, a knowledge of rhetoric helps us understand our world. Kenneth Burke's definition of the art, quoted at the beginning of this chapter, asserts that all human beings practice rhetoric and come under its influence. Every day we use words to shape attitudes and encourage people to act in certain ways. Teaching is a rhetorical art, and language used "as a symbolic means of inducing cooperation" appears all around us, in literature, advertising, broadcast journalism, politics, religion, art, films, and conversation. Not all communication has a rhetorical purpose, but much of what we say, hear, read, and do involves someone's influencing someone else to make choices. Rhetoric enables us to understand those choices and the processes whereby we make them.

Important though they may be, none of these reasons for studying rhetoric applies to this chapter. Although the chapter surveys a great deal of history, that isn't its primary purpose. Nor will the chapter help you understand, except perhaps incidentally, how rhetoric functions in contemporary society. Instead, we will examine here a few significant developments that have influenced how we were taught, and how we teach, composition. As part of a centuries-old rhetorical tradition, these developments explain many contemporary teaching practices.[1] Because our profession has seen a resurgence of interest in the rhetorical tradition, we need to understand its history. Specifically, we want to answer the following questions:

- What is *rhetoric* (and why do people say bad things about it)?
- Why do we discuss writing in terms of writer, reader, and subject?
- What is a topic?
- Where did the five-paragraph theme come from?
- What is *style* and what explains our preference for plain, clear writing?
- Why do traditional courses concern themselves with grammar instruction, imitating models of good prose, and studying literature?
- What is a mode?
- How does "new" rhetoric differ from classical rhetoric?

1. One of the best brief historical surveys of rhetorical developments up to the twentieth century is Edward P. J. Corbett and Robert Connors, *Classical Rhetoric for the Modern Student*, 4th ed. (New York: Oxford University Press, 1999), pp. 489–543. For longer treatments, see James L. Golden, Goodwin F. Berquist, and William E. Coleman, *The Rhetoric of Western Thought*, 2d ed. (Dubuque, IA: Kendall Hunt, 1978); George A. Kennedy, *A New History of Classical Rhetoric* (Princeton, NJ: Princeton University Press, 1994); Aldo Scaglione, *The Classical Theory of Composition from Its Origins to the Present: A Historical Survey* (Chapel Hill: University of North Carolina Press, 1972); James J. Murphy, ed., *A Short History of Writing Instruction from Ancient Greece to Twentieth-Century America* (Davis, CA: Hermagoras Press, 1990); Thomas M. Conley, *Rhetoric in the European Tradition* (Chicago: University of Chicago Press, 1990); and Andrea A. Lunsford, ed. *Reclaiming Rhetorica: Women in the Rhetorical Tradition* (Pittsburgh Series in Composition, Literacy, and Culture; Pittsburgh: University of Pittsburgh Press, 1995). For discussions of primary works and secondary scholarship, see Patricia Bizzell and Bruce Herzberg, eds., *The Rhetorical Tradition: Readings from Classical Times to the Present* (Boston: Bedford Books, 1990); and Winifred B. Horner, ed., *The Present State of Scholarship in Historical and Contemporary Rhetoric*, rev. ed. (Columbia: University of Missouri Press, 1990).

Keep these questions in mind as you read. The chapter examines them in order. You will find that many current definitions and teaching practices were first codified thousands of years ago. Other developments evolved fairly recently. Still other customs significantly reinterpret earlier practices. A historical perspective helps us understand these principles in the context in which they developed and adapt them to contemporary circumstances. More important, a sense of the past prevents us from becoming trapped by tradition and allows us to see rhetoric as an ongoing process, meeting the needs of different cultures in different ways.

WHAT IS RHETORIC?

In 2500 years the word *rhetoric* has taken on a range of meanings. People may use the term to refer to skillful, but often deceptive, eloquence. They point to the empty pomposity of political oratory, the slick language of advertising, or the verbal sparring of heated discussions and claim, "That's all rhetoric, empty hot air with no substance behind it." Rhetoric, so defined, is a fraudulent practice intended to give some people an advantage over others by appealing to their emotions or prejudices, but not to their intelligence. Allied with this view is the notion that rhetoric deals exclusively with language rather than with ideas. Flowery figures of speech and double-talk give the appearance of substance, while the "real questions" go unanswered. "The rhetoric was impressive," some people might say, "but he didn't tell us much." This view has had formidable support, most notably from Socrates and from Plato, who claims in the *Gorgias*, "The rhetorician need not know the truth about things; he has only to discover some way of persuading the ignorant that he has more knowledge than those who know." Although many people still attach negative connotations to the term *rhetoric*, most scholars do not. They now regard all uses of language as inherently suasive, in effect removing the onus of deception or manipulation evident in earlier discussions of the art.

Historically, *rhetoric* also has had positive connotations, suggesting a commendable skill with words. The Declaration of Independence, for example, eloquently expresses the consensus of a people persuaded to uphold certain self-evident truths. Similarly, writers of great literature have employed powerful language to make us cry, to poke fun at our human frailties, and to command our support for important causes. Those who believe that rhetoric has a useful function see it as a tool, inherently neither good nor bad. A deceitful person will use the art to deceive; an ethical person, to make truth and justice prevail. Aristotle, who regards rhetoric both as a practical art and as a way of knowing, defines it in the *Rhetoric* as "an ability, in each [particular] case, to see the available means of persuasion" (p. 36). When rightly practiced, Aristotle argues, rhetoric serves an honest and useful purpose. "And if it is argued that great harm can be done by unjustly using such power of words, this objection applies to all good things . . . for by using these justly one would do the greatest good and unjustly, the greatest harm" (p. 35).

As we shall see, every historical period characterizes the rhetorical tradition differently, sometimes focusing on oral discourse, sometimes on written texts. Some rhetoricians concern themselves exclusively with style (narrowly defined), or delivery, or invention, while others enlarge the discipline to include many arts and forms of communication. Currently, the term *rhetoric* can even refer to books—"Open your rhetorics to page 109"—and courses—"She teaches rhetoric"—that may not, in fact, treat rhetorical principles at all or that subordinate them to the study of grammar or literature.

Given the multiplicity of meanings *rhetoric* has accumulated, it may be foolish to attempt a working definition here. Yet the term identifies a discipline fundamental to this book, as its title makes clear. To insure that we are attaching roughly similar connotations to the word, let me spell out five assumptions governing my use of the term:

1. Rhetoric is both a field of humane study and a pragmatic art; that is, we can read about it as well as practice it.
2. The practice of rhetoric is a culturally determined, dynamic process. Rhetoric enables writers and speakers to design messages for particular audiences and purposes, but because people in various cultures and historical periods have assumed different definitions of what makes communication effective, rhetorical principles change. Although Aristotle's description of the art is still relevant, we must not assume that rhetorical principles articulated in the past *necessarily* determine or reflect contemporary practices.
3. When we practice rhetoric, we use language, either spoken or written, to "induce cooperation" in an audience.
4. The purpose of rhetoric, inducing cooperation, involves more than mere persuasion, narrowly defined. Discourse that affects an audience, that informs, moves, delights, and teaches, has a rhetorical aim. Not all verbal or written communication aims to create an effect in an audience; the brief exchanges between people engaged in informal conversation usually do not have a rhetorical purpose. But when we use language in more formal ways, with the intention of changing attitudes or behaviors, of explaining a subject matter, of expressing the self, or of calling attention to a text that can be appreciated for its artistic merits, our purpose is rhetorical.
5. Rhetoric implies choices, for both the speaker or writer and the audience. When we practice rhetoric we make decisions about our subject, audience, point of view, purpose, and message. We select our best evidence, the best order in which to

present our ideas, and the best resources of language to express them. Our choices aim to create an effect in our audience. However, the notion of choice carries with it an important ethical responsibility. Our strategies must be reasonable and honest. Furthermore, the audience must have a choice in responding to the message, must be able to adopt, modify, or reject it. A burglar who holds a gun to my head and calmly expresses an intention to rob me may induce my cooperation, but not by means of rhetoric. Similarly, a formal argument that urges human beings not to age is not rhetorical. Many modern rhetoricians agree that rhetoric is inoperative when the audience lacks the power to respond freely to the message.

CLASSICAL RHETORIC

Many contemporary practices in teaching writing have antecedents in classical (Greek and Roman) rhetoric. Aristotle's three appeals—to the good will of the speaker, to the nature of the audience, to the logic of the subject matter—are the basis for the discussion of the writer-reader-subject relationships in Chapter 1. Aristotle also introduces the term *topic*, still in use today, although our definition of it differs from Aristotle's. Classical rhetoricians consider style one of the five "departments" of rhetoric, and by Cicero's time, three levels of style had evolved, each intended to achieve a different purpose. Even in this early period, we find a school of rhetoricians, the sophists, whose emphasis on style prompted Plato's criticism that rhetoric amounted to no more than deceitful flattery. Prewriting also has its roots in classical rhetoric, for invention or ways of discovering lines of argument is another one of rhetoric's five departments. Finally, the five-paragraph theme, the staple of many writing classes, has analogues in formulas classical rhetoricians proposed for structuring arguments. Corax of Syracuse (fl. 460 B.C.E.), generally thought to have composed the first rhetorical treatise to help Sicilian landowners win title to disputed property, proposed that legal arguments have four parts. Aristotle adopted the same four divisions, and Cicero expanded them to six. Quintilian recommended that speeches arguing court cases have five parts. Although classical rhetoricians differed on precisely how many sections an argument should have, they established principles of arrangement that structured speeches in clearly defined sections, each part contributing to the whole in a particular way.

Certain practices distinguish classical rhetoric from the rhetorics of other periods. First, it was primarily a spoken, not a written, art. Second, it focused primarily on persuasive discourse, as traditionally defined. Rhetoric enabled politicians, lawyers, and statesmen to argue court cases (forensic or judicial rhetoric), shape political decisions about the nation's future (deliberative rhetoric), or make speeches of praise or blame on ceremonial occasions (epideictic rhetoric). When classical rhetoricians codified what had already become accepted practice, they divided rhetoric into five parts or departments: invention (*inventio*, ways of discovering arguments and supporting evidence), arrangement (*dispositio*, ways of organizing the parts of a discourse), style (*elocutio*, ways of ornamenting discourse), memory (*memoria*, mnemonic techniques), and delivery (*pronuntiatio*, techniques for practicing and giving oral speeches). The most influential works that describe the practice of classical rhetoricians are Aristotle's *Rhetoric* (c. 335 B.C.E.), Cicero's *De Inventione* (86 B.C.E.) and *De Oratore* (55 B.C.E.), and Quintilian's *Institutio Oratoria* (C.E. 94–95).

Aristotle's life's work (384–322 B.C.E.) was to understand intellectual activity and the relationships among the theoretical sciences and the practical and productive arts. Logic and rhetoric represented for Aristotle important tools (*organa*) or methods of knowing applicable to both the arts and the sciences. The *Rhetoric* is divided into three books, which treat respectively the nature of rhetoric, of invention, and of arrangement and style. For Aristotle, universal and verifiable truths belong to logic; rhetoric deals with *probable* truth, with opinions and beliefs that can be advanced with greater or lesser certainty. Rhetoric is a form of reasoning about probabilities, based on assumptions people share as members of a community. Aristotle groups all rhetorical arguments into two categories based on the means of persuasion used to support what the speaker believes to be true. Inartistic proofs make use of external evidence such as witnesses, contracts, evidence based on torture. Artistic proofs, on the other hand, are those proofs marshaled by the orator, who may rely on three means of persuasion. The orator may compose the speech in such a way as to create a favorable impression of himself as a wise, virtuous man of good will (*ethos*). The speaker also may appeal to the character or mental state of the audience (*pathos*). And he may argue from the subject matter (*logos*) by using the inductive logic of examples and the deductive logic of enthymemes.

Book Two of the *Rhetoric* explains each of these three means of persuasion and introduces the notion of topics (*topoi* or commonplaces). By *topoi* (Greek for "places") Aristotle does not mean a list of subjects, but rather ways of discovering arguments applying to any subject matter. All subjects, says Aristotle, can be argued on the grounds that a thing is possible or impossible, that it did or didn't happen, that it will or won't happen, or that it is relatively greater or lesser, better or worse, than something else. These four grounds are known as the *common topoi*. Also in Book Two of the *Rhetoric*, Aristotle discusses a second grouping of twenty-eight *topoi* for inventing enthymemes. These *topoi* represent lines of inquiry—such as arguing from opposites, from cause and effect, from the definitions of words, from parts to the whole, and so on. Aristotle's discovery procedures receive further elaboration in his *Topics*, a work Cicero later interpreted to include topics-as-subjects as well as topics-as-methods-of-inquiry. Much later, in Renaissance England, the *topoi* came to mean "commonplaces," subjects to write about. The usual definition of *topic* in today's English classes is "subject for writing about," not "way of approaching a subject." Some of Aristotle's *topoi*, however, survive in contemporary composition textbooks as methods of paragraph development: definition, comparison, cause-effect, and example.

In Book Three Aristotle maintains that arguments should have two parts; the first part states the case, and the second part proves it. At most, arguments should have only four sections: the introduction (*proem*), the outline or narration of the subject (*statement* of the case), the proofs for and against the case (the *argument*), and the summary (*epilogue*). Believing that a discourse persuades by reason rather than by calling attention to itself as a work of art, Aristotle advocates a plain or natural style that exhibits the virtues of clarity, dignity, propriety, and correctness. This view of style contrasts significantly with rhetorical traditions that precede and follow Aristotle—the Greek sophistic tradition of the fifth and fourth centuries B.C.E. and the Ciceronian tradition. The sophists emphasized style above all. It is to this dependence on ornamentation that Plato responds in the *Gorgias* by castigating rhetoric as an ignoble deceit, an attempt to flatter the audience. Aristotle defends rhetoric from those who would use its principles to persuade an audience of what is untrue or evil, arguing that rhetoric is a useful, practical art, dependent on logical argumentation.

Cicero (106–43 B.C.E.), a brilliant Roman politician, philosopher, and speaker, expected the orator to command a broad understanding of culture:

> no one should be numbered with the orators who is not accomplished in all those arts that befit the well-bred; for though we do not actually parade these in our discourse, it is none the less made clear to demonstration whether we are strangers to them or have learned to know them. (*De Oratore*, p. 100)

The orator must know a great deal about human experience in order to defend the political state eloquently. For Cicero, rhetoric is a branch of political science, if we define *political science* broadly to include all of the liberal arts.

Cicero composed at least seven rhetorical treatises, one on invention when he was only nineteen years old. He also wrote numerous orations and epistles, which generations of students studied as models of Cicero's theoretical principles. He expanded the parts of an argument from four to six, dividing Aristotle's section on the proofs into separate categories: *exordium* (introduction), *narratio* (a discussion of what has occurred to generate the issue to be resolved), *partitio* (an exposition of the points to be proven or a division of the argument), *confirmatio* (proofs "for" or confirmation of the argument), *refutatio* (proofs disproving the opponent's arguments), and *conclusio* (a review of the argument and a final appeal to the audience). Over time, these sections became discrete forms, which students practiced piecemeal as school exercises. Eventually the exercises, separated from the whole discourse of which they originally were a part, gave rise to the "modes" of composition. *Narratio* became a narrative essay; *partitio*, an expository essay; *confirmatio*, an argumentative essay.

Because the *Rhetorica ad Herennium* (c. 86–82 B.C.E.) for centuries was thought to have been written by Cicero, we credit him with having suggested three levels of style—high, middle, and low—intended respectively to move, delight, and teach the audience. Cicero's treatises tend to emphasize forensics, the use of rhetoric to argue legal cases, but because he believed that the orator needed to know many subjects, Cicero's influence had special significance during the Renaissance, with its emphasis on the humanistic training of clergy and statesmen.

Quintilian (35–100 C.E.) was born in Spain but later became a prominent teacher of rhetoric in Rome. He agrees with Cicero that the rhetor must be educated broadly but asserts that he must also be a good and moral man. Educational institutions from the Middle Ages to the twentieth century reflect Quintilian's insistence on the moral as well as the intellectual training of students. Although books three through twelve of Quintilian's *Institutio Oratoria* represent traditional Ciceronian discussions of the five departments of rhetoric, books one and two detail an educational program for training the ideal orator of strong moral character.

As soon as a child was able to read and write, he received instruction in grammar, which was for Quintilian a twofold science that encompassed speaking and writing correctly as well as interpreting the poets. The grammar teacher (*grammaticus*) taught rules for proper word order, agreement, and word choice, and gave lectures on every kind of writer. In this way students could learn by imitation to recite and comment on literature, noting the type of feet in a metrical line, the parts of speech in a line, and so on. Then students proceeded to write their own imitations of fables and verse as well as aphorisms, character sketches, and moral essays. Paraphrasing or imitating models was the major method of teaching grammar. After the child completed grammar instruction, the *rhetoricus*, a second teacher, managed the student's education. The *rhetoricus* taught more advanced rhetorical studies and assigned exercises in epideictic speaking and disputation. In general, he taught students to master the five departments of classical rhetoric. Grammatical studies, then, gave students an understanding of what correct discourse and poetic interpretation entail (knowledge of *what*); rhetorical studies equipped students to accomplish things by action (knowledge of *how*).

Quintilian's curriculum sounds similar to some contemporary writing courses, doesn't it? Even though classical rhetoric excluded grammar (grammar, like logic, was a separate discipline), Quintilian codified a hierarchy of instruction that began with grammar and proceeded to rhetorical studies. Quintilian's influence on the curriculum was so strong historically that even today many people believe that students must first study formal grammar and read "good writers" before they can learn to write well. Quintilian also incorporated writing into the curriculum; he valued training in writing as a means of reinforcing speaking skills. Then, as now, literature served an important function in the classroom, for the most important methods Quintilian used to develop writing skills were imitating, translating, or paraphrasing literary models. Quintilian's model certainly isn't the only design for a writing course, and many contemporary writing teachers give the study of grammar and literature much less prominence than Quintilian did. Nevertheless, most of us probably learned to write by methods at least indirectly traceable to Quintilian.

MEDIEVAL AND RENAISSANCE RHETORIC

The enormous social and political upheaval following the fall of Rome put much of the classical rhetorical tradition in jeopardy. During the Middle Ages and the Renaissance, rhetoric underwent several transformations, becoming increasingly adapted to the needs of the Christian Church and the emerging nations of Europe. Two developments especially interest us as writing teachers. First, the period saw a shift in emphasis among the five departments of classical rhetoric. Although Aristotle had assigned invention primary importance, medieval and Renaissance rhetoricians tended to emphasize style (*elocutio*). Through the influence of Christianity, invention became less significant, for biblical truths were inspired or "invented" by God; principles of style, however, helped men study God's Word and explain it to others. This attention to the Bible as a text, aided later by the development of the printing press, gave rhetoric a new focus. Whereas classical rhetoric had been concerned primarily with spoken discourse, medieval and Renaissance scholars increasingly applied rhetorical principles to written discourse.

Saint Augustine (354–430 C.E.) was a particularly influential figure in establishing this new focus. He not only upheld classical learning but also put it to use in the study of Christian texts, thereby redirecting rhetoric from being a public, oral form of persuasion to a private, written form of literary interpretation. Trained in classical rhetoric and, for a time, a teacher of rhetoric while he studied law, Aurelius Augustinus converted to Christianity in 386. He became a monk and wrote many letters, treatises, sermons, and hermeneutical works. Initially, he used his training in rhetoric and the law to defend Christian doctrine from contemporary heresies. He had read Cicero's works and appears to have been familiar with Platonic and Aristotelian thought through Latin treatises. At a time when many Christian scholars found no value in pagan, classical learning, Augustine argued that rhetorical principles could serve preaching and biblical interpretation. In *De Doctrina Christiana* (396–427 C.E.), he advises Christian scholars and orators (preachers) to take from the classical tradition those practices useful to understanding biblical truths and to teaching converts how to live their lives. In attempting to accommodate classical learning to Christian theology, Augustine found rhetoric a useful tool for interpreting scriptural truths and persuading people to live by them.

A second development during this period saw rhetoric become both a practical art and an academic subject. As a practical art, rhetoric served the clergy, whose sermons persuaded congregations to adopt Christian principles. Rhetoric was also a practical tool in secular and ecclesiastical courts, where letter writing became an important means of conducting legal and diplomatic transactions. As an academic subject, rhetoric shaped treatises and commentaries studied by scholastic philosophers. Cicero was favored as a classical authority until about the thirteenth century, when Aristotle's *Rhetoric* was recovered in a Latin translation.

In the Middle Ages, undergraduate students pursuing the bachelor of arts degree studied the *trivium*: grammar (*ars poetria* or verse writing), logic, and rhetoric. Graduate students received additional training in the disciplines making up the *quadrivium*: arithmetic, astronomy, music, and geometry. The study of rhetoric focused on two arts, letter writing (*ars dictaminis*) and preaching (*ars praedicandi*).[2] Both arts were heavily influenced by the so-called "Second Sophistic Tradition" (ca. 100–500 C.E.) and by writers like Cassiodorus and Bishop Isidore of Seville.

Cassiodorus (490–586 C.E.), minister to an illiterate Italian king, compiled twelve books of letters under the title *Variae*. Kings and nobles during this period often depended on literate servants to compose, write down, and deliver orally messages of considerable political importance. Students in the Middle Ages studied model letters like those of Cassiodorus and learned how to imitate their formulas and stylistic embellishments.

Style is also the chief concern of Bishop Isidore of Seville (c. 570–636 C.E.). His work, known variously as *Origenes* or *Etymologiae*, devotes considerable attention to summarizing the arts of grammar, rhetoric, and dialectic. "Like other encyclopedists," writes James Murphy, "he was trying merely to salvage what he could from the ancient heritage" (*Rhetoric in the Middle Ages*, p. 76). In cataloguing many traditional rhetorical figures, Isidore slights invention and arrangement and altogether ignores memory and delivery.

The sophists' concern with ornamentation can be traced back to the three Ciceronian levels of style: the grand style intended to move an audience, the middle style intended to delight an audience, and the plain style intended to teach an audience. To move a congregation to accept Christianity or to teach Christian precepts, the clergy ornamented sermons and letters with "figures," conveniently catalogued in many stylistic compendia. The anonymously authored *Rhetorica ad Herennium*

---

2. For a fuller discussion of medieval rhetoric, consult James J. Murphy, *Rhetoric in the Middle Ages* (Berkeley: University of California Press, 1974).

(c. 86 B.C.E.) enjoyed enormous popularity as a standard list. Although the "doctrine of figures" had been well established in Quintilian's day, the tradition has defied the attempts of scholars to trace its shifting, growing classifications. Essentially, the figures were of two kinds: (1) *tropes*, figures of thought or sense (e.g., metaphor, metonymy, synecdoche), and (2) *schemes*, figures of words and arrangement (e.g., amplifying or repeating an idea, alliteration, assonance). The figures weren't merely ornamental; they often reflected strategies of invention and arrangement.

Renaissance rhetoricians also concerned themselves with words, particularly with the distinction between words and the "things" they stood for, between *verba* and *res*, form and matter. Sister Miriam Joseph divides Renaissance rhetoricians into three groups: the traditionalists, the figurists, and the Ramists. The differences among them, she suggests, center on whether they viewed the topics of invention as belonging to rhetoric, to logic, or to both—a moot question really because "notwithstanding the variety of opinion as to the number of topics or places, there was complete unanimity among all Renaissance groups as to their nature, use, and importance" (*Rhetoric in Shakespeare's Time*, p. 30).

The traditionalists, among them Desiderius Erasmus and Thomas Wilson, tended to appreciate the importance of all five departments of rhetoric. Erasmus' *De Copia* (1512) is divided into two parts, the first teaching students how to vary their arguments by means of schemes and tropes and the second encouraging students to master lines of inquiry (topics) to invent subjects in various ways. Even though Erasmus treats words and things, form and matter, separately, he maintains a close Aristotelian connection between them. Erasmus was probably the first to advocate constant practice in writing rather than rote drill as a teaching technique. He encouraged students to keep commonplace books as an aid to invention. He also urged them to express the same argument in a variety of styles and to treat the same topic along several lines of reasoning. Thomas Wilson's *Arte of Rhetorique* (1553) presents the whole classical tradition in its five parts. It reintroduces a discussion of memory and delivery, often slighted in earlier works, and because it was one of the first rhetorics written in English instead of Latin, it enjoyed considerable popularity as a model of English prose style.

The second group of rhetoricians, the figurists, subordinated logic to rhetoric, emphasizing above all the importance of style. George Puttenham's *The Arte of English Poesie* (1589), which treats 107 figures, and Henry Peacham's *The Garden of Eloquence* (1577), which catalogues 184 figures, are important representatives of this tradition. A third group, the Ramists, tended to subordinate rhetoric to logic. They assigned invention, arrangement, and memory to logic and defined rhetoric as concerned with style and delivery. This regrouping of classical rhetoric's five departments created a dichotomy between matter and form, between processes that were said to belong to the intellect (logic) and those springing from the imagination (rhetoric).

Renaissance rhetoricians were master classifiers and cataloguers concerned primarily about the matter of *copia*, literally "abundance." *Copia* refers not only to various techniques for embellishing the argument but also to the many ways in which arguments could be invented. The poets and prose writers who studied these techniques produced a literature as rich in imagery and sound patterns as it was thoughtful and deeply rooted in logic.

THE RENAISSANCE TO THE TWENTIETH CENTURY

In the centuries following the Renaissance several approaches to rhetoric held the field in what W. Ross Winterowd calls "the war between the plain, unadorned method of human discourse and the elegant and ornate" (*Rhetoric: A Synthesis*, p. 46). The war centered on a difference of opinion among prominent scholars seeking to adapt classical principles to new developments in literature and the sciences. In blending the old and new, they tended to emphasize different elements of the tradition. Throughout this period, at least three points of view shaped rhetorical theory: the scientific, elocutionary, and literary perspectives. Although none of these perspectives significantly influenced current methods of teaching writing, except perhaps the literary, all three demonstrate how dynamic a process rhetoric is. It finds its roots not only in the past but also responds to contemporary concerns. People change the art to suit their purposes.

The scientific perspective stresses the importance of invention and advocates a plain style. It represents an attempt to adapt rhetoric to the emerging natural and social sciences. Although Francis Bacon (1561–1626) wrote no rhetorical treatises, many of his writings suggest new directions for rhetoric in the service of scientific studies. Bacon separates logic and rhetoric, reason and imagination, as distinct faculties that nevertheless must work harmoniously. "The duty and office of rhetoric is to apply reason to imagination for the better moving of the will," writes Bacon in *Advancement of Learning* (p. 66). In redefining invention, he minimizes the classical penchant for the deductive enthymeme, giving greater significance to inductive processes and memory, which help the scientist unlock knowledge stored in the mind. Bacon also advocates a "Senecan style," characterized by relatively short sentences, simple words, and little ornamentation. In his view, the style should suit the subject matter and the audience. A plain style, a code similar to mathematics, best expresses the precise, objective observations of scientists.

In some ways, George Campbell (1719–1796) also approaches rhetoric scientifically by incorporating principles from what we now call the social and behavioral sciences. Although upholding many precepts of classical rhetoric, Campbell's work is also influenced by Bacon, Locke, Hume, and Hartley, writers who attempt to explain the workings of the human mind. As the first sentence of Campbell's *The Philosophy of Rheto-*

ric (1776) reveals, rhetoric is a process of effecting change in an audience; "In speaking there is always some end proposed, or some effect which the speaker intends to produce on the hearer." To be effective, rhetoricians must understand human nature, must analyze the audience they hope to influence. Elaborating on Locke and Hume's discussions, Campbell proposes a hierarchy of four mental "faculties" common to all human beings: an understanding, an imagination, passions, and a will. Although the speaker may have one predominant purpose—"to enlighten the understanding, to please the imagination, to move the passions, or to influence the will"—a speech may introduce secondary rhetorical aims that enhance its persuasive power. Campbell is best known for reestablishing an important connection between rhetoric and psychology, between the arts of eloquence a speaker uses and their effect on an audience. He also explores the use of wit, humor, and ridicule as rhetorical strategies; examines the limitations of the deductive syllogism; enlarges the kinds of evidence that could be used to support arguments, including common sense, experience, analogy, testimony, and "calculations concerning chances"; and establishes what is now known as the "doctrine of usage," which suggests that generalizations about language should be based not on classical "authorities" but on the contemporary practices of reputable English authors.

A second perspective on rhetoric emphasized delivery. Like Bacon and Campbell, the elocutionists hoped to give classical rhetoric a contemporary focus, but their principle aim was to advance the art of public speaking. For too long, elocutionists claimed, rhetoricians had ignored delivery and emphasized almost exclusively the written word. But now public lectures, oral reading, parliamentary debates, and pulpit oratory offered numerous opportunities to express ideas orally. Thomas Sheridan's *Lectures on Elocution* (1762) and John Walker's *Elements of Elocution* (1781) offered speakers advice about pronunciation, gestures, voice control, and accent. Other elocutionary textbooks listed tropes and schemes for ornamenting speeches and provided models, often in the form of letters, for addressing various audiences in an elegant, genteel style. Prose and verse passages often were included so that students could practice reading material aloud. Although elocutionists didn't ignore invention, they concerned themselves primarily with delivery and style and upheld rhetoric as the practice of effective speaking in formal contexts. As public speaking declined in importance, so did the elocutionary movement. Nevertheless, the elocutionists demonstrated that delivery could be studied seriously and could win for its ablest practitioners international acclaim.

The third perspective focused not so much on public speaking or on the new science as on literary texts. The literary perspective, however, encompassed a spectrum of views concerning style. First, the neoclassicists, men like Jonathan Swift (1667–1745) and Jonathan Ward (d. 1758), revered the ancients and sought to reassert principles of taste built on classical precepts. A good writer, they maintained, studies classical authors and then imitates their style. The works of Horace, Homer, Virgil, and Cicero represented especially significant models. A good style, said the neoclassicists, need not show complete originality, need not be "modern." Rather, it should be relatively unadorned, free of ambiguity, and "correct," conforming to the style of Greek and Latin models. *Propriety* and *perspicuity* were the watchwords, and rhetorical choices tended to be primarily a matter of doctrine and rule. In reestablishing the importance of classical learning, these prominent men of letters hoped to give English the same power of expression so admired in Greek and Latin literature. Unfortunately, by slavishly adhering to classical principles and denigrating modern tastes, many neoclassicists reduced stylistic precepts to absolute law.

At the other end of the scale were literary scholars who admired the ornate style and revived the study of invention. They claimed as their authority Longinus, a third-century Roman whose treatise *On the Sublime* had been translated into English in 1674. Longinus recognized enthusiasm as a respectable source of ideas. Rhetoric, he claimed, need not merely persuade audiences; it also could transport them. Writers such as Joseph Addison (1672–1719) and Edmund Burke (1729–1797) placed great emphasis on sublimity of thought as well as style. The "sublime" that Longinus discussed arises from contemplating greatness, from permitting the beautiful to act on the mind through the senses. Sublimity of style moves an audience with irresistible power, grand thoughts, and eloquent expression. The followers of Longinus yielded to their emotions, to forces of enthusiasm, in order to create, especially through metaphor, expressions that would transport their audiences.

In between these two groups, the proponents of enthusiasm and the advocates of propriety, we find a large group of rhetoricians who blended the old and the new. They combined rhetoric and poetics, which the classical tradition had treated as separate verbal arts. They illustrated rhetorical principles, not by quoting Greek and Latin models, but by citing English literature. They looked to classical theories but also took into account contemporary discussions concerning genius, reason, and imagination. This synthesis represents the beginning of modern literary criticism and is best illustrated in the work of Hugh Blair (1718–1800).

Blair, a well-known preacher, was Regius Professor of Rhetoric and Belles Lettres at the University of Edinburgh for more than twenty years, retiring in 1783. *Lectures on Rhetoric and Belles Lettres* was published in the same year. "Blair explains in the preface that many students, relying on superficial notes, were circulating imperfect copies of his lectures. The purpose of the volume, therefore, was to give to the public an accurate account of his teachings."[3] Addressing his forty-seven lectures

3. Golden, Berquist, and Coleman, p. 95; see also James L. Golden and Edward P. J. Corbett, eds., *The Rhetoric of Blair, Campbell, and Whately* (New York: Holt, Rinehart and Winston, 1968).

to beginners, Blair presents a systematic overview of rhetoric-as-verbal-art. He deals with matters of taste and aesthetics, surveys classical and contemporary rhetoric, reviews grammar, offers a history of elocution, and explains stylistic principles by analyzing the prose of Addison and Swift. Although he prefers the plain style, he doesn't refute the Longinians' emphasis on the sublime. The sublime, he maintains, rests not in words but in things, not in stylistic adroitness but in noble and pleasurable ideas. For their time Blair's lectures offered the most comprehensive survey of the rhetorical tradition. They were enormously popular. In addition to summarizing the old, they also forged a new alliance between rhetoric and other verbal arts. Blair's rhetoric doesn't focus merely on style, plain or ornate, but on culture, on human beings and how they use language to communicate with different audiences for different purposes.

Blair's *Lectures on Rhetoric and Belles Lettres* became a popular textbook in colleges and universities, not only in England and Scotland but in America as well. Yale adopted it in 1785, Harvard in 1788, and Dartmouth in 1822.[4] Shortly after the University of North Carolina opened in 1795, the plan of education assigned the president the responsibility for lectures in "Rhetoric on the plan of Sheridan" and "Belles-Lettres on the plan of Blair and [Charles] Rollin." The study of rhetoric in American universities is a relatively recent development, generally considered to have begun in 1806, when John Quincy Adams became Boyleston Professor of Rhetoric and Oratory at Harvard. Throughout the first half of the nineteenth century, the study of rhetoric gained support from scholarly developments in philology, the forerunner of modern linguistics, and by a popular interest in public lectures and debates. At first, these courses emphasized oratory, rhetoric, and the study of language and logic; as a rule, they were taught by clergymen or moral philosophers. In addition to Blair's *Lectures*, other works enjoyed considerable influence: Thomas Sheridan's *Lectures on Elocution* (1762), Lord Kames' *Elements of Criticism* (1762), and Richard Whately's *Elements of Rhetoric* (1828).

Beyond attending lectures on rhetoric and writing compositions for professors, early nineteenth-century college students formed debating

---

4. William Riley Parker, "Where Do English Departments Come From?" *College English* 28 (1967), 343. The history of teaching rhetoric and composition in American colleges receives thorough discussion in James A. Berlin, *Writing Instruction in Nineteenth-Century American Colleges* (Studies in Writing and Rhetoric; Carbondale: Southern Illinois University Press, 1984); Albert Kitzhaber, *Rhetoric in American Colleges, 1850–1900* (SMU Studies in Composition and Rhetoric; Dallas: Southern Methodist University Press, 1990); Robert J. Connors, *Composition-Rhetoric: Backgrounds, Theory, and Pedagogy* (Pittsburgh Series in Composition, Literacy, and Culture; Pittsburgh: University of Pittsburgh Press, 1997); John C. Brereton, ed., *The Origins of Composition Studies in the American College, 1875–1925* (Pittsburgh Series in Composition, Literacy, and Culture; Pittsburgh: University of Pittsburgh Press, 1995); and Sharon Crowley, *Composition in the University: Historical and Polemical Essays* (Pittsburgh Series in Composition, Literacy, and Culture; Pittsburgh: University of Pittsburgh Press, 1998).

societies, some of which still survive today. As a rule, these extracurricular clubs were completely run by students. They wrote compositions, organized debates, and prepared extracts from works they admired to read aloud or declaim. They corrected one another's writing and critiqued the debates. Some societies sponsored literary magazines, amassed large libraries, and raised funds to build dormitories. As Anne Ruggles Gere has pointed out in *Writing Groups: History, Theory, and Implications*, college debating societies provided a forum for discussing political issues, contacts that sustained students professionally long after graduation, and opportunities to socialize in colleges that lacked cultural resources, constructive diversions, and few opportunities to meet women.

Courses in the reading and analysis of English literature were not to become part of the curriculum until the second half of the nineteenth century. Prior to that time, students enrolled in a uniform college curriculum, some attending school for only a year or two. After the Civil War, however, curricula became increasingly diversified into departments and specialized majors. By 1883 forty college teachers, representing twenty institutions, met in New York to establish the Modern Language Association. Most of the faculty members present taught modern foreign languages, but English teachers joined them in asserting "the disciplinary value of the modern as compared with the ancient languages" [Latin and Greek].[5] By the end of the century, the contributions of British and Scottish rhetoricians and philosophers to the history of rhetoric had found a place in the curriculum of most major American universities.

CONTEMPORARY RHETORIC

The twentieth century has seen a resurgence of interest in rhetoric. Modern scholars have continued to build on centuries-old traditions, reinterpreting them to assert the importance of human communication here and now. Scholars such as I. A. Richards, Kenneth Burke, Chaim Perelman, Richard Weaver, and Stephen Toulmin view rhetoric from quite different perspectives, but they're all principally concerned with contemporary uses of language in a complex society. Some focus on questions of meaning, on how we use language and other media to make sense of our world. Others, Weaver among them, concern themselves with ethics: "As rhetoric confronts us with choices involving values, the rhetorician is a preacher to us, noble if he tries to direct our passion toward noble ends and base if he uses our passion to confuse and degrade us" ("Language Is Sermonic," p. 210). Still others value rhetoric as a means of knowing. For them, language is crucial to thinking,

5. [George Winchester Stone], "The Beginning, Development and Impact of the MLA as a Learned Society: 1883–1958," *Publications of the Modern Language Association of America* 73 (December 1958), 25.

to advancing human knowledge. Toulmin, for example, who finds for-mal syllogistic logic impractical, develops a model for arguments that use language not so much to proclaim truth but to foster understanding. Finally, some contemporary rhetoricians explore the impact of language on political and social relationships, viewing rhetoric as an instrument of social change. In some ways, of course, the "new" rhetoric isn't new; it reaches back to the classical tradition. But it also incorporates recent perspectives from linguistics, anthropology, psychology, philosophy, semantics, politics, and even advertising to synthesize the arts of rheto-ric our culture now practices.

We won't survey here all of the significant contemporary develop-ments in rhetoric. Some of them will be discussed later, when we examine particular teaching strategies in light of current rhetorical theories. Pre-writing strategies, for example, reflect a renewed interest in invention, a development discussed in Chapters 6 and 7. Here we want to focus on two major contemporary figures often cited in the professional literature English teachers read, Kenneth Burke and James Kinneavy.

Kenneth Burke (1897–1993) has had the greatest impact on rhetoric in the twentieth century. Since the publication of *Counter-Statement* (1931), a succession of books articulate Burke's concern with the problem of language. "To his thorough knowledge of classical tradition," writes Marie Hochmuth, "he has added rich insights gained from serious study of anthropology, sociology, history, psychology, philosophy, and the whole body of humane letters."[6] Although essentially a philosopher, Burke views rhetoric so comprehensively that scholars in many disci-plines find his work valuable. Instead of placing inordinate emphasis on persuasion, or style, or literary criticism, Burke enlarges the scope of rhetoric to include all of the "symbolic means of inducing coopera-tion in beings that by nature respond to symbols" (*A Rhetoric of Motives*, p. 43).

Human beings, asserts Burke, are linguistic animals, using and misus-ing symbols. Rhetoric is a function of language that enables human beings to overcome the divisions separating them. Because human be-ings are, most of the time, at odds with one another, language permits them to "induce cooperation," to identify themselves with other individ-uals:

> If I had to sum up in one word the differences between the "old" rhetoric and a "new" (a rhetoric reinvigorated by fresh insights which the "new sciences" contributed to the subject), I would reduce it to this: The key term for the old rhetoric was "persuasion" and its stress was upon deliberate design. The key term for the "new" rhetoric would be "identifi-cation," which can include a partially "unconscious" factor in appeal.

6. Marie Hochmuth, "Kenneth Burke and the 'New Rhetoric,'" *Quarterly Journal of Speech* 38 (April 1952), 144. This essay offers an excellent overview of Burke's work and serves as my principal source for the following discussion.

> "Identification" at its simplest is also a deliberative device, as when the politician seeks to identify himself with his audience. In this respect, its equivalents are plentiful in Aristotle's *Rhetoric*. But identification can also be an end, as when people earnestly yearn to identify themselves with some group or other. Here they are not necessarily being acted upon by a conscious external agent, but may be acting upon themselves to this end. ("Rhetoric—Old and New," p. 63)

Identification is a key concept in Burke's theory of rhetoric; it explains why human beings act rhetorically on one another—to promote social cohesion.

The central question Burke investigates is, "What is involved, when we say what people are doing and why they are doing it?" (*A Grammar of Motives*, p. xv). In other words, he concerns himself with attributing motives to human actions. Instead of viewing motive in simple, mechanistic terms like "cause and effect" or "stimulus and response," Burke approaches the study of motivation through the analysis of drama. *Motive* acts as a kind of shorthand term for *situation*:

> In a rounded statement about motives, you must have some word that names the *act* (names what took place, in thought or deed), and another that names the *scene* (the background of the act, the situation in which it occurred); also, you must indicate what person or kind of person (*agent*) performed the act, what means or instruments he used (*agency*) and the *purpose*. Men may violently disagree about the purposes behind a given act, or about the character of the person who did it, or how he did it, or in what kind of situation he acted; or they may even insist upon totally different words to name the act itself. But be that as it may, any complete statement about motives will offer *some kind* of answers to these five questions: what was done (act), when or where it was done (scene), who did it (agent), how he did it (agency), and why (purpose). (p. xv)

These five terms—act, scene, agent, agency, and purpose—become the "pentad" for examining human motivation dramatistically, in terms of action and its ends.

Burke's rhetoric of motives interprets human relations in terms of "signs," not just spoken language but also nonverbal communication that achieves identification. For example, regardless of what my department head may say to me when he visits my office, the visit itself represents a symbolic, nonverbal action associated with administrative rhetoric. Meeting me on my "territory" suggests that he identifies himself with my concerns, a rhetorical strategy more likely to induce my cooperation than if he had summoned me to his office. The tendency toward identification also promotes symbolic actions such as signing a petition, attending a social function because we ought to make an appearance, remembering someone's birthday, or carefully selecting the clothes we wear on the first day of class.

Burke's major contribution to rhetorical theory is his attempt to broaden its scope and to connect all acts of language to the social fabric of the culture in which they occur. In *A Rhetoric of Motives*, he redefines *persuasion*: "All told, persuasion ranges from the bluntest quest of advantage, as in sales promotion or propaganda, through courtship, social etiquette, education, and the sermon, to a 'pure' form that delights in the process of appeal for itself alone, without ulterior purpose" (p. xiv). More important, Burke reasserts the importance of rhetoric at a time when most people have become conscious of the dehumanizing influence of technology. Rhetoric functions, he argues, not to ornament arguments or even to assert truths. Rather, it uses symbols as a means whereby human beings act out with one another the drama of life.

James Kinneavy's *A Theory of Discourse* (1971) brings together with extraordinary comprehensiveness classical and contemporary developments in rhetoric. His theory is essentially Aristotelian, but it also incorporates the perspectives of modern linguists, logicians, semioticians, propaganda analysts, literary critics, philosophers, information theorists, and social scientists. Kinneavy avoids the term *rhetoric*, primarily because it has taken on meanings as broad as "the general science or art of communication" and as restricted as "style." He focuses instead on the term *discourse*, "the full text . . . of an oral or written situation."[7] His work gives us a framework for understanding what is produced when people practice rhetoric, using language purposefully to communicate ideas to an audience. His theory certainly includes rhetoric-as-persuasion, but it also examines other purposes for oral and written communication.

Beginning with the communication triangle (encoder, decoder, reality, signal), Kinneavy divides the field of English into three areas of study that explain human experience with language: syntactics, semantics, and pragmatics. Only pragmatics concerns us here. Pragmatics studies the actual *use* of meaningful signals by encoders and decoders. Viewed as the study of texts, pragmatics depends on all four terms in the communication triangle because every discourse, every spoken or written text, reflects an author who uses signals to communicate a reality for a particular purpose.

Kinneavy subdivides pragmatics into the arts, media, modes, and aims of discourse (see Fig. 4.1). The arts—speaking, writing, listening, and reading—differ according to the kinds of signals that encoders and decoders use and how they process these signals. The media define the *channels* through which the signal is transmitted. "In other words, arts of discourse are signals transmitted through various media of discourse" (p. 33). Media can be classified according to the number of encoders

---

7. James Kinneavy, *A Theory of Discourse* (New York: W. W. Norton, 1980), p. 4. Kinneavy summarizes his *Theory of Discourse* and compares it to James Moffett's *Teaching the Universe of Discourse*, Frank D'Angelo's *A Conceptual Theory of Rhetoric*, and James Britton's *The Development of Writing Abilities, 11–18*, in "A Pluralistic Synthesis of Four Contemporary Models for Teaching Composition," in *Reinventing the Rhetorical Tradition*, ed. Aviva Freedman and Ian Pringle (Conway, AR: L & S Books, 1980), pp. 37–52.

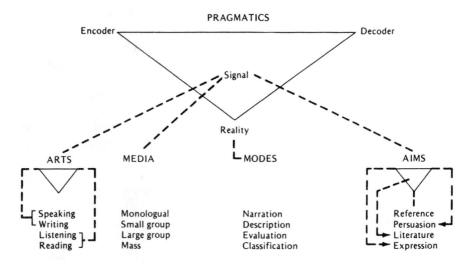

FIGURE 4.1 Pragmatics: The Study of Texts
Source: Adapted from James Kinneavy, *A Theory of Discourse*, p. 31.

and decoders using the channels at a given time. From monologual to mass media, Kinneavy's classification includes lectures, soliloquies, telephone calls, counseling sessions, panels, questionnaires, conventions, newspapers, and television.

For Kinneavy, the term *mode* is difficult to define because it has accumulated multiple meanings over the years. Alexander Bain, in *English Composition and Rhetoric* (1866), established five modes, four of which are still found in many contemporary textbooks: narration, description, exposition, and persuasion. (Bain's fifth mode was poetry). However, Kinneavy notes that argumentation or persuasion is not a mode, but an aim of discourse, not a method or way of discussing reality, but a reason or purpose for using language. Consequently, he revises the traditional classification of modes to include narration, description, evaluation, and classification.

The term *mode* denotes the kinds of realities discourse refers to. Modes answer the question, "What is this text about?" We're naming modes when we respond to this question with "It's a story (narration)," "It's a description of my dog," "It's a criticism (evaluation) of the president's foreign policy," or "It's a discussion of the types (classification) of college students." Each mode, Kinneavy maintains, is grounded in a principle of thought that permits us to view reality a certain way. "Therefore," he claims, "each of the modes has its own peculiar logic. It also has its own organizational patterns and, to some extent, its own stylistic characteristics" (p. 37). Furthermore, the modes of discourse overlap; a given text may have a dominant mode, but "[i]n actuality, it is impossible to have pure narration, description, evaluation, or classification" (p. 37).

Having defined the arts, media, and modes of discourse, Kinneavy devotes the rest of his book to a discussion of aims. The aims of discourse reflect the writer's or speaker's purpose for using language. They are perhaps the most significant subdivision of pragmatics in Kinneavy's theory because purpose determines everything else about the discourse. When our purpose is to discuss reality, we may produce what Kinneavy calls *reference discourse*. There are three kinds of reference discourse. If we know the reality and simply want to relay facts about it, we use language to inform; Kinneavy cites weather reports, news stories, and telephone directories as examples of informative discourse. Second, "[i]f this information is systematized and accompanied by demonstrative proof of its validity, there is a scientific use of language" (p. 39); some literary criticism and much historical writing represents scientific discourse. Third, if we don't know the reality but our purpose is to explore it, we stress the exploratory use of language; exploratory discourse may include interviews, questionnaires, and some seminars.

Whereas reference discourse is reality-centered, the other three aims of discourse focus on other components of the communication triangle (see Fig. 4.2). Persuasive discourse uses language to persuade the audience; our primary purpose is to prompt a response in the reader or listener. Literary discourse calls attention to itself as a text; our primary purpose is to create artifacts "worthy of contemplation in their own

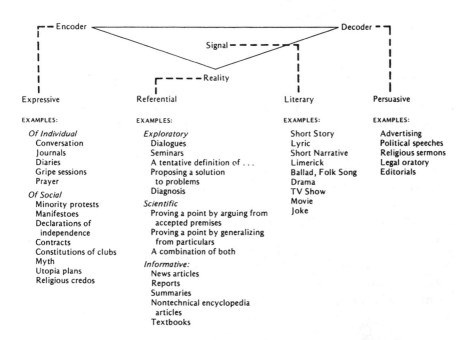

FIGURE 4.2 The Aims of Discourse
Source: James Kinneavy, *A Theory of Discourse*, p. 61.

right" (p. 39). Expressive discourse emphasizes the encoder, either a person or a group, using language to assert the self. The four aims, like the four modes, overlap. We may use language primarily to emphasize one element of the communication triangle, but that doesn't deny the presence of lesser purposes and other uses of language: "Persuasion as a matter of course incorporates information about the product [being advertised], maybe even some valid scientific proof of its superiority, and it may use such literary techniques as rhythm, rhyme, and alliteration in its slogan" (p. 60).

Each of these four uses of language, governed by the writer's or speaker's purpose, has its own logic, organizational patterns, and stylistic peculiarities. Kinneavy's discussion of these distinguishing characteristics occupies most of his book. Essentially, he applies the traditional departments of rhetoric—especially invention, arrangement, and style—to each of the four aims, consequently generating four "rhetorics." Rhetoric, traditionally viewed as the art of persuasion, is for Kinneavy only one use of language, only one aspect of a much larger study that describes how human beings use language to realize certain purposes in communicating with one another:

> Language is like a windowpane. I may throw bricks at it to vent my feelings about something; I may use a chunk of it to chase away an intruder; I may use it to mirror or explore reality; and I may use a stained-glass windowpane to call attention to itself. Windows can be used expressively, persuasively, referentially, and artistically. (p. 40)

CONCLUSION

We must now return to the question the title of this chapter poses: What do teachers need to know about rhetoric? Embedded in the historical summaries you've read here lie terms, principles, and emphases writing teachers encounter in every aspect of their work. The rhetorical tradition influences how you studied the uses of English in the writing and literature courses you took as a student. It informs the scholarship of our profession and the ways in which we discuss our work. It offers a framework for the textbooks we adopt. It provides useful principles for improving our students' writing and our oratorical performances in the classroom. Outside the classroom, we all practice rhetoric and come under its influence, composing and responding to discourses written and spoken for varied purposes and audiences. This chapter demonstrates, in part, how influential the rhetorical tradition has been in shaping contemporary perspectives on the teaching of writing. The more you know about these influences, the better able you are to make self-conscious choices among the uses of language you observe and teach.

One conclusion you might have reached is that the terms associated with rhetoric change. *Rhetoric* itself is difficult to define, for it denotes both a practice and a body of knowledge describing the practice. We need to understand what people mean when they use the term. Are they referring to a theory? If so, whose? To a practice? If so, what does the practice involve? In what contexts does it occur? Similarly, when we hear words like *persuasion, communication, style,* and *mode,* what do they mean? Does *style* simply refer to the kinds of words writers use, or does it rather reflect all of the rhetorical choices writers make? Concerns about stylistic "correctness" or "propriety," for example, represent only one definition of style. Textbooks urging students to "be clear, precise, and concise" reflect a neoclassical preference for the plain style, a view that has been questioned recently in studies of women's language, the language of power relationships, and the different registers sanctioned by diverse academic disciplines and professions.

The rhetorical tradition is shaped by cultural emphases that change over time. Even classical rhetoric was not a uniform theory or practice. For Aristotle, the essence of language was social, the character of the courts, deliberative assemblies, and ceremonial occasions of Athenian democracy shaping the goals and strategies of the orator. Subsequent writers modified this tradition to reflect the practices of their day. As a result, various departments of rhetoric fluctuated in prominence. In the Middle Ages and the Renaissance, then again in the eighteenth century, rhetoricians focused primarily on style. Elocutionists concerned themselves principally with delivery. Longinians asserted the primacy of sublime thoughts or invention as well as sublimity of style. In the twentieth century, especially among writing teachers, rhetorical theory has seen a resurgence of interest in invention or prewriting, in part to counter a preoccupation with the written product.

For some time now, the narrower definition of rhetoric as the art of persuasion has failed to describe adequately contemporary uses of language. That is why in this century the definition incorporates aims of discourse beyond persuasion. Knowing that rhetorical principles reflect dynamic cultural practices permits us to question traditional assumptions and definitions of the art. It makes no more sense to assert that rhetoric is principally concerned with persuasion, or with stylistic flair, or with literary analysis, than it does to ask our students to demonstrate the elocutionary skills of medieval preachers. If we view rhetorical theory and practice as an irrelevant archaism, we will become trapped by the tradition. If we understand, instead, the varied and changing purposes people have for using language, we will be better equipped to teach effectively the arts of rhetoric our culture now practices.

five

What Do Teachers Need to Know about Linguistics?

It is still our custom unhesitatingly and unthinkingly to demand that the clocks of language all be set to Central Standard Time.

MARTIN JOOS

Because we use English every day, we all know quite a bit about how it functions. We've developed an intuitive, largely unconscious ability to create and comprehend statements that conform to the rules of English. That knowledge—linguists call it *competence*—enables us to understand sentences we've never heard or read before, sentences we may read or hear only once in a lifetime. As writing teachers, however, we have a professional need to know considerably more about language than our experiences as language users provide. As Charles Hockett points out in *A Course in Modern Linguistics*, "Native control of a language does not in itself imply conscious understanding of how the language works, or ability to teach it—any more than having cancer automatically makes one a specialist in cancer diagnosis and therapy" (p. 2). To *teach* English requires a second kind of knowledge, a "conscious understanding" of linguistic principles.

One purpose for this chapter, then, is to examine the role language plays in composing, especially at the writing and rewriting stages. That is when students are principally concerned with manipulating language, putting ideas into words and examining the words to determine if they express ideas effectively. The more we know about how English works, the more linguistic options we can suggest to students struggling to get the words right. As this chapter will make clear, what teachers must know about written English is not necessarily the same body of information that our students must be required to memorize.

Hockett's cancer analogy suggests another reason why writing teachers need a secure knowledge of linguistic principles. Many people, including English teachers, would characterize student writing as "diseased" prose. Shocked by what they see, the public expects writing teachers to become therapists, remedying students' deficiencies and thereby restoring the English language to its former healthy state. For many people, a "healthy" respect for English also will solve complicated social problems, the kind that English-only legislation attempts to address. Perhaps the most controversial questions writing teachers confront focus on language: By what standards should we judge student writing? Is it an English teacher's primary responsibility to teach standard English? What right have we to force a particular language or dialect on speakers of other languages and dialects? If there really is a literacy crisis in this country, what can we do about it? What's the best way to test the language skills of students? Responsible answers to questions such as these require an understanding of linguistic principles.

A second purpose for this chapter then is to examine some assumptions people make when they discuss language. Many notions about language have no basis in linguistic fact. Instead, they derive their strength from tradition and from the enormous value we attach to our own personal variety of English. Linguists, who analyze languages objectively and systematically, can help us sort through these assumptions, question the methods we use to discuss language with our students, and revise those practices that research has shown to be unproductive. We may not agree with all of their findings; we may want to adapt their discussions to the particular needs of our students; but we cannot ignore the significant contributions linguists have made in studying how people learn and use English.

Linguistics comprises a large body of organized information about language, not only spoken and written English but other languages as well.[1] Linguists study how we learn language (language acquisition), what features characterize a language (descriptive or synchronic linguistics; phonology, morphology, and syntax), how social contexts shape people's use of language (sociolinguistics), what characteristics languages have in common (comparative linguistics), how languages change (historical or diachronic linguistics), how we attach meaning to sounds (semantics), even how dictionaries are made (lexicography). In this chapter we will limit our discussion of linguistic principles to four topics: the relationship between writing and speech; the nature of lan-

---

1. A useful bibliographic survey of linguistic theories that bear on the teaching of composition is W. Ross Winterowd's "Literacy, Linguistics, and Rhetoric," in *Teaching Composition: Twelve Bibliographical Essays*, ed. Gary Tate (Fort Worth: Texas Christian University Press, 1987), pp. 265–90. Although this chapter does not discuss language acquisition, teachers, especially at elementary levels, will find useful Roger Brown, *A First Language: The Early Stages* (Cambridge, MA: Harvard University Press, 1973), and Courtney B. Cazden, *Child Language and Education* (New York: Holt, Rinehart and Winston, 1972).

guage; grammar and usage; and three approaches to grammar. These topics focus on areas of linguistics most writing teachers want to know something about. They also allow us to construct a theoretical framework for Chapters 8 through 12, which apply linguistic principles to the teaching of writing.

WRITING AND SPEECH

In Chapter 2, we discussed *code* as one of the elements of Jakobson's diagram. The English graphic system, we noted, comprises (1) alphabet letters and conventions for arranging them into words, sentences, and paragraphs; (2) a system of punctuation marks that separate the structural units of a message; and (3) mechanical customs that determine what the text looks like. The most important thing to remember about codes is that they're arbitrary and conventional. To illustrate this principle, try decoding the following sentences:

1. txetnoc morf sesseug redaer ehT
   spiks tsuj esle ro ,sdrow railimafnu
   .meht
2. The as he reader reads or though sense text the make expects she to.
3. gsv ivzwvi nzpvh fhv lu ivwfmwzmxrvh—ligsltizksrx, hbmgzxgrx, zmw hvnzmgrx—gl ivwfxv fmxvigzrmgb zylfg nvzmrmt.

Which of the sentences is easiest to read? Why? Although all three sentences use English alphabet letters and punctuation marks, what conventions govern their use? The first sentence arranges English alphabet letters from right to left across the page. The second sentence rearranges whole English words in an unconventional, random order. The third sentence, like many secret codes children devise, assigns new values to English alphabet letters: z = a, y = b, x = c, and so on.

Although some writers—e. e. cummings and George Herbert, for example—deliberately manipulate graphic conventions in their poetry, readers and writers most of the time agree to use the English symbol system in certain ways, respecting the shape of the symbols and their order. The symbols also have linguistic values; they correspond to sounds in spoken English. Writing and speech, however, are not isomorphic. The graphic symbols and the sounds they represent do not share a strict one-to-one correspondence. For example, the single sound at the beginning and end of *church* (/č/ in the phonemic alphabet linguists use) must be represented by two alphabet letters. Conversely, the alphabet letters *th* represent two different "th" sounds, as in *thigh* (/θaɪ/) and *thy* (/ðaɪ/). The symbol *a* represents at least six sounds: *father, ask, all, sensation, around, mare.*

One of the reasons alphabet letters and speech sounds don't "fit" is that writing systems change more slowly than spoken languages do.

When printing presses made books available to an educated middle class, spelling became relatively fixed, even though the language continued to change. We still spell *know* with an initial *k*, a sound speakers of Old English once pronounced. Speakers of Middle English would have pronounced *hope* as a two-syllable word, whereas today we regard *e* as "silent." To complicate matters further, some Renaissance printers added so-called silent *e*'s to words such as *life* and *come*, originally spelled without *e*, to make them analogous to other words or to justify lines of type and make the margins even.

Although written and spoken English share many features, they're different systems. People often confuse them by suggesting that what is true of one system also should be true of the other. A woman once approached me after a talk I'd given and quietly, so as not to embarrass me, encouraged me not to "drop the *g*'s" at the ends of my words. "After all," she whispered, "you're an English teacher." I thanked her because she meant to help me but, like many people, she assumed that words should be pronounced as they're spelled. They rarely are. Shakespeare's compositors also had some difficulty determining when to spell a final *g* that was no longer pronounced. They "corrected" the pronunciations of *napkin* and *javelins* by spelling them as *napking* and *javelings*.

Because language is a powerful means of expressing ourselves, making value judgments about what "sounds good" and "looks right" is natural. Each of us can name what, for us, represents the most beautiful and ugliest sounding languages. We might even justify our preferences with statements such as "Russian sounds harsh; French sounds melodious." Such statements, however, represent opinions, not facts. Many people would say that French and Italian, the languages of love and opera, sound beautiful, whereas German and Russian sound ugly, preferences no doubt shaped by World War II and cold war propaganda. Like all matters of taste, our assumptions about what language should and shouldn't be reflect personal and cultural values. It's difficult to set these biases aside when discussing linguistic issues. It's even more difficult to avoid imposing our values on the students we teach. As teachers our best defense may be acknowledging the problem. Students need to know that all writers make choices based on what they believe constitutes "effective English." They can't make those choices freely if we treat language as an absolute, a system of right and wrong rules. Reducing written and spoken English to inflexible rules is linguistically inaccurate and also increases students' fears of making mistakes. When we discourage students' curiosity about language, we prevent them from appreciating the very power of expression that so attracted us to the study of English in the first place.

THE NATURE OF LANGUAGE

Most linguists define *language* as "a learned system of sounds having an arbitrary value that meets a social need to communicate." For linguists, then, language is sound, not writing. The sounds (phones) vary from culture to culture, but the organs used to produce them are common to all human beings. Neither climate nor race has a role in speech production. The southern American drawl, for example, isn't the result of hot weather or inherent laziness among southerners; speakers in equally hot or hotter climates in Africa and South America produce speech at relatively fast tempos.

As the definition notes, language also is a social, not a biological, necessity. We don't need language to survive. Feral children, raised in the wild without other human beings around them, and mutes, who for some physiological reason aren't able to speak, can survive without language. But language enables us to satisfy an important need for human contact. We are social animals who depend on one another and spend a lifetime maintaining mutually sustaining relationships by sharing our experiences and ideas. Language is an important way of establishing contact, of realizing a psychological need to live in societies rather than as isolated individuals.

Because we make meaning of our world through language, it reveals what a society regards as being important. Groups of sounds that have meaning—linguists call them *morphs*—denote the realities of our culture and connote the values we assign those realities. Terms for kinship, colors, technological innovations, the euphemisms we invent to discuss taboo subjects, indicate how we perceive ourselves and others. Keep in mind, however, that the sounds of English are themselves neutral; /t/ is neither a "good" nor a "bad" sound. When we say, "*Spit* is an ugly word," we really mean that the action of spitting in public is socially unacceptable in our culture, not that the sequence of sounds is ugly. The same sequence is found in the word *hospitality*, which has favorable connotations, not because the sounds are "good" but because the reality to which the sounds refer has a positive value in our culture.

That there's nothing intrinsically "good" or "bad" about the sequence of sounds /spɪt/ brings us to another term in our definition of language, *arbitrary*. The sounds of English "have an arbitrary value." Like the symbols in the English graphic system, speech sounds are conventional. We mutually agree to use the system in certain ways. We might just as well call a student a *klib*, and if all of us agreed that *klib* refers to a student, we'd communicate quite well. Similarly, the entire system of English is arbitrary. Its sounds, its vocabulary, its sentence structures have been sanctioned by history, tradition, and the consent of those who hold power in our culture. Any of these conventions may change, so long as speakers and hearers agree to adopt the new arrangement.

Languages do change—constantly. People change them by adopting new features. Over time, they redefine what is "acceptable" in speech and writing. In the fourteenth century it was rhetorically effective for Chaucer to intensify negation by piling up four negatives in the lines, "he *nevere* yet *no* vileynye *ne* sayde/In al his lyf unto *no* maner wight"

(*Canterbury Tales*, Prologue, lines 70–71). Because we no longer observe the conventions of Chaucer's day, modern writers are more likely to emphasize negation by writing, "He NEVER used foul language." Despite the opinions of eighteenth-century grammarians, we also know that double negatives don't make a statement positive. No native speaker of English would understand "He ain' no foul-mouthed liar" to mean "He *is* a foul-mouthed liar." What is "acceptable" in written or spoken English depends on the context in which a feature is used. "Acceptable" always presupposes "to whom?"

Notions about what is grammatical also change. The writers of the King James Bible (1611) didn't subscribe to the later convention of using *who* as a predicate nominative after the verb "to be." For them, "to be," like any other verb, required the objective case: "*Whom* do men say that I the Son of man am?" (Matt. 16:13). Today the use of 's to indicate possession seems to be giving way to possessive constructions involving prepositions. We're more likely to say "the top of the house" than "the house's top." Some dialects indicate possession by juxtaposing the noun and its modifier, as in "Mary hat" for "Mary's hat," or "up on the house top" for "up on the top of the house." Do writing teachers read a great deal of "student writing" or "students' writing?"

As a rule, innovations or changes in language occur slowly. Usually they become acceptable in speech before they're acceptable in writing. Children are responsible for much language change because as each younger generation attempts to conform its language to that of adults a perfect match is unlikely. Over time, those changes most likely to become preferred usages are the features adopted by politically, socially, and culturally influential speakers and writers. For us, changes in vocabulary may be the easiest to observe. As events and inventions change our world, we develop new words—*smog, pulsars, television, cloning*—to talk about them. Conversely, some words diminish in importance as we no longer need them. *Forecastle*, for example, still occurs in written form, but people rarely pronounce it in two syllables /fóksəl/ as an experienced sailor would. Nor would we now understand, as Winfred Lehmann has pointed out, the technical terms once used in astrology. Change has affected and continues to affect every level of the language. For at least 5,000 years speakers and writers of English have altered our system of meaningful speech sounds (phonemes); how we combine them into units of meaning (morphemes); and how we arrange those units into phrases, clauses, and sentences (syntax).[2]

Although, change is a constant in all languages, conscious attempts by government agencies or professional organizations to alter the language rarely have been successful. Users of a language will express themselves

2. Especially thorough introductory surveys of these developments are Albert C. Baugh and Thomas Cable, *A History of the English Language*, 4th ed. (Englewood Cliffs, NJ: Prentice Hall, 1993), and Thomas Pyles, *The Origins and Development of the English Language*, 3d ed. (New York: Harcourt Brace Jovanovich, 1982).

despite the efforts of others to regulate their communication. Language change follows social change, not the other way around. But over time, if enough influential users consent to new conventions, the spoken language may begin to reflect the change. The gender bias in English, for example, reflects the gender bias in cultures that use English. As attitudes toward women change, the language may too. Even though style manuals, handbooks, and publishers now recommend gender-neutral substitutions—*fire fighters* for *firemen*—not all of these suggestions will endure. Some seem awkward; many Americans prefer *chair* to *chairman* and *chairperson*, but in selecting the gender-neutral term *chair*, we have dehumanized presiding officers by referring to them as a piece of furniture. Other substitutions, writing *s/he* for example, may fail to gain widespread acceptance because they have no counterparts in spoken English. Similarly, proposals to level the system of pronouns in English are unlikely to win widespread support, perhaps because we want to keep the *I*s, *you*s, *he*s, *she*s, and *it*s of our experience distinct. Writing teachers will find their students eager to discuss these changes and the reasons for them.

As the authors of "Students' Right to Their Own Language" observe, "past change is considered normal, but current change is viewed by some as degradation. From Chaucer to Shakespeare to Faulkner, the language assuredly changed, and yet no one speaks of the primitive language of Chaucer or the impoverished language of Shakespeare" (p. 18). Language change is neither good nor bad; it simply *is*. As English teachers, we have no hope of halting or hastening innovations in language, but if we understand the factors that underlie language change and explain them to our students, they may learn to regard language as a resource they can manipulate to express themselves to others.

GRAMMAR AND USAGE

People who don't understand linguistic principles generally confuse the terms *grammar* and *usage*. English teachers, like linguists, must keep them distinct. *Grammar* has several meanings.[3] First, it denotes that internalized knowledge of language human beings gain by about age five. In this sense, $grammar_1$ means "a capacity for language," a native ability to create and comprehend English utterances. The term also refers to various formal systems ($grammar_2$) scholars have developed to explain and analyze language. Three such systems have been important in American language study: traditional grammar, structural grammar, and generative-transformational grammar.

---

3. See W. Nelson Francis, "Revolution in Grammar," *Quarterly Journal of Speech* 40 (October 1954), 299–312. Patrick Hartwell discusses five meanings of *grammar* in "Grammar, Grammars, and the Teaching of Grammar," *College English* 47 (February 1985), 105–27.

Usage, on the other hand, refers to linguistic etiquette, to socially sanctioned styles of language appropriate to given situations and audiences.[4] If I address my class with profanity, I am demonstrating an insensitivity to usage. My speech would be grammatical because it conforms to the standard word order for English, but profane language is judged socially unacceptable in a classroom. Similarly, lacing my responses to questions in a job interview with double negatives wouldn't be consistent with the formality of that situation. Conversely, answering the telephone with "It is I" instead of "It's me," or using the conventions of formal writing in conversations with a close friend would doubtless create the impression that I'm a snob. Formal styles of written English conventionally avoid ending sentences with prepositions, but in informal writing and spoken English, we often place prepositions at the ends of sentences. Winston Churchill maintained it was "a rule up with which I will not put." Modern grammarians would agree with Churchill; they regard *up* as a verb particle, not a preposition. Usage, then, refers to language in a context, for a particular audience.

Many people link usage to standard English, implying that there's an absolute right and wrong way to use the language. The wrong way denotes nonstandard English; the right way defines the standard. In practice, however, "the wrong way" also defines standard English; that is, people find it much easier to say what standard English is *not* than to describe what it is. By implying that there's only one way to use the language, such definitions also are linguistically inaccurate. Like many styles of dress appropriate to different social occasions, English permits several "standards." Edited American English—often called "standard edited English"—comprises many literary dialects. Its conventions tend to be more conservative than those of spoken English, but they define a spectrum of styles useful in writing everything from very formal essays to informal notes. Similarly, standard spoken English consists of many regional, social, and occupational dialects, each of which has several registers or levels of usage. The speech of presidents Kennedy, Johnson, and Carter represents several regional varieties of standard spoken English. We may define standard spoken English as that variety of English used by the educated upper middle class, Americans who historically wield the greatest social, political, and economic clout, but we must remember that the definition incorporates many levels of usage employed in very formal to quite informal situations.

Each of us speaks a variety of English, called an idiolect, that differs in details of pronunciation, vocabulary, and syntax from every other idiolect. Like fingerprints, idiolects are unique; no two people share precisely the same idiolect. Many forces shape these individual language

---

4. For helpful discussions of usage, see Dennis E. Baron, *Grammar and Good Taste: Reforming the American Language* (New Haven, CN: Yale University Press, 1982); and Baron's *Declining Grammar and Other Essays on the English Vocabulary* (Urbana, IL: NCTE, 1989).

patterns: social, cultural, geographical, economic, and educational influences, even our sex and age. Strictly speaking, dialects represent collections of features idiolects have in common, shared similarities in pronunciation, vocabulary, and syntax. Dialectologists, linguistic geographers, and sociolinguists study dialects and the forces that propagate them.[5]

Dialectal differences depend on the historical character of settlements, geographical features, political or ecclesiastical boundaries, cultural centers, and routes of migration. Other forces promote uniformity among dialects: mass education, urbanization, industrialization, geographic and social mobility. Unlike England or France, where London and Paris are major cultural centers, the United States has no single dominant cultural capital. Consequently, American English comprises several regional dialects. In a project known as the Linguistic Atlas of the United States and Canada (LAUSC), dialectologists have undertaken to survey the English dialects of North America. LAUSC actually represents several autonomous regional surveys that share a common methodology. Using a finely graded phonetic alphabet and elaborate questionnaires, trained investigators have made firsthand observations of local speechways, data that reveal the normal usage on hundreds of points of grammar, vocabulary, and pronunciation among speakers in a network of communities throughout the United States and Canada. The results of this fieldwork appear in several atlases. The *Linguistic Atlas of New England* (1939–1943) was the first to be published, followed by the *Linguistic Atlas of the Upper Midwest* (1973–1976), the *Linguistic Atlas of the Middle and South Atlantic States* (1980–), and the *Linguistic Atlas of the Gulf States* (1986–1992). Materials for linguistic atlases of the north central states, of Oklahoma, of Missouri, of the Rocky Mountain states, and of the Pacific coast are in archival form, and Canadian dialectologists have completed extensive fieldwork. These materials together with other published summaries of information from the Linguistic Atlas records provide an essential foundation for the study of variation in American speech.

The materials also offer practical guidance to writing teachers. Let's examine a simple, fairly uncontroversial usage problem. Suppose you read in a student's paper, "She dove into the pool." Should you mark out *dove* and replace it with *dived*? Which form is more acceptable?

---

5. An excellent introduction to varieties of American English is Raven I. McDavid's "The Dialects of American English," in W. Nelson Francis, *The Structure of American English* (New York: Ronald Press, 1958), pp. 480–543. McDavid's "American English: A Bibliographic Essay," *American Studies International* 17 (Winter 1979), 3–45, discusses numerous resources for investigating the pronunciation, spelling, grammar, usage, names, slang, and regional, social, and literary dialects of American English. I am indebted to Professor McDavid and Raymond O'Cain for making available materials on which I have based my discussion of American dialects and for developing from Linguistic Atlas records the maps on pp. 71–72.

You consult several handbooks and dictionaries to discover conflicting information.[6] Some claim that *dove* is "restricted"; its use is limited to particular contexts or is disapproved altogether. Others label *dove* as "colloquial," which, according to many traditional textbooks, also means "don't use it." Still other handbooks judge both forms "acceptable." Despite what some handbooks maintain, the Linguistic Atlas records reveal that both *dived* and *dove* (even /dəv/ and /dɪv/) are legitimate past tense forms of the verb "to dive." Notice their distribution on the maps in Figures 5.1 and 5.2.

Dove has a clearly defined regional distribution that extends from the northeast United States westward along migration routes across the Great Lakes to the North Central states and Upper Midwest. Correcting *dove* amounts to insisting on an *ungrammatical* past tense if the student's dialect permits only *dove*, not *dived*. *Dived* represents unconventional usage for speakers who grew up in these areas, even though they may no longer live there.

On matters of divided or disputed usage, it's best to give student writers options. Send them to *several* dictionaries and usage handbooks. If students can support a usage item with at least one outside reference, permit it. Their investigation, in the meantime, also will increase their sensitivity to and tolerance for varieties of English.

One of the most difficult issues facing writing teachers is this matter of "linguistic tolerance," which some critics view as the surest course to "corrupting" the English language. Generally, the value judgments we make about another's speech are ethnocentric; they assume the superiority of our own dialect. Few of us would label our own speech "corrupt" or "unacceptable," but we're all tempted to account for differences in speech—like taste in music, clothes, or food—by questioning the intelligence or heritage of others. The error of their ways is just as obvious as the propriety of ours. It's this tendency we must resist, in ourselves and in our students, for the judgments we make about another person on the basis of language reflect personal values, not linguistic facts. Still, even well-educated people construct elaborate rationalizations to buttress their attitudes about cultural, social, and linguistic differences. Several studies have proven such logic fallacious. Let's examine some of them.

Which of the following statements are true, and which are false? If you consider a statement misleading or believe that "it depends," can you explain why?

1. Textbooks are a reliable resource for determining the conventions of edited American English.

---

6. Thomas J. Creswell, *Usage in Dictionaries and Dictionaries of Usage* (Publication of the American Dialect Society, Nos. 63–64; University: University of Alabama Press, 1975), examines how contemporary American dictionaries, usage guides, and studies of usage differ in their treatment of usage items.

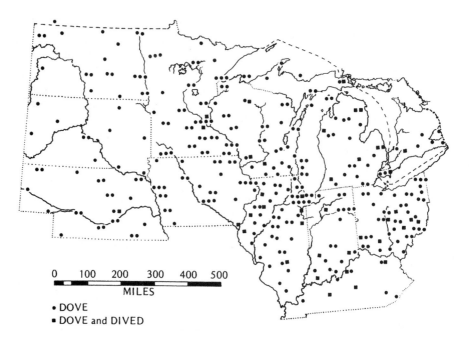

0   100   200   300   400   500

MILES

• DOVE
■ DOVE and DIVED

FIGURE 5.1 Linguistic Atlas Map of Upper Midwest and North Central States

2. Teachers are a reliable resource for determining the acceptability of certain words or phrases, for arbitrating usage.
3. Anybody can learn grammar.
4. Teaching grammar—memorizing parts of speech, diagramming sentences—improves writing ability.
5. Dialects interfere with the ability to read.
6. Dialects interfere with the ability to think.
7. Dialects interfere with the ability to write.

The first six statements are predominantly false either because they confuse the terms *grammar* and *usage* or because they imply that what's true for one language operation is also true for another.

Statement 1. Using Linguistic Atlas findings, Malmstrom[7] compares fifty-seven items of current American usage with the advice of 312 textbooks published between 1940 and 1955. Not only is the advice of textbooks inconsistent, but pronouncements about edited American English also contradict what speakers of American English actually do when they use the language. More recently, Creswell has examined the "variations in treatment of usage matters and in judgments about individual locutions in a selected list of recent and contemporary American dictionaries,

7. Jean Malmstrom, "Linguistic Atlas Findings Versus Textbook Pronouncements on Current American Usage," *English Journal* 48 (April 1959), 191–98.

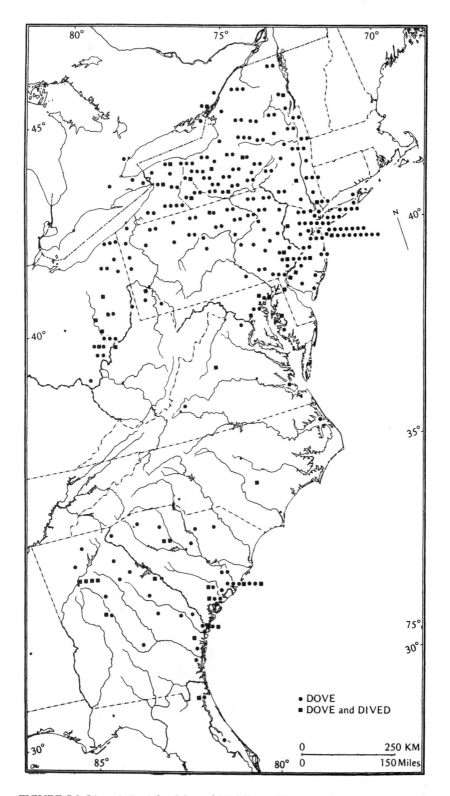

FIGURE 5.2 Linguistic Atlas Map of Middle and South Atlantic States

usage guides, and studies of usage" (*Usage in Dictionaries and Dictionaries of Usage*, p. 7). His study is based on 226 usage items that editors of the *American Heritage Dictionary* (1969) "deemed of questionable acceptability."

Statement 2. Some individual teachers may indeed be reliable usage arbiters. As a group, however, English teachers tend to be far more conservative than the rest of the population about *rejecting* usages that current practice and much published information support as acceptable. Womack[8] demonstrates that the most conservative judgments about fifty disputed usage items tended to come from high school teachers with B.A. or M.A. degrees who had taught in small towns for more than ten years; teachers who held a Ph.D. and had been teaching less than ten years in cities of over 50,000 people were more likely to accept disputed usages. The study also finds that, despite considerable published new information on current American usage, the opinions of English teachers do not conform to these findings.

Statement 3. Meade[9] compares the intelligence quotients of 104 high school seniors to their performance on items from several standardized grammar tests. He concludes that even the brightest students (114–152 I.Q.) have difficulty making a "creditable showing" on the tests; ten of the twenty-six students in the "bright" group couldn't complete at least 75 percent of the test correctly. English teachers who feel confident about "knowing grammar" consequently may assume that their students can easily master it. Meade's study suggests that perhaps teachers should revise their expectations. Most students find learning formal grammar difficult and not very enjoyable. In Donelson's study[10] of effective and ineffective tenth-grade writers, the students' fondness for grammar instruction was a significant variable. The better writers *least* preferred studying grammar, even though they enjoyed other activities in their English classes. Many experienced teachers won't be startled by these findings. We know our students have trouble learning formal grammar, dislike it, and seem not to retain for very long what they've learned. Nevertheless, we continue to teach it in the belief that "it's good for them," that it improves their writing. But does grammar instruction actually improve writing ability?

Statement 4. Beginning with Braddock, Lloyd-Jones, and Schoer and continuing through George Hillocks, Jr.'s comprehensive review of em-

---

8. Thurston Womack, "Teachers' Attitudes toward Current Usage," *English Journal* 48 (April 1959), 186–90.
9. Richard A. Meade, "Who Can Learn Grammar?" *English Journal* 50 (February 1961), 87–92.
10. K. L. Donelson, "Variables Distinguishing between Effective and Ineffective Writers in the Tenth Grade," *Journal of Experimental Education* 35 (Summer 1967), 37–41.

pirical research,[11] scholars repeatedly have concluded that formal grammar instruction doesn't improve writing ability, principally because writing involves a great deal more than merely editing a written product. Students learn to write by writing, not by analyzing or diagramming sentences someone else has written, not by memorizing parts of speech divorced from the context of student prose. Unless grammar instruction derives from actual discussions of student papers, these studies conclude, it has no useful connection to composing. As Weaver points out, learning grammar is not useful for attaining any other goal except learning grammar:

> As long ago as 1950, the *Encyclopedia of Educational Research* summarized the available research (pp. 392–96), concluding that the study of grammar has a negligible effect in helping people think more clearly, and that a knowledge of English grammar does not contribute significantly to achievement in foreign language. Furthermore, the results from tests in grammar, composition, and literary interpretation led to the conclusion that there was little or no relationship between grammar and composition or between grammar and literary interpretation. Further evidence supplementing the early studies indicated that training in formal grammar did not transfer to any significant extent to writing or to recognizing correct English. In general, the experimental evidence revealed a discouraging lack of relationship between grammatical knowledge and the better utilization of expressional skills. Recently grammar has been held to contribute to the better understanding of the sentence. Yet even here, there is discouragingly little relationship between sentence sense and grammatical knowledge of subjects and predicates. On the whole, the more recent research supports the conclusion that the study of grammar in, of, and by itself has little positive effect upon anything else. . . . Indeed, even the grammatical knowledge itself is not long retained. (*Grammar for Teachers*, p. 4)

Statement 5. Gunderson[12] compiles much useful information on theories, research, problems, and practices of teaching reading, and Baratz and Shuy's collection of articles[13] suggests that the teacher's attitudes toward dialects, not the dialects themselves, can interfere with the complex process of learning to read. Each of us understands many varieties of

11. Richard Braddock, Richard Lloyd-Jones and Lowell Schoer, *Research in Written Composition* (Urbana, IL: NCTE, 1963); "Grammar and the Manipulation of Syntax," in George Hillocks, Jr., *Research on Written Composition: New Directions for Teaching* (Urbana, IL: ERIC Clearinghouse on Reading and Communication Skills and the National Conference on Research in English, 1986), pp. 133–51: "None of the studies reviewed for the present report provides any support for teaching grammar as a means of improving composition skills. If schools insist upon teaching the identification of parts of speech, the parsing or diagramming of sentences, or other concepts of traditional school grammar (as many still do), they cannot defend it as a means of improving the quality of writing" (p. 138).
12. Doris V. Gunderson, ed., *Language and Reading* (Washington, DC: Center for Applied Linguistics, 1970).
13. Joan C. Baratz and Roger W. Shuy, eds., *Teaching Black Children to Read* (Washington, DC: Center for Applied Linguistics, 1969).

English, even dialects we don't ourselves speak. It follows then that we don't need to speak Milton's English to be able to read his work. We read texts to understand their meaning, not to speak them.

Statement 6. Similarly, students who write "he walk" and "Mary hat" aren't deficient thinkers who lack "concepts" of tense or possession. They are applying a grammar that differs from edited American English. "Mary hat" is a grammatical phrase in certain dialects; it does not represent a thinking problem that requires endless drilling and workbook exercises on the metaphysics of ownership.

The 129-item bibliography appended to "The Students' Right to Their Own Language" cites many useful resources that review the distinctions between speech, writing, thinking, and reading. These authors rightly insist that basing our teaching on value judgments about dialects not only is inconsistent with linguistic fact but also can harm students. It is doubly dangerous, therefore, to assume that particular patterns of speech characterize deficiencies in other, quite different mental processes—thinking, reading, and writing.

Statement 7. Although some students experience difficulty mastering edited American English, a particular written code, they need not change their spoken dialect to write effectively. Speaking and writing are different language operations, and if students see a need to write edited American English, they will use it. To return to a previous example, presidents Kennedy, Johnson, and Carter mastered edited American English without changing the ways in which they talked. Although regional accents characterized their speech, they nevertheless spoke standard English. Students who do not speak standard English, can learn to switch codes, writing edited American English when necessary regardless of the dialect they speak. Marcia Farr and Harvey Daniels offer writing teachers a convenient survey of research on language variation and useful advice about teaching writing to nonmainstream students in *Language Diversity and Writing Instruction* (1986).

We teach students the conventions of edited American English because many parents, teachers, administrators, and employers believe that it's a code essential to social and professional advancement. But the code, as we know, represents only one element of Jakobson's diagram. To focus our teaching exclusively on code is to ignore other equally important elements of the composing process.

APPROACHES TO GRAMMAR

If teaching grammar per se doesn't improve writing ability, why include in this chapter a section called "Approaches to Grammar"? Because a knowledge of grammar translates into a knowledge of language. Beginning teachers, especially, should know that language and grammar can be approached from several perspectives. Each perspective can help students expand their powers of expression and increase their linguistic options. Furthermore, when teachers understand grammatical theories, they can respond to concerns that parents, administrators, and other teachers express about what should be basic in a writing course. Grammatical knowledge also helps teachers evaluate curricula, instructional materials, and teaching practices.

Many contemporary methods of teaching English originate in past theories about language that ought to be reexamined. The teaching of English as a school subject began in the seventeenth century, when England was filled with foreigners and members of the middle class who wanted to read and write English. Formerly, education had belonged to the nobility and the clergy, but in the Renaissance teachers quickly needed to adapt old methods of teaching Latin and Greek to new students and a new subject, English.

Even though English is structurally quite different from Latin and Greek, English instruction nevertheless was modeled on methods for teaching classical languages. As early as 100 B.C.E., Dionysius Thrax had compiled a grammar of Greek, based on the written, not the spoken, language. He classified Greek into parts of speech. Latin grammar books adopted the Greek classification system. They also included material on metrics and established the practice of imitating literary models. The tradition of teaching parts of speech, of asking students to memorize verb, noun, and pronoun paradigms, of defining *excellence* with reference to great works of literature, remains virtually unchanged after centuries of employing the classical tradition to teach English.

A second characteristic of English education, making judgments about language, legislating correctness, stems from classical precepts reinforced during the Middle Ages, when the Church fostered education. Christian theology tended to view change negatively, as emblematic of the human condition since the fall from grace in the Garden of Eden. Language was believed to be devolving from Hebrew (erroneously thought to be the oldest language). Language change was seen as further evidence that sin pervaded human existence. To prevent further degeneration, scholars and teachers sought to fix language by rigid rules, by establishing classical models and the formal writing of the Church Fathers as standards for correctness. Language study became error oriented. Students needed to learn the rules and practice recognizing "deviant" constructions.

These two traditions, a reliance on classical models and an orientation toward correctness, were reemphasized in the eighteenth century, when scientific rationalism exerted tremendous influence on the study of language. Scholars of this period sought to make language logical, reasonable in a scientific, mathematical sense. Wherever possible, they reinforced their explanations of logical rules with examples from classical authors. In an effort to promote and codify the logic of English, eighteenth-century grammarians adopted the following aims:[14]

1. To devise rules governing "correct" English usage. Many rules resorted to mathematical principles. For example, writing two negatives in a sentence began to be "incorrect," given the logic of mathematics. Similarly, because the verb *to be* was viewed as a mathematical equals sign, the nominative, not the objective, case became the appropriate form to use after *to be*:

It is I (not *me*).

Nominative = Nominative

2. To refine the language, removing "deviant" constructions and introducing "improvements." Regarding words of Anglo-Saxon origin inferior, scholars sought to replace them with Latinate vocabulary. Dr. Samuel Johnson's *Dictionary of the English Language* (1755), the first true English dictionary and a remarkable achievement in its day, often resorts to Latin terms in defining English words. His definition of *network*, for example, reads: "Any thing reticulated or decussated, at equal distances, with interstices between the intersections." Many of the terms we encounter in studying grammar—*antecedent, accusative, intransitive, passive*—originate in this period and reflect a preference for Latin, the "superior" authority as a model.

3. To fix the English language and prevent further deterioration. Working from the mistaken notion that Greek and Latin hadn't changed, grammarians wanted to codify the new refinements and rules they had developed for English. In this way, they thought, the collective wisdom of textbooks and other reference works could guide writers and speakers. Samuel Johnson's *Dictionary* (1755) and the grammar books of Robert Lowth (1762) and Lindley Murray (1795) became important school texts, prototypes of instructional materials used for the past 150 years.

Traditional grammar reflects this legacy. It is rules-oriented, Latin-based, prescriptive and proscriptive. It legislates constructions that must be adhered to or avoided. It focuses on the written language. The principal method of teaching traditional grammar is called *parsing*, a rote process that analyzes a given sentence in four steps:

1. By identifying the largest structural components of the sentence (subject and predicate, dependent and independent clauses);

14. For a detailed discussion of these aims, see Baugh and Cable, Chapter 9.

2. By classifying each word as one of eight parts of speech (nouns, pronouns, verbs, adverbs, adjectives, prepositions, conjunctions, interjections);
3. By describing individual words in terms of their inflectional or derivational prefixes or suffixes;
4. By explaining the relationship of each word to other words in the sentence through a sentence diagram.

Traditional grammarians developed terminology useful to discussing language and codified many conventions governing edited American English. Nevertheless, the traditional approach to grammar has many disadvantages. In the first place, traditional grammarians did not describe what spoken English was but rather legislated what written English ought to be. They failed to respect the role of change in language and refused to recognize that forms appropriate in some kinds of writing might not be appropriate for other audiences.

Second, they based their approach on Latin and Greek, assuming that what was logical for those languages was also logical for English. They failed to recognize English's unique logic and structure. Because English has lost most of its inflectional endings, it differs in many significant ways from its distant Latin and Greek cousins. For example, a paradigm may be useful for teaching the Latin verb *amo* ("I love") in the present tense indicative mood. All the endings are different. In English, however, most verbs show only one inflectional variant in the third person singular; modal verbs show no variants at all.

Latin		*English*			
amo	amamus	love	love	may	may
amas	amatis	love	love	may	may
amat	amant	loves	love	may	may

A paradigm such as the one above represents a time-consuming, inefficient means of teaching students where English requires a final -s on present tense verbs.

Third, traditional grammar's preoccupation with terminology shifts the focus of instruction to what things are called, not how to use them. We've probably memorized the definitions so well that we don't recognize how vague some of them are: "A sentence expresses a *complete thought*." (What, then, is an "incomplete" thought?) "A verb expresses action or *state of being*." (How do you explain "being-ness" to a tenth grader?) Some definitions are circular: "An adverb modifies a verb, adjective, or *another adverb*." Other definitions seem inconsistent, some explaining what a part of speech *means* and others describing what the part of speech *does*, how it functions.

Finally, although traditional grammar claims to study the sentence, the approach focuses on taking language apart, not on putting it together.

Students analyze and dissect sentences by diagramming them or classifying each word as a part of speech. Generally, they are someone else's sentences, not the students'. Although students may learn terminology and perhaps some principles of editing, they haven't learned how to *create* their own discourse. They have only practiced labeling, diagramming, or analyzing someone else's. All grammar instruction should be connected directly to writing instruction. That is, the student's own prose, not the chapter-by-chapter arrangement of a textbook, should govern which grammatical principles need review.

STRUCTURAL GRAMMAR

Although descriptive approaches to the study of language developed more slowly than the traditional prescriptive approach, they have found favor among many modern linguists as well as writing teachers. As long ago as the eighteenth century, Joseph Priestley (*Rudiments of English Grammar*, 1761) and George Campbell (*The Philosophy of Rhetoric*, 1776) advanced the theory that contemporary usage, not classical authority, must determine what's appropriate or standard in English. For them, English speakers, not Latin models, were the best authority for describing the grammar of English. When Darwin's studies (1859) asserted that "progress" was beneficial, not harmful, people also began to view change in language more positively. Scholars became more interested in what changes had occurred than in determining whether those changes were right or wrong. In contrast to the prescriptivists, descriptive linguists are primarily interested in examining the language as it is, not advancing notions about what it should be.

In 1933 Leonard Bloomfield, widely regarded as the father of modern linguistics in America, published *Language*, which defines the methodology of the descriptive linguist. Working only with data that can be verified objectively, the descriptive linguist describes, classifies, and analyzes samples of language before making generalizations about the evidence. Limiting himself only to that which is measurable, Bloomfield relegated the rest of language study, especially thought processes, to other disciplines.

FIGURE 5.3 PEANUTS, reprinted by permission of United Feature Syndicate, Inc.

The structural grammarian, one kind of descriptive linguist, sorts language data into three levels: the smallest units of language or individual sounds (phonology), groups of sounds that have meaning (morphology), and the arrangement of morphs that signal complex relationships in phrases, clauses, and sentences (syntax). Structural grammarians treat the parts of speech differently from traditional grammarians. Unwilling to classify nouns, for example, on the basis of a word's meaning, structuralists use other evidence. *Gangsters* is a noun, not because it names persons, but because it shows an inflectional plural *-s* and because the derivational suffix *-ster* is a morph reserved exclusively for nouns in English. In addition to form-criteria, position-criteria (syntax) also may determine "nounness." In the sentence, "The gangsters robbed the bank," *gangsters* occupies one of many slots or positions nouns hold in English sentence patterns. Students find these criteria—what a word looks like and where it appears in the sentence—much more reliable and concrete than criteria that resort to meaning.

The structuralists' descriptions of basic English sentence patterns also help students identify the order and arrangement of sentence elements. Without making abstract determinations about a clause's "dependence" or "independence," students can study how words behave by examining where they appear. A common technique structuralists use for teaching syntax asks students to analyze nonsense sentences such as "The trasky gleebers were miffling holps wombly." Deprived of clues to a word's meaning, students must base their understanding of sentence construction on morphological and syntactic evidence. An important feature of structural grammar, then, is that it emphasizes the relationships that exist among words and phrases in a given sentence.

These and other techniques derived from structural grammar help us teach students about words and sentences more objectively, concretely, and descriptively than the traditional approach permits. We'll examine them in more detail in Chapters 10 and 11. Structural principles also inform Chapter 14, which approaches students' papers descriptively, as evidence of how students use language, not as proof that they committed errors.

GENERATIVE-TRANSFORMATIONAL GRAMMAR

Oddly enough, our ability to decode nonsense sentences has caused some linguists such as Noam Chomsky to argue that structural grammar is deficient in approach and methodology. In *Syntactic Structures* (1957), Chomsky asserts that the structuralist can't explain how speakers of a language constantly create sentences they've never heard before. Structuralists aren't able to analyze the infinite possibilities of a complex, living language because they limit themselves to investigating only measurable spoken data. They exclude from their studies mental processes, what speakers know, and focus only on performance, the results of speakers' putting what they know to use.

Generative-transformational grammarians distinguish between *competence* and *performance*, which for our purpose here may be thought of as the "innate ability to make grammatical judgments" and the "application of grammar rules," respectively. Generative-transformationalists attempt to explain how speakers and hearers of English create and understand unique sentences, based on the same code, yet permitting infinite variations. All human beings acquire the ability to use language without formal instruction. We master the code we share with other English speakers long before we know (if ever) that English has a grammar. The generative-transformational grammarian seeks to describe this grammatical knowledge and what it consists of.

Chomsky and his followers maintain that native speakers know the grammar of their language inductively. By *grammar* they mean not only the rules whereby we combine words into sentences (syntax), but also our knowledge of sounds (phonology) and units of meaning (morphology). Such linguistic knowledge, a grammar, would govern all our uses of language, as speakers, hearers, writers, or readers. Whereas structuralists begin their study with the smallest units of speech, individual sounds, and proceed to analyze ever larger units of language, the transformationalist describes the native speaker's grammar beginning with the sentence. Defining *sentence* is the heart of transformational grammar. An analogy to mathematics may help to explain the transformationalist's approach.[15]

When we learn mathematics, we don't have to store in our memories the fact that $126 \times 157 = 19,782$. We simply learn a finite set of multiplication tables and then memorize a few simple rules—how to "carry" numbers, shift columns, add the columns—for reusing the basic tables. Given a finite set of multiplication tables and a finite set of rules for using them, we can perform an infinite number of math problems. Similarly, the transformationalist suggests that we learn as children a finite set of phrase-structure rules and a second finite set of transformation rules that give us the linguistic capability of generating an infinite number of sentences.

Transformation rules, therefore, build on phrase-structure rules. Phrase-structure rules, corresponding to multiplication tables in math, describe the nature and order of the parts in a simple declarative sentence. Written in mathematical notation, the phrase-structure rule S → NP + VP reads, "The sentence may be rewritten or defined as noun

15. The analogy was suggested by Jeanne Herndon, *A Survey of Modern Grammars* (New York: Holt, Rinehart and Winston, 1970). The second edition (1976) offers an overview of traditional, structural, and transformational approaches to the study of language. For a brief, readable discussion of transformational grammar alone, consult Suzette Haden Elgin, *A Primer of Transformational Grammar: For the Rank Beginner* (Urbana, IL: NCTE, 1975).

phrase plus verb phrase." That is, all declarative sentences *in English* must contain a noun phrase and a verb phrase. A second phrase-structure rule defines NP:

$$NP \rightarrow \left\{ \begin{array}{c} (\text{Determiner}) + N \\ \text{Pronoun} \end{array} \right\}$$

As the braces indicate, all English noun phrases must contain *either* a pronoun *or* a noun. If a noun is present, a determiner or article also *may* be present. In English, then, we may generate three kinds of noun phrases:

1. N	Dogs
2. Determiner + N	The dogs — barked.
3. Pronoun	They

Notice, too, that phrase-structure rules describe the order of the parts; determiners, if present, always precede the noun. Because phrase-structure rules are recursive, a noun phrase, regardless of where it appears in a sentence, always will have the same components.

Phrase-structure rules explain the underlying structures of simple declarative sentences. But because we do not write and speak only simple declarative sentences, grammarians also must explain constructions such as questions, compound sentences, and dependent clauses. Transformation rules are applied to sentences described through phrase-structure rules. These grammatical operations are analogous to the multiplication rules for carrying numbers, shifting columns, and adding them up. Each transformation modifies a sentence's underlying structure in a specific way. Some transformations are obligatory; others are optional. In any event, transformation rules perform four operations: they add, delete, substitute, or reorder parts of a sentence. Transformations performed on a single sentence are known as *single-base transformations*. Transformations that embed one sentence within a second sentence are called *double-base* (or *multiple-base*) *transformations*. The following sentences, then, are said to be transformationally related to the simple declarative sentence, "Michael painted the picture":

Single-Base Transformations

Did Michael paint the picture? (*Yes-No* question transformation)

The picture was painted by Michael. (Passive transformation)

What was Michael painting? (*Wh*-question transformation)

Double-Base Transformations (*embedding or sentence combining*)

Michael, who painted the picture, won first prize. (Relative clause transformation)

The picture that Michael painted was beautiful. (Relative clause transformation)

Michael painted the picture and cleaned the brushes. (Conjunctive transformation)

Michael painted the beautiful picture. (Adjective transformation)

Generating a simple declarative sentence and transforming it are mental operations that yield ordered slots for vocabulary items. The sentence to this point is said to have a *deep structure*, as contrasted with a *surface structure*, the appearance it has when it's spoken or written. The sentences "Michael painted the picture" and "The picture was painted by Michael" show a difference in surface structure only; underlying both is the same deep structure, the same meanings, and the same relationships between parts. Their surface structures differ because the second example underwent a passive transformation that wasn't applied to the first sentence.

A sentence receives a surface structure when we fill the ordered slots of a transformed sentence with appropriate selections from the English lexicon, a kind of internalized, mental dictionary in which we store the countless vocabulary items we learn throughout life. When we learn new words, we remember not only their pronunciations and meanings, but also other information about their use.

Generative-transformationalists characterize this information by marking the features of words with a plus or minus. Feature analysis assumes importance in the final stages of creating sentences, when we give sentences a surface structure by selecting lexical items that share compatible features. Although "The building is eating a steak" sounds English and conforms to English sentence structure, as defined by phrase-structure rules, it doesn't make sense (though it might appear in a story or other text that deliberately manipulates sense into nonsense). The "sense" is disturbed because we assign *building* −animate and −human features, whereas the verb *eat* shows +animate and +human features. Substituting a +animate and +human noun for *building* rids the sentence of semantic distortions: "The boy is eating a steak."

Generative-transformationalists focus on the creative aspect of language, on the ability of human beings regularly to produce and understand new utterances, on a language system that holds an infinite number of possible sentences. Furthermore, the approach assumes that native speakers intuitively "know" how English works. Students have a competence for language that writing teachers should not ignore. Sentence combining, a technique we will examine in more detail in Chapter 10, represents one way of tapping this resource. Through sentence combining, students transform simple declarative sentences and construct increasingly complex sentences, enlarging their repertoire of syntactic options and improving their ability to "perform" sentences. As Frank

O'Hare and John Mellon have demonstrated,[16] sentence combining may increase "syntactic fluency" without formal grammar instruction or a dependence on terminology.

If grammatical competence is intuitive, why do students have sentence problems? Generative-transformationalists would claim that sentence fragments, run-on sentences, and confused syntax reflect difficulties in performance, not deficient competence. They represent problems in translating spoken English into writing. Because written English requires punctuation, for example, which speech handles with pauses, students may be uncertain about "performing" commas and terminal punctuation marks. Apostrophes too can be troublesome because they have no equivalents in spoken English, which signals "possession" by means of several sounds. Both the written and spoken codes are systematic, but the systems don't always overlap. Strategies such as sentence combining and reading aloud may improve performance by tapping the competence older students already have for language and by giving students a greater conscious awareness of their linguistic options.

THE ASSOCIATION MODEL

Although this chapter discusses several formal systems that attempt to explain our capacity for language, a word of caution is in order. All grammars are theoretical. That is, they make assumptions about how people learn and use language. Every approach to grammar is grounded in a model of language learning. As scholars in various disciplines study this complicated ability to make meaning through symbol systems, they test and revise previous models, constructing new theories to explain what human beings do with such apparent ease.

The models we have examined here are rule-driven. Traditional grammar assumes a fallen world in which all human behavior is corrupt. By teaching people prescriptive rules drawn from logic and prestige dialects (including the example of great literature), traditional grammarians sought to halt linguistic decay and make language orderly, especially in its written form. Structural grammarians, in their attempts to describe languages threatened with extinction, also constructed models based on rules. They realized that the rules governing English presented problems in analyzing languages that had no written form and were structurally

16. John C. Mellon, *Transformational Sentence-Combining: A Method for Enhancing the Development of Syntactic Fluency in English Composition* (NCTE Research Report No. 10; Champaign, IL: NCTE, 1967), and Frank O'Hare, *Sentence Combining: Improving Student Writing without Formal Grammar Instruction* (1973), describe the effects of this technique on groups of students participating in research studies. Two sentence-combining textbooks for students are Max Morenberg, Jeffrey Sommers, Donald Daiker, and Andrew Kerek, *The Writer's Options: Lessons in Style and Arrangement*, 6th ed. (New York: Addison-Wesley Longman, 1999); and Walter Beale, Karen Meyers, and Laurie White, *Stylistic Options: The Sentence and the Paragraph* (Glenview, IL: Scott, Foresman, 1982). The best resource for sentence-combining practice remains the students' own writing.

different from English. Approaching each language as a unique code, they attempted to describe its components and how they were assembled. Though correctness and value judgments have no place in these descriptions, structuralists developed formulas and rules to explain what the phonemes, morphemes, and syntactic units of a language are and the contexts in which they occur. Generative-transformationalists, seeking to explain the human capacity to generate an infinite number of possible sentences, developed a computational model of linguistic competence. This model, based on mathematics, assumes that input precedes output, that human beings are language-processing machines who formulate the rules of a language as young children and then use those rules over and over again to produce a lifetime of utterances.

Rule-governed models have a prominent place in the study of writing. As we have seen, they have a long and respected history. Although scholars have questioned these models from time to time, they nevertheless revise their assumptions with reference to new formulas and rules. They may revise the mathematical model but do not altogether reject it. That is because the idea that the mind employs rules to organize reality is very powerful.

Alternative models exist, however. Beginning in the 1980s, a group of scholars increasingly dissatisfied with rule-driven models began reassessing how the mind processes information. One of the problems they saw is that rule-driven models are deterministic, which makes it difficult to account for the errors people make when performing mental operations or using language. Another problem is that rule-driven models propose that people induce rules on the basis of highly distorted and incomplete input, somehow sorting through the "noise" surrounding grammar rules, for example, that supposedly underlie language. To solve these and other problems, the group constructed models that depend on the human ability to recognize patterns of regularity in stimuli and to make associations among similar sets of information.

In "Rule-Governed Approaches to Language and Composition," James D. Williams discusses the shortcomings of rule-governed models, particularly in regard to grammar, and contrasts these models with the newer ones, focusing on what is called "parallel distributed processing." He states, "This [newer] model proposes that there are no rules associated with mental activities. Instead, logical thinking, language, and so forth, are governed probabilistically by patterns of regularity through a matching procedure" (p. 557). An association model assumes that human beings interpret the world by identifying patterns of regularity that allow us to compare and match new information with old.

This process establishes powerful connections among categories of information that share similar features. For instance, in the presence of a dog, a child's parents are likely to point to the animal and say, "Dog." The result is that the child's brain builds a neural network that connects the mental image of a dog to the word *dog*. The next time the child sees an animal that resembles a dog, the mental image will activate the connected word. Williams and others argue that this process also accounts for syntax. That is, children don't induce the "rules" of language governing the position of and relationships among subject, verb, object; instead they identify the pattern of regularity that characterizes these factors much in the same way that they identify the pattern of regularity (fur, four legs, lolling tongue, and so on) that characterizes dogs. Certain types of experience and their related mental images are connected to these patterns of regularity, thereby resulting in appropriate syntax. Grammar in this view consists of the system we have developed to talk about the patterns of regularity evident in language: nouns, verbs, predicates, modifiers, and so on. Grammar does not consist of a set of rules that govern the mental operations involved in language processing.

The absence of rules in this model suggests that every encounter with language requires us to connect what we know from past experiences as language users to new circumstances. We constantly are manipulating our environment and being manipulated by it as patterns of regularity emerge, resulting in new neural networks, which we then apply. In an important sense, Williams claims, we approach each writing task anew, as an individual act of creation. We must match the demands of the new task to previous mental models we have constructed around such concepts as audience, sentence structure, the essay, and so forth. We elaborate and complicate these models by experience, which allows us to build bridges between our intentions and our words. Writing in this view is not merely a matter of transcribing thought. It calls up all of our past experiences with life, knowledge, and language. It evokes the models and patterns we have developed though repeated encounters with reading, speaking, listening, and writing.

Furthermore, the association model assumes that linguistic behavior never occurs in a vacuum. We cannot perform language as isolated individuals following rules. Our ability to perceive patterns and make models depends on others. From birth, we encounter an environment filled with language, which the experience of living helps us shape and revise. Facility with language then results from interacting with others, encountering new uses of language and developing increasingly complex procedures and models for using symbols to express our ideas.

As the association model implies, the study of grammar in isolation from actual experience with writing is ineffective. Student writers don't need to "know" grammar in the same way that linguists and teachers do. If we teach grammar as a subject matter, we isolate language study from language use. If, on the other hand, we apply what we know about grammar to helping writers use language, our students will become more proficient in negotiating increasingly complex encounters with language.

six

What Do Teachers Need to Know about Cognition?

I know what I know and I write it.

OCTAVIO PAZ

Most students believe that good writers are born, not made. Some have the gift; some don't. For those who do, the right words somehow move magically from the mind to the page. For those who don't, writing is pretty tough work. Most students think they belong to this latter group. Because writing is a struggle, they assume that they must lack the talent for it. Their teachers, unfortunately, often agree with them. "My students just can't think," protests one. "Susan has absolutely no imagination," complains another. Such opinions, born of frustration, cannot be taken literally, but they imply that writing has a great deal to do with thinking and creativity.

This chapter explores the creative process. It explains how seeing and thinking help writers generate ideas, and why prewriting is crucial to composing. The discussion is by no means comprehensive. In the first place, we know very little about how the mind functions. In the second place, a single chapter can't summarize what we do know. However, it can help us understand why "finding a topic" may not be as simple as most textbooks assume. We also may discover tentative answers to other questions: How do people learn to think? How do writers interpret experience? Why do people who've been through the same experience describe it differently? How can we sequence writing instruction to develop our students' powers of observation and thinking?

CREATIVITY

Many scholars, particularly in this century, have sought to explain creativity. Janet Emig summarizes several important discussions of the creative process in Chapter One of *The Composing Processes of Twelfth Graders* (1971). Her review suggests two ways of viewing creativity: (1) as a tension or moment of intersection between two or more opposing variables, and (2) as a series of several aligned stages. The second perspective is best illustrated by Graham Wallas' *The Art of Thought* (1926), which defines four stages of creative problem-solving. In the first stage, called *preparation*, we become aware of the problem, exploring and investigating its dimensions. In the second stage, *incubation*, we mull the problem over subconsciously. At the point of *illumination*, a sudden insight or "Eureka moment" propels us toward a possible solution. Finally, we test the potential or hypothetical solution in the fourth stage, *verification*. Viewed as a sequence of stages, creativity involves several mental operations. When we become conscious of a problem, we explore it from several angles, searching for some unknown. Having discovered it, we make an imaginative leap toward a solution that we can attempt to test or verify.

Although we still have much to learn about how the brain functions, current theories agree on one significant point: "To create" is not beyond the capacity of any normal human being. If creativity is somehow a special ability, it is special for us all. With the possible exception of brain-damaged individuals, we all develop modes of consciousness that have physiological origins in the brain. Our culture tends to place greater emphasis on cognitive modes of thought, on logic, reason, and "literacy." However, affective modes such as imagination and feeling also represent important ways of thinking. Writers must respect both the affective and cognitive dimensions of thought, developing a feeling for and an intuition about their work as well as a sense of its logic.

The subject of this chapter, however, is *cognition*, which means "knowing." Psychologists generally use the term to describe at least two kinds of knowledge: (1) knowledge through awareness, seeing, or perception; and (2) knowledge through judgment, thinking, or conception. To separate cognition into seeing and thinking forces an artificial distinction between two processes that must work together. Many textbooks foster a similar division when they suggest, for example, that descriptive writing emphasizes the writer's powers of observation, whereas persuasive writing focuses on the ability to reason. Such distinctions fail to consider that writers see and think regardless of their aim or mode of discourse. Nevertheless, by examining separately these two cognitive processes, perception and conception, we may better understand what they contribute to composing. Both the eye and the brain serve as essential tools for writers.

PERCEPTION

Perception or seeing is far more complex than most of us consciously realize.[1] Almost everyone has seen a deck of playing cards, for example. Stop reading and try to sketch the five of hearts *from memory*. Now, compare your drawing to the actual card reproduced in Figure 6.4. Very few people can draw the five of hearts accurately on the first try. Why? Must we conclude that reasonably intelligent human beings can't remember what they've obviously seen many times? Not really. Gestalt psychologists maintain that we don't just perceive stimuli; we impose patterns on stimuli. We compose them.

At this moment your eyes are taking in thousands of bits of data, but reading specialists tell us that we don't read every word, much less every letter. It's impossible for us to comprehend so many stimuli at once. If we had to see every line and curve of every letter in every word, we could only read about one word every 1.75 seconds, or roughly thirty-five words per minute.[2] Fluent readers, however, comprehend anywhere from 180 to 600 words per minute, depending on their familiarity with the material.[3] That's because we don't allow masses of stimuli to overwhelm us; instead, we select those that are significant and ignore or deemphasize what doesn't matter at the moment. We compose the selected stimuli into patterns consistent with other patterns we have created from other stimuli. We build categories, making choices about what to highlight and what to place into the background. That's why different people can observe the same phenomenon—an automobile accident, a film, a Rorschach drawing—and see them differently.

Let's consider another example. What do you see in the drawing in Figure 6.1, a goblet or two faces? What you see depends on whether you select white or black as the background for the picture. Similar choices determine how we see "Day and Night," a woodcut by Maurits Escher, who produced fascinating art by manipulating principles of perception. By forcing black into the background at the top of the picture, we observe white geese flying east through the night sky. Reversing fields by selecting white as the background, we see black geese flying west in the daytime.

Not only do we compose stimuli into patterns; we also translate two-dimensional images into hypotheses about three-dimensional realities. The Necker cube illustrates this principle. If you look steadily at corner A, you may see it two ways, as part of the front of the cube or as part of the back. The first view you decide on may actually interfere with

---

1. For many of the principles discussed in this section and for the five-of-hearts exercise, I am indebted to Richard M. Coe, *Process, Form, and Substance: A Rhetoric for Advanced Writers*, 2d ed. (Englewood Cliffs, NJ: Prentice Hall, 1990).
2. Paul A. Kolers, "Experiments in Reading," *Scientific American* 227 (July 1972), 84.
3. Charles Cooper and Anthony R. Petrosky, "A Psycholinguistic View of the Fluent Reading Process," *Journal of Reading* 19 (December 1976), 194.

FIGURE 6.1 The Goblet and Two Faces

your seeing the cube from the other perspective. Neither view is right or wrong; the drawing just represents two valid hypotheses about three-dimensional cubes. We simply don't get enough contextual information from the drawing to relate the pattern of stimuli to a familiar surrounding.

The decisions we make about which stimuli to select and which pat-

FIGURE 6.2 Maurits-Coenelis Escher, "Day and Night" (color woodcut, 1938) Yale University Art Gallery. Gift of George Hopper Fitch, B.A., 1932, and Mrs. Fitch.

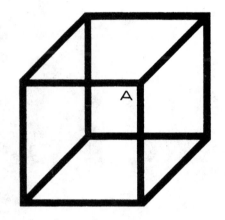

FIGURE 6.3 The Necker Cube

terns to impose on them are based largely on what we already "know."
James Britton describes this decision-making process as follows:

> I look at the world in the light of what I have learned to expect from
> past experience of the world. That is to say, there is on the one hand
> my world representation—the accumulated record of my past experi-
> ence—and there is on the other hand the process of representing to
> myself whatever of the world confronts me at any given moment. It is
> as though, in confrontation, my world representation were a body of
> expectations from which I select and match: the selecting and matching
> being in response to whatever cues the situation offers (but influenced
> also by my mood of the moment). What takes place in the confrontation
> may contradict or modify or confirm my expectations. My expectations
> are hypotheses which I submit to the test of encounter with the actual.
> The outcome affects not only my representation of the present moment,
> but, if necessary, my whole accumulated representation of the world.
> *Every encounter with the actual is an experimental committal of all I have
> learned from experience.* (*Language and Learning*, p. 15)

Who we are, then, determines how we see. And who we are, in turn,
depends on how we have been socialized. In our culture, for example,
we have come to associate the color black with death, dirt, and predominantly unfavorable images. Writers may consciously play up this color
stereotype to create various moods and symbols in their works. In Japan,
however, and in some African tribes white is the color of death. Because
different cultures dissect the universe in different ways, our perceptions
are influenced by the culture in which we live. To some extent we share
perceptual patterns with everyone else in our culture.

Context also determines what we see. Because the mind can't sort all
of the stimuli the eye sees, we select those bits of information that have
meaning for us *in a certain context*. Your attempt to draw the five of

FIGURE 6.4 The Five of Hearts

hearts illustrates this principle. Your picture probably didn't reproduce every detail of the card, even though you had seen it many times. However, most people who attempt to draw it do include the heart symbol and some way of representing the notion "five." That's because, in the context of card games, the number and suit matter most to us. We have sorted the information from our perceptions into categories necessary to playing card games. Designers of playing cards, however, must keep in mind something we rarely consider: for convenience, the suit and number should appear at the "top" of the card regardless of how the player holds it. In other words, your drawing suggests that context assumes greater importance than the evidence of your senses.

Other drawings illustrate this same principle: context overrides visual evidence (see Fig. 6.5). Try as we might, we have difficulty believing

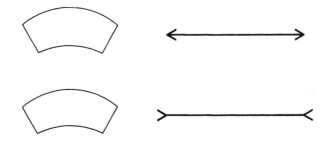

FIGURE 6.5 Muller-Lyer Drawings

that the curved figures are identical in size or that the two horizontal lines are equally long.[4]

So far we have examined sensory or visual contexts that determine what we see, but verbal contexts also shape perceptions. As Stuart Chase explains, "We cut up the seamless web of nature, gather the pieces into concepts, because, within our speech community, we are parties to an agreement to organize things that way, an agreement codified in the patterns of language" ("How Language Shapes Our Thoughts," p. 33). Language shapes our view of reality, and according to Benjamin Lee Whorf, people who speak different languages see the world differently. An investigator for an insurance company, Whorf describes a fire that was caused by language, because a worker responded to the way a situation was named, not the way it really was.

> An electric glow heater on the wall was little used and for one workman had the meaning of a convenient coathanger. At night a watchman entered and snapped a switch, which action he verbalized as "turning on the light." No light appeared, and this result he verbalized as "light is burned out." He could not see the glow of the heater because of the old coat hung on it. Soon the heater ignited the coat, which set fire to the building.[5]

I've had a similar experience in which language determined reality. Needing 100 copies of a handout, I placed the original into the photocopier and pressed C, which I interpreted as the Roman numeral C for 100. Ten minutes later, the machine was still spitting out copies, so I concluded that it must have been malfunctioning and turned it off. By that time, it had copied the handout 245 times! When I reported the problem to the secretary, she laughed. "Oh, there's nothing wrong with the machine. C means 'continuous'; the machine just keeps making copies until you turn it off."

Different languages express reality in different ways. The world of color, for example, may be the same reality for all people, but other languages dissect the color spectrum in ways English doesn't. Zuni, a Southwestern American Indian language, uses a single word for English's *yellow* and *orange*. Other realities—actions, kinship, parts of the body—also are treated differently by speakers of other languages. The English word *eat*, for example, names an activity that, in German, represents two distinct actions: *essen*, "to eat like a human being," and *fressen*, "to eat like an animal."

Whorf isn't the only one to suggest that verbal contexts determine

4. The goblet and two faces, the Necker cube, and the Muller-Lyer drawings appear in R. L. Gregory, *The Intelligent Eye* (New York: McGraw-Hill, 1970), a detailed, thoroughly illustrated discussion of perception.
5. Coe, p. 272. See also Benjamin Lee Whorf, *Language, Thought and Reality*, ed. John B. Carroll (Cambridge, MA: MIT Press, 1967).

how we perceive the world. Francis Bacon in *Novum Organum* (1620) views language, the Idol of the Market, as an obstruction to thinking: "For men believe that their reason governs words; but it is also true that words react on the understanding." George Orwell's *Nineteen Eighty-Four* (1949) proposes a society in which the thoughts of individuals can be controlled by controlling their language. Politicians and advertisers also attempt to shape our thoughts and experiences through language.

We need to know much more about the complex relations between language, perception, and thought. Sometimes we seem to think in words, talking to ourselves as we sort out a problem or grope for an idea. At other times, we seem to think nonverbally, in pictures. All of us have experienced the feeling that we know what we mean but can't put it into words. A colleague whose hobby is woodworking "thinks" in terms of the materials he works with: "When I design a piece of furniture, I do not think in words, but in images of the areas to be joined, and I solve problems of construction by manipulating images of the pieces to be joined."

Sometimes we control language, and at other times it controls us. We succumb to linguistic, cultural, and perceptual stereotypes as well as break through them now and then. Prewriting helps us question these stereotypes. When we probe a subject matter thoroughly and systematically, we begin to see it differently. We examine the topic from various perspectives. We place it in different contexts, breaking out of the sensory, verbal, emotional, or cultural limitations on what we see. The specific prewriting activities in Chapter 7 invite students to question perceptual patterns, to see the subject from many angles so that they can discover a message that is truly their own.

CONCEPTION

Not only does prewriting encourage students to see their subject and envision an audience, perceptual problems all writers must solve, it also aids thinking. It helps us relate perceptions, to understand differences and similarities in what we observe, to make inferences. Although seeing and thinking are closely related, for our purposes here, thinking or conception refers to a more abstract process. In perception the eye and the mind collect, sort out, and impose patterns on visual, verbal, and auditory stimuli. In conception, the mind relates these patterns to other patterns, enlarging, reinterpreting, and giving meaning to our experiences and observations. "By 'thinking,'" writes D. Gordon Rohman, "we refer to that activity of mind which *brings forth* and develops ideas, plans, designs, not merely the entrance of an idea into one's mind [perception]; an active, not a passive enlistment in the 'cause' of an idea; conceiving, which includes consecutive logical thinking but much more besides; essentially the imposition of pattern upon experience" ("Pre-Writing," p. 106).

Whenever we complain "My students can't think," we imply that conceptual processes are crucial to composing. Furthermore, we expect "thought-provoking" writing from our students. Perhaps if we understood conceptual processes better, we might be able to show students how to probe their topics more efficiently, how to make effective choices, how to think through a writing assignment. Unfortunately, experts can't tell us much about conception. They haven't yet been able to identify, much less explain, the complex mental processes we call "thinking."[6] Moreover, good thinkers do not always produce good writing; good writing or reading "great books" does not always produce good thinkers.

For many people, thinking and writing enjoy a reciprocal, dynamic relationship to each other. Each ability enhances the other, but neither faculty can be defined apart from the social and cultural contexts in which writers and thinkers find themselves. Because we understand what is involved in teaching, for example, we can think and write about the subject in ways that other teachers might find meaningful. On the other hand, if you ask me to think and write intelligently about chaos theory, I wouldn't know where to begin. Even though I am educated, command reasonable powers of thought, and understand the English language, I am not a participant in the discourse community that engages in discussions of chaos theory. Some of the assignments we give our students similarly are challenging because their worlds do not sufficiently overlap with academic culture. Conversely, if our assignments tap subjects, purposes, and audiences familiar to students, their writing can be quite powerful.

Though we still have much to learn about the relationship between mind and language among adults, we do know some things about how children grow to be thinkers, about intellectual development. Social scientists, especially those who conduct research in several subspecialties of psychology and education, insist that human intellectual development never occurs in isolation. It remains inextricably bound to physical, social, and emotional growth and to language acquisition.

PIAGET

Perhaps no other individual has made a greater impact on educational theory in this century than Jean Piaget (1896–1980). His research concerns itself with two questions: What mechanisms permit human beings to adapt efficiently to their environment? How can we classify the progressively complex adaptations human beings make as they grow older?

---

6. A comprehensive, readable survey of research on the relationship between language and mind is James D. Williams, "The Psychology of Writing," in *Preparing to Teach Writing*, 2d ed. (Mahwah, NJ: Lawrence Erlbaum Associates, 1998), pp. 219–41.

Problem solving is one technique Piaget uses to study intellectual development. A typical problem for children eleven years old or older requires them to supply a missing letter, figure, or object in a collection.[7]
Can you determine what symbol belongs in the blank section of the
circle? Solving the problem made me feel like a slow seven-year-old
because my perceptions inhibited my powers of reasoning. The difficulty
lies in classifying the letters to determine how they correspond to one
another. To solve the problem I must recognize that the symbols I, V,
and X represent Roman numerals, that A and J represent the first and
tenth letters of the alphabet, and that the alphabet letters and Roman
numerals are arranged in an "opposite to" relationship within the circle.
Thus, the letter opposite Roman numeral V must be the fifth letter of
the alphabet or E. To arrive at that conclusion requires a complicated
understanding of space, numbers, letters, correspondences, sequences,
and relationships.

Were we born with this understanding? It seems not. We learn these
concepts slowly, generally through flexible processes of trial and error.
As infants, we gradually learn to recognize sizes and shapes, and not
until much later do we learn that objects have permanence. Two underlying processes explain how we learn these things and thereby gradually
adapt to our environment. First, we use the environment to learn a new
behavior, a process Piaget calls *assimilation*. Second, the environment
modifies behaviors we have already learned, a process called *accommodation*. In other words, we are constantly drawing the environment to us
or adapting ourselves to it: "assimilation involves reacting on the basis
of previous learning and understanding; accommodation involves a
change in understanding and the interplay of assimilation and accommodation leads to adaptation" (Guy Lefrancois, *Of Children*, p. 76).

By repeatedly responding to our environment, assimilating it or accommodating ourselves to it, we organize our behavior into habits,
sequences of actions that Piaget calls *schemes*. We incorporate new experiences into these schemes (assimilation) until the environment presents some unfamiliar problem that requires us to modify, extend, or
combine the schemes (accommodation). Piaget defines four stages of

7. Ruth M. Beard, *An Outline of Piaget's Developmental Psychology for Students and Teachers*
(Students Library of Education; London: Routledge and Kegan Paul, 1969), pp. 1–2.

intellectual development. Each stage is characterized by schemes the child learned during the previous stage as well as by new adaptations that prepare for the next stage. Like slowly blowing up a balloon, we progress through each stage with schemes we have already organized, adjusting them gradually to incorporate new concepts. Table 6.1 describes the major characteristics of each stage.

Given the ages of our students, high school and college teachers are most interested in the fourth stage, the stage of formal operations. Before we examine its characteristics, let's review what children can already do by the time they are eleven or twelve years old. They have acquired language, and they can comprehend all of its uses. They can reverse thoughts or actions, whereas younger children can't; if two-year-old Jimmy, *in the process* of pulling on a sock, is asked to take it off, he can't do it. Older students also can symbolize. They can construct classifications and recognize that objects belonging to the same class have unique identities; preschool children can't, which is why they can still believe in Santa Claus even though they've seen several different Santas, several members of the class, on the same day in the same department store.

Older children also have learned what Piaget calls *conservation*, that objects don't change unless something's been added or taken away. Preoperational children wouldn't be able to reason that Figures A and B (p. 97) contain the same number of dots. Children able to "conserve" understand that the dots in the two figures have merely been rearranged. By the time they are twelve, children have developed rules of logic

TABLE 6.1 Piaget's Stages of Cognitive Development

Stage	Approximate Age	Some Major Characteristics
Sensorimotor	0–2 years	Motoric intelligence. World of the here and now. No language, no thought in early stages. No notion of objective reality.
Preoperational Preconceptual Intuitive	2–7 years 2–4 years 4–7 years	Egocentric thought. Reason dominated by perception. Intuitive rather than logical solutions. Inability to conserve.
Concrete Operations	7–11 or 12 years	Ability to conserve. Logic of classes and relations. Understanding of number. Thinking bound to the concrete. Development of reversibility in thought.
Formal Operations	11 or 12–14 or 15 years	Complete generality of thought. Propositional thinking. Ability to deal with the hypothetical. Development of strong idealism.

Source: Guy R. Lefrancois, *Of Children: An Introduction to Child Development,* p. 77.

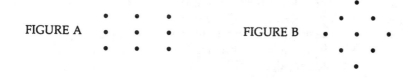

FIGURE A

FIGURE B

governing numbers, area, volume, liquids, and so on. They can construct series, order classes into hierarchies, imagine perspectives other than their own, make substitutions, and combine operations in various ways to yield the same result. They also are less egocentric and, instead of playing by themselves, demonstrate increased cooperation with and interest in others. Although they can reason inductively and deductively, their thinking is still tied to the concrete, to this world or to objects easily imagined.

During the period of formal operations, young adults develop abilities to use logic as we usually define it, inductive and deductive reasoning from the concrete to the abstract and vice versa. They can now express and test hypotheses, accept assumptions for the sake of argument, deal with more complex concepts (including "infinity," "correlation," and "probability"), and compare ideal or imagined concepts with actuality. This ability to reason from the real to the possible prompts the intense idealism and frustration of adolescents. They now become aware of discrepancies between the actual world and the utopia they contemplate, between who they think they are and who they want to be. Although intellectual as well as emotional turmoil seems unavoidable at this stage (at least in Western cultures), young adults spend most of their teens applying their recently developed inductive and deductive powers to the problems they perceive in themselves and in their world. They are practicing conceptual processes that, in increasingly efficient, effective ways, help them adapt to an ever more complex environment, the world of an independent adult.

Although some scholars have criticized Piaget's work and others have elaborated his findings, Piaget helps us become teachers who foster rather than frustrate the progress of children learning to adapt to their world. Because children don't develop the capacity for operational thinking until they are teenagers, we can't expect them to be able to do certain kinds of writing until then.

Prior to about the ninth grade, writing courses should emphasize self-expressive writing, description, simple stories, fairly concrete subject matters. As Piaget tells us, students at this age tend to be preoccupied with themselves and concerned with their immediate environment. They are their own best audience. After grade nine, however, they can reason in progressively abstract ways either from memory or from present phenomena. It makes sense then to focus on more complex categories of writing to reinforce the development of operational thinking.

Although Piaget's work doesn't directly suggest specific teaching techniques, other investigators, working from Piaget's description, have developed curricula and instructional materials that foster cognitive development. English teachers are especially fortunate in finding many of Piaget's principles applied to the teaching of writing in James Moffett's work.

MOFFETT

James Moffett's *Teaching the Universe of Discourse* (1968) presents a rationale for a student-centered, process-oriented language arts curriculum. A companion volume, *Student-Centered Language Arts and Reading, K–13: A Handbook for Teachers* (4th ed., 1991) translates Moffett's theory of discourse into practice, offering specific suggestions for teaching techniques, classroom activities, and instructional materials. Moffett's *Active Voice* (1992) outlines a cross-curricular writing program based on his *Teaching the Universe of Discourse*. For Moffett, communication is a process of overcoming an imbalance in knowledge by means of a symbol system; "the great thing to learn about symbol systems is how to manipulate them, not how to analyze them" (*Teaching the Universe of Discourse*, p. viii). He rejects approaches that dissect the traditional subject matters of English classes into elements, categories, and units—he calls it "the particle approach"—rather than seeing things holistically. Students learn to write by writing, Moffett maintains, not by talking about writing. The student consequently is the focus of Moffett's curriculum.

When Moffett suggests that writing "overcomes an imbalance in knowledge," he means that communication requires adjusting the relationships among writer, reader, and subject.

If readers are to comprehend our message, we must effectively manipulate two relationships, how we view the subject and how we view our readers. Moffett calls the relation between writers and their subjects the "I–it," or referential, relation. Defining this relationship requires exercising perception, memory, and reason. The I–it relation becomes increasingly abstract as we select, incorporate, and reorganize the features of the subject, as we generalize about it or create hierarchies of

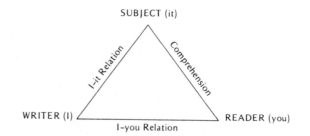

classes and subclasses, as we extend it into time and space, and as we remember our experiences. For example, if I were discussing with another teacher how a student's paper is organized, there wouldn't be much distance between me and the experience. I am participating in a drama, recording the event through my perceptions of it.

However, if months or years later I were to combine what I remember of that experience with recollections of other experiences, I would be generalizing from the events, drawing conclusions from them at a fairly high level of abstraction. Now my memory, not my perceptual apparatus, is more active in helping me select the details.

Moffett describes a spectrum of four I–it relations, each one at a higher level of abstraction. The lowest level, "what is happening," corresponds most nearly to the reality of the experience itself and entails the least processing of events by the mind. Higher levels of abstraction require more complex conceptual processes and manipulations of logic; the "subject becomes less and less matter and more and more idea" ("I, You, and It," p. 246). The list below illustrates the continuum of I–it relations by posing questions with different verb tenses, "which indicate when events occurred in relation to when the speaker is speaking of them" (p. 244). Each level supports its own form of discourse symbolizing the experience and its own abstractive process defining the logic of each level.

What may happen?	Argumentation	Theorizing about experience
What happens?	Exposition	Generalizing from experience
What happened?	Narrative	Reporting experience
What is happening?	Drama	Recording experience

Moffett's I–you relation, on the other hand, defines degrees of distance, not between writer and subject, but between writer and reader. "We abstract not only from something," Moffett claims, "but for someone" (p. 246). Beginning with self-verbalization, in which "I" and "you" are the same person (Piaget's "egocentric speech"), the spectrum of I–you relations expands to include audiences in the same time or place as the writer or in progressively distant times and places. The audience also may grow to include more than one reader. Each kind of discourse becomes more and more public and offers less and less immediate feedback for the writer. Moffett suggests that students need to develop, in an orderly fashion, "voices" and rhetorical stances useful in addressing a variety of these audiences. Unfortunately most students are not really writing for a "you." They have learned to address most of their academic writing to an "it," an abstraction of an authority figure they presume to be The English Teacher.

To produce authentic discourse, writers must mesh both the I–it and I–you relationships. They must practice increasing the distance between themselves and their audience, simultaneously adjusting the abstractive attitude between themselves and the subject matter. A writing curriculum, in Moffett's view, should move students through a spiral of writing assignments that require progressively complex cognitive processes and progressively larger or more distant audiences. Students would first record the drama of "what is happening" for several kinds of audiences, recreating the experience for themselves, for a close friend sitting within speaking distance, in a letter to someone they know, in a formal essay addressed to a public audience. Then, students would move to the next level of the spiral, reporting the narrative of "what happened" for a variety of audiences. And so on. In Moffett's curriculum, each turn of the spiral builds on the previous one and leads to the next. As students speak, read, and write progressively more abstract discourse, they learn to differentiate and integrate the mental operations each kind of discourse requires. "The movement is from self to world, from point to an area, from a private world of egocentric chatter to a public universe of discourse" (p. 246), from concrete experience to abstract idea, from first-person observation to third-person theorizing.

In Moffett's view, writing teachers must have as their primary aim encouraging a student's intellectual and social development. They act as one kind of audience, offering a point of view that helps the student manipulate effectively the I–you and I–it relations. Teachers also provide important feedback for writers who have encountered problems or can't see what the problem is. Instead of assuming roles as a "parental substitute, civic authority, and the wielder of marks" (*Teaching the Universe of Discourse*, p. 193), instead of explaining what's in the textbook, teachers using Moffett's student-centered curriculum encourage students to teach one another. Writing assignments aren't restricted to academic prose practical only in schools; students practice writing many forms of discourse, for many audiences.

PERRY AND MAGOLDA

Piaget's work has contributed much to our understanding of cognitive development in children, but it also has been criticized for overgeneralizing the nature and progression of cognitive change. Some preschoolers, for example, may be more competent thinkers than Piaget believed. For all children, cognitive advances may occur in some areas of thinking and not in others, and ways of knowing are dependent on race and class, social relations, and the nature of individual experiences. Each child, in other words, may have a unique rate of development, generally consistent with Piaget's schemes but also influenced more than Piaget acknowledged by social forces shaping the child's home life and schooling.

Piaget also offers little help to college writing teachers because their students are older than those he studied. To understand the cognitive processes of late adolescents and adults, we must turn to developmental psychologists who study people throughout the life span. They have found that as adults age their intellectual skills become more specialized, experiential, and integrative. Unlike adolescents, who attempt to distill universal truths from personal experience and who try to resolve the world's problems in terms of rational absolutes, adults tend to accept inconsistencies in experience. We learn to adopt provisional rather than definitive solutions to problems and come to understand that our own view of things is only one of many valid perspectives. We adapt our thinking to particular contexts. For most adults the process involves understanding the pros and cons of a situation or idea and continually integrating our experiences and beliefs with the inconsistencies encountered in daily life. This process is called dialectical thinking. Every new idea or truth (thesis) implies one or more opposing ideas (antithesis), which, considered simultaneously, must be reconciled into a synthesis. Adults come to understand that this dialectical process is continual throughout life, that change is constant, and that our views of ourselves and the world are continually evolving as each new synthesis revises ideas previously held.

For college students, late adolescents becoming adults, dialectical thinking is an unfamiliar form of reasoning. Their thinking strategies lie somewhere between Piaget's stage of formal operations and the process of dialectical reasoning. Descriptions of these strategies can be found in the work of William G. Perry, Jr., and Marcia B. Baxter Magolda. Perry, who studied Harvard University students intensively in the 1950s and 1960s, found that they progressed through nine "positions," grouped into three phases of cognitive development (*Forms of Intellectual and Ethical Development in the College Years: A Scheme*, 1970). Most beginning college students, he observed, view the world in a dualistic fashion. They think in terms of polarities such as right and wrong, we and they, success and failure. They believe that answers to questions are absolutes. As they gradually become aware of differing opinions on a subject and learn that authorities may not have all the answers, they begin questioning their values, even the notion of truth itself. Students in Perry's second phase of intellectual development discover relativism. They may assert that everyone is entitled to his or her own opinion, that one perspective is as good as another, and that everything is relative. When others challenge this relativism, young adults come to recognize that, while knowledge and values may be relative, not all ideas are equally valid. They begin to see theories, not as Truth, but as metaphors for interpreting experience. They learn to think about their thinking as they consciously pursue and evaluate knowledge. Finally, in Perry's third phase, students become committed to certain values and ideas, nevertheless realizing that they must remain open to change. They understand that the meaning of an event is related to the context in which it occurs, that in life, not just in the academic world, knowledge is constructed, not given.

Perry's scheme does not predict that college students necessarily will abandon conservative values and adopt liberal ones, though certainly some do. Rather, Perry charts how the knowledge and values students acquire are challenged, redefined, and eventually held—with greater confidence, tolerance, and flexibility. Especially influential in the progression Perry describes are the academic and social experiences of college life that stimulate new questions, create disequilibrium, and expose students to diverse points of view. A college education, then, fosters intellectual growth, not only by exposing students to new ideas and ways of thinking, but also by making the views of others less threatening, which promotes flexible attitudes and an acceptance of difference.

Perry acknowledged that the developmental process he observed continues throughout adulthood. His work has been challenged, however, because it was based on male students and did not take into account differences between men and women. An important study that does examine gender in the context of college students' intellectual development is Marcia B. Baxter Magolda's *Knowing and Reasoning in College* (1992). Elaborating on Perry's work and on studies of women's ways of knowing, Magolda bases her Epistemological Reflection Model on interviews over a five-year period with 101 men and women attending Miami University in Ohio. Her work is especially valuable because it includes generous excerpts from her interviews, which trace changes in students' evolving patterns of cognitive growth. She constructs four qualitatively different ways of knowing evident among the students she interviewed: absolute knowing, transitional knowing, independent knowing, and contextual knowing. These ways of knowing are summarized in Table 6.2.

Absolute knowers, like Perry's dualists, believe that knowledge is absolute. It resides with authorities such as teachers and textbooks. Jim, a student quoted in Magolda's study, is an absolute knower: "The information is cut and dried. It is either right or wrong. If you know the information, you can do well. It is easy because you just read or listen to a lecture about the ideas, then present it back to the teacher" (p. xi). Absolute knowers approach educational decisions, including decisions about majors, roommates, and romances, by looking for right and wrong answers. They do not see peers as playing a significant role in learning because peers are not creators of knowledge; at best, they usefully can explain what teachers may be talking about and can share what they have learned from other authorities. Approaching a writing assignment, an absolute knower is likely to be preeminently concerned with what the teacher wants and may doubt that peers can or should offer advice in planning or revising a draft.

Among absolute knowers, Magolda found that women tended to take a more private approach to receiving knowledge than men, who mastered knowledge more publicly. Women, more often than men, described listening and taking notes as their primary activities in class. They did

TABLE 6.2 Magolda's Epistemological Reflection Model

Domains	Absolute Knowing	Transitional Knowing	Independent Knowing	Contextual Knowing
Role of learner	• Obtains knowledge from instructor	• Understands knowledge	• Thinks for self • Shares views with others • Creates own perspective	• Exchanges and compares perspectives • Thinks through problems • Integrates and applies knowledge
Role of peers	• Share materials • Explain what they have learned to each other	• Provide active exchanges • Share views • Serve as a source of knowledge	• Enhance learning via quality contributions	
Role of instructor	• Communicates knowledge appropriately • Ensures that students understand knowledge	• Uses methods aimed at understanding • Employs methods that help apply knowledge	• Promotes independent thinking • Promotes exchange of opinions	• Promotes application of knowledge in context • Promotes evaluative discussion of perspectives • Student and teacher critique each other
Evaluation	• Provides vehicle to show instructor what was learned	• Measures students' understanding of the material	• Rewards independent thinking	• Accurately measures competence • Student and teacher work toward goal and measure progress
Nature of knowledge	• Is certain or absolute	• Is partially certain and partially uncertain	• Is uncertain—everyone has own beliefs	• Is contextual; judge on basis of evidence in context

Source: Marcia B. Baxter Magolda, Knowing and Reasoning in College, p. 30.

not expect interactions with teachers, used peers as a support network, and when discrepancies among knowledge claims arose, relied on their own interpretations rather than consulting authorities. Men, on the other hand, tended to "embrace a public role in class to demonstrate their interest to the instructor, expect interchanges with teachers, view peers as partners in arguing and quizzing each other to master the material, value evaluation that helps them improve their mastery, and appeal to authority to resolve differences in knowledge claims" (p. 38). Although these public and private approaches to learning were not exclusively determined by gender, more men than women used public, "mastery-pattern" methods instead of private "receiving-pattern" methods.

Transitional knowing among Magolda's students was signaled by the important discovery that authorities do not have all the answers. Teachers themselves often prompted this revelation, which sometimes distressed, even angered, students. Confronted by uncertainty about the omniscience of authorities, transitional knowers shifted their focus from receiving or mastering knowledge to understanding it. "If you want to be a thinking person," Sean reported, "you have to take them [many viewpoints] into account, instead of just saying 'that's right' because my teacher said it" (p. 104). Transitional knowers did not immediately abandon the idea that knowledge is absolute, but they found it necessary to balance its certainty in some areas with uncertainty in others. They recognized that instructors often asked students to apply knowledge, not merely receive it, and preferred hands-on methods of learning. Transitional knowers also viewed peers in more active roles, as people who could help explore knowledge from different perspectives, whose voices represented "something more than an echo of authorities" (p. 111). In the absence of right and wrong answers, "what would work out best" became a way to resolve uncertainty.

Transitional knowers who embraced uncertainty assigned legitimacy to classmates' ideas more readily than those who did not. These "interpersonal-pattern" learners sought greater interaction with teachers and peers and valued classes that encouraged self-expression and involvement. They tended to be women. Many men adopted an "impersonal pattern" of transitional knowing, regarding relationships as less important than women did. Many men's ways of learning were individually focused, a matter of defending their positions, sorting out their ideas, and eventually deciding for themselves what to believe.

Magolda's third category, independent knowers, responded to differences among authorities by changing both the source and the process of their thinking. They did not regard authorities as the only source of knowledge but also held their own opinions as valid. Peers became legitimate sources for knowledge too. Independent knowers expected instructors to promote the expression of personal viewpoints, to reward independent thinking, and to avoid penalizing students for holding views different from the teacher or the authors of textbooks. Like Perry's relativists, they emphasized being open-minded, letting everyone believe what they will. Because knowledge is open to many interpretations, open-mindedness and maintaining a variety of perspectives are core assumptions of independent knowers. Though people should be receptive to others' ideas, independent knowers do not feel obliged to judge among ideas or to identify the criteria upon which personal beliefs are based.

Among the independent knowers Magolda interviewed, many men were slightly threatened by regarding the voices of others as equal to their own. These "individual-pattern" learners had to find a balance between their own views and those held by authorities and classmates. "Inter-individual-pattern learners," on the other hand, often women, tended to be more open to the views of peers but sometimes found it difficult to express their own views unless the threat of criticism was removed by regarding all views as equal. Each group, however, seemed to move closer to the other than in previous stages, coming to terms in different ways with the need to remain open to others' views as well as to generate knowledge for themselves.

Thinking for oneself remains the most prominent characteristic of contextual knowing, the fourth pattern in Magolda's scheme. Instead of regarding all views as equally valid, as independent knowers do, contextual knowers think for themselves within the context of knowledge generated by others. Such knowing requires judgment. The "everything goes" approach no longer holds. Contextual knowers weigh facts and opinions against what they already know, judging the degree to which others can support their stance and making adjustments as they encounter new information. What counts as evidence may come from teachers and books, but in some contexts, expertise may rest with peers. Contextual knowers appreciate classmates who are knowledgeable and willing to share their expertise, instructors who promote discussions that evaluate ideas, and forms of evaluation whereby students and instructors work together to set goals and determine progress. Students writing a senior thesis, for example, understand that they must take responsibility for the project, but they also may solicit criticism and direction from a thesis advisor, other teachers, friends, and students enrolled in a thesis seminar group.

Magolda suggests that gender-related patterns of knowing found in the first three stages may converge in the fourth. Contextual knowers integrate thinking for themselves with genuine consideration of others' views, central features of receiving-, interpersonal-, and interindividual-pattern learners in previous stages. Contextual knowers also assume ultimate responsibility for their own judgments and constructed perspectives, characteristics found among mastery-, impersonal-, and individual-pattern learners.

Although all four types of knowing were evident among the students Magolda interviewed, most of them were absolute and transitional knowers:

> Absolute knowing was most prevalent in the first year of college (68 percent). Fewer students were absolute knowers as sophomores (46 percent) and very few juniors (11 percent) and seniors (2 percent). This approach to knowing had disappeared by the year following graduation. Whereas absolute knowing decreased with each year, the transitional perspective increased during the first three years of college. Thirty-two percent of the first-year students were transitional knowers. This number rose to 53 percent for sophomores and 83 percent for juniors. Transitional knowing declined slightly for seniors (80 percent) and substantially the year following graduation (31 percent). Thus, transitional knowing was most prevalent in the junior and senior years. (p. 70)

Independent knowing, Magolda concluded, was absent among first-year students and only minimally evident among sophomores and juniors. Contextual knowing was rarely evident among college students. Most college students, then, can be characterized as absolute and transitional knowers, their learning strategies differing significantly from those of teachers, who are likely to be independent and contextual knowers.

IMPLICATIONS

So, what do teachers need to know about cognition? Though we should avoid overgeneralizing what researchers tell us about how people learn and allow for differences among individuals, research on cognitive development offers useful principles for writing teachers to consider. First, teachers should be aware that they employ different strategies for thinking than their students do. Teachers nevertheless have an important role to play in helping students adopt new ways of thinking. They can and should intervene to make a difference between what students will learn on their own and what they can learn with guidance. The evolving mind is not awaiting some transformation from within but responds to external influences.

Second, learning depends on relationships with others. It requires a social network of teachers, classmates, friends, and family members, all of whom are essential to intellectual development. Many students, however, perceive education as an isolating experience. Knowledge seems divorced from their interests and lived experiences. Students rarely talk to one another in class. Intense competition for individual grades prevents students from regarding classmates as sources of support, advice, and knowledge. Large classes make it difficult for students and teachers to get to know one another. Yet, integrating knowledge and experience and comparing what we know with what others know are fundamental to learning. Teachers, then, must find ways to work against perceptions and policies that separate learners from their learning. Writing classes can help overcome this separation if they tap students' interests and experiences, ask students to interact with the world outside the classroom, and give them frequent opportunities to learn from and teach one another.

Third, the research summarized in this chapter urges high school and college teachers to respect each others' teaching spaces. Because the students they teach are in unique stages of intellectual development, each group of teachers plays an important role in promoting cognitive growth. Although high school teachers can prepare their college-bound students up to a point, they cannot anticipate or address those ways of knowing that will emerge only after students have spent a year or two on a college campus. High school writing courses should support the important intellectual and social growth of fascinating teenagers. College teachers, on the other hand, should define their work, not as a remedial enactment of what students experienced in high school, but as a valuable opportunity to support and extend students' ways of knowing into adulthood.

Fourth, intellectual growth occurs when people are required to exercise high-level thinking, "high" relative to their own stage of development, but not so high as to represent a stage that they have not yet attained. This principle can help us design and sequence writing assignments as well as plan class activities. If I know, for example, that first-year college students tend to regard peers as knowledge-sharers, not as knowledge-makers, I can help students question that view by encouraging them to learn from their classmates. Reaching such a goal would require establishing peer groups in my writing class, designing a sequence of tasks that gives the groups increasing responsibility for creating knowledge together, modeling the kinds of work I want the groups to do, discussing how groups work effectively, asking students to examine how their own group functions, holding conferences with groups to assess progress, and so on.

Knowing generally what constitutes "high-level thinking" for particular students also can help teachers establish or modify expectations for their writing. Some kinds of writing will present difficulties even for high school and college students. Many can handle descriptive and narrative modes of discourse confidently, but evaluation, classification, argumentation, writing for a mixed audience, and topics that require theorizing, abstracting, or predictions about the future can be troublesome. High school students, for example, may have difficulty analyzing someone else's argument, and first-year college students may be frustrated by assignments that require dialectical reasoning (thesis-antithesis-synthesis). That doesn't mean that they should avoid challenging work. On the contrary, practicing difficult modes of thought encourages their mastery. But it does mean that our expectations for such work must be tempered by the knowledge that some ways of thinking that seem "natural" to us involve cognitive processes that our students have only recently begun to exercise. They do not yet command securely the "logics" of the academic world, ways of thinking that we teachers grew to adopt only after four years of college and perhaps a few years of graduate school.

A writing class offers excellent opportunities to reinforce our students' cognitive development. In our haste to teach a subject matter, we sometimes forget that we're teaching, first and foremost, a complex human being. We shouldn't be concerned as much with the facts we want students to know as with those processes that help students learn whatever facts they have a need to know. By posing unfamiliar problems that require students to see, talk, think, and write, we encourage them to modify the cognitive schemes that they have developed and to adopt progressively more complex ways of knowing.

As we have seen in this chapter, what we write has a lot to do with what we see, how we learn, and how we solve problems. As we grapple with the rhetorical problem a writing assignment poses, we also confront problems in managing what we know and in choosing effective ways to express it. To solve these problems, we develop sophisticated hierarchies of goals, consolidating, revising, and generating new agendas as we plan, draft, and revise a piece of writing. The cognitive processes brought to bear on any writing problem are far more complex than most of us consciously realize. Prewriting triggers some of these mental processes, enabling writers to set productive goals that will help them discover their words and ideas.

seven

Prewriting Techniques

This is the first requirement for good writing: truth; not the truth . . . but some kind of truth—a connection between the things written about, the words used in the writing, and the author's real experience in the world he knows well—whether in fact or dream or imagination.

KEN MACRORIE

Prewriting refers to those activities that precede composing a draft. They may involve reading, thinking, talking with others, as well as writing. The term *prewriting* originally referred to three kinds of exploratory writing—journals, meditation, and analogy—that were popularized by D. Gordon Rohman and Albert O. Wlecke in the 1960s, techniques that emphasized creative thinking and the self-actualization of the writer.[1] Nowadays *prewriting* refers to a variety of strategies writers use to generate and organize their material. Some teachers prefer the term *invention*, borrowed from classical rhetoric, because *prewriting* can imply "what the writer does before writing," even though many prewriting techniques use writing to explore a subject. Others prefer *prewriting* because they wish to avoid the Latinate term *invention*, which has mechanistic connotations for today's students. Many teachers use *prewriting* and *invention* interchangeably. I've chosen to use *prewriting* throughout this book to maintain (perhaps artificially) consistent terms built on *writing* when discussing the stages of composing, broadly defined.

The prewriting techniques discussed in this chapter help students assess the dimensions of a rhetorical problem and plan its solution. They

1. D. Gordon Rohman, "Pre-Writing: The Stage of Discovery in the Writing Process," *College Composition and Communication* 16 (May 1965), 106–12. An indispensable survey of methods of invention as well as a history of the art is Richard Young, "Recent Developments in Rhetorical Invention," in *Teaching Composition: Twelve Bibliographical Essays,* ed. Gary Tate (Fort Worth: Texas Christian University Press, 1987), pp. 1–38.

trigger perceptual and conceptual processes, permitting writers to re-call experiences, break through stereotyped thinking, examine relation-ships between ideas, assess the expectations of their audience, find an implicit order in their subject matter, and discover how they feel about the work. Some prewriting activities enable writers to probe the subject from several perspectives; others help writers assess their relationship to an audience. Some use pictures, talk, or pantomime to generate ideas, while others ask students to write lists, notes, and scratch outlines.

As a rule, the more time students spend on a variety of prewriting activities, the more successful the paper will be. In working out the possibilities an assignment suggests, students discover what they hon-estly want to say and address some of the decisions they must make if the paper is to express a message effectively. Writing the first draft becomes easier because some writing—notes, lists, freewriting—has al-ready taken place. Drafting also becomes more productive because stu-dents are less preoccupied with formulating ideas from scratch and freer to discover new messages as the words appear on the page.

In many composition textbooks, the only prewriting technique dis-cussed is the formal outline. Although writers rarely construct elaborate outlines, informal outlines serve a useful purpose. Outlining can help students shape raw material generated by other prewriting activities. Outlining also can serve revision because when students outline a draft they may discover digressions, inconsistencies, or other organizational problems to work on. Nevertheless, outlining represents only one of many prewriting activities.

Because prewriting is a means to an end, I don't grade the notes, lists, and miscellaneous scratch work my students turn in with their final drafts. I look through the material, however, to discover which students need help generating more support for their topics or making prewrit-ing work more efficiently for them. I also involve students in several prewriting activities, not just one, for each assignment. Sequencing sev-eral kinds of prewriting activities encourages students to explore their subjects thoroughly, planning their response to an assignment gradually, moving tentatively but then more confidently toward a first draft. Even-tually, students modify and combine in whatever ways work best for them the techniques discussed in this chapter. All of them offer writers places to begin, keys of different shapes and sizes that grant access to experience, memory, and intuition.

PERCEPTION EXERCISES

Thinking games, "conceptual blockbusting," and sense-scrambling ac-tivities encourage students to think about how they think. By analyzing the steps they go through to "have ideas" or solve problems, they discover barriers that block perceptions.[2] Much of the material in Chapter 6, including the five-of-hearts exercise, can prompt a discussion of these perceptual, cultural, emotional, and intellectual barriers. To demonstrate these principles, you might ask students to pair up and by turns lead each other blindfolded on a tour of the building or some other familiar place. Deprived of their visual orientations, they can appreciate perceptions gained through other senses: smell, touch, hearing. Students also might discuss pictures, a busy city street for example, and then draw the scene from various perspectives. What would a bird's-eye view of the picture look like? How would you draw it if you were standing at the right-hand side of the picture looking left? After students have compared their drawings and discussed the differences in perspective, the class can move on to other prewriting activities directly relevant to a particular assignment.

For many students, arts and media that don't involve writing offer a comfortable place to begin probing a subject. Pantomime and role-playing encourage students to act out a subject before translating it into written form. Especially when an issue admits several points of view or when an audience may hold diverse opinions about a subject, role-playing clarifies the options students must consider. Assignments involving argumentation can begin with impromptu debates, which might then be worked into brief written dialogues and from there into more formal kinds of discourse. Similarly, students can translate reading assignments, pictures, or music from one medium to another, then to a third and finally to a written form. The assumption behind these activities is that similar principles govern communication in various media. When students practice the "language" of pictorial art, of gesture, and of music, they also learn principles that reinforce their use of the spoken and written word. Furthermore, in responding to cartoons, music, and pantomime, students become more sensitive observers of their world.

Not every piece of writing, of course, finds a convenient beginning in art, music, or drama, but all writing can begin with speech, a comfortable means of expression for most people. As Robert Zoellner and others have suggested, talking out a rhetorical problem helps students define and solve it: "Since students have a greater fluency in speaking than in writing because they practice it more, speaking can be used as a stage prior to writing and can provide the basis for moving through increasingly adequate written versions of a unit of discourse."[3] All students, especially those whose fear of failure makes writing anything, even

2. James L. Adams, *Conceptual Blockbusting: A Pleasurable Guide to Better Problem Solving* (San Francisco: W. H. Freeman, 1974), is a useful discussion of how to cultivate thinking and problem-solving abilities. The book analyzes barriers to thinking and suggests strategies for breaking through them.
3. Young, p. 37; cf. Robert Zoellner, "A Behavioral Approach to Writing," *College English* 30 (January 1969), 267–320.

scratch notes, difficult, need opportunities to explain their plans to them-selves or discuss them with other students, a sympathetic teacher, or even a tape recorder. Every assignment should provide several opportu-nities for students to discuss their work-in-progress with one another.

BRAINSTORMING AND CLUSTERING

Brainstorming is an unstructured probing of a topic. Like free associa-tion, brainstorming allows writers to venture whatever comes to mind about a subject, no matter how obvious or strange the ideas might be. When the entire class brainstorms a topic, the teacher generally writes on the board whatever words and phrases students call out. When students brainstorm topics on their own, they list whatever details occur to them. As a rule, general or superficial observations head the list, but as students begin to examine the subject more closely, useful and interesting details begin to appear. To be useful, of course, the list must contain abundant raw material.

Sometimes, however, brainstorming yields only rambling, unfocused, or repetitive generalizations. If the teacher has presented the technique as an end in itself, students may conclude, "Okay, she wants a list of 100 details, so I'll give her a list of 100 details." The purpose of brain-storming is neither list making nor reaching a precise number of details. As Donald Murray advises in *A Writer Teaches Writing*, "The teacher must, in such lists as this, begin to encourage honesty, to have the student look into himself and into his subject with candor and vigor. The list also gives the teacher a chance to defeat the cliché and the vague general-ization by saying to the student, 'What does that mean? Can you be more specific?' The teacher should praise a student when he gets a good concrete detail which has the ring of reality" (1st ed., p. 78). At least initially, students need guidance in generating *useful* details and enough of them to permit discarding those that seem irrelevant. Students also need reminding that list making serves a larger purpose, to explore the subject thoroughly and discover what makes it interesting or important.

Teachers can go over these lists with individual students in brief conferences during class. An especially rich list can be the subject of whole-class discussion, followed by groups of students reviewing their own lists with one another. What details seem most forceful? In what ways could details be grouped? What patterns have emerged in the list? What dimensions of the subject seemed to attract the writer's interest? What details must be left out at this point if the first draft is to hang together? A discussion along these lines helps students discover organi-zational possibilities in the raw material and suggests options for devel-oping the paper.

Following such a discussion, students might begin clustering their material, grouping and regrouping items into a diagram such as the one in Figure 7.1. Called "mapping," "clustering," or "webbing," the process

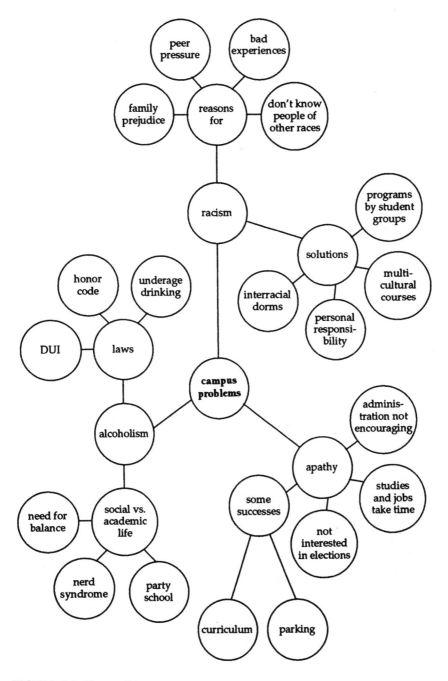

FIGURE 7.1 Cluster Diagram

of creating such drawings helps writers explore the organizational possibilities in their material. Unlike formal outlines, with their restrictive system of Roman and Arabic numerals and their need for parallelism, cluster diagrams represent provisional representations of the relationships among topics, subtopics, and supporting evidence. If one area of the diagram looks skimpy, additional brainstorming will provide more material (or the writer may abandon it altogether). Heavy branches may need subdividing.

The clusters in Figure 7.1 grew out of a brainstorming session on the topic "campus problems." As it happened, the class creating the diagram eventually abandoned "campus problems" as the topic because the material in some of the subtopics—"alcoholism," "racism," and "apathy"— seemed more interesting. As with most cluster diagrams, any branch could be developed into a new, more detailed diagram. The purpose of clustering is to help a writer discover order in a subject and to transform lists of details into meaningful groupings, some of which eventually may find a place in a first draft.

FREEWRITING

Freewriting, a technique advocated by Peter Elbow and Ken Macrorie, offers students a risk-free way of getting words onto a page without having to worry about their correctness. Elbow explains the technique this way:

> The idea is simply to write for ten minutes (later on, perhaps fifteen or twenty). Don't stop for anything. Go quickly without rushing. Never stop to look back, to cross something out, to wonder how to spell something, to wonder what word or thought to use, or to think about what you are doing. If you can't think of a word or a spelling, just use a squiggle or else write, "I can't think of it." Just put down something. The easiest thing is just to put down whatever is in your mind. If you get stuck it's fine to write "I can't think what to say, I can't think what to say" as many times as you want: or repeat the last word you wrote over and over again: or anything else. The only requirement is that you *never* stop. (*Writing without Teachers*, p. 3)

Elbow recommends that students freewrite at least three times a week. Freewritings, he insists, should *never* be graded. Their primary purpose is to get something on paper, and "it's an unnecessary burden to try to think of words and also worry at the same time whether they're the right words" (p. 5). Macrorie advocates freewriting because it produces honest writing, writing that is free from phoniness or pretension. The writer must write fast enough to use "his own natural language without thinking of his expression" (*Telling Writing*, p. 9).

Some teachers do not constrain freewriting in any way; others offer a phrase or the beginning of a sentence to help students get started. Teachers also can sequence freewriting exercises in several ways to move students closer to more formal drafts. For example, after students have completed a freewriting, they may read it aloud or silently to find words, phrases, a sentence or two that seem especially appealing. These words then offer a place to begin a second freewriting. The second freewriting may suggest ideas for a third and so on.

Murray sequences freewritings by incorporating student response at each stage.[4] First, students write freely for five minutes or so. Then, working in pairs, they discuss the freewriting by answering a question about it: "What appeared on the page that you didn't expect?" After a few minutes of discussion, students complete a second freewriting and stop to discuss it: "What idea do you want to develop in the next freewriting?" The procedure is repeated six or seven times, a new question guiding the students' discussion after each period of writing. The questions help students focus on what has appeared, on where the composing process is taking them. Teachers and students may substitute their own questions to guide the discussion, focusing on the writing but at the same time leaving students free to let their own language take charge of the page: What is the writing telling you? How do you (the writer) feel about what is appearing on the page? What do you (the reader) need to know that I haven't told you yet?

Freewriting encourages students to overcome their fear of the blank page and their stifling preoccupation with correctness. The technique encourages play with language and uses language as an aid to thinking. A freewriting represents a writer talking out an idea; it is not a polished communication intended for an outside audience. Needless to say, if teachers grade freewritings, they are no longer "free." Threatened by grades, students will shift their attention from generating and developing ideas to editing a finished product.

JOURNALS

Journals, commonplace books, or writer's notebooks have been indispensable tools for many writers, the famous and not so famous. Some journals, like diaries, record experiences and observations meant only to be read by their authors. Other journals, Virginia Woolf's *Writer's Diary* and Ralph Waldo Emerson's *Journals* for example, contain such significant information about an author's life and work that they reach a large public audience. Many professional writers use journals to sketch out, organize, draft, and revise their work before they submit it for publication.

4. Donald Murray, workshop presentation, South Carolina English Teachers Conference, University of South Carolina, October 21, 1978. See also "The Listening Eye: Reflections on the Writing Conference," *College English* 41 (September 1979), 13–18. "Looping" and "cubing," which also depend on completing series of freewritings, are described in Elizabeth Cowan Neeld, *Writing*, 3d ed. (Glenview, IL: Scott, Foresman, 1990), pp. 20–21 and 315–16 respectively.

The journal has several uses in a writing class. Many teachers set aside the first few minutes of every class period for journal writing. While the teacher checks the roll, returns papers, or reviews the lesson plan, students use the time to write whatever they want in their journals. The procedure settles the class down to work and gives students daily writing practice. To avoid treating the journal as inconsequential busywork, students should have opportunities to develop the material recorded in their journals into more formal assignments. Journals also can become workbooks for the course. In them, students may practice freewriting, respond to reading assignments, jot down leading ideas in preparation for class discussion, work out plans for papers, complete sentence-combining exercises, work on revisions, experiment with stylistic effects, keep track of spelling demons, and note which writing problems they have conquered and which still need work.

Unaccustomed to writing without some teacher-made assignment in front of them, students may protest that they can't think of anything to write in their journals, or they may devote several entries to deliberately "detached" topics: "I got up at eight, skipped breakfast, and went to class. Nothing much happened today." When this happens, teachers can discuss the difference between simply recording experiences and the more productive activity of reacting to or reflecting on events. They might also suggest that students capture a feeling in words or speculate about some imaginary, "what if" situation. If these open-ended, deliberately vague suggestions don't work, the following list might help, at least until students become comfortable pursuing their own interests.[5]

1. Speculate. Why do you spend so much time in a certain place? Why do you read a certain book or see a particular movie more than once?
2. Sketch in words a person who doesn't know you're watching: a woman studying her reflection in a store window, a spectator at a sports event, a student studying desperately.
3. Record some observations about a current song, book, movie, television program.
4. React to something you've read recently. Was it well written? Why or why not? What strategies did the writer use to get you to like or dislike the piece?
5. Try to capture an incident of night fear—when a bush became a bear, for example—so that a reader might feel the same way you did.
6. Explain an important lesson you learned as a child.
7. If peace were a way of life and not merely a sentiment, what would you have to give up?

5. Adapted from a list developed by Connie Pritchard, University of South Carolina, Fall 1977. See also Macrorie, *Telling Writing*, pp. 140–51.

8. Describe your idea of paradise or hell.
9. Write a nasty letter complaining about some product that didn't work or some service that was performed poorly.
10. Pretend you're the consumer relations official for the company in number 9. Write a calm, convincing response to your complaint.
11. If you were an administrator in this school, what's the first change you'd make? Why?
12. Tell what season of the year brings the things you like best.
13. You have been given the power to make one person, and only one, disappear. Whom would you eliminate and why?

Most teachers read their students' journals periodically, every few weeks or so. Eventually, they may assign the entire journal a percentage of the final grade; students receive credit simply for writing regularly. Other teachers base the grade for the journal on the quantity of writing it contains, thirty entries receiving an A, twenty to twenty-nine entries earning a B, and so on. Grading individual entries in journals is counterproductive because it discourages provisional thinking and regular practice with writing. Journals offer students a place to write without fear of making mistakes or facing criticism for what they have to say. Comments on journal entries should be positive, encouraging further writing or deeper exploration of an idea: "I felt that way too when my best friend misunderstood what I said." "It must have taken courage to tell your parents this; why not write an entry as if you were telling the story from their point of view?" Students should feel free to write "Do not read" across the top of an entry they don't want anyone else to see or to fold the page over and staple it. A teacher unable to resist temptation should ask students to remove personal entries before the journals are turned in.

When I read a set of journals, occasionally I'll come across an entry full of obscenities. They're meant to shock me. Generally, I ignore them the first time around; if they appear again, I usually discuss the journal with the student. In a fit of frustration, I once asked a student to write another entry defining some of the four-letter words he'd used. He never did. Much more common are the touchingly painful accounts of personal traumas students sometimes share with their English teachers. If I ignore the entry because it makes me uncomfortable, the student will conclude that I can't handle honest, sensitive topics and prefer to read only about "safe," academic subjects. If I write some gratuitous comment in the margin, I belittle the experience. When I discover students working out difficult experiences by writing them down in a journal, I generally encourage them to tackle the problem in several entries. They may have detected an irony in the experience, a weakness or strength in themselves, or a serious flaw in their idealistic notions about people. They need to examine further what they have found, first to understand it for themselves and perhaps later to share it with a larger audience. Precisely because such entries contain honest statements about important problems, they deserve to be treated seriously.

HEURISTICS

Heuristics derive ultimately from the *topoi* of classical rhetoric. In Book Two of the *Rhetoric*, Aristotle discusses twenty-eight "universal topics for enthymemes on all matters," among them, arguing from opposites, dividing the subject, exploring various senses of an ambiguous term, examining cause and effect. Although the classical *topoi* represent lines of reasoning speakers might pursue to invent arguments, heuristics prompt thinking by means of questions. The questions are ordered so that writers can explore the subject systematically and efficiently, but they also are open-ended to stimulate intuition and memory as well as reason. Most students are already familiar with the heuristic procedure journalists use: Who? What? When? Where? How? These questions help reporters compose effective lead paragraphs in news stories. Conditioned by years of testing, students often think that heuristic questions must have right and wrong answers; they don't. They increase the possibilities for probing a topic thoroughly, and they usually generate provisional answers. Ideally, those tentative answers should lead students to formulate further questions.

In *Writing* (3d ed., pp. 328–29), Elizabeth Cowan Neeld presents a heuristic derived from the categories "definition," "comparison," "relationship," "testimony," and "circumstance." The author encourages students to take the questions one at a time, thoughtfully, replacing the blank with a subject they want to explore and writing brief notes to answer the questions. If students get stuck on a question, they should move on. When they have finished the entire list, they should reread their notes, starring the material that looks promising.

Definition

1. How does the dictionary define _____ ?
2. What earlier words did _____ come from?
3. What do *I* mean by _____ ?
4. What group of things does _____ seem to belong to? How is _____ different from other things in this group?
5. What parts can _____ be divided into?
6. Did _____ mean something in the past that it doesn't mean now? If so, what? What does this former meaning tell us about how the idea grew and developed?
7. Does _____ mean something now that it didn't years ago? If so, what?

8. What other words mean approximately the same as _____ ?
9. What are some concrete examples of _____ ?
10. When is the meaning of _____ misunderstood?

Comparison

1. What is _____ similar to? In what ways?
2. What is _____ different from? In what ways?
3. _____ is superior to what? In what ways?
4. _____ is inferior to what? In what ways?
5. _____ is most unlike what? (What is it opposite to?) In what ways?
6. _____ is most like what? In what ways?

Relationship

1. What causes _____ ?
2. What is the purpose of _____ ?
3. Why does _____ happen?
4. What comes before _____ ?
5. What comes after _____ ?

Circumstance

1. Is _____ possible or impossible?
2. What qualities, conditions, or circumstances make _____ possible or impossible?
3. Supposing that _____ is possible, is it also desirable? Why?
4. When did _____ happen previously?
5. Who has done or experienced _____ ?
6. Who can do _____ ?
7. If _____ starts, what makes it end?
8. What would it take for _____ to happen now?
9. What would prevent _____ from happening?

Testimony

1. What have I heard people say about _____ ?
2. Do I know any facts or statistics about _____ ? If so, what?
3. Have I talked with anyone about _____ ?
4. Do I know any famous or well-known saying (e.g., "A bird in the hand is worth two in the bush") about _____ ?
5. Can I quote any proverbs or any poems about _____ ?
6. Are there any laws about _____ ?
7. Do I remember any songs about _____ ? Do I remember anything I've read about _____ in books or magazines? Anything I've seen in a movie or on television?
8. Do I want to do any research on _____ ?

The dramatistic pentad is a heuristic derived from Kenneth Burke's rhetoric of human motives discussed in Chapter 4:

What was done? (act)

Where or when was it done? (scene)

Who did it? (agent)

How was it done? (agency)

Why was it done? (purpose)

Although Burke originally posed these questions to explore the complicated motives of human actions, most composition teachers use the heuristic with a simpler aim in mind: to help students generate descriptive or narrative material. As a prewriting technique, the pentad works well for investigating literary topics, historical or current events, and biographical subjects. The pentad gains additional heuristic power when any two of the five terms are regarded together, as "ratios." Consider, for example, how the act:scene ratio informs the plot of any murder mystery. Or how the act:purpose ratio characterizes what some people call *euthanasia* and others, *murder*.

William Irmscher has elaborated on Burke's pentad by expanding the questions. In the *Holt Guide to English* (pp. 35–40), he uses the following questions to generate material about the painting *Nighthawks* by American artist Edward Hopper:

Action

1. What happened?
2. What is happening?
3. What will happen?
4. What could happen?
5. What is it?

Actor or agent

1. Who did it?
2. Who is doing it?
3. What did it?
4. What is causing it?
5. What kind of agent is it?

Scene

1. Where did it happen?
2. Where is it happening?
3. Where will it happen?
4. When did it happen?
5. What is the background?

Means or agency

1. How did the agent do it?
2. What means were used?

Purpose

1. Why? Why not?

In answering such questions about a painting, the material we will generate depends on our perspective. If we take the "action" to be Hopper's physically painting his work of art, he is the agent, and we will generate one set of answers. However, if the action is understood to be what is occurring inside the painting, in a transfixed moment, different possibilities emerge. Neither set of answers to Irmscher's questions would be correct or incorrect; they simply represent different ways of defining the subject.

Because students sometimes assume that every question must have a right answer, they need to see a demonstration to use the questions effectively. A teacher might bring a large picture or poster to class, choose a current event of interest to students, or base the demonstration on the subject of an assignment. Using the board, the teacher can guide students through the questions, writing down their answers, then reviewing the material to evaluate which answers seem most insightful or productive. The pentad will be most helpful in generating material about topics involving human activity. It is less likely to help students determine the audience and purpose for a piece of writing.

Another series of questions, adapted from Richard Larson's problem-solving model, suggests ways to engage issues-oriented subjects, the sort teachers often assign for persuasive papers. Students also may find the heuristic useful in sorting through other problems: personal difficulties, writing problems, or the problem posed by a writing assignment.

> What is the problem?
>
> Why is the problem indeed a problem?
>
> What goals must be served by whatever action or solution that is taken?
>
> Which goals have the highest priority?
>
> What procedures might attain the stated goals?
>
> What can I predict about the consequences of each possible action?
>
> How do the actions compare with each other as potential solutions to the problem?
>
> Which course of action is best?

In answering these questions, students define the problem, analyze it, formulate several potential solutions, and select the best solution. "In every problem," writes Edward P. J. Corbett, "there are some things that you know or can easily find out, but there is something too that you don't know. It is the *unknown* that creates the problem. When confronted with a problem, you have to take note of all the things you do know. Then, by a series of inferences from the known, you try to form a hypothesis to determine whether your theory leads you to discover the unknown that is causing the problem" (*The Little Rhetoric and Handbook*, p. 44). Teachers too can employ the heuristic to define, analyze, and solve teaching problems or conduct research.

Because most writing teachers also teach literature courses, a heuristic for analyzing, interpreting, and evaluating literature can pose useful questions to guide students' reading or help them explore literary topics. Corbett devised the following series of questions, which have been adapted from *The Little Rhetoric and Handbook* (pp. 186–221):

I. Analyzing the work

    A. What is the work about?

        1. What kind of work is it? (genre)

        2. What happens or what is said? (plot)

        3. What is the source of conflict?

    B. How is the work put together?

        1. What is the setting?

        2. What is the style of the work?

        3. How is the work organized and structured?

        4. What is the point of view from which the story is told?

        5. Why did the author choose this point of view from which to tell the story?

II. Interpreting the work

    A. What did the author mean?

        1. What is the theme of the work?

        2. In what way is (a particular incident or passage) related to the theme of the work?

        3. What did (a particular character) mean when he/she said, "(quotation of the statement)"?

        4. What is the symbolism of (a particular event or object in the work)?

        5. What patterns do you find in the (incidents, characters, diction, figures of speech)?

    B. What did the work mean to you?

        1. How is the ending of the work related to other parts of the work?

        2. Why did (a particular character) do what he/she did?

        3. What kind of person is (a particular character in a story or the persona that speaks in a poem)?

    4. What attitude does the narrator have toward (a particular character) and how is the attitude revealed?

III. Evaluating the work

    A. How well does the author accomplish what he/she set out to do?

        1. Was the work true-to-life?

        2. Was the action plausible?

        3. Were the characters believable and consistent?

        4. Was the author's style clear and pleasing?

    B. Was the work worth your time and attention?

        1. Did the work capture and hold your interest?

        2. How does the work compare with other literary works you have read or with some movie, play, or television drama you have seen?

        3. Do you agree or disagree with what other critics have said about the work?

        4. If you were writing a review of the work for a newspaper, what would you say to encourage others to read or not read the work?

        5. What have you learned from reading this work that could make your life better or different?

Obviously, students don't need to answer all of Corbett's questions every time they read a literary work. Routinely dragging the class through each question would be boring busywork. The questions have value insofar as they guide reading, suggest new ideas to explore, or encourage a closer examination of the text. The questions can be broken apart, altered, or culled selectively. At some point, students need to frame their own questions to explain their response to the work.

Because most textbooks devote little attention to audience, students may need help defining for whom they are writing and why. A heuristic for assessing the audience provides such help. Audience analysis not only generates content, depending on what a reader already knows about a subject, but it also encourages writers to think early on about their tone and point of view. The following questions, adapted from Karl R. Wallace's "*Topoi* and the Problem of Invention," ask writers to identify several characteristics of an audience:

How old is the audience?

What is the economic or social condition of the audience?

What is the educational status of the audience?

What general philosophies of government or politics does the audience hold?

What values and beliefs would be common to an audience of this age?

What economic or social values is the audience likely to hold?

What value does the audience place on education, religion, work?

Which of these values—economic, social, political, educational—is most important to the audience? Least important?

In general, how does the audience feel about its heritage or events that happened in the past? That are going on in the present? What hopes for the future does the audience hold?

In general, does the audience expect certain patterns of thought in what it reads? Should I include a lot of data to convince the audience of my point? What authorities would be most convincing? Does the audience need to see the causes and effects of my proposals? Would stories and analogies confuse my readers or encourage them to understand what I want to say? What terms will I need to define, and what terms can I assume are already understood?

What sorts of issues most frequently make the audience angry or defensive?

What things can I say without antagonizing my audience?

What options do I have for presenting unpopular opinions to my audience?

What is the most convincing appeal I could make? Should I try to convince by being reasonable and logical? Should I appeal to the emotions? Or should I demonstrate that I am an honest, trustworthy, sympathetic expert whom the audience can trust?

Have I stereotyped my audience, overlooking individuals who may hold views that are different from those the rest of my audience believes in?

Am I just saying what my audience wants to hear or am I also saying what I honestly believe to be true?

After students have grown comfortable with relatively simple prewriting techniques—brainstorming, clustering, freewriting, answering questions—they may want to use more elaborate heuristics to probe the subject even further.[6]

The following heuristic is adapted from Richard Young, Alton Becker, and Kenneth Pike's *Rhetoric: Discovery and Change* (1970) and permits us to examine a subject systematically from several perspectives. Although we customarily consider a subject from only one point of view, tagmemic invention forces us to shift mental gears to see it differently. According

6. See, for example, Richard L. Larson, "Discovery through Questioning: A Plan for Teaching Rhetorical Invention," *College English* 30 (November 1968), 126–34; and Tommy J. Boley, "A Heuristic for Persuasion," *College Composition and Communication* 30 (May 1979), 187–91.

to Young, Becker, and Pike, anything—an object, event, concept—can be viewed from three perspectives. We usually regard an oak tree, to use their example, as an isolated, static entity, as a "thing" or particle. But we also could view the oak as a process (wave), as a participant in the natural growth cycle that begins with an acorn and ends when the tree rots or is cut into lumber. Or we may regard the tree as a system (field) of roots, trunk, branches, and leaves. These three perspectives—particle, wave, field—permit us to consider the same subject from three angles: as a static entity, as a dynamic process, and as a system.

Furthermore, in order to "know" this oak tree, we must be able to figure out three aspects of its existence (regardless of which perspective we assume):

1. *How is it unique?* As an entity, process, or system, how does it differ from everything else? Young, Becker, and Pike label this aspect "contrast."
2. *How much can it change and still be itself?* How much "variation" is possible in the oak (viewed as entity, process, or system) before it becomes something other than an oak?
3. *How does it fit into larger systems of which it is a part?* What is its "distribution"? In other words, the oak tree not only *is* a system, but it also belongs to other systems. It is affected by a system of seasonal changes; it participates in the ecosystem of the surrounding countryside; it plays a role in an economic system to which lumber production, tourism, and national parks belong.

The six concepts—particle, wave, field, contrast, variation, and distribution—can be arranged to produce a nine-cell chart, often referred to as a *tagmemic grid* or *matrix* (see *Rhetoric: Discovery and Change*, p. 127).

Although the nine-cell matrix can generate enormous amounts of material about a subject, most students need considerable practice using the technique before they find it helpful and comfortable. For this reason, you may prefer to introduce students to a simplified version of the matrix such as the one W. Ross Winterowd includes in *The Contemporary Writer* (p. 94):

The Los Angeles freeway system, for instance, can be viewed

1. *As an Isolated, Static Entity.* We ask, What features characterize it? We can draw a map of it; we can measure its total length; we can count the number of overpasses and underpasses. We can describe it in great detail. In fact, such a description could well demand a number of thick volumes. But the point is that we can view anything as an isolated, static entity and begin to find those features that characterize it.
2. *As One Among Many of a Class.* We ask, How does it differ from others in its class? From this point of view, we would compare the Los Angeles freeway system with others like it. I, for instance, immediately

think of the difference between the L. A. freeway system and the turnpikes of the East and Midwest, as well as the German Autobahnen.

3. *As Part of a Larger System.* We ask, How does it fit into larger systems of which it is a part? The L. A. freeway system would be worthless if it did not integrate with national, state, and county highway systems; therefore, its place in these larger systems is crucial.

4. *As a Process, Rather Than as a Static Entity.* We ask, How is it changing? In regard to the L. A. freeway system, this question brings up the whole problem of planning for the future, which implies the problem of history, or how the system got to be the way it currently is.

5. *As a System, Rather Than as an Entity.* We ask, What are the parts, and how do they work together? Now we are focusing on the L. A. freeways as a transportation system, each part of which must integrate and function with the whole.

MODELS

Discussing models for student writers to emulate is a technique as old as rhetoric itself. For centuries, teachers of rhetoric and composition have asked students to imitate noteworthy essays, aphorisms, fables, speeches, and excerpts from works by great writers. Advocates of the practice believe that it exposes students to important cultural values and helps them develop their sense of style. To imitate an excellent writer, students have to read carefully, analyze the text closely, and then use similar constructions in creating their own texts. Although close imitation is no longer a staple of contemporary writing classes, most writing teachers still present models that illustrate approaches students may take in responding to assignments.

The most common model in today's writing course is the expository essay, perhaps because it is the most frequent form of discourse students write. Despite a long tradition of using essays to teach writing, we ought to question their purpose. What kinds of models are appropriate? In what ways are they helpful? When should they be introduced? How should they be discussed?

First, the models don't always have to be essays. Letters, advertisements, reports, memoranda, newspapers, policy statements, even junk mail, can illustrate rhetorical strategies. Students themselves can bring these materials to class, providing their own examples of the kinds of writing they are practicing.

Second, the models discussed in class don't have to be written by professionals. Good student writing should serve as a model most of the time because it best exemplifies those rhetorical strategies we expect to find in students' papers. Good student writing teaches writers of similar age and experience how to plan their work, how to anticipate problems of organization and language, and how to frame their notions of audience, purpose, subject, and persona. Furthermore, student models have an important advantage over professional models: the author is sitting in the class, a live, present author who can help us sort out intended meanings or points of confusion. Student writing also represents a more realistic, attainable model than the writing of professionals. Students know that they aren't the kind of writer Montaigne or Martin Luther King, Jr., were. Nor do we want them to be. Instead, we want them to use their own voices to express their own messages, to discover their own purposes for writing. From time to time, we may even want to discuss examples of atrocious professional prose to reinforce the notion that students sometimes write better than professionals.

Third, in discussing any model, the focus should be primarily on *how* the writer solves problems. Of course, we also have some responsibility for helping students understand *what* the writer says, for teaching students to read critically and carefully. But we should avoid approaching models, especially those written by professionals, as literary works subject to intense critical analysis. In a writing course, unlike a literature course, models serve not so much as literary artifacts to interpret, but as examples of the rhetorical problems, decisions, and choices student writers confront.

Fourth, most writing teachers introduce models prematurely. The best time to discuss a model is *after* students have already completed some prewriting and perhaps an early draft. That is when they are most likely to appreciate the rhetorical problem an assignment poses and to benefit from discovering how another writer addresses similar difficulties. Students cannot value the strategies a model illustrates if their own writing projects are not yet very far along. After students understand by experience the demands an assignment makes of them, examining a model can be instructive. Then they can know firsthand what options the writer had in presenting a subject, what choices he or she made and perhaps rejected, and how the strategies evident in the model apply to the student's work-in-progress.

The value of a model is what it can teach us about our own writing projects. Consequently, we don't need to belabor their discussion. One or two models for each assignment should be plenty. Most of the time, devoting fifteen to twenty minutes of a class period for their discussion should be adequate if we ask the right questions.

What are the right questions? Robert Bain's "Framework for Judging" is a good place to begin.[7]

Framework for Judging

1. A writer promises to do something. What does this writer promise to do? Does the writer keep that promise? If not, where and why does she or he fail to do so?
2. What seems to be the writer's attitude toward the reader?

---

7. The framework is adapted from Robert A. Bain, "Reading Student Papers," *College Composition and Communication* 25 (October 1974), 307–09.

Does the writer treat the audience playfully, seriously, with sarcasm? What does the writer's attitude toward the audience say about him/her and his/her subject?

3. Is the writer's attitude toward the subject convincing? Is the writer simply filling space or writing about feelings and ideas that matter? How can we tell?

4. Is there a perceivable order to the presentation? Can we follow and describe that order? If not, where does the writer lose us and why?

5. Has the writer omitted any important details or arguments that would help us understand the piece? Has the writer included details or arguments not connected with the ideas and feelings being discussed?

6. Does each paragraph signal clearly to the reader the direction in which the writer's ideas and feelings are moving? Does each paragraph develop and complete the idea it introduces? If we lose our way in a paragraph, where and why do we get lost?

7. Are the rhythms and patterns of sentences appropriate to the writer's subject and voice? If the sentences seem to be "Dick-and-Jane sentences," how could the writer combine them to break up this pattern? If the sentences are so long that we get lost in them, where could the writer break sentences into shorter units? Does the writer use passive voice excessively? If so, is that usage justified?

8. Is the language of the piece appropriate to the writer's voice and subject? If the writer uses big words, is she or he showing off or trying to help us understand better? Is the language fairly free of clichés, jargon, and worn-out words and phrases? If the writer ignores conventions of language, making up new words or running them together, what are some reasons for doing so?

9. Has the writer observed the conventions of grammar, punctuation, spelling, and capitalization? If not, is there a good reason for not doing so?

This sequence of questions places larger rhetorical concerns first, asking students to consider subject, audience, purpose, paragraphs, and sentences before attending to matters of punctuation and usage. Bain's questions also serve several functions. Because the framework helps writers discover what they propose to do and how they intend to go about it, the questions provide an excellent heuristic for planning responses to writing assignments. They also can organize discussions of student writing or some other model. Applied to student or professional models, the framework focuses discussion on *how* the model works, on ways to solve problems in writing. The questions serve revision too.

Students can work through them, on their own or in a draft workshop with other students, as they review their drafts. Not all of the questions need answering all of the time. A fifteen-minute class discussion of a student's paper, for example, might cover only the first four sets of questions; a draft workshop early in the term, only the questions in the fourth set.

Eventually, writers must stop generating answers to questions and begin organizing their raw material. They must evaluate what prewriting has yielded, identify hierarchies and classes, assign importance to some ideas and abandon others, and tentatively arrange whatever materials belong in a draft. It's difficult to say when generating material stops and shaping it begins because prewriting, writing, and rewriting don't follow a strict linear sequence. Sometimes prewriting activities generate material that reveals its own implicit organization. Sometimes writers don't discover the best way to organize their material until they've completed two or three drafts. Furthermore, as writers draft and rewrite their work, they often discover "holes" in the discourse. They stop drafting and return to prewriting, generating additional material to fill the gaps.

Most students begin drafting too soon, before they have sufficiently probed the subject, developed their own point of view, and made a commitment to the message. Their papers remain general because they haven't found enough interesting possibilities to pursue in their raw material or have failed to develop meaningful plans and goals to guide subsequent work. To address these problems, we must teach prewriting. We must give students a repertoire of planning strategies that, used in various combinations, will yield abundant raw material. Students need specific instruction in how to use a particular prewriting technique and enough practice with it to gain a sense of its potential. We can give them this practice if we structure writing assignments to move from brainstorming and freewriting to research and note-taking to responding to a heuristic, from role-playing to talking out ideas with classmates to writing them down. We also can collect scratch work and jotted notes from time to time, not merely to ensure that students give adequate time to prewriting, but also to guide them in developing more efficient, effective plans. Students should view these prewriting activities, not as isolated events, but as parts of a process that always looks ahead to drafting and revising. They are ways to let a piece of writing grow, ways to let us find a topic but also to let the topic find us.

eight

Shaping Discourse

Prose is architecture, not interior decoration.

ERNEST HEMINGWAY

In school as well as in the professional world, writers must observe formal requirements. Business letters, technical reports, and legal documents, for example, arrange material in prescribed ways, according to patterns sanctioned by convention and tradition. In these contexts, effective communication depends partly on writing-by-formula. Writing-by-formula also is necessary when teachers specify how they want students to organize book reports, term projects, and footnote or bibliographical citations. Formulas also save students time when they are writing under pressure. Because they have only a few minutes for prewriting during an examination period, a repertoire of formulas for organizing essay exams helps them plan their answers quickly and efficiently. Prescribed patterns of organization, then, serve a useful purpose, especially when time or tradition limits the choices writers have in shaping their work.

This chapter focuses primarily on organizing another kind of writing, writing that allows students more time to discover their purpose and message and that permits several options for arranging the material. This category includes most self-expressive writing and responses to assignments in many composition, creative writing, and journalism classes. It also covers the kind of writing students and professionals do whenever the audience—a teacher, an employer, a committee, a consumer group—considers any number of organizational patterns acceptable. This kind of writing confronts students with many possibilities for shaping their work. Students need to know what their options are and how to make effective choices.

FORM CONSCIOUSNESS

Form is everywhere. Although we rarely pay attention to how the world around us is organized, we encounter form not only in printed material but also in nature, the arts, and social and religious rituals. Discussions about form can begin by examining how artists—painters, sculptors, photographers, cartoonists, architects, fashion designers, and musicians—create form in media other than words, or how scientists and social scientists organize the phenomena they study. As we learned in Chapter 6, we impose patterns on our world, creating categories and relationships and making choices about what is significant and what is not.

Form exists in language too. In spoken English, the sequence of sounds, their arrangement into words and sentences, even the way we take turns in conversation "compose" speech into comprehensible utterances. If we didn't understand these patterns at some level, we would have difficulty making ourselves understood. In written English, we find form in the system of alphabet letters and other symbols that comprise the code. Formal conventions also govern how we arrange words on a page.

Although we know a good bit about how children acquire language and eventually manage to manipulate both the spoken and written code, we know less about how people become conscious of form in discourse. Most likely, form consciousness, like everything else in language, is the product of social interaction with others. Young children learn how to shape stories by hearing them and then inventing their own to tell to their teddy bears and imaginary playmates. Over time, as we read and write other genres, we begin building a repertoire of forms for poems, dialogues, explanations, and arguments. High school and college students, for example, have begun to develop skill in argumentation, but they often construct arguments by repeating the claim—"But I need to borrow the car"—instead of marshaling evidence to make the claim persuasive. Graduate students, confronted with the need to write a prospectus, a thesis, or a dissertation, spend considerable time trying to assess what these forms require. We learn how to organize different kinds of writing by becoming members of the culture that customarily uses those forms.

To some extent, then, others help us develop a conscious sense of form. We write to be read, and what our readers expect influences our decisions about how to organize and present our ideas. In early stages of composing, we devote most of our energies to organizing our ideas to suit ourselves, but eventually they also must make sense to a reader. To help our students become conscious of forms they may be unfamiliar with, we need to do what we ourselves would do: look at examples, analyze them to determine what principles govern the presentation of material, and practice the form in the context of sympathetic responses from readers.

DISCOVERING FORM

Most writers discover the shape of the whole discourse as they write. We may begin with a general plan in mind, but we work out the specific relationships between parts and wholes in the writing and rewriting stages. The general plan develops from prewriting decisions. As we probe the subject to discover what we want to say, as we define our purpose and assess the expectations of our readers, we make choices that will characterize the organization. A subject probed thoroughly enough begins to organize itself, begins to suggest possibilities for arranging the material. As we draft the piece, executing some of these preliminary decisions, new possibilities emerge, and we may decide to modify or abandon altogether our original plan. Then in reviewing the draft, we may discover holes or overlapping material; sections may need condensing, expanding, or rearranging. Most writers complete several drafts before the shape of the discourse suits them.

Some prewriting techniques discussed in Chapter 7 imply patterns of arrangement. Mapping or clustering, for example, tentatively arranges topics, subtopics, and supporting details in groups that offer a writer a place to begin. Larson's problem-solving heuristic suggests an organizational scheme in eight parts, each discussing one question or step in a process we can use to assess and solve problems. Corbett's heuristic implies a scheme for organizing discussions of literary works: analyze the work, interpret the work, evaluate the work. Both Larson and Corbett would argue that these schemes aren't the only ones we can use to discuss problems or works of literature, and they would urge us, furthermore, not to view any organizational model as a rigid formula, incapable of accepting revisions.

Because writers discover form at every stage of composing, teachers should stress planning strategies but also encourage students to be flexible about them. Inflexible plans that slavishly follow an outline or cram ideas into a prescribed form can undermine the effectiveness of a student's work. When students adhere too rigidly to their original intention, they seem less likely to make choices that might improve the piece. They also prevent themselves from discovering the material's organic unity and finding new implications in the subject. When we give students plenty of time for prewriting and frequent opportunities to examine where their writing is taking them, they will be more likely to modify or wisely abandon their original plan when necessary, without feeling that they have failed by not sticking to it.

One common organizational pattern, the five-paragraph theme, remains a persistent staple of many high school and college writing courses. Historically, it may survive from the era of Quintilian, who identified five sections in speeches arguing court cases:

> ... in all forensic cases the speech consists of five parts, the *exordium* designed to conciliate the audience, the *statement of facts* designed to instruct him, the *proof* which confirms our own propositions, the *refutation* which overthrows the arguments of our opponents, and the *peroration*

which either refreshes the memory of our hearers or plays upon their emotions. (*The Institutio Oratoria of Quintilian*, Vol. III, p. 183)

Because student writers rarely develop forensic orations nowadays, teachers must have other reasons for prescribing the five-paragraph form (or its three- and seven-paragraph cousins). Most teachers believe that it gives students a place to start, a simple way of developing form consciousness. By practicing the five-paragraph theme, students ostensibly will gain a stronger sense of how to divide material into an introduction, body, and conclusion.

In practice, however, the five-paragraph theme teaches students less about form than most of us would hope. Truthfully, the five-paragraph theme rarely appears in the real world; it survives primarily in some English classes. Many students also find it difficult to transfer what they have learned about the five-paragraph form to contexts requiring different organizational strategies. Writers sometimes need six or eight or twenty paragraphs to develop their subjects adequately, but students wed to five paragraphs incorrectly assume that all topics, especially in academic contexts, must be made to fit the mold they have learned. They have learned a particular form, not form consciousness.

Writing teachers often spend considerable time relaxing their students' grip on the five-paragraph model. Students who cling to the model usually do not know that they have choices about form, what those choices are, or how to choose wisely. We need to encourage them to listen to their material and help them discover options for organizing it. The college student who wrote the following essay obviously kept in mind the five-paragraph form, but the paper suffers because her ideas are disconnected and undeveloped. Caroline is writing off the top of her head, as if filling five "boxes" were more important than discussing how her life differs from her parents':

> The greatest contribution to ones' life are the exposures in which he or she become familiar with. These exposures are what basically effect ones' life and mold the way a person will live their remaining life.
>
> Exposure is the greatest attribute to ones' life. From what I've seen and what my parents saw at my age, what I saw was more. The world is smaller now because of mass transit. You can now fly all over the world in one day. Drive three hundred miles in one day. To be able to go to more places and see more things affects ones' future.
>
> It all amounts to the constant change in life style. Back in my parents' childhood, they could not have dreamed of having their own car. And my grandmother would have killed my mother for smoking a cigarette or drinking a beer.

Of course there is education. Education is a great contribution to how one is going to live their life. Education has become much better than that of my parents.

In conclusion the exposures that one encounters in the early portion of a life time contribute to ones' latter life. The exposures in which I have encountered are greater than my parents, so my life will be better.

For Caroline, form precedes content. The five-paragraph model, a conventional form, limits what she might say. It requires her to divide her topic into three subtopics, whether or not her subject matter lends itself to such a division, and to repeat in the fifth paragraph what was said in the first. As most students understand the form, it amounts to "telling them what you're going to tell them, telling them, and then telling them what you've told them." Because real writers rarely use the five-paragraph model, it is an irrelevant form. At the same time, because students can successfully learn to "fill the boxes," we need not abandon conventional forms altogether. Some conventional forms are useful.

Many of the forms that adult writers encounter have conventional arrangements. Résumés, for example, require that personal data (name, address, telephone number, and e-mail address) appear at the top of the page. Educational background and work experiences come next; references appear last. Furthermore, résumés conventionally omit some kinds of personal information—age and marital status, for example— and arrange work experiences with the most recent jobs first. Writing a résumé also invokes rules about how many headings and type faces to use, what verbs will best represent an applicant's qualifications, and how important proofreading can be. Successful résumés, job application letters, memos, grant proposals, educational research studies, and many other kinds of writing depend in part on a writer's managing the formal requirements. Content matters, of course, but readers also expect the content to appear in particular places. We learn how to compose such conventional forms by consulting models and adapting them to specific circumstances.

Writing courses rarely take advantage of relevant conventional forms, one reason perhaps why teaching form may be so difficult. Our courses usually focus instead on the composition, essay, or theme, a type of writing that, on the whole, exhibits relatively few formal constraints. Although readers make certain assumptions about how sentences and paragraphs will be constructed, they approach the organization of whole essays with a much more flexible set of expectations, willing to follow a writer through the piece so long as they encounter organizational clues or structural signposts now and then. One conventional form that may be relevant in a writing class that focuses primarily on essays is a form for constructing arguments. The form originates with Aristotle, but

Quintilian's version of it, quoted above, will work just as well if we adapt it to the needs of contemporary writers and readers. As Quintilian explains, an argument can have five parts:

1. The *exordium* or introduction tells readers what the argument is about and why it matters. The introduction must also "conciliate the audience," meaning it should establish a rapport with the reader by demonstrating that the writer is knowledgeable, trustworthy, and mindful of people's best interests.

2. The statement of facts or *narratio* offers background information. It states a thesis or makes a proposition that the rest of the argument will develop. If appropriate, it may divide the proposition into several parts, presenting a brief outline of the points to be covered. Quintilian advises that this section be "lucid, brief, and plausible"(IV, p. 67); it should avoid loaded language, irrelevant details, or meanness toward one's opponents.

3. The proof or confirmation may be the most important and longest part of the argument. It spells out the writer's position and elaborates it with reasons and evidence. Generally speaking, the strongest, most compelling evidence should come last so that it will be freshest in a reader's mind.[1]

4. The refutation treats objections that others might raise to the position that the writer supports. Dealing with opposing arguments so late in the essay can be tricky because writers easily can undermine themselves, but they also can strengthen their case and credibility if they treat opponents fairly, acknowledge or minimize legitimate differences, and construct powerful counterarguments.

5. The peroration, epilogue, or conclusion serves two purposes. It summarizes the main points of the argument and, more important, urges readers to adopt the writer's position. Emotional appeals have a place in the conclusion, but to be effective they should not be overdone.

Quintilian's model offers an effective scheme for organizing some kinds of arguments. It requires students to develop the pros and cons of their position, the thesis and antithesis essential to dialectical thinking. It also helps them practice the three appeals of classical rhetoric: logical reasoning, emotional appeals intended to move an audience, and ethical appeals that present the writer as a knowledgeable person of good will. Its disadvantage is that it encourages students to think of propositions

---

1. Arguments can come from many sources, as treatises on invention in classical rhetoric reveal. For contemporary discussions of sources for arguments, see Jeanne Fahnestock and Marie Secor, "Teaching Argument: A Theory of Types," *College Composition and Communication* 34 (February 1983), 20–30; and Richard Fulkerson, *Teaching the Argument in Writing* (Urbana, IL: NCTE, 1996).

as having "sides," that argumentation is a matter of "winning" by demonstrating that one position is superior to another. Consequently, the classical form will not lend itself well to arguments that require finding a common ground among legitimate alternatives or that develop a synthesis of divergent views of a subject.

Genres that permit several options for organizing material require a different approach to form. "The job of teaching structure," William Irmscher writes, "is not to prescribe it, but to help students realize how they can perceive and create the patterns of their own thoughts"(*Teaching Expository Writing*, p. 105). In other words, students "need to learn more about linking the 'inner parts' than designing the outer shape" (p. 104). In order to link inner parts, writers must do enough prewriting to develop sufficient material to link. Then they must see connections among their ideas, the relationships parts have to the whole. Teaching students to shape discourse is like teaching them to structure sentences and paragraphs. Form in discourse is "architecture." It's a way of expressing relationships among ideas.

STRATEGIES FOR TEACHING FORM

One of the most useful maxims for teaching form is Kenneth Burke's definition in *Counter-Statement*: "Form . . . is an arousing and fulfillment of desire. A work has form in so far as one part of it leads a reader to anticipate another part, to be gratified by the sequence" (p. 124). Form raises and fulfills a reader's expectations. When we write, we begin with a promise to our readers that the rest of the piece should keep. If we look back at the first paragraph of Caroline's paper, we can see that she is unsure about the promise she wants to make. She wants to discuss the effect of "exposures" on a person's life, but she hasn't defined for herself yet what she means by "exposures." Nor has she brought herself into the essay; she's looking abstractly, from a considerable distance, at "exposures" and their effect on her life.

In short essays, but in other kinds of discourse too, writers raise a reader's expectations early, generally in the first few sentences. Form is a way of fulfilling those expectations, of arranging material in ways a reader can follow. Because most readers are flexible and tolerant, we usually have several options for shaping the text. But we will lose our readers if we make too many promises, fail to keep them, or become too unpredictable.

Because students are readers as well as writers, a useful way of introducing them to form is to discuss the expectations raised by sentences they might encounter early in a text. Suppose, for example, that the following sentence appears in the opening paragraph of a student's paper: "People have speculated about the nature of language for a long time." What expectations does this sentence raise? What might the writer do in the rest of the essay to fulfill our expectations? Well, probably the writer will give us some examples of the "speculations" and maybe we'd find them arranged chronologically, because "for a long time" implies a historical context.

Let's consider another example: "Paid political advertising is expensive, deceptive, and ineffective in helping to educate voters." If we encountered such a sentence early in an essay, we'd expect a three-part argument treating the expense, the deceptive tactics, and the ineffectiveness of paid political advertising *in that order*. If the discussion fails to follow the order promised in the sentence, we might become confused. Furthermore, we might legitimately expect different methods of development in each of the three sections. Statistics might demonstrate that paid political advertising is expensive; examples could illustrate deceptive tactics; reasons would demonstrate why the writer believes that such advertising is ineffective. Readers would tolerate other approaches to the material. Our expectations also would be fulfilled if the writer chose several examples of political advertising and discussed the expense, deceptive tactics, and ineffectiveness of each example. The writer has several options for keeping the promise to the reader, and interested readers will accept almost any approach a writer has prepared them to anticipate. Indeed, the essay might be a five-paragraph theme, not because the teacher stipulates the form, but because the writer chose to divide the material into five sections.

A final example: "There are many differences between high school and college." My students call such a promise sentence a "throwaway sentence." It's a self-evident statement that arouses no desire in a reader. The response it raises is "So what?" As readers, we would engage the text more enthusiastically if we knew how many points of contrast we might expect to find, what areas of high school and college life we'll be reading about, and why the differences might be important. Like Caroline's opening paragraph, the throwaway sentence should prompt the writer to examine the material again to discover a message readers might be interested in.

Discussing promise sentences such as these, gleaned from student or professional writing, represents only one way of helping students understand how form affects a reader. Students also can investigate their options for organizing prose by bringing to class examples of the sorts of writing their assignments call for. How do writers organize these documents? Working in groups, students might outline these samples, not only to understand their contents, but also to examine how each section of the document fulfills the promise. As Kinneavy demonstrates, each aim of discourse supports its own patterns of organization; the expectations we bring to newspaper editorials differ from those that guide our reading of the sports pages. For this reason, if students are writing arguments, they should be analyzing arguments in editorials, professional publications, textbooks, and other materials. Such an analysis reveals how writers construct their claims and define their assumptions, what kinds of evidence they use and where they place it, and how they signal important subtopics.

We also can encourage students to consider their readers by giving them frequent opportunities to discuss their plans and eventually their drafts with one another. These activities promote audience awareness, reminding students about what their readers expect. With practice, students can become astute critics of one another's plans and drafts, pointing out gaps in the material, questioning its order, and testing the writer's assumptions and evidence. This feedback helps writers gain confidence in sorting claims and evidence, shaping them into parts and wholes, and arranging them in ways that are "logical" but invented anew for each subject, purpose, and audience.

BLOCKING

Although many teachers ask students to organize their material into an outline, formal outlines have several disadvantages. They can be too inflexible to guide composing, especially if the formal requirements of the outline—its sequence of Roman and Arabic numerals, its need for parallelism—assume greater importance than its content. When teachers insist on outlines, many students draft them after they have written the paper. They regard the formal outline almost as a separate assignment, with rules of form all its own and only a tangential connection to the paper. Formal outlines also can be inadequate and incomplete. Although they may list in order the points a writer wishes to cover, they may offer little help in determining proportions or deciding what rhetorical strategies to use in developing each section. Outlines also do not encourage provisional planning; they are supposed to be neat, final, and rigidly adhered to. Most writers, however, need at least one draft to work out the shape of the discourse. An outline can force premature decisions and limit options. Because formal outlines also focus attention on the content or subject matter, they may prevent writers from adequately considering audience and purpose.

Most experienced writers (and doubtless most writing teachers) do not work from the kinds of outlines described in composition textbooks. Rather, they develop informal written plans, rough blueprints that represent their intentions for a draft. Blocking or "chunking" resembles more closely than constructing formal outlines what writers do as they shape a draft. Blocking asks students to draw a picture of what they propose to write. Guided by questions they ask of their material, their audience, and their purpose, they fill in their drawing one layer at a time. Although students eventually develop their own styles of blocking, a finished block plan might look like this:

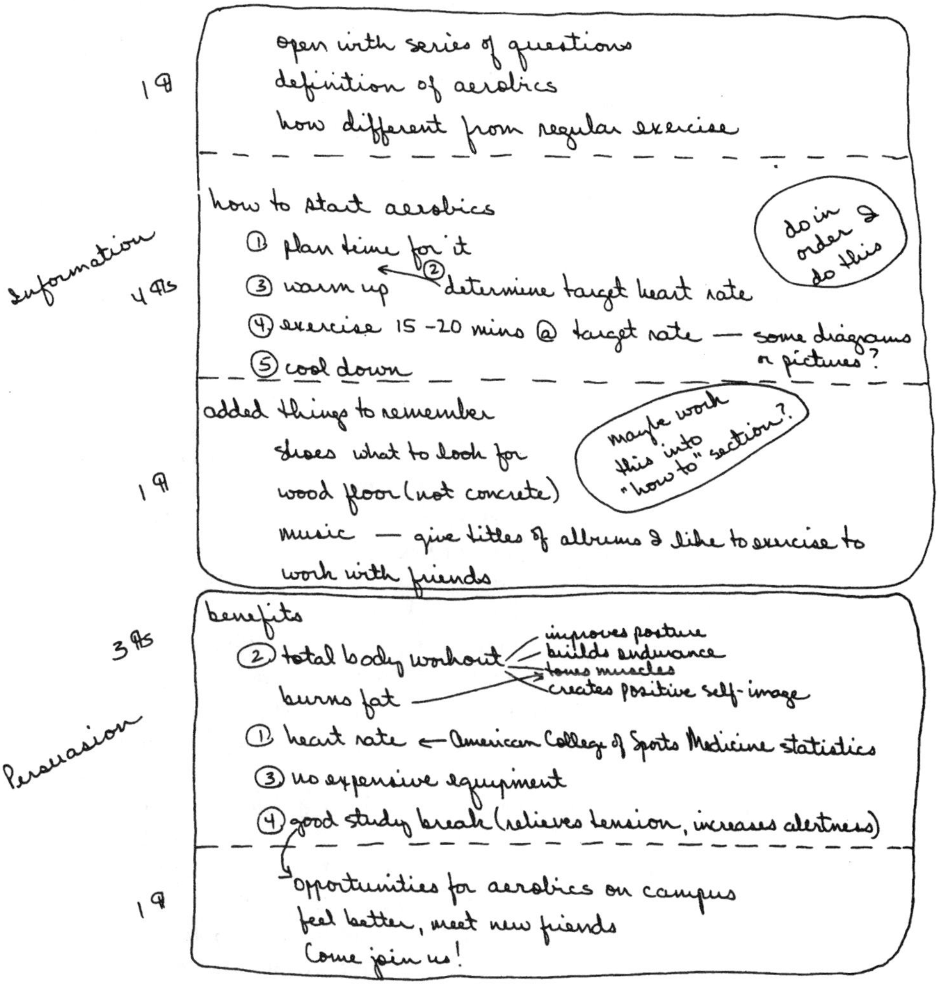

Block plan (handwritten notes):

1 ¶
- open with series of questions
- definition of aerobics
- how different from regular exercise

information
4 ¶s
- how to start aerobics
  - ① plan time for it
  - ③ warm up ← ② determine target heart rate
  - ④ exercise 15–20 mins @ target rate — some diagrams n pictures?
  - ⑤ cool down

(circled note: do in order & do this)

1 ¶
- added things to remember
  - shoes — what to look for
  - wood floor (not concrete)
  - music — give titles of albums I like to exercise to
  - work with friends

(circled note: maybe work this into "how to" section?)

persuasion
3 ¶s
- benefits
  - ② total body workout ← improves posture / builds endurance / tones muscles / creates positive self-image
  - burns fat
  - ① heart rate ← American College of Sports Medicine statistics
  - ③ no expensive equipment
  - ④ good study break (relieves tension, increases alertness)

1 ¶
- opportunities for aerobics on campus
- feel better, meet new friends
- Come join us!

Robert's block plan, shown here, helped him draft an effective essay for an audience of college students on the importance of aerobic exercise. Prior to blocking the plan, he had reviewed a brainstormed list and completed two freewritings in response to the questions "What do I know about aerobic exercise?" and "What do college students want to know about aerobic exercise?" He also had decided that his primary purpose would be to give his readers information about aerobic exercise (an expository or referential purpose) but that he would end the essay with an exhortation encouraging students to begin some kind of regular program of aerobic exercise (a persuasive purpose).

In developing the plan, Robert first asked himself, "How many blocks of material will it take to do what I want to do?" Some students may need to break this question into two questions if they are uncertain of their purpose: "How many blocks of material will I need?" and "What job is each block supposed to do?" Robert thought he'd need basically two blocks: one informative, one persuasive.

Then he asked himself, "What material goes into each block?" Returning to his brainstormed list and freewritings, he began moving material into the two blocks, developing smaller chunks (separated by dotted lines on the plan). Then he asked of his plan, "What order for these chunks would best help my audience get through my essay?" In testing the order of the chunks, Robert added arrows and numbers to indicate the arrangement he wanted and transitions from one chunk to another. In discussing the plan with classmates during a workshop session, he subsequently changed the order of some chunks, but because he regarded the plan as provisional, capable of being messy, he wasn't reluctant to revise it.

Next he asked, "How much space *roughly* do I want each chunk to take up?" Notes in the left-hand margin helped him decide tentatively how elaborately or briefly to develop each section. In determining the proportions of his essay, he considered both how much material he had and how much his projected audience already knew about the subject. Finally, he asked himself, "How do I want to develop each chunk?" He shifted his attention from the content of his essay to the rhetorical strategies he wanted to use, from *what* to say to *how* to say it. His notes about "titles," "diagrams or pictures," "do in order I do this," and "maybe work this into 'how to' section" reflect decisions about his approach to the material.

The plan Robert developed isn't an outline, although it has some of the characteristics of one. It's more like a carpenter's working drawing, complete with notes and revisions, illustrating how he proposes to lead the reader through the house he's building. His material, purpose, and sense of audience have helped him construct the rooms, but he still has some choices about how to furnish them, even about knocking out a wall here or adding a window there.

Blocking helps students shape their writing by looking simultaneously at their materials, their purpose, and the expectations of an audience. The questions Robert asked (or appropriate variations of them) could be typed onto a handout and distributed with the assignment. After students have developed their plans, they will want to discuss them with one another in a "planning workshop." Introducing a workshop at this point helps reinforce the sense of audience that should guide such plans and gives the writer an opportunity to hear alternatives or resolve confusion. After the writer has finished a draft, similar questions could structure a second workshop that allows students to offer one another suggestions for revision.

Teaching students how to block their papers requires more than telling them to do it. They need the guidance the questions offer; they need practice; they need some kind of response to the plan from other students. Block plans don't have to be graded. Their strengths and weaknesses will show up in the papers developed from the plan. However, the paper is likely to be more effective because the writer has taken the time to review prewriting decisions, creating a visual representation of how the inner parts and the outer shape of the piece might work together to convey a message to a reader.

D'ANGELO'S PARADIGMS

Another way of looking at form in discourse is to see it as a manifestation of thinking. Frank D'Angelo assumes a close connection between invention and arrangement, between thought processes and the organizational patterns or paradigms that express ideas. "The value of paradigms," D'Angelo explains, "is that they enable you to move your thinking in an orderly manner from the beginning of an essay to its conclusion. In some respects, paradigms are like maps. Maps are representations of a part or a whole of a city or a geographical region. They enable you to get around in the environment. Paradigms are mental representations of some course of action. They are mental anticipations of a plan that you expect to carry out. They are maps in your head that help you get around in your writing."[2] Because the mind composes perceptions, organizing them into temporal, spatial, and logical patterns, D'Angelo's paradigms reflect those mental processes at work in a piece of writing. The classification paradigm, for example, symbolizes a thought process we use every day. As we perceive the world around us, we constantly create categories, grouping phenomena that share some common characteristic. To express those categories in writing is to reveal how we think.

D'Angelo divides the paradigms into two groups, "static" and "progressive." The static paradigms arrange topics that can be viewed as entities, fixed in time and space; the progressive paradigms order topics such as narration and process that occur *through* time and space, that is, in several time-states. In their skeletal form, the most commonly used paradigms look like this:

Static Topics

1. Description Paradigm
   Paradigm 1: Vertical Order (bottom to top, top to bottom)
   Paradigm 2: Horizontal Order (left to right, right to left)
   Paradigm 3: Depth Order (inside, outside)
   Paradigm 4: Circular Order (clockwise, counterclockwise)

---

2. Frank D'Angelo, *Process and Thought in Composition*, 3d ed. (Boston: Little, Brown, 1985), p. 53. For a fuller explanation of the theory on which D'Angelo's textbook is based, see his *A Conceptual Theory of Rhetoric* (Boston: Little, Brown, 1975).

2. Definition Paradigm
     Extended Definition A
          1 Introduction (includes logical definition)
          2 Expansion of the genus
          3 Expansion of the differentia
          4 Conclusion (includes clincher sentence)
     Extended Definition B
          1 Introduction (includes logical definition)
          2 Supporting details
          3 Supporting details . . .
          4 Conclusion (includes clincher sentence)
     Extended Definition C
          1 Introduction (includes thesis)
          2 Meaning 1 (partial definition of key term)
          3 Meaning 2 (partial definition of key term)
          4 Meanings 3, 4, 5, . . .
          5 Conclusion (includes clincher sentence)
3. Analysis Paradigm
          1 Introduction (includes thesis)
          2 Characteristic 1
          3 Characteristic 2
          4 Characteristics 3, 4, 5, . . .
          5 Conclusion (includes clincher sentence)
4. Enumeration Paradigm
          1 Introduction (includes thesis)
          2 First (the first, one)
          3 Second (the next, two)
          4 Third (another, three)
          5 Finally (the final, four)
          6 Conclusion (summary, return to beginning)
5. Classification Paradigm
          1 Introduction (includes thesis)
          2 Type 1 (or subclass 1)
          3 Type 2 (or subclass 2)
          4 Types 3, 4, 5, . . .
          5 Conclusion (includes clincher sentence)
6. Exemplification Paradigm
          1 Introduction (includes thesis)
          2 Example 1 (or cluster of examples)
          3 Example 2 (or cluster of examples)
          4 Examples 3, 4, 5, . . .
          5 Conclusion (includes clincher sentence)
7. Comparison Paradigms
     Half and Half Pattern
          1 Introduction (includes thesis, sets up comparison)
          2 Subject 1

       a Characteristic 1
       b Characteristic 2 . . .
    3 Subject 2
       a Characteristic 1
       b Characteristic 2 . . .
    4 Conclusion (includes clincher sentence)
Characteristics Pattern
    1 Introduction (includes thesis, sets up comparison)
    2 Characteristic 1
       a Subject 1
       b Subject 2
    3 Characteristic 2 . . .
       a Subject 1
       b Subject 2
    4 Conclusion (includes clincher sentence)
Point by Point Pattern
    1 Introduction (includes thesis, sets up comparison)
    2 Subject 1 is similar (dissimilar) to Subject 2 in this respect
    3 Subject 1 is similar (dissimilar) to Subject 2 in this respect . . .
    4 Conclusion (therefore, subject 1 is similar [dissimilar] to subject 2 in some respect known about 1 but not about 2)

Progressive Topics

1. Narration Paradigm
    1 Introduction (setting, character)
    2 Event or Incident 1
    3 Events or Incidents 2, 3, 4, . . .
    4 Conclusion
2. Process Paradigm
    1 Introduction (organizing sentence, description of the materials, principles, implements)
    2 Step or Phase 1
    3 Steps or Phases 2, 3, 4, . . .
    4 Conclusion (includes clincher sentence, summary)
3. Cause and Effect Paradigms
    Cause to Effect Pattern A
       1 Introduction (includes background material, thesis)
       2 Cause 1
       3 Causes 2, 3, 4, . . .
       4 Effect
       5 Conclusion (includes clincher sentence)
    Cause to Effect Pattern B
       1 Introduction (includes background material, thesis)

2 Cause
3 Effect 1
4 Effects 2, 3, 4, . . .
5 Conclusion (includes clincher sentence)
Effect to Cause Pattern A
    1 Introduction (includes thesis)
    2 Effect 1
    3 Effects 2, 3, 4, . . .
    4 Cause
    5 Conclusion (includes clincher sentence)
Effect to Cause Pattern B
    1 Introduction (includes thesis)
    2 Effect
    3 Cause 1
    4 Causes 2, 3, 4, . . .
    5 Conclusion (includes clincher sentence)
(*Process and Thought in Composition*, 3d ed., pp. 72–73,
81, 91, 110, 119, 133–34, 144, 147, 157, 166, 181, 194–96)

Like any model, the paradigms are means to an end. Students should view them as options for discovering inherent organizational possibilities in ideas and experiences; "each of these paradigms can be shortened, lengthened, or modified to suit your own purpose," advises D'Angelo (p. 47). Depending on the material, students may need several paragraphs for introductions and conclusions. They may want to subordinate one paradigm to another. For example, each "type" in the classification paradigm could be developed by a series of examples, definitions, comparisons, and so on.

Before we leave these paradigms, we ought to notice something else about them, a feature that will shape our discussion of paragraphs and sentences in Chapters 9 and 10. The paradigms relate material by one of only two methods: coordination and subordination. In the classification paradigm, for example, the "types" all share coordinate relationships with one another; each type is an equal member of a larger class. Consequently, each type also is subordinate to the larger class mentioned in the introduction and conclusion. Similarly, because the process paradigm divides a whole into parts, a process into steps, the steps all share a coordinate relationship with one another, and each step is subordinate to the whole process. The paradigms illustrate that form expresses relationships. We express these relationships either by subdividing material (subordination) or by giving it equal status (coordination).

In "A Generative Rhetoric of the Essay," D'Angelo suggests that an essay, like a sentence and a paragraph, links its material by coordination and subordination. We can see these relationships at every level of language, from the coordination evident in compound sentences, to the repetition of examples in a paragraph, to the elaborated, extended examples of the exemplification paradigm for an entire essay. Although the parts and wholes of a complete essay encompass larger chunks of material than paragraphs and sentences do, the relationships will be the same. The same patterns of coordination and subordination that link the inner parts of an essay to one another and to the "main idea" or thesis are also at work in paragraphs and sentences. Writers express coordination and subordination either in grammatical structures or in meaning. Grammatical coordination occurs when sentences, paragraphs, and essays show parallel structures; meaning coordination depends on grouping similar examples, reasons, or details. Subordination, on the other hand, either within or between sentences, paragraphs, and parts of essays can be expressed in several ways:

> Some typical examples of grammatical subordination include: the use of a pronoun in one sentence to refer to a noun in the previous sentence; the use of transitional markers, such as *therefore, nevertheless, thus,* and the like, to tie sentences together; the repetition of a word or a part of a word (based on the same root) in a subsequent sentence to link it to a similar word in the previous sentence; and the use of a synonym to refer to an equivalent word in a previous sentence. Semantic relationships are much more difficult to discern, but in general . . . a sentence which gives an example, a reason, a statistic, a fact, or a detail is considered to be subordinate to a more general statement that precedes it. (p. 389)

We will examine these principles of subordination and coordination in greater detail in the next two chapters. D'Angelo sees these similarities in the relationships that organize essays, paragraphs, and sentences because he believes that thinking is relational; it forges links. The paradigms reflect these thought processes and express the relationships, associations, hierarchies, and categories that the mind has made of experience.

All of the strategies discussed in this chapter—examining the organizational schemes implicit in heuristics, adopting conventional forms, making and fulfilling promises to readers, block plans, and D'Angelo's paradigms—illustrate that the process of shaping discourse begins with prewriting and continues through rewriting. As means to an end, these strategies help students plot, at least provisionally, how a draft should proceed. Block plans and paradigms also support careful reading, allowing students to abstract ideas in an essay and discover its underlying patterns. Such a skill has value outside an English class, but it also serves revision because it gives writers new ways to read their drafts, eyes open to alternatives for organizing their material. If we encourage students to find form in discourse at each stage of composing, they will understand that a paper's organization derives from a range of choices writers control when they perceive relationships to express.

nine

Teaching Paragraphing

> In every structure we may distinguish the *relation* or *relations*, and the items *related*.
>
> SUZANNE LANGER

TRADITIONAL VIEWS OF THE PARAGRAPH

Perhaps nowhere else is the tendency to teach writing-as-product more evident than in the teaching of paragraphs. We may not be able to remember *how* we learned to group ideas into paragraphs, but we know by rote *what* paragraphs are: "a distinct unit of thought," "a group of logically related sentences," "a set of sentences, all of which deal with a common topic." Effective paragraphs, we tell our students, exhibit "unity, coherence, and emphasis," abstract qualities difficult to define. Traditionally, we have treated paragraphs as "things," as entities. They represent boxes students must wedge ideas into, adjusting their material until it fills out the specified shape. Paragraphs also have been taught through models and imitation. Students examine models in their reading assignments, label them as one of several "methods of paragraph development," and imitate the method in a series of paragraph-writing exercises.

Let's examine some of the assumptions governing these traditional methods of teaching paragraphs. Although the methods of paragraph development discussed in modern textbooks vary, the following catalogue is a standard list: narration, description, details, definition, comparison or contrast, cause or effect, examples and illustration, enumeration, classification. The list has a long history. It may derive from Aristotle's *Rhetoric*, which catalogues twenty-eight *topoi* for inventing enthymemes. But Aristotle wasn't describing structural units in a finished piece of writing or methods of arranging material. He was discussing means of generating subject matter, lines of inquiry that could be used to invent an argument. Over the years, however, terms that had originally defined techniques of invention or prewriting may have come to describe structures of arrangement. Terms referring to a process now appear to label parts of the written product.

By contrast, the terms we use to describe effective paragraphs—*unity, coherence,* and *emphasis*—are relatively recent. They derive from Alexander Bain's *English Composition and Rhetoric* (1866), which stipulates "seven laws" for effective paragraphs:

1. Distribution into Sentences: The consideration of the Unity of the individual Sentence leads up to the structure of the Paragraph, as composed of sentences properly parted off.
2. Explicit Reference: The bearing of each sentence of a Paragraph on the sentences preceding needs to be explicit.
3. Parallel Construction: When several consecutive sentences iterate or illustrate the same idea, they should, as far as possible, be formed alike.
4. Indication of the Theme: The opening sentence, unless obviously preparatory, is expected to indicate the scope of the paragraph.
5. Unity: Unity in a Paragraph implies a sustained purpose, and forbids digressions and irrelevant matter.
6. Consecutive Arrangement: The first thing involved in Consecutive Arrangement is, that related topics should be kept close together: in other words, Proximity has to be governed by Affinity.
7. Marking of Subordination: As in the Sentence, so in the Paragraph, Principal and Subordinate Statements should have their relative importance clearly indicated. (pp. 92–134)

Bain's principles serve a useful purpose when students want to examine, in literature or in their own writing, the effectiveness of written paragraphs; however, the laws are not so helpful when students want to know how to draft paragraphs from scratch. In the first place, several of Bain's principles of paragraph construction apply equally well to entire essays and books; Bain himself notes that "the internal arrangement of the paragraph comes under laws that are essentially the same as in the sentence, but on a greater scale" (p. 31). Second, the laws describe *what* characterizes an effective paragraph, not *how* a writer achieves the effect. Although keeping related topics close together is a commendable goal, the principles don't explain *how* that's to be done. Like the advice in many contemporary textbooks, Bain's principles describe the qualities of paragraphs-as-products but offer student writers inadequate help with paragraphing-as-process.

HOW WRITERS PARAGRAPH

One way to balance the view of paragraphs-as-products is to examine our own writing practices. When and why do we indent material? Sometimes we want to shift to a different idea, or to a different perspective, or to a new subset of material within the larger subject. Paragraphing signals changes to a reader. At other times, we begin new paragraphs to restate a point, to emphasize it, or to provide additional support for an idea. Paragraphing signals similarities in our treatment of the subject, allowing us to accumulate details. Finally, all writers begin new paragraphs from time to time simply because it seems convenient. In reading over a draft, we may notice that a paragraph contains only two or three sentences; so, we decide to combine those sentences with others to create a longer unit. Or, as I've discovered time and again in drafting this book, a paragraph may simply look too long; so, I find a place to break it into two or three smaller chunks. When we shape paragraphs according to how they look on the page—too long, too short, just right— we're basing our decisions first on formal considerations and only secondarily on the logical connections among ideas. We're approaching the material as a reader does, accustomed to seeing a line indented every so often.

Because readers want to comprehend ideas in manageable chunks, writers attempt to oblige them. How we define "manageable chunks," however, depends very much on convention. Medieval monks, concerned about saving parchment, rarely indented manuscripts. Instead, they began new sections by enlarging the first line of script or decorating the initial character. Nowadays, the kind of writing we're doing often determines how much material constitutes a "manageable chunk." Informal letters, newspaper articles, and advertising copy contain "over-differentiated" or short paragraphs. "Underdifferentiated" or long paragraphs occur in formal essays, encyclopedia articles, and some legal documents. Paragraph lengths also seem to reflect cultural and historical preferences. Eighteenth- and nineteenth-century prose may impress us as having extremely long paragraphs, perhaps because we're more used to reading the shorter paragraphs of modern newspapers and news magazines.

Examining our own writing habits also forces us to admit that we don't compose paragraphs as textbooks tell us to. Rarely do we consciously construct a topic sentence and then deliberately choose a method of developing it. We may keep a general plan in mind as we write, but actual drafting requires too much concentration to stop every few sentences and ask, "Now, what will my next topic sentence say, and what method of development will I use for this paragraph?" For most writers, the difficult process of generating words shuts out conscious decisions about form. That's why, it seems, we reparagraph at the rewriting stage, when we're relatively less preoccupied with ideas and can attend to form.

Despite textbook pronouncements, anywhere from 50 percent to 80 percent of the paragraphs written by accomplished professionals do *not* contain topic sentences.[1] Furthermore, they don't observe the methods of development listed in most textbooks. As Richard Meade and Geiger Ellis discovered when they examined 300 paragraphs selected at random from *Saturday Review, English Journal,* and letters to the editor of the *Richmond Times-Dispatch,* "56 percent (168) of the three hundred paragraphs were not developed by any textbook method. The remaining 44 percent followed only two of the textbook methods to any appreciable extent: reasons and examples" ("Paragraph Development in the Modern Age of Rhetoric," p. 222). Meade and Ellis conclude that, despite the variety of methods textbooks mention, "writers generally use paragraphs which reflect development by additional *comment, reasons,* or *examples,* either separately or in combination" (p. 225).

In addition to perpetuating myths about topic sentences and methods of development, most textbooks overlook a much more important truth about paragraphs: writers create complex internal relationships among the sentences *within* a paragraph. Traditionally, paragraphs are treated as units of prose that have two parts, a topic sentence and support. Some textbooks even quantify the amount of support a paragraph must have, claiming that paragraphs aren't paragraphs unless they contain at least three, five, or seven sentences. Such talk obscures how writers, on the creating end of paragraphs, treat them. First, writers use paragraphs to bring ideas and evidence together, to forge relationships between the so-called topic sentence and its support. Second, however long the supporting section of a paragraph may be, writers relate those sentences not only to the topic sentence (if there is one), but also to other sentences in the paragraph. Third, writers rarely give paragraphs an independent existence; paragraphs in continuous discourse are surrounded by other paragraphs.

Although we don't yet understand as much as we'd like to about the process of shaping discourse, apparently writers, in drafting the first sentence of a paragraph, commit themselves to a topic and establish a purpose for subsequent sentences. The first sentence may suggest a range of possibilities for developing an idea, but with each subsequent sentence the writer has less flexibility, fewer options. A writer who becomes committed to a generalization in the first few sentences of a paragraph, for example, still has some choice about supporting it with reasons or examples. Having chosen to present a reason, the writer is almost obliged to cite a second reason or to support the reason with an

1. William Irmscher, *Teaching Expository Writing* (New York: Holt, Rinehart and Winston, 1979), p. 98, reports that his graduate students found topic sentences in an average of 40 percent to 50 percent of the paragraphs they examined, whereas Richard Braddock found them only 13 percent of the time [see Braddock's "The Frequency and Placement of Topic Sentences in Expository Prose," *Research in the Teaching of English* 8 (1974), 287–302]. As Irmscher points out (p. 98), "Part of the problem is determining exactly what a topic sentence is"; he also notes that "percentages vary greatly among individual writers."

example. In this way, each decision dictates the range of choices for writing the next sentence.

From the reader's point of view, paragraphs make promises. As we saw in the previous chapter, form raises and fulfills a reader's expectations. Experienced readers know that indenting (or white space) "means" something. It may signal a subdivision of a topic, an example, a reason, a counterargument, a new speaker in a dialogue, perhaps a transition if the indented material is brief. Reader's expectations are flexible but not without limits. Reading the first sentence of this paragraph, you may have agreed with it, at least provisionally, but you probably also had some questions in mind, "What does she mean by *promises*? What kinds of promises do paragraphs make? How do paragraphs make these promises?" If the paragraph I wrote answers some of those questions for you, I have fulfilled your expectations; if not, I need to revise this group of sentences.

In writing paragraphs, as in shaping larger units of discourse, we continually discover form. To use Irmscher's simile, "The writer writes more like a sculptor who finds form *while* sculpting than like a bricklayer who piles bricks to construct a wall" (*Teaching Expository Writing*, p. 99, my italics). We don't begin with the parts, with paragraph-bricks, but with the whole, with ideas to express and a purpose for communicating them. We may set boundaries for the whole, deciding where we want our subject to begin and end, what we want to include and exclude, but in generating language to express the whole we choose to reveal it a certain way. We discover its parts and pieces and their relationships to one another, shaping paragraphs to demonstrate those relationships. We don't begin with forms, pouring content into paragraph molds; rather, we begin with content, and in the act of drafting discover form.

RELATING PART TO WHOLE

If indenting permits writers to relate parts to wholes, what is the nature of those relationships? As many teachers recognize, methods of paragraph development "overlap." Narrative paragraphs often incorporate description; definition paragraphs frequently include examples; comparison paragraphs may resort to point-by-point classifications. Although the so-called "combination of methods" paragraph occurs frequently, textbooks must treat it as an anomaly because there's no room for it in the traditional scheme for classifying paragraph types.

Frank D'Angelo suggests, however, that overlapping categories seem to be the rule rather than the exception. Paragraph types, he maintains, manifest underlying thought processes and consequently are related to the ways we organize perceptions. Although we can assign labels to logical mental operations, what we're doing when we think transcends terminology:

> Description, for example, is related to definition. Describing something provides a means of analyzing and identifying it. Defining is a kind of abstract description. Definition, division into parts, and classification share fundamental relationships: to define is to limit or set boundaries to a thing by separating it from other things (division); to define is to put the thing to be defined into a class (classification): to classify is to divide into categories, so classification and division are related categories. Exemplification is related to definition (giving examples is one way of defining), to division in parts (examples are parts of wholes), and to classification (each example is a member of a group or class of persons and things). (*A Conceptual Theory of Rhetoric*, p. 44)

In other words, thinking is *relational*. When we perceive objects and events, we don't merely isolate or identify them; we relate them to other objects and events, to our own past experiences. If thought processes relate perceptions, organizing them into patterns, then it follows that paragraphs will express those relationships. Not only paragraphs, but also sentences and whole discourse.

Teaching paragraphs-as-process implies, then, that we teach students how to discover relationships among ideas, words, and sentences. Instead of focusing instruction on *what* paragraphs are, we need to teach students *how* to discover relationships and express them in units of discourse. To be sure, it's much easier to teach students "about" paragraphs, isolating the shapes and labeling them, but if we want students to "do" paragraphs, we must teach paragraph*ing*, not paragraphs.[2]

GENERATIVE RHETORIC OF THE PARAGRAPH

In teaching students how sentences may relate to one another, we might begin with speech, a more comfortable medium for most students than writing. Patrick Hartwell suggests recording some informal conversations, "then noting the patterns of connection between sentences."[3] As a rule, the patterns of connection will be one of two kinds: coordination

2. This thesis—that paragraphs, sentences, and essays express relationships—governs my selection of methods for teaching paragraphing. As a result, I omit other useful techniques. Teachers may want to consult Sheridan Baker, *The Practical Stylist*, 8th ed. (New York: Addison-Wesley, 1998), especially his discussion of "funnel" paragraphs; Alton L. Becker, "A Tagmemic Approach to Paragraph Analysis," *College Composition and Communication* 16 (December 1965), 237–42; Willis L. Pitkin, Jr., "Discourse Blocs," *College Composition and Communication* 20 (May 1969), 138–48; Paul C. Rodgers, Jr., "A Discourse-Centered Rhetoric of the Paragraph," *College Composition and Communication* 17 (February 1966), 2–11; and *The Sentence and the Paragraph* (Urbana, IL: NCTE, 1966). For an extended discussion of the relationships among elements of discourse, see Richard M. Coe, *Toward a Grammar of Passages* (Studies in Writing and Rhetoric; Carbondale: Southern Illinois University Press, 1988).

3. Patrick Hartwell, "Teaching Arrangement: A Pedagogy," *College English* 40 (January 1979), 548–54, outlines a sequence of instruction that "begins with the tacit knowledge of organizing speech that we all share and ends with the 'fixed forms' of certain writing situations" (p. 550).

or subordination. We express coordinate relationships between groups of words (within as well as across sentences) by *and, but*, and *or*. As W. Ross Winterowd demonstrates,[4] each linking word effects a slightly different kind of coordination, but they all grant equal status to the elements being linked. *And* stresses similarities between equal elements; *but* contrasts equal elements; *or* establishes alternatives between equal elements. We express subordinate relationships, Winterowd notes, by *because* (literally "by cause"), by *so*, and by the colon. *Because* and *for* subordinate causes to effects (or vice versa, effects to causes); *so* subordinates examples or other evidence to a conclusion; the colon signals a list of objects or events that represent particular members of a more general class.

Students have been expressing these subordinate and coordinate relationships in speech for most of their lives. Making them conscious of their tacit knowledge can help them control these relationships in sentences, paragraphs, and even larger units of discourse. Because coordination and subordination in speech often are implied rather than stated, the linking words may be omitted. For this reason, it's helpful to analyze spoken conversation so that students develop a conscious vocabulary of linking words that express these coordinate and subordinate relationships.

Once students understand how conversation proceeds, they can practice creating subordinate and coordinate relationships of various kinds in writing. Brief sentence-combining problems, for example, give writers practice emphasizing ideas through coordination and subordination, highlighting one element while diminishing another, or giving equal importance to each element. What happens to the meaning of the following groups of statements when we use *and, but, or, because, so*, and a colon (or list) to combine them?

> He eats spinach. He eats broccoli. He likes them.
> Jane went to a movie. Harry went to a party.
> Men can be teachers. Women can be lawyers.

An exercise such as this one permits students to discuss differences in meaning expressed by various linking words. It also allows students to suggest additional vocabulary for expressing coordinate and subordinate relationships.

4. W. Ross Winterowd, "The Grammar of Coherence," in *Contemporary Rhetoric: A Conceptual Background with Readings*, ed. W. Ross Winterowd (New York: Harcourt Brace Jovanovich, 1975), pp. 225–33; reprinted from *College English* (May 1970). Winterowd argues that coherence has three levels, expressed by means of case relationships, syntax, and transitions or relationships beyond the sentence. Although he originally posited seven transitions, he labels the six relationships I discuss as follows: coordinate (*and*), obversative (*but*), alternative (*or*), causative (*because* or *for*), conclusive (*so*), and inclusive (colon). Since we express these relationship in different ways, not merely with six conjunctions, beginning teachers will find it helpful to read his article in its entirety.

Generative rhetoric offers another way of looking at coordination and subordination in discourse. Originally developed to examine sentence structure, the principles of generative rhetoric apply equally well to paragraphs. The best explanation of these principles appears in Francis Christensen's *Notes toward a New Rhetoric* (1978), a work we will examine in greater detail in Chapter 10. At the level of the sentence, Christensen explains, writers can elaborate any base clause by attaching to it coordinate and subordinate word groups. Christensen calls such a sentence a "cumulative sentence," a base clause together with all of its modifiers. These modifiers are groups of words that refer to elements of the base clause and consequently express a coordinate or subordinate relationship to it. Christensen diagrams subordinate relationships between the base clause and its supporting material by indenting word groups and numbering them consecutively. In the following sentence, for example, each indented word group elaborates a word in the preceding phrase and, consequently, is subordinate to it:

> 1 He dipped his hands in the bichloride solution and shook them,
>   2 a quick shake,
>   3 fingers down,
>   4 like the fingers of a pianist above the keys.
>   (Sinclair Lewis, *Main Street*)

On the other hand, cumulative sentences may coordinate word groups rather than subordinate them. When they do, Christensen assigns word groups the same number and the same level of indentation. In the following sentence, all of the level-2 word groups are subordinate to the base clause or level 1. But all of the level-2 constructions are coordinate with respect to each other. They are all grammatically the same, and they all modify "He" in the base clause.

> 1 He could sail for hours,
>   2 searching the blanched grasses below him with his telescopic eyes,
>   2 gaining height against the wind,
>   2 descending in mile-long, gently declining swoops when he curved and rode back,
>   2 never beating a wing.
>   (Walter Van Tilburg Clark, *The Ox-Bow Incident*)

So too with paragraphs. "The topic sentence of a paragraph," Christensen maintains, "is analogous to the base clause of such a cumulative sentence, and the supporting sentences of a paragraph are analogous to the added levels of the sentence" (*Notes toward a New Rhetoric*, p. 75). Stated another way, we create a paragraph by beginning with a sentence that makes a promise to a reader. If the paragraph is to fulfill the promise, if it is to have coherence, the second sentence must relate to the first. The second sentence must be either coordinate with or subordinate to the first sentence. In the following paragraph, the first sentence promises to discuss writing that leaves "a record of ourselves." The second sentence is subordinate to the first because it gives a specific example of writing that records the self. The rest of the sentences give additional examples and consequently develop the paragraph by coordination:

1 We write to leave a record of ourselves.
   2 Your name was probably the first word you learned to write, and you were probably very proud of yourself when you recorded who you were on a sheet of paper.
   2 Now, some of you love to put your names on desks or bathroom walls.
   2 Some of you keep diaries or write poems to express your secret thoughts and feelings.
   2 Some of you write emotional letters to friends, recording in writing what you cannot express orally.

A colon-relationship holds this paragraph together. Sentence one makes an assertion about a class or category, writing that leaves a record of the self. Sentences two through five are subordinate to sentence one because they specify members of the class writing-as-record: writing that records our name, diaries and poems that record our secret thoughts and feelings, and letters that record what we cannot say. Sentences two through five are coordinate with respect to one another; the repetitious "some of you" reinforces this parallelism.

On the other hand, writers also can choose to continue subordinating sentences once they have written the "promise" (or topic) sentence:

1 The process of learning is essential to our lives.
  2 All higher animals seek it deliberately.
    3 They are inquisitive and they experiment.
      4 An experiment is a sort of harmless trial run of some action which we shall have to make in the real world; and this, whether it is made in the laboratory by scientists or by fox-cubs outside their earth den.
        5 The scientist experiments and the cub plays; both are learning to correct their errors of judgment in a setting in which errors are not fatal.
          6 Perhaps this is what gives them both their air of happiness and freedom in these activities.

              (J. Bronowski, *The Common Sense of Science*)

Although *within* sentences three through five the two halves of the sentence are related by coordination, each complete sentence in the paragraph is subordinate to the sentence preceding it. Sentences one and two express a cause and effect relationship to each other, in Winterowd's terms a *because*-relationship. Sentence three specifies qualities implied by the general verb *seek* in sentence two, establishing a colon-relationship between sentences two and three. Sentence four elaborates the general term *experiment* in sentence three and defines the general category *they* in sentence three to include *scientists* and *fox-cubs*; both functions constitute colon-relationships. Sentence five specifies the meaning of *harmless trial run* in sentence four, another kind of colon-relationship. Sentence six represents a conclusion drawn from sentence five, a *so*-relationship. In this paragraph, the same three forms of subordination that may relate parts of sentences—*because, so,* colon—establish connections among whole sentences.

Notice that Bronowski's paragraph develops its promise sentence by a variety of methods. It constructs an argument of premises and conclusions; it cites examples of what scientists and fox cubs do to learn; it compares scientists and cubs; it defines *experiment* as "a sort of harmless trial run"; and it establishes a cause-effect relationship between play and learning. Given traditional labels for methods of paragraph development, we'd have difficulty assigning one label to a paragraph such as this one.

Because Bronowski is an experienced writer, his paragraph is especially complex. All the same, students can construct similar coordinate and subordinate relationships in their work, as the following examples attest:

Coordinate Sequence

1   Racism is everywhere.
   2   In our homes we are taught to grin in people's faces, even though we may not like them, and believe that our culture is superior.
   2   In classrooms we snicker when students of other races miss an answer to the teacher's question.
   2   Although some racism may be evident verbally, it can also be found in a simple Band-Aid box and a pantyhose pack that have no flesh color for African Americans.

Subordinate Sequence

1   Although Ms. Jane Elliott, a race relations expert on the *Oprah Winfrey Show*, was popular with the audience, her message was ineffective.
   2   She was extremely hostile, arrogant, and rude in her approach to the other guests.
      3   Instead of listening to Ron's opinions, she criticized him, pointing her finger in his face and yelling at him.
         4   She told him, "If you weren't a racist, you'd be a miracle. You don't look like a miracle to me."

A SEQUENCE OF LESSONS

To give students practice creating their own paragraphs, this chapter concludes with a sequence of lessons that group progressively larger amounts of material. The sequence moves from creating single sentences through building paragraphs to rewriting them. Although designed for whole-class discussion and groupwork, the activities could be modified to help individual students. As with any lesson plan, the ten activities outlined below should be adjusted to meet students' needs. Some activities will take longer than others; some can be handled quickly if students already understand the principle. Whenever possible, focus the discussion on student writing, using professional models only to supplement or reinforce the students' work.

1. Discuss how writers and speakers connect material. Record informal conversations and trace the implied or stated relationships among groups of utterances. Examine sentence-combining exercises or groups of sentences from students' previous papers to derive lists of words that express the coordinate and subordinate relationships between word groups. Ask students to combine a group of short, choppy sentences in various ways using a progressively larger vocabulary of linking words:

Coordinate Relationships	Additional Linking Words
and-relationship	furthermore, also, too, again, similarly, in addition
but-relationship	yet, however, still, on the other hand, nevertheless
or-relationship	nor

Subordinate Relationships	Additional Linking Words
because-relationships	for, as a result, consequently
so-relationships	therefore, thus, for this reason
colon-relationships	first, second, third; who, which, that; for example, to illustrate

2. Because textbook authors deliberately select model paragraphs to reflect the traditional methods of development, students should have opportunities to examine "natural" paragraphs. Ask them to collect paragraphs from a variety of sources: textbooks, novels, business letters, poems, newspapers, popular magazines, advertisements. Then discuss why writers seem to be grouping material in certain ways. If paragraphs act as signals to a reader, what sorts of signals are possible? What purposes does indentation (or white space) serve? Discussing the work that paragraphs do clarifies myths about how long they should be and whether or not they all have topic sentences and a single method of development.

3. Let groups of students examine the signals writers use within paragraphs. Delete the linking words from student (or professional) paragraphs, and ask the groups to fill in the blanks with appropriate choices. After the groups have read their versions to the whole class, discuss

alternate wordings the class may have overlooked. The following paragraph reproduces Theron Alexander's words, but similar relationships within and between sentences could be expressed with different words:

> Social change takes many forms in modern society, *and* people are affected by it in several different ways. *For example*, in the past, a man's prestige *as well as* much of his life satisfaction lay in his occupation and in his work. *However*, signs indicate that the traditional basis for satisfaction is changing. *Now*, the source often lies outside of "work." The satisfaction formerly obtained in an occupation is being pursued in clubs, sports, and many kinds of projects. This change in attitude toward work stems *not only* from the character of job duties, *but also* from shorter work hours and higher incomes. (Theron Alexander, "The Individual and Social Change," *Intellect* [December 1974])

4. After students have completed some prewriting on a topic, let them practice writing topic or promise sentences. Such sentences usually show the following characteristics:

a. They express an opinion or fact.

   Historians interpret written records.

b. They express an attitude toward or give an impression of a whole experience.

   Since my automobile accident, I have learned to drive more carefully.

c. They specify how many parts are contained in the whole.

   My English class has three types of students.
   My brother did not finish school for four reasons.

d. They ask a question, which the paragraph answers.

   Why are low-calorie diets dangerous?

e. They present a problem, to which the paragraph offers solutions.[5]

   More and more people are discovering that they live near unsafe toxic waste dumps.

Groups of students can help one another evaluate and revise their promise sentences.

5. Using a student's promise sentence, guide the whole class in developing it by coordinating and subordinating other sentences to it. Repeat

---

5. For further discussion of the question-answer and problem-solution paragraph (d and e in the list), see Alton L. Becker, "A Tagmemic Approach to Paragraph Analysis," *College Composition and Communication* 16 (December 1965), 237–42.

the procedure, then let students try it on their own, first in groups and then individually. Two ways of developing the question "Why are low-calorie diets dangerous?" (d above) might look like this:

Coordinate Relationships

1 Why are low-calorie diets dangerous?
   2 One reason is that, when people reduce the amount of food they eat, they also deprive themselves of essential nutrients, fiber, and water.
   2 They may also overlook the importance of eating foods in the right proportions: 55 percent carbohydrates, 15 percent protein, and 30 percent fat.
   2 Because dieters focus on food, they may neglect aerobic exercise, the only way to thin the fat layer covering muscle tissue.
   2 Perhaps the worst danger is that, psychologically, most dieters find themselves defeated again and again, unable to understand why counting calories hasn't yielded more dramatic progress.

Subordinate Relationships

1 Why are low-calorie diets dangerous?
   2 Basically, they prevent us from getting all the nutrients we need.
      3 When we reduce our intake of food, we also cut back on essential vitamins and minerals needed to stay healthy.
         4 One recent survey of a dozen popular diets found all of them deficient in the U.S. Recommended Daily Allowances for thirteen vitamins and minerals.
      3 Even though vitamin supplements may correct some nutritional deficiencies, dieters may not notice that they are also getting less fiber and water than they were before.

6. Scramble the sentences of a student's paragraph and type the random order of sentences onto a handout, numbering the sentences consecutively. Have groups of students put the sentences into any order that makes sense to them, so long as they can explain how the sentences relate to one another. After the groups have reported their justifications to the class, show the students the original paragraph and discuss its arrangement.

7. Diagram the coordinate and subordinate relationships in a model paragraph. Christensen's "A Generative Rhetoric of the Paragraph" offers several examples by professional writers, but student paragraphs will work better. Ask students to imitate the pattern of sentence relationships in constructing paragraphs on topics of their own choosing.

8. Discuss with the class a student's paragraph that needs revising.

Draw arrows and circles all over it (rewriting is messy work). How could we express the relationships between sentences more clearly? Where could we add linking words? How could we make sentence subjects (circled in the examples below) more consistent? Can we repeat key words or substitute pronouns? Do we need to change the promise sentence? Are sentence patterns disrupting the unity of the paragraph?

Original

Many suburban (homeowners) have become slaves to lawns. The (time and money) spent on lawns are ridiculous. (Weekends and evenings) are devoted to mowing, raking, trimming, watering, weeding, and feeding the grass. (Lawns) are cursed and slaved over.

[Notice that each sentence shifts to a new subject. Sentences are all the same type and about the same length.]

Revision

Many suburban (homeowners) have become slaves to their lawns. (They) spend a ridiculous amount of time and money on their yards, devoting weekends and evenings to the care and feeding of the green monsters. Instead of enjoying their leisure time, (these suburbanites) constantly mow, rake, trim, water, weed, and feed their turf. Although most (property owners) curse their lawns, (they) slavishly continue to care for the grass.

(Adapted from William E. Mahaney,
Workbook of Current English, p. 292)

9. Have students examine their previous writings for paragraphs that need rewriting. Guided by questions similar to those in 8 above, let them work in groups or individually to analyze and revise their paragraphs. Discuss several "before" and "after" paragraphs.

10. After considerable practice creating paragraphs, students may want to examine and label various paragraph "shapes," a way of reinforcing a skill they have already acquired. Paragraph shapes—inverted and regular triangles, diamonds, and hourglasses—represent ways of

"stacking" sentences that relate to one another. Like Christensen's indented levels of generality, paragraph shapes depict where the most general statement appears and how other material is arranged in relation to it. The inverted triangle, for example, begins with the topic sentence, the level-1 sentence as Christensen would have it, and subordinates subsequent sentences. For ease of comparison, the following paragraph is reproduced first with indented levels of generality and then as a geometric shape:[6]

1 Typhoon Chris hit with full fury today on the central coast of Japan.
  2 High waves carried many homes into the sea.
  2 Heavy rain from the storm flooded the area.
    3 People now fear that the heavy rains may have caused mud slides in the central part of the country.
      4 The number of victims buried under the mud may climb past the 200 mark by Saturday.

Typhoon Chris hit with full fury today on the central coast of Japan. High waves carried many homes into the sea. Heavy rain from the storm flooded the area. People now fear that the heavy rains may have caused mud slides in the central part of the country. The number of victims buried under the mud may climb past the 200 mark by Saturday.

The regular triangle places the topic sentence last and arranges subordinate sentences to lead up to it:

  2 If the wind becomes gusty suddenly after being calm, you may need to start looking for shelter.
  2 If you see clouds becoming darker, you may need shelter right away.
  2 Naturally, you know that thunder and lightning mean a storm is coming.
    3 Keep in mind that bright lightning doesn't mean a storm is coming.
    3 The number of lightning flashes is important, though.
      4 The more lightning flashes, the worse the storm is likely to be.
1 The signs of a thunderstorm are many, and being able to understand them can be important.

6. The examples illustrating paragraph shapes have been adapted from Glenn R. Williston, *Understanding the Main Idea, Middle Level* (Providence, RI: Jamestown Publishers, 1976), pp. 14–17, 43.

If the wind becomes
gusty suddenly after being
calm, you may need to start looking
for shelter. If you see clouds becoming
darker, you may need shelter right away.
Naturally, you know that thunder and lightning mean
a storm is coming. Keep in mind that bright lightning
doesn't mean a storm is coming. The number of lightning
flashes is important, though. The more lightening flashes, the
worse the storm is likely to be. *The signs of a thunderstorm
are many, and being able to understand them can be important.*

In the diamond-shaped paragraph, the topic sentence appears near
the middle, the subordinate sentences leading up to and then away
from it:

    2 Dark green, leafy vegetables such as kale and spinach are
      good sources of vitamin C and iron.
    2 Carrots, squash, and sweet potatoes are good sources of
      carotene, which the body changes to vitamin A.
  1 All vegetables are good for us because they provide important
     vitamins and minerals that build cells and keep us healthy.
    2 Vitamin C, for example, builds strong teeth and helps us
      resist infections.
    2 Vitamin A keeps skin healthy and protects our eyes.
    2 Iron, also an important part of vegetables, builds red blood
      cells.

Dark green, leafy
vegetables such as kale and
spinach are good sources of vitamin C
and iron. Carrots, squash, and sweet potatoes are
good sources of carotene, which the body changes to vitamin A.
*All vegetables are good for us because they provide important
vitamins and minerals that build cells and keep us healthy.*
Vitamin C, for example, builds strong teeth and helps
us resist infections. Vitamin A keeps skin
healthy and protects our eyes. Iron, also
an important part of vegetables,
builds red blood cells.

Hourglass- or I-shaped paragraphs begin with the topic sentence and
end with a restatement of it, sandwiching the supporting material in
between:

  1 Houdini, the famous magician, began his career with a traveling
    circus at the age of nine.
    2 His first trick was to pick up needles with his eyelids while he
      was hanging by his heels, head downward.

    3 He slowly perfected this trick in secret in the family wood-
       shed.
    2 He was world famous for his escapes—from handcuffs, strait-
       jackets, prison cells, and sealed chambers.
    3 He even escaped from a grave six feet in the ground.
 1 When he died on October 31, 1926, he had been a public per-
    former for forty-three years.

Houdini, the famous magician, began his career with a traveling
       circus at the age of nine. His first trick was to pick up
          needles with his eyelids while he was hanging by
             his heels, head downward. He slowly
                perfected this trick in secret
                   in the family woodshed.
             He was world famous for his
          escapes—from handcuffs, straitjackets,
    prison cells, and sealed chambers. He even escaped from
 a grave six feet in the ground. *When he died on October 31,*
 1926, he had been a public performer for forty-three years.

The value of studying model paragraphs lies not in labeling their
shapes but in illustrating options, in showing students *how* writers link
their sentences one by one, expressing with each new sentence a coordinate or subordinate relationship to those already written. Students should
apply the model's strategies to drafting or rewriting their own paragraphs, so that they may practice tightening or clarifying intersentence
relationships.

When we help writers create sentences, paragraphs, and larger units
of prose, using consistent methods and terminology is useful. Unfortunately, traditional practice establishes one set of terms for sentence types
and a different set of labels for methods of paragraph and essay development. Because traditional methods emphasize labels, they offer students
little help in creating the forms themselves. Christensen's generative
rhetoric and Winterowd's grammar of coherence, on the other hand,
describe relationships within and between units of language with the
same set of terms. The same six relationships—three expressing coordination and three expressing subordination—link word groups within
sentences, sentences within paragraphs, and paragraphs within whole
discourse. When students learn how to establish these relationships
confidently, they will be able to make and keep their promises to readers.

ten

Teaching about Sentences

A sentence should read as if its author, had he held a plow instead of a pen, could have drawn a furrow deep and straight to the end.

HENRY DAVID THOREAU

All of us have an intuitive understanding of sentence structures and their use. We've all been talking in sentences since childhood, rarely stopping to consider whether or not our speech represents a "complete thought," contains a subject and predicate, or shows "dependent" and "independent" clauses. Our sentences, most of which we've never heard or said before, get the message across. All native speakers *do* know what a sentence is; they can create complex sentences without knowing the names for the constructions they produce.

If that's so, why spend time in a writing class on sentences? To be sure, some types of sentence instruction do not use class time productively. Too much time spent analyzing someone else's sentences gives students too little practice generating their own. Too much attention to labeling sentence types or classifying phrases and clauses may teach terminology—*what* to call a construction—but not writing—*how* to create it. Although human beings have an intuitive competence for creating sentences, many student writers need practice translating competence into fluent performance.

A major reason why "performing" written sentences is difficult stems from differences between speech and writing. Spoken communication, which may be highly elliptical, generally succeeds without complicated syntax. Gestures, facial expressions, and the habit of taking turns reinforce the message. Although high school and college students are capable of writing complicated sentences, they're unaccustomed to using their entire syntactic repertoire, especially if they habitually write as they talk. Second, writing sentences presents considerable risk. Every word added to a sentence increases the possibility of misspellings, punctuation mistakes, or other errors that jeopardize students' grades. Short, simple sentences are safest. Third, some students have trouble with sentences because they can't depend on the eye or ear to help them identify prose rhythms. If they read poorly, rarely read for pleasure, converse infrequently with adults, or passively watch a great deal of television, they may have difficulty imagining comfortable options for sentences. Television commercials, for example, are usually scripted in sentence fragments, a style that may influence our students' "ear" for sentences to a greater extent than we realize. Finally, writing sentences requires punctuation marks that have few equivalents in speech. Yes, we pause for longer or shorter periods as we speak, but writing indicates "pauses" with a confusing array of symbols, with commas, dashes, colons, semicolons, periods, and other marks. Conversely, we don't "speak" apostrophes. Performing written sentences, then, requires confidence in manipulating symbols that have no true counterparts in spoken English.

For these reasons, students need risk-free opportunities to practice sentences, especially complex sentences. Such practice should take place in the context of composing longer stretches of discourse. When students study and practice sentences, they must be able to apply what they're learning *about* sentences to composing. They must translate knowledge into performance. Instead of analyzing sentences in a textbook, we can help students discover what kinds of sentences their own writing contains. Instead of drilling students on punctuation rules, we can encourage them to practice unfamiliar constructions and address the punctuation problems as they arise. Instead of discussing sentence patterns students have already mastered, we can help them practice types they may be avoiding for fear of making mistakes in punctuation or subject-verb agreement. The goal of our teaching should be to enlarge the student's repertoire of sentence options and rhetorical choices.

One relatively simple way to discuss sentences involves talking about readers. Reader's expect sentences to conform to conventional punctuation, but they have other expectations as well.[1] Readers expect the most important information in a sentence to appear at the beginning and at the end. The beginning of a sentence names the actors and either establishes a context for information to come or links the sentence to the one before it by providing transitional, old information. The end of the sentence stresses new information. Information buried in the middle gets the least attention. Putting important information in the right slot helps readers follow along. What is "important" depends on the context in which the sentence appears. That is, writers do not compose individual sentences; they put sentences together into paragraphs and larger units of dis-

---

1. See Joseph M. Williams, *Style: Ten Lessons in Clarity and Grace*, 6th ed. (New York: Addison-Wesley, 1999). I also draw on unpublished material developed by George Gopen, Duke University.

course. In reading the following student's paragraph, notice which words Roger has put in the most emphatic positions, the beginning and end of the sentence:

> In some cultures it is the men who are more conscious of non-verbal communication than *the women are.* That is not true *in North America.* In our culture it seems that of both groups the women are more aware of body language, voice tone, and *other nonverbal messages.* This was brought to my attention by a *man,* but it was only after I became more sensitive myself that *I really believed him.*

Although Roger's paragraph is about men's awareness of nonverbal communication, *men, I* (Roger), or *nonverbal communication* rarely appear in emphatic sentence positions. The paragraph's implicit story of how Roger "became more sensitive" never gets told. Discussing such a paragraph with students shows them how to reorder sentence elements so that important information appears where a reader expects to find it. Roger's revised paragraph is more specific, shows better sentence variety, and also makes more effective use of sentence positions to advance the story of what Roger learned:

> While men in some cultures are more conscious than women of *nonverbal communication,* I haven't always been. I learned from my girlfriend's brother that body language, tone of voice, and gestures are less important to me than *they are to my girlfriend.* Through his advice, I learned *what my girlfriend's signals meant.* For example, I realized that when she leaned back in her chair, *she was saying, "I'm upset."* By watching my girlfriend's nonverbal messages, I became *more sensitive* to them.

In addition to discussing how readers regard sentences, two other techniques for teaching sentences in the context of composing are popular with writing teachers: sentence combining and generating cumulative sentences. Both techniques can increase the "syntactic fluency" of students' writing. At the same time, writing teachers must guard against the exaggerated claims of some proponents of these techniques, especially of sentence combining. Kellogg Hunt, for example, suggests structuring an entire writing course around sentence combining: "In every sense, sentence combining can be a comprehensive writing program in and of itself, for at least one semester. It is nonsense, rather than common sense, to suggest that sentence combining can't be the one and only instructional strategy, at least for one term."[2] Nonsense or not, many writing teachers

2. Kellogg W. Hunt, "Anybody Can Teach English," in *Sentence Combining and the Teaching of Writing,* ed. Donald A. Daiker, Andrew Kerek, and Max Morenberg (Conway, AR: L & S Books, 1979), p. 156. Although I disagree with Hunt, I recommend this collection of essays for those who want to know more about sentence combining. I also recommend Stephen P. Witte's review of the book in *College Composition and Communication* 31 (Decem-

and researchers *do* express misgivings about the efficacy of sentence combining as the sole instructional method in a writing course and have doubts about the syntactic gains attributed to sentence-combining practice. Some of these gains, in fact, may result from instruction in semantics and rhetoric that accompanies discussions of sentence-combining problems. More important, because composing involves more than mastering sentences, no single instructional method, including sentence combining or work with cumulative sentences, will transform poor writers into accomplished ones. Although both techniques have advantages, neither should become the exclusive focus of a writing class.

SENTENCE COMBINING

Generative-transformational theory suggests that we transform sentences intuitively by adding to, deleting from, or rearranging sentence elements. Sentence combining applies this principle to writing instruction.[3] As Charles Cooper explains, sentence-combining problems "confront the student with sentences more complex than ones he would be likely to write at that point in his development; they ask the student to write out fully-formed sentences and they provide him the content of the sentences so that his attention can remain focused on the *structural* aspects of the problem."[4] To combine the following sentences, for example, students would insert information from the indented sentence into the first sentence:

> The canary flew out the window.
>> The canary is yellow.
> *Student's response:* The yellow canary flew out the window.

Some sentence-combining problems offer clues about which words to add or delete:

> SOMETHING made her angry.
>> She read something in the note. (what)
> *Student's response:* What she read in the note made her angry.

ber 1980), 433–37, which discusses some of the reservations writing teachers have about sentence-combining research. A useful summary of research on sentence combining is George Hillocks, Jr., *Research on Written Composition: New Directions for Teaching* (Urbana, IL: ERIC Clearinghouse on Reading and Communication Skills and the National Conference on Research in English, 1986), pp. 141–51.

3. Frank O'Hare, *Sentence Combining: Improving Student Writing without Formal Grammar Instruction* (NCTE Research Report No. 15; Urbana, IL: NCTE, 1973), reviews research on the relationship between grammar study and improvement in writing and describes his own investigation. O'Hare's study demonstrates that written and oral sentence-combining exercises helped seventh graders "write compositions that could be described as syntactically more elaborated or mature" and "better in overall quality" (p. 67).

4. Charles Cooper, "An Outline for Writing Sentence-Combining Problems," *English Journal* 62 (January 1973). The next three sample problems appear in Cooper.

Multiple embeddings are also possible:

> My friends and I enjoy SOMETHING.
> We race our bicycles around the paths in the park. (racing)
>> Our bicycles are lightweight.
>> Our bicycles are ten-speed.
>> The paths are narrow.
>> The paths are winding.
>
> *Student's response:* My friends and I enjoy racing our lightweight, ten-speed bicycles around the narrow, winding paths in the park.

Exercises that contain transformation cues require students to combine the sentences in a specified way. Cued exercises can give students confidence in generating syntactic structures that they may be avoiding. The cues show students *how* to combine the sentences, providing a repertoire of connectives that hold phrases and clauses together. As students work through the exercises, teachers can introduce terminology and whatever punctuation conventions a particular transformation requires.

Open-ended exercises, which offer no cues, may be more difficult for some students, but they permit more choices and encourage students to consider the rhetorical effects of possible combinations:

> The national debt concerns Americans.
> The national debt grows five hundred dollars every second.
> The national debt totals nearly six trillion dollars.
>
> *Possible student responses, each of which achieves a different rhetorical effect:* The national debt concerns Americans because it grows five hundred dollars every second and totals nearly six trillion dollars. The national debt, a concern for Americans, grows five hundred dollars every second and totals nearly six trillion dollars. The national debt, growing five hundred dollars every second and totaling nearly six trillion dollars, concerns Americans. Americans are concerned about the national debt, which grows five hundred dollars every second and totals nearly six trillion dollars. Because the national debt grows five hundred dollars every second and totals nearly six trillion dollars, it concerns Americans.

When students combine sentences in as many ways as they know how, read them aloud, and discuss which versions they like best, they're not only exercising syntactic muscles but also making rhetorical choices. Like professional writers, students develop an eye and ear for prose rhythms. "In addition to playing with transformations and making their choices," writes William Strong, "professional writers also seem to spend considerable time hearing the way sentences fit together to make up the 'melody' of their writing. They listen for the dips and swaying curves of some phrases, the hard, rhythmic, regular punch of others. They sensitize themselves to avoid sentences where meaning is almost obscured within the lengthy confines of the sentence itself; they study those sentences where pause, and momentary reflection, have their impact" (*Sentence Combining*, p. xv).

Discussing sentence-combining exercises also helps students become confident about punctuation. My own students shun participial modifiers, appositives, and relative clauses because they aren't sure how to use commas to set them off. They avoid introductory adverb clauses for similar reasons. Students who have learned to be careful about commas understandably "write around" the problem. Sentence-combining exercises illustrate how punctuation organizes sentence elements for a reader and offer risk-free opportunities to solve punctuation problems that have baffled students for years. Sometimes an exercise exposes a punctuation rule misunderstood in a previous English class. A former student of mine consistently placed commas behind words such as *because, since,* and *if* when they began a sentence: "Because, I didn't have a car I couldn't date Susan." When I asked him why he thought the comma belonged there, he explained, "My English teacher told me to set off *because* words; she called them 'introductory' something-or-other." Doubtless, his teacher encouraged him to set off the entire introductory clause, but the student had heard only part of the rule. He solved the problem by practicing a few sentence-combining exercises. My student's problem also illustrates another point; grammatical terminology sometimes creates punctuation problems. Sentence combining allows teachers to dispense with terminology altogether or, if they wish, to name constructions *after* students have practiced them.

Other students may need practice "decombining" sentences. Older students sometimes attempt such extraordinarily complicated sentences that the syntax gets twisted. They may be writing to please teachers who implicitly praise "long" sentences; nevertheless, they develop a style that obscures ideas in hopelessly convoluted syntax. Here's an example from a first-year college student's paper:

> The things that people go to the pharmacist for sometimes are just to get the pharmacist to prescribe them something for their illness, and he can not do any prescribing for anyone for medicine.

Prepositions are part of the problem here, but Kenny loses his reader by piling too much information into one sentence. When he read the sentence out loud, he said it sounded "weird," but he didn't know how to revise it. I asked him to "decombine" the sentence, breaking it into simple sentences. We came up with the following two lists, which reproduce the simple sentences embedded in his original:

> People go to the pharmacist for things.
> People go to the pharmacist sometimes.
> People just get the pharmacist to do SOMETHING. (to)
>   The pharmacist prescribes them something for their illness.

and

> ⌐ He cannot do any SOMETHING. (-ing)
> | He prescribes for anyone.
> ∟ He prescribes medicine.

At this point, Kenny could understand why the sentence seems "weird." It lacks a single focus. Two or three subjects—"people," "pharmacist," and perhaps "things"—vie for attention. Recombining the sentences to emphasize only one subject, "people" or "pharmacist," might yield the following options:

"People" Sentences

1. People sometimes go to the pharmacist, who cannot prescribe medicine for anyone, just to get him to prescribe something for their illness.
2. Sometimes people go to the pharmacist just to get him to prescribe medicine for their illness, something he cannot do.

"Pharmacist" Sentences

1. The pharmacist cannot prescribe medicine for anyone's illness, even though people sometimes ask him to.
2. Although people sometimes ask the pharmacist to prescribe medicine for their illness, he cannot write prescriptions.

The two-step decombining and recombining procedure now gives Kenny several sentences to choose from in revising his paper.

Decombining and recombining sentences can help students untangle, tighten, and rewrite sentences too complex for a reader to follow easily. After a while, students also discover which transformations create convoluted sentences. For Kenny, beginning sentences with noun clauses and piling up infinitives creates problems. For other students, passive constructions or beginning sentences with "There are" and "It is" tangle the syntax. Different kinds of sentence-combining exercises help students detect and solve these problems.

To improve their skill in manipulating sentence structures, students need regular sentence-combining practice over a long period, ideally two or three times a week throughout the entire course of instruction. The exercises can begin as early as the fourth grade and increase in complexity through college. Inundating students with sentence-combining problems, however, turns a means into an end. Assigning too many problems too frequently bores students, who begin to regard the exercises as busywork. Because the exercises focus only on sentences, not longer stretches of discourse, and because the content of the sentences is predetermined, not invented by the student, sentence combining should supplement, not replace, students' own writing.

All the same, sentence combining has several advantages. Used correctly, the technique *does* increase students' syntactic fluency. Teachers can assign the exercises as individual homework or as in-class group-work, students pooling their intuitive linguistic resources to solve the problems. Teachers can design their own exercises, use those available in published textbooks, or best of all, glean them from students' papers. Grading the work is inappropriate because it attaches risks to the exercises. To be effective, sentence-combining must remain risk free, a way of experimenting with syntactic structures students avoid for fear of making low marks. Some teachers post or pass out answers for the problems so that students can check their sentences against the key.

Besides increasing the complexity of students' sentences, the exercises have other advantages. They demonstrate how to construct sentences without resorting to grammatical terms or singling out errors in students' papers. They permit us to avoid terminology altogether or introduce it after students understand how to perform a particular transformation. They offer plenty of examples for describing punctuation, mechanics, and conventions of edited American English in the context of writing, not isolated from it. And because students will combine sentences in many interesting ways, the exercises allow us to discuss rhetorical choices, differences in emphasis that might work more effectively in some contexts than in others. Open-ended exercises work especially well in this regard. They help students discover, not the one "right" sentence, but a range of options. Students also can apply the technique to their own drafts, rewriting sentences to emphasize ideas differently, change the focus, coordinate or subordinate material, and achieve sentence variety.

CUMULATIVE SENTENCES

In *Notes toward a New Rhetoric* (1978), Francis Christensen expresses considerable dissatisfaction with traditional methods of teaching sentences. "We need," he says, "a rhetoric of the sentence that will do more than combine the ideas of primer sentences. We need one that will *generate* ideas" (p. 26). Instead of teaching sentences based on rhetorical classifications (loose, balanced, and periodic sentences) or grammatical categories (simple, compound, complex, and compound-complex sentences), Christensen offers an alternative method, generative rhetoric. It's a rhetoric that generates ideas, not words. According to Christensen, students don't need to write longer, more complex sentences simply to produce more words; rather, the sentence-as-form encourages writers to examine the ideas expressed by the words, to sharpen or add to them, and then to reproduce the idea more effectively. The "cumulative sentence," the heart of Christensen's generative rhetoric, compels writers to examine their thoughts, the meanings words convey. Consequently, generative rhetoric serves prewriting as well as rewriting.

Christensen bases his generative rhetoric on four principles derived from his study of prose style and the works of contemporary authors. He maintains, first, that "composition is essentially a process of addition"; nouns, verbs, or main clauses serve as a foundation or base to which we add details, qualifications, new meanings. Second, Christensen's "principle of modification" suggests that we can add these new meanings either before or after some noun, verb, or base clause. The "direction of movement" for the sentence changes, depending on where we've added modifiers and new meaning. When modifiers appear before the noun, verb, or base clause (which Christensen calls the "head" of the construction), the sentence "moves" forward. Modifiers placed after the noun, verb, or base clause move the sentence backward because they require readers to relate the new details, qualifications, and meanings *back* to the head appearing earlier in the sentence. Christensen's third principle states that, depending on the meanings of the words we add, the head becomes either more concrete or less so. The base word or clause together with one or more modifying additions expresses several "levels of generality or abstraction." Finally, Christensen's "principle of texture" describes and evaluates a writer's style. He characterizes style as relatively "dense" or "plain," depending on the number and variety of additions writers make to nouns, verbs, and base clauses.

We don't need to explain Christensen's four principles to students before asking them to create cumulative sentences. Native speakers form such sentences naturally. When I introduce my class to cumulative sentences, I begin by asking students to add words and phrases to the following sentence, written on the blackboard: "The horse galloped." I provide a base clause and deliberately ask the class to "load the pattern," a practice that Christensen would condemn but that gives me a starting point. After students suggest additions to the sentence for three to five minutes, it might look like the following monstrosity: "Because Farmer Brown didn't notice the swarm of bees in the appletree and hadn't tightened the cinch on the old, brown leather saddle securely, the horse galloped off through the orchard, throwing the startled rider to the ground, terrified by the bees buzzing around his head, until he reached the weathered board fence, where he stopped."

Although the sentence is unwieldy, students seem pleased to discover that they *can* compose complicated sentences like this one. Initially, quantity not quality intrigues them. That's fine for now; we'll get to quality soon enough (and fix that misplaced modifier). Generally, students add material at the end of the base clause first. Then, prompted by prewriting questions—Who? What? When? Where? How? Why?—they begin to place modifiers at the beginning or in the middle of the sentence: appositives, participial constructions, relative clauses, adverb and adjective constructions. After they have created the sentence, we discuss the kinds of grammatical structures and relationships the sentence expresses as well as punctuation problems we have encountered. Finally, we assess its rhetorical effectiveness, concluding that writing long sentences per se isn't a virtue and that our example needs revising. So, we tighten it, rearranging and deleting elements, reading versions aloud to evaluate their rhythm, and finally, imagining the larger context of the paragraph in which revised versions of our sentence might appear. Although the sample sentence enables us to take up several grammatical, rhetorical, and mechanical concerns, we will explore them in detail for several class meetings.

In one class period, for example, we might examine the kinds of additions that expand the base clause, discussing sentences from students' papers or a reading assignment. Although I avoid grammatical terms, Christensen uses them. In contrast to traditional methods, however, he limits the number of modifiers added to base clauses to only seven grammatical constructions:

PP   Prepositional phrase
NC   Noun cluster (appositives)
VC   Verb cluster (present and past participles, infinitives)
Abs   Absolute construction (a participial construction with its
      own subject)
Adv   Adverb clauses
AC   Adjective clauses
Rel   Relative clauses

Each of these additions adjusts the meaning of the base clause (or other clauses added to the base). "The main or base clause," Christensen explains, "is likely to be stated in general or abstract or plural terms. With the main clause stated, the forward movement of the sentence stops: The writer instead of going on to something new shifts down to a lower level of generality or abstraction or to singular terms, and goes back over the same ground at this lower level" (p. 29).

If we indent and number the levels of generality in the sample sentence discussed earlier, it looks like this:

```
  2 Because Farmer Brown didn't notice the swarm of bees/ . . .
    and (Adv)
    3 in the appletree (PP)
  2 (because he) hadn't tightened the cinch/ . . . securely, (Adv)
    3 on the old, brown leather saddle (PP)
1 the horse galloped off
  2 through the orchard, (PP)
  2 throwing the startled rider (VC)
    3 to the ground (PP)
  2 terrified (VC)
    3 by the bees (PP)
      4 buzzing around his head, (VC)
  2 until he reached the weathered board fence, (Adv)
    3 where he stopped. (Rel)
```

Christensen calls this a four-level sentence. The base clause is always numbered "level 1," regardless of where it appears in the sentence. All of the level-2 additions modify "horse" and "galloped off," words in the base or level-1 clause. The level-3 modifiers refer back to and elaborate elements of level-2 constructions; level-4 modifiers particularize elements in level 3. Indenting each level helps students see what kinds of additions have been made and where they appear (before, after, or as the slash indicates, in the middle of a group of words). The diagram also reveals whether or not groups of words are grammatically similar or parallel, and how they relate to one another by qualifying or elaborating material elsewhere in the sentence. It's not necessary that students always label the modifiers correctly or number the levels the same way. What's important is seeing how the parts of the sentence work together.

Although our Farmer Brown sentence contains four levels, it is uncharacteristically "dense." Most high school and college students write one-, or at best, two-level sentences. Their "texture" is thin or plain. They resemble lists of information that have no shape because the writer hasn't figured out what relationship the details have to some larger idea. Here's an example of a one-level sentence, written by Maria, a first-year college student who is describing an advertisement.

> 1 The background is a dull, white film while
> 1 the caption shows black type.

Because Maria had practiced expanding sentences with level-2 and -3 modifiers, she knew how and where to improve the sentence with details. Here's her revision:

>   2 Cloudy and misty, (AC)
> 1 the background looks like a soft, white film,
>   2 draped behind bold, black type, (VC)
>   3 which catches the reader's eye. (Rel)

Out of context, this revision may sound flowery, but it demonstrates the generative power of Christensen's cumulative sentence. In reviewing her first sentence, Maria was able to generate additional details about the background and caption, features of the advertisement she wanted to discuss. Her revised sentence is longer—not necessarily a virtue—but it also relates the details instead of merely listing them. It subordinates the "bold, black type" of the caption (level 2) to the background (level 1).

Generative rhetoric helps students attend to the ways sentences express relationships among ideas.

> 1 The cumulative sentence in unskillful hands is unsteady,
>   2 allowing a writer to ramble on, (VC)
>   3 adding modifier after modifier, (VC)
>   4 until the reader is almost overwhelmed (Adv)
>   5 because the writer's central idea is lost. (Adv)

Cumulative sentences are not merely multilevel constructions that string together modifiers one after another. Students also must control the placement of modifiers, drawing them out of ideas in the base clause. They must see the idea again, sharpen the image, the object, the action. In exploring the implications of what they've said, they will generate or reinvent additional meanings to express. At the level of the sentence, the new meanings become cumulative modifiers. At the level of the paragraph and whole discourse, as we've already seen, the generative principles of Christensen's rhetoric can shape new sentences, paragraphs, and sections.

eleven

Teaching about Words

The Tough Talker . . . is a man dramatized as centrally concerned with himself—his style is I-talk. The Sweet Talker goes out of his way to be nice to us—his style is you-talk. The Stuffy Talker expresses no concern either for himself or his reader—his style is it-talk.

WALKER GIBSON

Writing, the second stage of composing, requires considerable concentration. The best way to teach it is to give students considerable help with prewriting and then step back while they rough out a draft. Advocates of freewriting recommend just such an approach. The teacher's guidance, they suggest, is most useful later, after students have put some words on paper and are ready to review the material.

Most students, however, don't feel free to let their own linguistic resources take over in drafting. Writing, they believe, is constrained by rules. Paragraphs, sentence structures, punctuation, and spelling must all be perfect the first time around. Attempting to manage everything at once, student writers often disrupt the flow of ideas to attend to individual words. Their past experiences have taught them to equate the first draft with the final product, with a perfect performance worthy of a good grade. From their perspective, writing and rewriting are concurrent activities.

In teaching about words, the subject of this chapter, the first lesson must be that words can change. All writers rewrite their work many times before it expresses what they want to say. They play with words, recognizing that nothing about the first draft is carved in stone. They compose several drafts, focusing each time on different problems they have discovered in listening to a previous draft. As Donald Murray explains, "The writer toys with language, knowing that out of his most irresponsible word play may come his most responsible writing. His drafts, both in his mind and on the page, are filled with words, tried out and discarded, arranged, and rearranged—evidence of language that is always changing, flexible, usable" (*Learning by Teaching*, p. 10).

A second principle students need to learn is that writers view words in the context of other words. In one sense, a word by itself has no meaning, not even a "part of speech," until the writer relates it to some other word. Most grammar instruction separates words from their context, treating them as isolated entities, whereas writers must do just the reverse, make meaning by putting words together. It's not the word that creates meaning, but rather the writer's ability to relate words. Students must discover what writers such as Murray know: "The writer doesn't write down words to photograph what is in his head; he uses words to set an experiment in motion. Words are put down so he can find out what they reveal when they bump into other words on the page" (p. 9).

For Murray, watching words "bump into other words on the page" produces an excitement and surprise many student writers never experience. They've learned an unfortunate lesson: words have to be "right." For these students, working with words is like crossing a minefield. Any false step lowers the paper's grade. Because taking risks with language is suicidal, the safest course is following whatever rules about words students believe are most important. They know that words must observe not only conventions of grammar, spelling, and punctuation, but also confusing and sometimes contradictory prescriptions about style: "Don't use *I*"; "Never begin a sentence with *and*"; "Avoid fancy words"; "Avoid colloquial English."

Teachers who encourage students to play with words free young writers from the trap written language represents for them. That's an important responsibility because students who fear the rules can't use language effectively to give their ideas power. They also can't appreciate the reasons for following conventions when it's necessary.

This chapter, then, treats words in a special way. It will *not* outline a typical grammar unit, although it will discuss some grammatical problems student writers encounter. It will *not* spell out all there is to know about style, although it will present some strategies for helping students become aware of a variety of styles. The purpose of this chapter is to suggest some ways of talking with students about words in the special context of a writer at work.

What can we assume about that special context? First, writers at work need to be able to *use* words, not just know about them. Most grammar books divorce words from writing, isolating words in lockstep units peppered with terminology and exercises asking students to analyze someone else's writing. By contrast, this chapter encourages students to examine their own writing to discover how their words work. Second, writers at work need to look at language in ways that encourage rewriting. They need practice choosing words to realize particular rhetorical effects, and those choices must be governed by their subject, audience, and purpose for writing.

Finally, writers at work need the kind of instruction in language that capitalizes on what they already know. As Chapter 5 makes clear, students already know a great deal about how English works. A good way to begin discussing written English, then, is to tap the native speaker's knowledge of spoken English. But because spoken English also differs from edited American English, we also must illustrate for students the differences between the two systems. Sometimes we can do that in discussions involving the whole class. Often we must do it individually or in small groups because the points of confusion between the two codes will differ from student to student.

The pages that follow offer some suggestions for helping students understand the grammatical form and function of parts of speech, especially verbs and nouns. Beyond that, we want to look at some ways of teaching style, of encouraging students to become sensitive to the varieties of language that give writing power, clarity, and when appropriate, a sense of playfulness.

PARTS OF SPEECH

Traditionally, students learn parts of speech deductively. They memorize terminology, definitions, rules, and paradigms and then reproduce the constructions in their own writing. However, as most teachers know, students can quote the definition for *verb* much more readily than they can remember to write the final -s when they need to. Perhaps, then, we should be teaching inductively, beginning with the students' considerable competence for language.

For example, if students have trouble with verbs, we might discuss some nonsense verbs that have no meaning, observing how they behave in different contexts. Without knowing if *glork* represents "an action or state of being," students can generate appropriate forms of the word in sentences such as the following:

1. I don't like to _____ when I'm sleepy.
2. She always _____ in the morning.
3. As a matter of fact, she _____ yesterday.
4. Tomorrow she will _____ again.
5. She has _____ every day for the past three years.
6. She is _____ all the time.
7. Her _____ doesn't bother anybody.

Now students can work from "correct" forms they've generated, not from "errors"; from strengths, not weaknesses. By discussing these sentences, students can derive the "rules" that describe verb behavior in written English. They'll be concentrating primarily on how verbs look in various written contexts and how writers manipulate the form and position of verbs to express different meanings. Most important, they'll discover how much grammar they already know.

ACTIVE AND PASSIVE VOICE

The passive voice has legitimate uses. When Willa Cather begins *O Pioneers!* she establishes the wind as the powerful agent of the opening scene by referring to other details in the landscape with passive voice verbs:

> One January day, thirty years ago, the little town of Hanover, anchored on a windy Nebraska tableland, was trying not *to be blown away*. A mist of fine snowflakes was curling and eddying about the cluster of low drab buildings huddled on the gray prairie, under a gray sky. The dwelling-houses *were set about* haphazard on the tough prairie sod; some of them looked as if they *had been moved in* overnight, and others as if they were straying off by themselves, headed straight for the open plain. None of them had any appearance of permanence, and the howling wind blew under them as well as over them. (p. 3)

Although we sometimes use the passive voice for special effect, generally we write in the active voice because it makes the message more emphatic and less wordy. Students often have difficulty detecting passive constructions because they have been told to focus on the meaning of the sentence: "Who is doing what to whom?" At best, meaning offers slippery clues. Students seem to feel more secure when the words themselves, their form not their meaning, identify the construction. Students can begin the search for passive constructions in their drafts by finding forms of the verb "to be." Passive sentences always introduce the verb "to be" plus a past participle (a verb form usually ending in *-ed, -en*; other forms also are possible: *done, hit, had*).

> Passive: The college *was founded* in 1901.
> Passive: The books *were taken.*

So far so good. But not all "to be" verbs are passive. The verb "to be" also functions as an auxiliary verb in active voice constructions. When this is the case, a present participle ending in *-ing* will always follow the *be* verb:

> Active: She *is glorking* all the time.
> Active: Carlos *was making* good grades.

Most of the time, students can identify passive constructions simply by scanning their papers for *be* verbs (*is/am/are/was/were/being/been*) and then noticing what the next verb looks like. If the verb behind the *be* verb ends in *-ing*, the sentence is active; if the verb behind a form of *be* ends in *-ed, -en,* or something else, the sentence is probably passive.

Active: Carlos has *been making* good grades.

Passive: The candy has *been hidden* all over the house.

Once students know how to find passive constructions, they need specific instruction in rewriting them. Other clues about the form and position of words in active and passive sentences can help. I generally begin talking about the two kinds of sentences by writing on the board a passive sentence taken from a student's paper and its active counterpart:

Active: Our class *discussed* Susan's draft.

Passive: Susan's draft *was discussed* by our class.

Discussing paired sentences, students can easily identify how they differ and how to restore the passive sentence to the active voice. I lead the discussion toward the following conclusions:

1. The passive sentence reverses the order of two noun phrases.

   Active: *Our class* discussed *Susan's draft.*

   Passive: *Susan's draft* was discussed by *our class.*

2. Even simple passive sentences are wordy because they intro-duce a form of the verb "to be" and the preposition *by*.

3. The *by* phrase is optional. Some writers deliberately omit the *by* phrase to avoid giving "actors" responsibility for their actions. Susan's draft was discussed.
   Our taxes were increased.

4. To make passive sentences active, begin the revised sentence with the noun in the *by* phase, inventing a new subject if the *by* phrase has been omitted. Then delete the *be* verb and place the first noun phrase of the passive sentence behind the verb phrase of the active sentence.

   Passive: *Our taxes* were increased (by X).

   Revision: *The city council increased our taxes.*

   Passive: *The books were taken* (by X).

   Revision: *Someone took the books.*

   Passive: *The candy has been hidden all over the house* (by X).

   Revision: *Mother has hidden the candy* all over the house.

Because verb phrases represent complex grammatical constructions, their variety gives writers considerable flexibility in composing. Consequently, students need to know not only *how* to make passive sentences active but also *when* such a revision improves the draft. Encouraging students to become conscious of their options means approaching constructions descriptively, discussing first the variety of forms and positions verbs assume in sentence patterns. Then, we can label the constructions, explore their meaning, and judge their effectiveness in specific rhetorical contexts.

DERIVATIONAL AND INFLECTIONAL AFFIXES

Many teachers use a poem such as "Jabberwocky" (or their own nonsense sentences) to review the contextual clues readers and writers use to determine the form and position of words:

> 'Twas brillig and the slithy toves
> Did gyre and gimble in the wabe.

How do we know that *slithy* is an adjective? We can't decipher its meaning to determine if it tells "how many" or "what kind," but its form and position define its "adjectiveness." Like many adjectives *slithy* ends in -*y*, a clue about its form. *Slithy* also occupies a slot between *the* and *toves*, which looks like a noun. By position, then, *slithy* also appears to be an adjective. How do we know that *toves* is a noun? Though we can't tell if it names persons, places, or things, it ends in -*s*, a form clue. Although both nouns and verbs may end in -*s*, *toves* occupies a position in the sentence reserved for nouns. It appears after *the* and before "did gyre and gimble," in a nominal position common to many English sentence patterns. The form and position of a word in a sentence yield useful information about its function. When we confront new vocabulary, form and position clues often enable us to comprehend the author's message without referring to a dictionary. We infer roughly what the word means from where it appears and how it looks.

Much of the evidence about a word's form comes from affixes, units of meaning attached to a base or root. English permits adding affixes in front of the base (prefixes), behind the base (suffixes), or inside the base (infixes, the past tense affix placed inside "irregular verbs" such as *ran*, for example). Affixes are said to be *derivational* or *inflectional* depending on their function. Affixes that change a word's part of speech or its meaning are derivational. The suffix -*fy* is derivational because it creates verbs out of nouns: *beautify, liquify*. The prefix *anti-* also is derivational because it changes a word's meaning: *anti-Semitic, antisocial, antitrust*. On the other hand, inflectional affixes (all of them are suffixes) don't change a word's part of speech or its meaning; they adapt words to grammatical functions. *Dog* and *dogs* remain nouns denoting "domesticated mammals of the family *Canis familiaris*," even though *dogs* shows an inflectional plural suffix. In the following sentence, derivational and inflectional affixes have been marked with *D* or *I*:

The boys slowly walked backwards, carefully dragging the youngest
    I   D   I   D   D D   I   I
child's wooden sled.
    I   D

Although English once had many inflectional endings, now only eight
major suffixes remain:

1.	$-s_1$	noun possessive	boy's
2.	$-s_2$	noun plural	dogs, cats, oxen
3.	$-s_3$	3rd person present singular	learns
4.	-ing	present participle	They were *writing* letters.
5.	$-d_1$	past tense	climbed, walked, rode
6.	$-d_2$	past participle	She has *walked* home.
			She was *chosen* by him.
7.	-er	comparative degree	sweeter, deadlier
8.	-est	superlative degree	sweetest, deadliest

Few in number, inflectional endings nevertheless present problems for
some students. Our use of final -s seems especially confusing and inconsistent.[1] We add -s to verbs to make them singular, but we add -s to
nouns to make them plural. Moreover, we only add -s sometimes. English
doesn't permit such constructions as "He cans walk" or "Two oxes
plowed the field." Too, some dialects differ from edited American English on the matter of final -s. As Mina Shaughnessy suggests, writers
often see no need for the pluralizing -s in such phrases as "these two
suggestion" and "four year of college" because quantifiers (*these, two,
four*) already indicate plurality. Some students neither write nor pronounce -s in such constructions as "many scientist." Because *many* signals
plurality, adding -s to *scientist* seems redundant. Or, students may omit
-s because they're spelling the word as they pronounce it, with a simplified final consonant cluster.

Possessive final -s is similarly troublesome. Shaughnessy suggests
that some students consider such phrases as "42 percent of this nation
youth" analogous to compound nouns such as "child welfare" and "student activities." Possession by juxtaposition is common in English and
may explain why a student writes "Mary hat" for "Mary's hat." In these
examples, final -s does not appear in some students' writing because it
does not appear in their speech. Conversely, students may have difficulty transcribing possessive forms that *do* have spoken counterparts. Students who write "it's cover" have applied the rule for possessive -s to a
pronoun. If possessive nouns end in 's, they reason, so should possessive
pronouns. In English, however, possessive pronouns omit the apostro-

1. Mina Shaughnessy, *Errors and Expectations: A Guide for the Teacher of Basic Writing*
(New York: Oxford University Press, 1977), remains an important discussion of the logic
governing students' writing problems. An extensive discussion of final -s appears in
Chapter 4, "Common Errors," pp. 90–159.

phe. We need to explain that English has two ways of showing possession: nouns add 's ("the book's cover") but pronouns add only s ("its
cover"). Students who misuse it's are not confusing a possessive pronoun
("its") with a contraction ("it's"). They are confusing two methods of
showing possession in written English.

Inflectional endings create problems for students because some conventions of edited American English are redundant and inconsistent.
The student's "logic" produces an error because the "logic" of written
English requires a different form. To help students become confident
about these forms, we must remain sensitive not only to the conventional
behavior of English words, but also to the ingeniously unconventional
ways in which students sometimes use them.

STYLE

What do we mean by *style* in writing? Some writers define *style* broadly,
as the "characteristic means of expressing ideas" used by an individual,
by a group of writers in a certain period, or even by a whole nation of
writers. Broad definitions view style as the sum total of all the decisions
writers make in selecting, arranging, and expressing their ideas. Other
writers find broad definitions unhelpful. Although they acknowledge
the influence a writer's sense of audience and purpose has on style,
they define *style* more narrowly. For them, *style* refers to choices writers
make about words or diction and sometimes sentence structure.

For our purposes in this chapter, we will adopt the narrower view
that style is word choice. Writers create a style by selecting words that
give ideas clarity, emphasis, specificity, and variety. Though style is
seen in words, it always involves larger considerations of audience,
subject, and purpose, which change from one piece of writing to the
next. In some contexts, for example, writers must be deliberately obscure,
wordy, or pseudoerudite. Most high school and college students, however, need practice being precise and direct. Cultural and historical
preferences also may influence the choices writers make in selecting one
style over another. Writers in past centuries, for example, sometimes
delighted in ornate linguistic displays. Nowadays, readers prefer plain
prose.

In a writing class, then, students need opportunities to discover what
stylistic choices are possible and how to choose wisely. We can introduce
students to these choices by asking them to examine two or more passages representing quite different styles of contemporary prose. Read
the following examples out loud. Good writing affects the ear and the
mouth as well as the eye:

Example A:

The problem of order, and thus of the nature of the integration of stable
systems of social interaction, that is, of social structure, thus focuses on

the integration of the motivation of actors with the normative cultural standards which integrate the action system, in our context interpersonally. These standards are, in the terms used in the preceding chapter, patterns of value-orientation, and as such are a particularly crucial part of the cultural tradition of the social system. (Talcott Parsons, *The Social System*, pp. 36–37)

Example B:

I don't know about you, but I have this voice that goes:

"*What?* NAW. That ain't no way to write a damn sentence! That's the limpest damn piddliest damn saddest-looking most clogged and whiney damn hitching-around piss-and-corruption-covered damn sentence I ever saw.

"*Boy!* Anybody can snuffle along through the pine straw! I want to see you down with your teeth in the dirt! Reaching and gnawing and chewing and gnashing on some *oak tree roots!* Right on down through to where the *juice is. Git* it. *Drive.* Show me something!" (Roy Blount, Jr., *Crackers*, p. 1)

In discussing these passages, we might ask several questions: Why did you like one better than the other? Which author would you rather meet? In what ways are the passages different? Similar? Which author seems to know his subject better? His audience? In what circumstances might you choose a style such as Parsons'? Blount's? In what circumstances would neither style be appropriate?

Having discussed the models, give students an opportunity to imitate them, not to grade their performance, but to help them stretch their stylistic muscles. Give them a plain idea, "I failed the course," and ask them to write a paragraph in each of the styles they have just examined. Repeat that process several times, each time selecting models that permit students to discuss and imitate a variety of styles, both contemporary and historical. Although imitation is difficult work, students will enjoy the exercise if they can assume playful personas and don't have to worry about a grade on the exercise. They also will learn how flexible written English can be and how to control their choices to achieve a consistent tone of voice.

At some point, students must apply what they have learned to their own drafts, testing their choices and improving language that fails adequately to capture their ideas. Perhaps the best way to guide students in examining their own drafts is to work through sections of sample student papers in class or in groups, line by line and sometimes word by word. As classmates suggest revisions and point out sources of confusion, the author of the paper learns where ideas are muddy, where an extended figure becomes overworked, where an imprecise word reveals imprecise thinking.

Discussing students' drafts permits us to cover the same elements of style we might find in a textbook. Unlike a textbook, though, the examples will be in the students' own words, and we can discuss them in the larger rhetorical context of an entire paper, something that one-sentence exercises in textbooks discourage. When the class examines why and how stylistic revisions improve a draft, students gain a clear sense of what questions to ask of their writing. Using students' papers to teach style isn't as tidy as following the carefully laid out chapters in a textbook; the papers themselves determine which elements of style will receive attention. We won't find them all in one or two papers, and we won't be able to cover them all in one day. But with careful planning, we can examine style in every paper discussed in class, in time addressing most of the elements in the following list:

concrete and abstract diction	parts of speech
denotation and connotation	nominalization
synonyms and antonyms	passive voice
figurative language	trite diction and clichés
jargon, doublespeak, pomposity	idioms
repetition, deadwood	usage
dialects, levels of diction	gendered language
coordination and subordination	coherence
clarity, specificity, detail	word etymologies
using a thesaurus and dictionary	emphatic word orders

ADDITIONAL RESOURCES

A number of useful textbooks discuss style. As resources for teachers, these books yield generous information about how words work and what problems of style student writers encounter. I have found the following works especially helpful:

> Donald Hall and Sven Birkerts, *Writing Well* (9th ed., 1997);
>
> Richard Lanham, *Revising Prose* (4th ed., 1999), and *The Revising Prose Videotape* (1981);
>
> Winston Weathers and Otis Winchester, *The New Strategy of Style* (2d ed., 1978);
>
> Joseph Williams, *Style: Ten Lessons in Clarity and Grace* (6th ed., 1999);
>
> William Zinsser, *On Writing Well* (6th ed., 1998).

In addition to serving teachers well, some of these books would be excellent resources for students. But we also can supplement traditional textbooks, handbooks, and dictionaries with other materials that stimulate an interest in style. Newspapers, magazines, advertisements, editorials, cartoons, memoranda, reports, and junk mail offer countless possibilities for discussing the purposeful word choices writers make. They illustrate rhetorical strategies and linguistic options that, for students, seem somehow more real than the examples in a textbook.

These materials can be especially useful in discussing dishonest uses of language. Doublespeak, gobbledygook, and jargon depend on passive constructions, piled-up prepositional phrases, abstract nouns, and nominalizations (nouns derived from verbs). The impenetrable pretentious prose many students write—Macrorie calls it "Engfish"[2]—also uses language dishonestly. To write honest prose, students must understand what Engfish looks like and why it's phony. The following memorandum, for example, begs for translation and offers generous material for discussing not only word choices but sentence structure, paragraph construction, and rhetorical principles as well.

MEMORANDUM

TO: Executive Director

FROM: Regional Planning Director

SUBJECT: **PLAN IMPLEMENTATION.** COMPREHENSIVE DEVELOPMENT PLAN, policy for

In the course of evolving a distinctively Regional program responsive to over-all area-wide goals and objectives for attaining the physical, social, and economic betterment of the Region, we are undertaking formulation of initial sets of compatible definitions of basic concepts in support of an optimal approach to the participatory processes essential for effectuation of achievable strategies that may demonstrate at least minimal promise of generating measurable progress toward alleviation of selected Regional-scale problems of priority concern, through implementation of an assertive action-oriented posture regarding topical issues of Regional import on the part of the Council, through both formal and informal mechanisms for eliciting and receiving citizen-participation impact at critical phases of the decision-making process, in concert with the advisory to responsible elected officials of units of local general government, to the maximum extent feasible at each step in the comprehensive planning process, and in harmony with area-wide functional planning and programming as well as established State policies having identifiable application in prescribing broad guidelines for the compatible ordering of intraregional development trends, all keyed to initial revised control projections for the horizon year. Periodically, revisions are considered in accordance with HUD guidelines.

cc: Local Planning Chief

Planning and Management Assistant

When we bring these materials into the English class, we also reinforce our contention that writing matters in the world of work. The state driver's handbook, for example, of special interest to high school students, can serve as a source for reading and writing assignments as well as discussions of language. Many so-called "survival documents" bear translating into styles appropriate for different audiences: income tax regulations, voter registration forms, owner's manuals for small appli-

2. See Ken Macrorie, *Telling Writing*, 4th ed. (Portsmouth, NH: Boynton/Cook, 1985), especially Chapter 1. For exercises focusing on irresponsible uses of language, see Daniel Dieterich, ed., *Teaching about Doublespeak* (Urbana, IL: NCTE, 1976).

ances, insurance policies, credit agreements, applications for college admission or a job. Students are likely to enjoy working with these materials because they symbolize adult responsibilities. They also represent a broad range of styles and language choices.

SUGGESTIONS FOR TEACHING STUDENTS ABOUT LANGUAGE

Teachers who want to help students enlarge their repertoire of stylistic options and master the conventions of edited American English often encounter apathy or resistance to the subject. For most students, the facts of how people use language have become so confused by rules and exceptions to rules, by shifting definitions, by rote memorization, and by boring homework assignments that language study is neither interesting nor related to anything worth mastering. "Language manipulates me," they conclude, "I can't possibly control it." They're trapped by rules.

But language is not just a set of rules. It's a tool people use to create meaning, an enormously flexible means of expression. To break out of language-manipulates-me thinking, students must first understand that language-users, not usage guides and handbooks, determine the conventions of English prose. Then students more confidently can discuss what language really is, what attitudes people have about it, how writers use it to express ideas purposefully to an audience. Yes, writers observe conventions, but excessive concern about them, especially in the early stages of composing, prevents students from recognizing that their own language permits infinite possibilities for expressing ideas. To foster that recognition, the following suggestions may help.

1. Whenever possible, begin discussions about language by asking students what they already know, or assume to be true, about the material you intend to cover. If you discover that they already understand the material, revise your discussion to help students *apply* the principle to their writing.
2. As students talk about their writing, listen for evidence of misinformation or confusion about rhetorical and linguistic principles. Explain how the confusion might have arisen. Perhaps a "rule" was only partially learned, or misapplied, or confused with some other principle. Because most misunderstandings contain partial truths, you may want to review the principle when it comes up; that's when students are most receptive to discussing it. Listen, too, for examples of linguistic and rhetorical principles in the spoken language students use in the classroom.
3. Whenever possible, base discussions of language on students' writing instead of examples in textbooks. Excellent papers show students that they can use language effectively, that what

you're asking them to do doesn't require some peculiar magical power granted only to professionals. Average papers permit the class to praise a student's achievements and suggest improvements. Avoid discussing weak papers, but remember that weak students occasionally write exemplary prose that merits class discussion. Some teachers discuss students' papers by granting the authors anonymity; others select sample papers from one class to show another class; still others regularly "publish" papers, names attached, from everyone in the class so that students have several opportunities to gain constructive responses to their work. Of course, these discussions must focus on both the strengths and weaknesses of the piece. With practice, students will become better able to articulate the principles of good writing in their own words, more proficient in analyzing and revising their own work, and more self-reliant critics.

4. Conduct discussions about language with a minimum of technical terms, at least at first. Writing, not learning terminology, should remain the focus of the course. You can label constructions after students have practiced a particular technique or become reasonably comfortable manipulating the language in certain ways: "These words we've been using to hook sentences together have a name; we call them 'subordinating and coordinating conjunctions.'"

5. To write well, students need practice using language, creating their own discourse. Avoid asking students to spend a great deal of time analyzing someone else's language. Most worksheets, programmed textbooks, and exercises don't encourage writing; they teach underlining, circling, and filling in blanks. They may be easy to grade, but they rarely engage students in composing. Furthermore, they assume that students must master "pieces" of language in isolation—words, sentences, paragraphs—before doing "real" writing. This piecemeal approach, argues David Bartholomae, contradicts the assumption that writing is a process of making decisions and exercising options:

Before students can be let loose to write, the argument goes, they need a semester to "work on" sentences or paragraphs, as if writing a sentence in a workbook or paragraph in isolation were somehow equivalent to producing those units in the midst of some extended act of writing, or as if the difficulties of writing sentences or paragraphs are concepts rather than intrinsic to the writer and his struggle to juggle the demands of a language, a rhetoric, and a task. ("Teaching Basic Writing: An Alternative to Basic Skills," p. 87)

All of us remember teachers who inadvertently attempted to subvert our love of English. Reviewing our own experiences in English classes can strengthen our teaching. What did we like most and least about studying the language? Did looking up all the words we didn't understand in a reading assignment really make us better word wizards? Was reading aloud in front of the class a humiliating torture? Were you proud to have mastered sentence diagramming, or did you never see the point of tearing up sentences that way? Did you enjoy filling out workbooks or doing homework assignments meant to keep you busy?

To be sure, writing is hard work, but it needn't be synonymous with pain and punishment. Writing, like reading, can have quite unpleasant associations for students, as John Holt points out:

> Mark Twain once said that a cat that sat on a hot stove lid would never sit on one again—but it would never sit on a cold one either. As true of children as of cats. If they, so to speak, sit on a hot book a few times, if books cause them humiliation and pain, they are likely to decide that the safest thing to do is to leave all books alone. ("How Teachers Make Children Hate Reading," p. 226)

The study of English doesn't need to be distasteful for our students if we can prevent them from constantly associating their use of language with mistakes, penalties, and humiliation, real or imagined. Most of us became teachers because we appreciate the enormous expressive power of our language. Inviting students to discover and appreciate their language reflects the essence of our teaching.

twelve

Teaching Rewriting

How do I know what I think until I see what I say?

E. M. FORSTER

CHANGING ATTITUDES

For most students, *rewriting* is a dirty word. It's a punishment, a penalty for writing poorly. This notion gains strength when teachers insist that students correct mistakes in papers already graded or complete workbook exercises on writing problems in someone else's prose. Rewriting the *whole* paper, students believe, means they've failed the assignment. Rewriting remains an unpleasant chore for almost all writers, a process that confronts them with countless inadequacies in the draft and convinces them that words manipulate writers, not the other way around. Students rewrite their papers reluctantly for many reasons, as the following comments attest:

1. I wait until the last minute, so there's no time to rewrite.
2. My first draft is the best I can do. I can't improve it.
3. I don't know whether my first draft is any good or not, so how can I improve it?
4. I don't know where to begin, and I wouldn't know when to stop.
5. Well, frankly, I'm lazy.
6. When I tinker with my sentences, they just turn out worse.
7. I don't really care about what I'm writing, so I just want to get it over with.
8. Rewriting is too messy. I like to work with clean looking pages.
9. I'm such a bad writer I hate to read my own writing.
10. Rewriting is my instructor's responsibility.

11. Rewriting is painful. I can't stand the agony.
12. If I can't get it right the first time, I must be stupid.
(Diana Hacker and Betty Renshaw, *Writing with a Voice*, p. 26)

Most of these attitudes developed slowly, as students sat year after year in English classes where rewriting *was* a form of punishment, where the teacher's comments on papers rarely praised strengths or offered practical suggestions for addressing weaknesses, where students never had opportunities to draft several versions of an assignment before it was due. The techniques discussed in this chapter are meant to correct students' perceptions of rewriting-as-punishment, to encourage the view that rewriting remains crucial to composing, not an afterthought.

Many good writers spend considerably more time rewriting their work than drafting it. "I can't write five words," Dorothy Parker claims, "but that I change seven." Bernard de Voto insists that "the best reason for putting anything down on paper is that one may then change it." The changes we make in a draft are fairly simple; we add, delete, substitute, or rearrange material. But each adjustment requires judgment, making choices about what to keep and what to discard. We must decide, first of all, whether what we've written suits us, represents what we honestly want to say; then we must determine if a reader can make sense of it. From the students' perspective, this process poses several obstacles.

First, if neatness matters, as it has mattered ever since handwriting was graded in elementary school, students will be reluctant to mess up their drafts with changes. Second, if they mistakenly believe that some mysterious genius explodes clearly articulated, perfectly punctuated sentences onto a page, they'll hesitate to admit that their "genius" has failed them. On the other hand, if they've psyched out the teacher correctly on the first draft, the grade should be high without revising the paper. Third, if they've had no opportunities to prewrite the paper, to develop an overabundance of material, they'll be reluctant to tamper with the piece for fear of having to endure again the agony of finding something to say and making the words come out right. Finally, students conclude, rewriting doesn't matter much anyway. Their teachers neglect it, rarely demonstrating *how* rewriting works. They only occasionally request "corrections," schedule assignments so as to preclude time for rewriting, and harp on the disadvantages of scissors and paste.

According to Nancy Sommers, many student writers use rewriting strategies different from those experienced writers employ. In "Revision Strategies of Student Writers and Experienced Writers," she notes that students see rewriting primarily as rewording, approaching the process with what she calls a "thesaurus philosophy of writing": "The students consider the thesaurus a harvest of lexical substitutions and believe that most problems in their essays can be solved by rewording" (p. 381). They worry most about eliminating lexical repetition, are predominantly concerned about vocabulary, and delete or substitute words much more frequently than adding or reordering material. Although occasionally they reword the introduction or reorder ideas, they generally limit themselves to matters covered by editing rules. "At best the students see their writing altogether passively through the eyes of former teachers or their surrogates, the textbooks, and are bound to the rules that they have been taught" (p. 383).

Experienced writers, Sommers concludes, approach rewriting differently, much more concerned about finding the shape of the argument and about the reader's expectations. Although they make changes primarily at the level of the sentence (predominantly by addition and deletion), the changes encompass the whole composition and take several cycles to complete, each cycle embracing a different objective:

> The experienced writers see their revision process as a recursive process—a process with significant recurring activities—with different levels of attention and different agenda for each cycle. During the first revision cycle their attention is primarily directed towards narrowing the topic and delimiting their ideas. At this point, they are not as concerned as they are later about vocabulary and style. The experienced writers explained that they get closer to the meaning by not limiting themselves too early to lexical concerns. (p. 386)

Whereas early cycles concentrate on finding form, discovering the message, and clarifying ideas, later cycles focus on stylistic concerns. Yet even though each cycle may have a primary focus, experienced writers subordinate other concerns to it, keeping the whole in mind as they concentrate on its parts.

Sommers' work helps us redefine *rewriting* to include both revising and editing. When we want students to polish a text, to clean up misspellings, to change punctuation, to straighten out grammatical problems, we're asking them to edit, not revise, their work. Editing usually takes place during one of the later cycles Sommers describes. Revising, however, is not, as many textbooks proclaim, the last stage of composing. "Instead of thinking of revision as an activity at the end of the process, what if we thought of revision as a process of making a work congruent with what a writer intends—a process that occurs throughout the writing of a work?"[1] The composing process is not a linear sequence of separable stages; prewriting, writing, and rewriting are concurrent activities, repeated over and over again as writers come progressively closer to resolving incongruities between what they intend to say and what the discourse actually says.

Let me illustrate some of the decisions writers must make by discussing several versions of the introductory paragraph for this chapter. Before

---

1. Nancy I. Sommers, "The Need for Theory in Composition Research," *College Composition and Communication* 30 (February 1979), 48. Sommers appears to use the term *revising* with the meaning I attach to *rewriting*; both of us agree that revising and rewriting amount to more than "editing," "proofreading," or "correcting" a text.

I drafted it, I compiled a list of notes and decided roughly what I wanted to do: to present the students' perspective on rewriting. Once I've discussed why students hate rewriting, I reasoned, I can then explain what we can do about the problem. When I wrote the paragraph the first time, in pencil on a long, yellow, legal tablet, I got stuck in several places. Instead of erasing my words, as I usually do, I simply crossed through them so that you could see the changes I made. Here's that early version of Chapter 12's opening paragraph:

Rewriting -- a swear word in most English classes. Most students consider it a punishment, ~~fo~~ a penalty for writing poorly in the first place. Many teachers, bent on beating comma faults out of ~~their~~ ~~students~~ ~~papers~~, require them to "correct" ~~misstype~~ submit pages of corrections ~~complete for each essay or sentence~~ ~~delinquents to complete~~ or to complete appropriate exercises in the composition handbook. ~~If writing represents in the minds of most~~ ~~students writing itself~~ If writing seems painful, as it ~~does~~ ~~you~~ for most ~~people~~ ~~students~~, surely rewriting prolongs and intensifies the agony. ~~Most~~ They remain ~~conf~~ convinced that, having ~~executed out the~~ ~~done their best work~~ given the paper their best effort, there is no way to improve it by revision. For almost all writers, rewriting is a frustrating chore, ~~It when we contemplate an almost alien draft, we~~ ~~a process that required us to admit~~ ~~tempts us to admit th~~ ~~It~~ must admit that, ~~some of~~ our ~~words~~ idea ~~and words~~ refuse to ~~submit to~~ ~~be governed by~~ ~~words~~ ~~our control,~~ that we ~~didn't intend to say this and left that point undeveloped~~ ~~haven't thought things through, that that~~ ~~in some sense we have failed to communicate~~ ~~didn't mean to say this and left that out,~~ that in ~~some~~ ~~many~~ ways the ~~writing has flaws~~ ~~communication is flawed~~ To protect ourselves from viewing our mistakes as a personal failure, we construct defenses which ~~prevent~~ ~~permit~~ us to ignore the draft altogether. Listen to these students as they ~~rationalize~~ their reluctance to rewrite their papers:

A week later, after I'd drafted the entire chapter, I reread it. What especially displeased me about the first paragraph was its lack of focus.

Although I had intended to present the students' perspective on rewriting, I shifted the focus several times from "rewriting" to "students" to "teachers" to "all writers/we" back to "students." I wasn't secure about my audience either. Although I wanted to communicate how students feel about rewriting papers, their teachers would be reading the book. Some readers surely would resent such phrases as "swear word" and "teachers bent on beating comma faults out of their students." Some would resent my aversion to handbook exercises. At the point in the paragraph where I've marked through "sweated out," I seem to have shifted my language to "talk up" to an audience of colleagues; words such as "contemplate," "alien," "be governed by," and "permit" represent, for me, a formal vocabulary, especially in a first draft. The last sentence didn't please me either. I needed a lead into the students' comments, but the alliterating r's seemed too fancy.

Keeping these judgments in mind, I rewrote the paragraph. Again, instead of erasing options I'd discarded, I left them for you to see. The second version is considerably shorter than the first, probably because I kept asking myself as I wrote, "What do *students* think about rewriting?" The last sentence gave me fits; for all my tinkering with it, I just couldn't get from my own paragraph to the quoted material. Changing "Most" to "Many" was necessary to avoid antagonizing my audience. Changing "Sometimes teachers" to "Some students" kept the focus of the paragraph on students (a deliberate passive construction helped). I changed "Revision," written too hastily, to "Rewriting" because the entire book organizes itself around words ending in -*writing*, a handy way to remember what the composing process entails.

Eight months later, when I rewrote the entire manuscript, I changed the paragraph again. Although the second version had persuaded me that I wasn't consciously alienating my readers, I wasn't pleased about the sentences. They were all about the same length and type. Comparing the first and second drafts of the paragraph also forced me to reconsider decisions I'd already made about my audience: "If I really don't think that 'correction exercises' help students," I thought, "I should say so honestly and explain why. If I've asserted throughout the book that teachers *and* students are writers, why not also make the point here?" The third version of my paragraph appeared in the first two editions of this book:

> For most students, *rewriting* is a dirty word. They see it as a punishment, a penalty for writing poorly in the first place. Many teachers reinforce this notion by insisting that students correct mistakes in papers already graded or complete workbook exercises on writing problems in someone else's prose. Rewriting the *whole* paper, students believe, means they've failed the assignment. For almost all writers, rewriting remains an unpleasant chore, a process which confronts them with countless inadequacies in the draft and convinces them that words manipulate writers, not the other way around. Students rewrite their papers reluctantly for many reasons, as the following comments attest:

In revising the chapter for the third edition, I reviewed the paragraph again. It still didn't satisfy me because the focus wasn't clear. Sentence subjects shifted from *rewriting* to *They* (students) to *Many teachers* back to *Rewriting* and then to *Students* again. "Surely," I thought to myself, "you can realign the sentence subjects so that most of them emphasize rewriting, the subject of the chapter." So, I reordered sentence elements again and trimmed a little fat. That fourth version now appears at the beginning of the chapter.

As you read this book, many years after I wrote the first draft, you may see further revisions I could have made just in that one paragraph. Although days, months, and years separate the different versions, a luxury most student writers don't have, the rewriting process was cyclical. I began with a purpose but didn't discover my message or clarify my audience until I'd examined the second draft. Sentence problems occupied my attention the second and third time I reviewed the paragraph, but I also addressed larger concerns, reconsidering my audience, my focus, and my own attitudes about teaching. In rewriting, then, as Sommers' research describes, writers review decisions they've made throughout the composing process. They redefine their purpose and audience, reassess the message, reshape the discourse, and realign their meaning with linguistic forms. For this reason, several strategies discussed earlier in the context of prewriting and writing reappear in this chapter. They serve to remind us that creating and recreating prose involve similar decisions.

Beyond redefining what rewriting entails, we also can encourage students to see it differently, dispelling some of their negative attitudes. We can adjust course schedules so that students have adequate time to plan, draft, and rewrite each assignment. At least one-third of our teaching should emphasize how writers rework drafts. We can discuss successive versions of novels, speeches, or other works by professional writers. We can encourage students to examine one another's drafts and together develop strategies for rewriting them. Students seem comfortable reworking their papers on word processors, in part because the terminal provides a clean copy of the text each time, in part because students have not yet learned to associate machine-edited texts with the teacher's red pen. We also can share our own writing with students, explaining problems we encountered and how we resolved them. This last suggestion is especially crucial for students who believe that writing is a magic talent peculiar to English teachers and novelists. Students need to see what rewriting looks like with all its false starts, messy pages, and momentary indecisions. My students have seen the several versions of this chapter's opening paragraph and reviewed with me the decisions I made. They're surprised to see how messy rewriting can be, but they also understand what choices writers must make and how to evaluate them. As long as I continue to let them see my work, they're willing to share theirs with other students.

WRITING STRATEGIES APPLIED TO REWRITING: FINDING THE SUBJECT

Because prewriting decisions affect every element of a composition, writers must review them when they rewrite a draft. For example, Caroline, the student whose paper appears in Chapter 8 (p. 133), could write a stronger essay if she reinvented her draft, redefining her subject, her audience, and her purpose. Although she promises to discuss "exposures," she hasn't yet decided how or why they "mold the way a person will live." "Exposure" may simply be an empty, fancy word intended to impress the teacher-audience. Although she subdivides her topic into travel, changes in life style, and education, she hasn't developed enough details to demonstrate how these contemporary advantages differ from those available to her parents and grandparents.

She might begin reinventing her draft by brainstorming "travel" and/or "education," clustering the topic, or applying heuristic questions to a sentence such as "The most important influence on my life has been (*person or experience*)." Freewriting also might make her more comfortable with her subject; the first and last paragraphs are written in "Engfish," the pretentiously formal style some students think their English teachers want to read. Perhaps addressing the paper to a classmate or younger sibling would help. The point is that Caroline can't improve this version of her paper significantly by repairing the sentence fragment and correcting "ones'." She needs to find her message and a purpose for expressing it. Like most students, she needs to probe the subject again and develop new rhetorical strategies for developing it. Then, using a traditional outline, a block plan, or one of D'Angelo's paradigms, she can redefine the shape she wants to give her material.

Of course, responses from classmates also would help Caroline find her message. Depending on how much experience she has with group-work and how comfortable she is sharing her writing, several activities are possible. Simply reading the paper aloud to a partner, who then might describe briefly one meritorious detail, would be an important first step. Reading aloud would give Caroline an opportunity to hear her own words, to share her work with a real audience, and to gain information about a strength that she could build on.

As students develop trust in group members, responses can become more elaborate. *Student Writing Groups* (1988) describes a three-step method for offering feedback. In step one, the writer simply reads the paper while group members listen. Then, as the writer reads the draft a second time, group members occasionally jot down words or phrases that they are hearing, recording them on a sheet of paper that has been divided into three columns headed with a plus sign, a minus sign, and a question mark. The plus column contains words that reso-nated positively with the listener; the minus column, words that sug-gested problems; the column headed by a question mark, words that the listener was confused by or unsure about. After the second reading and without additional comments from the writer, each member of the group comments on the words and phrases entered in each column. During this third step, the writer makes notes on what the listeners are saying. At the end of this process, the writer has gained important, specific information about the strengths and weaknesses group members heard in the draft. Where group members' comments contradict each other, the writer will have to resolve the conflict, but all of the comments will let the writer know what is and is not working in the piece.

In *Sharing and Responding* (2000), Peter Elbow and Pat Belanoff offer students numerous other ways of responding to one another's writing. Some methods simply call for descriptions or summaries of a draft or of the listener's responses to it. Others require judgment and analysis, invoking traditional criteria for organization, content, voice, style, and mechanics. "Sayback," for example, encourages responders to summa-rize for the writer what they have read or heard, to "say back" what the main ideas seem to be. The method can be especially useful when students are inexperienced in discussing drafts or when drafts represent early attempts to explore a topic. "Movies of the Reader's Mind" invites responders to describe in detail what happens in their minds as they read the draft: "I got lost here because I thought I would find out about the second kind of snail, but the paper talks about how escargot get cooked instead." "This part reminds me of how crazy some people get at rock concerts." "Believing and doubting," another of Elbow and Belanoff's techniques, requires responders first to pretend that they believe everything that the writer is saying. In this role they offer additional evidence, support, or details for the piece. Then, assuming the role of doubters, they produce all the evidence that they can think of against the writer's position. In providing writers with first a sympathetic and then a skeptical audience, "believing and doubting" responses and can help strengthen certain kinds of writing, especially arguments.

Elbow and Belanoff advise that students practice many methods of responding to drafts and then choose those strategies that best suit their needs. To reach this goal, students need to learn not only how to elicit effective advice but also which kinds of feedback may work best in particular situations. Caroline, for example, must realize that asking classmates for help with spelling will be less useful in rewriting her draft than seeking advice to clarify what she wants to say. Generally speaking, less structured responses are most appropriate early in the development of a draft, when writers are still exploring their message, or early in the term, as students learn to give and receive effective advice. Furthermore, students need to see these techniques demonstrated, the teacher modeling procedures and providing language that group members can emulate. Finally, they need opportunities to comment on the usefulness of various strategies. Assessing their merits will give students confidence in asking for forms of feedback most likely to move an evolving project forward.

REWRITING: FINDING THE SHAPE OF DISCOURSE

The following essay, a description of Megan's bedroom, shows organizational problems. It needs reshaping.

The Pink Bedroom

This bedroom is unique. The dresser has handmade items that match each other and contain make-up. The bedspread on the canopy bed matches the wallpaper. Under the bed and in the closet are treasured items. The objects on the walls illustrate the accomplishments made during the years at school.

The handmade items on the dresser are pink, and they match the pink and white striped wallpaper on three of the walls. These containers hold make up such as lotion, foundation base, powder, and lipstick. Also, the dresser is composed of a pink jewelry box. On either side of the jewelry box, consists a pink lamp. The dresser is white and has two drawers. This dresser is delicate and stays neat.

The canopy bed is also white. The top of the canopy and the ruffle on the bottom of the bed matches the flower wallpaper that it faces, and the bedspread is white and quilted. On the inside of the top of the canopy is a red rose, that is attractive to look at while in the bed. A few pillows and collected dolls are set on the bed. The mattress is soft, and the bed is high off the ground. This bed is comfortable and makes a nice picture to look at.

In different storage spots, numerous articles are found. Under the bed, boxes of letters and past schoolwork are kept. A scrapbook of different events that have happened is stored. In the closet, an array of clothing hangs and on the shelves collectors' items such as books, stamps, seashells, and coins are placed. A shoerack is also in the closet, so that shoes are neatly arranged. These items are in safe keeping in these different places.

Several plaques are displayed on the walls. Certain frames contain witty sayings, and others show the awards that were received in school. Some of these awards were for photography, biology, and acceptance into the honor society. Also, on the wall is a picture of the Virgin Mary and a crucifix, which shows a dedication to the church. Each of these objects on the wall is special and has a purpose in being there.

Overall, the room is neatly organized and delicate. Pink is the main color theme for the room, and the furniture is white. Several plaques and scrapbooks are selectively displayed in different parts of the room. The room is comfortable to live in, but it also makes an attractive picture for observers.

Megan generated plenty of details prior to drafting. She also had a plan for organizing the composition (although it wasn't an effective one). Outlining only the first three paragraphs of Megan's essay allows us to see that each sentence of the first paragraph establishes a general subtopic that subsequent paragraphs develop:

I. This bedroom is unique.
    A. The <u>dresser</u> has handmade items.
    B. The <u>bedspread</u> matches the wallpaper.
    C. <u>Treasured items</u> are stored under the bed and in the closet.
    D. <u>Plaques</u> hang on the walls.
II. <u>The items on the dresser</u> are pink.
    A. Several containers hold make up.
    B. There is a jewelry box.
    C. Pink lamps stand on either side of the dresser.
    D. The dresser is white.
    E. The dresser has two drawers.
    F. The dresser is delicate.
III. The <u>canopy bed</u> is white.
    A. The canopy and ruffle match the wall paper.
    B. The bedspread is quilted and white.
    C. A rose inside the top of the canopy is attractive to look at.
    D. Pillows and dolls are set on the bed.
    E. The mattress is soft.

F. The bed is high off the ground.
G. The bed is comfortable and nice to look at.

A major problem with this composition is attributable to the assignment, "Describe a person by describing his or her room." In all probability, Megan wasn't much interested in the topic, was reluctant to reveal herself, or wondered what purpose the teacher had in making such an assignment. Although she lists many details about her room, no "person" ever appears. She completes the paper only to satisfy the teacher.

On the other hand, she's organized the paper deliberately, listing her subtopics in the introductory paragraph. Because she has some sense of structure, reshaping the paper may be the best place to begin rewriting it. What would we tell her? First, the details in paragraph one aren't "unique," nor does she tell us her purpose for including them. She makes no promise to the reader that the rest of the paper can fulfill. The outline shows that she's merely listing "things" without linking them to a description of a person or supporting the "uniqueness" idea. The thesis, "This bedroom is unique," needs revising.

As Megan plans her next draft, she could ask herself some of the following questions about the outline: Do I really want to write about my room? If so, why begin with "dresser" and end with "plaques"? Is there a logic to moving around the room this way? What alternate description paradigms could I use? In what ways do the items I'm talking about reveal the kind of person I am? What's the purpose for each paragraph and how does it fulfill the promise I'm making at the beginning of my paper? Does each paragraph establish subordinate and coordinate relationships among its sentences? In answering these questions about the outline, Meagan will discover a problem in paragraph two, where II A–C specify items on the dresser while II D–F describe the dresser itself. Or she might see that paragraph three shifts the reader's attention spatially from the canopy to the ruffle to the bedspread back to the canopy to the pillows and dolls on the bedspread to the mattress to the floor. She can improve that order of details.

Sentence structure needs work too. Megan rarely subordinates word groups within sentences, a problem similar to the lack of confidence she shows in working out coordinate and subordinate relationships among sentences within paragraphs. But for now, Megan shouldn't worry about that, not until she's discovered what she wants to say about the bedroom, how to shape her message. She can concentrate on paragraphing and sentence structure in subsequent cycles of revision.

Outlining a draft can help students identify not only structural problems but also decisions about purpose and audience. As papers-in-miniature, outlines reveal where organizational tensions occur, where readers might get lost, where sections are skimpy, where details could be deleted, added, or rearranged. Outlines also may demonstrate that the draft doesn't address the assignment or fulfill its promise to a reader.

REWRITING: FINDING RELATIONSHIPS IN PARAGRAPHS

Attending to coordinate and subordinate relationships within and between paragraphs can become the goal of yet another rewriting cycle.
As students work through the draft a second or third time, they might
examine the density and forward movement of paragraphs. By diagramming a paragraph such as the one below, the student can see that it
contains only two levels of generality, merely lists details, and establishes
few subordinate relationships either within sentences or between them:

> 1 The inside of my jeep is filthy.
> 2 The ashtray hasn't been cleaned in weeks.
> 2 The floor is covered with corn and dirt from our farm.
> 2 The seats are dusty because I haven't driven it in months.
> 2 The ceiling has been spotted by beer and soda pop fights.

Ron did some prewriting, listing *ashtrays, floor, seats, ceiling* under the
general heading "My jeep is filthy," but he didn't probe the subject much
beyond that. Consequently, the draft only reproduces his prewriting list.

Fortunately, the draft eventually reveals Ron's purpose for discussing
the jeep. In the last sentence of his essay, he writes, "Nevertheless, I'll
never part with my jeep." Like many students, Ron wrote his way toward
the point he wanted to make, which appears at the end of his draft
rather than at the beginning, where a reader expects to find it. Ron
intended to describe his jeep in such a way that its imperfections "nevertheless" increase its value. Keeping the "nevertheless" intention in mind,
he can begin rewriting the paragraph. First, he must invent new material
to point up the contrast between "filth that most people object to" and
"filth that gives my jeep character." "If most people object to dirty
ashtrays," he might ask himself, "why don't I?" After he has explored
these contrasts, he must rework the sentences, incorporating more subordination to express the "nevertheless" relationship. The revised version
looks like this:

> 1 Although most people think my jeep is filthy, I can't bring myself
>   to clean it.
> 2 The ashtray hasn't been cleaned in weeks.
>   3 I won't empty it though because my parents won't let me
>   smoke in the house, and when I'm in my jeep I can do what
>   I want to.
> 2 The floor is covered with corn and dirt from our farm.
>   3 All the same, I haven't vacuumed it because I'm proud of
>   being a country boy and don't mind carrying my turf around
>   with me.
> 2 The seats stay dusty because I've had too much work to do
>   after school lately to take the jeep out of the driveway.
> 2 The interior is a mess, the ceiling and upholstery spotted by
>   beer and soda pop fights.

3 They remind me of all the good times I've had with my friends on weekends.

Although the paragraph could benefit from yet another revision to tighten sentences, at least now Ron's identified the relationships that hold the paragraph together. Furthermore, he's added reasons to support the bald statements in the first draft, decreased the distance between himself and his topic, and used the description of his filthy jeep to characterize himself. Rewriting has helped him clarify his purpose for the paper.

Some paragraphs require less substantial rewriting. Students can improve them by adjusting the topic or promise sentence, by adding, deleting, substituting, or reordering supporting details, by improving transitions, or by reorganizing sentences to take advantage of emphatic sentence position. In the following paragraph, the writer has established chains of equivalent terms to hold the paragraph together. These "equivalence chains" give readers recognizable signals for proceeding smoothly through the paragraph:[2]

> One of the functions of a society is to make its inhabitants feel safe, and Americans devote more of their time and collective resources to security than to any other need. Yet Americans do not feel safe, despite (or because of) shotguns in the closet and nuclear bombers patrolling overhead. With each decade we seem to accumulate more fears, and most of these fears seem to be about each other. In the fifties, we were afraid of Communists, and although we now feel sheepish about that moment of panic, we express today the same kinds of fear towards blacks and feminists; and in our reactions to all of these fears we have created some very real dangers.

Some paragraphs, however, can't be improved by removing irrelevant material, making sentence subjects similar, or establishing equivalence chains. The following paragraph already has consistent sentence subjects:

> *Draft:* The store went out of business. It did not attract enough customers. It had a good location, but its merchandise was over-

2. *Equivalence* is a technical term borrowed from structural linguists who study the linguistic features—the recurrence of words, parts of words, and phrases, for example—that give texts cohesion; see M. A. K. Halliday and Rugaiya Hasan, *Cohesion in English* (London: Longman, 1976). See also "Cohesion, Coherence, and Incoherence" in Marilyn M. Cooper and Michael Holzman, *Writing as Social Action* (Portsmouth, NH: Boynton/Cook, 1989), pp. 94–107.

priced. Its salespeople were not helpful. (William Mahaney, *Workbook of Current English*, p. 293)

The problem here is short, choppy sentences. The paragraph reads like a randomly ordered list of facts. If the writer were to combine the sentences, he'd realize that he doesn't have enough material for a paragraph:

> *Revision:* The store went out of business, in spite of its ideal location, because its overpriced merchandise and rude salespeople drove customers away.

Now the "paragraph" has become a tight topic or promise sentence. By inventing additional material, the writer can develop a new paragraph that explains why the "overpriced merchandise" and "rude salespeople" put the store out of business.

REWRITING: FINDING SENTENCE PROBLEMS

Because most writers have enough trouble simply getting their ideas onto the page in an initial draft, they can't worry about polishing sentences the first time around. Writers who do may have difficulty completing a draft. Sentence work can come later, when the message is clearer and supporting evidence seems in place. That is when sentence combining, for example, will help rid sentences of deadwood and create varied prose rhythms. Moving through a draft, a few sentences at a time, gives students a chance to review relationships between sentences, embedding one sentence into another, revising punctuation, condensing piled up prepositional phrases into single modifiers, adding adverbs and adjectives, substituting action verbs for lifeless *be* and *have*, weeding out unnecessary passive constructions, reordering phrases, and undangling participles.

Rewriting sentences will be especially troublesome for students who believe that fancy vocabulary and wordiness define "good writing." Their prose may contain one-third to one-half "lard," a term Richard Lanham uses to characterize stylistic problems that not only lengthen sentences unnecessarily but also obscure meaning. To reduce the lard, he recommends that writers analyze their sentences using the "Paramedic Method":

1. Circle the prepositions.
2. Circle the "is" forms.
3. Ask, "Where's the action?" "Who's kicking who?"
4. Put this "kicking" action into a simple (not compound) active verb.
5. Start fast—no slow windups.
6. Write out each sentence on a blank sheet of paper and mark off its basic rhythmic units with a "/".
7. Mark off sentence lengths in the passage with a big "/" between sentences.

8. Read the passage aloud with emphasis and feeling.

(*Revising Prose*, p. xii)

Guided by this method, students can "get the lard out" by rewriting sentences such as the following:

Original: This sentence is in need of an active verb.
Revision: This sentence needs an active verb. (6 words instead of 9; lard factor = 33%) (*Revising Prose*, p. 3)

Original: I think that all I can usefully say on this point is that in the normal course of their professional activities social anthropologists are usually concerned with the third of these alternatives, while the other two levels are treated as raw data for analysis.
Revision: Social anthropologists usually concentrate on the third alternative, treating the other two as raw data. (15 words instead of 44; lard factor = 66%) (*Revising Prose*, p. 47)

Lard adds up when it accumulates over several sentences. Removing it is sometimes simply a matter of making every word count—and deleting words that don't:

> The opening paragraph is an important one. It should announce your topic and the restrictions and limitations that you yourself have placed upon that topic. It should make clear your point of view, your style, and your tone. Moreover, it should demonstrate your confidence and control, the assurance that you as author know exactly where you want to go and how you plan to get there. Sounds easy and obvious. And yet opening paragraphs—or, to be more precise, effective opening paragraphs are often the most difficult of all to sit down and write.

Finally, writers must devote one reading of the draft to proofreading and editing. Students who tend to overlook misspellings may spot them by reading their papers backward, beginning with the last word. Reading the paper aloud also helps identify stilted phrases or unreasonably convoluted sentences that went undetected earlier.

Approached as a series of purposeful cycles, rewriting requires several readings of a draft, each with a different emphasis. We read it first to evaluate our message and the relationships we're establishing among writer, reader, and subject. Then we read to test the overall organization, rediscovering our message and strengthening the relationships between inner parts and outer shape. In another reading, we examine paragraph structure; in another, sentence construction and diction. Finally, we clean up the surface features, attending to punctuation, mechanics, and spelling.

Although experienced writers can juggle two or three objectives simultaneously, students may need to move more slowly until they get the hang of it. Some students find it helpful to recopy the draft after attending to global concerns and structural problems, say, and before moving on to sentence revision and editing. Others are more comfortable making several passes through a draft on a word processor, each time attending to a different concern. Although students should feel free to prepare a clean text at any time, I wouldn't require them to recopy their papers for two reasons. First, although each reading may focus on a particular set of decisions, those decisions are intimately related to other choices the writer has made. As students examine individual paragraphs, for example, they necessarily must evaluate sentences, consider the overall organization, and determine if the paragraph realizes prewriting decisions about purpose and audience. Recopying drafts too often removes the evidence of these decisions and forces writers to spend considerable time reconstructing them if it turns out later that they were effective choices after all. Second, recopying drafts is boring and inefficient. It reduces the amount of time students devote to reviewing their work, lengthens the time between cycles, and prevents students from applying what they've learned in one reading to subsequent readings. Students need to recopy drafts only when it helps to record on a clean page the changes made during one cycle before going on to the next. Several purposeful *readings* of the draft are necessary; endless drafts aren't. With practice, students can complete the cycles of rewriting in the second or third draft.

WRITING WORKSHOPS

We can promote careful attention to rewriting in several ways. My students turn in all of their drafts when they submit final copies of their papers. I don't grade their scratch work and drafts, but looking them over helps me determine what rewriting strategies students find useful and which ones they're avoiding. From time to time, I copy a "before" and "after" version of a student's paper to illustrate what messy, thoughtful rewriting looks like.

Commenting on drafts, rather than final papers, is also helpful. When we write comments on drafts or discuss them with students in conference, writers can benefit from our opinions and suggestions. They still have time before the assignment is due to take our feedback into account. Because we will discuss written responses to students' writing in the next chapter, we won't go into the subject in detail here. But for my money, commenting on drafts makes more sense than commenting on final versions. If we're going to spend the time it takes to offer students sound advice, let's offer it when it does some good, when students are still working on a project, not after it's finished.

We also can turn our classes into writing workshops. When the first edition of this book appeared, writing workshops were new. Now they are standard practice. Letting students help one another develop and rewrite their papers has several benefits.[3] Writing workshops insure that students compose papers in stages, not the night before they are due. They allow students to exchange solutions to writing problems and become responsible for their own learning. They provide an audience other than the teacher and immerse students in a community of readers and writers. Students in workshop settings see a great deal more writing than they would in a traditional writing class. As they give one another advice and use it to develop their own messages, they learn relatively quickly what good writing is. Good writing is no longer a matter of psyching out the teacher or conforming to standards in a handbook. It is writing that readers, including classmates, find interesting and effective. Writing workshops give teachers new roles too. We stop being lecturers and become enablers, planning activities to help students learn from one another, monitoring students' work, offering help when it's requested, and evaluating the effectiveness of groupwork.

To be effective, writing workshops need careful planning. For one thing, students aren't accustomed to working in groups. They're used to sitting passively or competing against one another for grades. Initially, students need explicit instructions for using their time in groups constructively. Second, when students "play teacher," they often adopt the hypercritical, authoritative tone of the comments they've read on their papers. They need guidance in giving constructive advice, even a language for offering helpful feedback. To encourage responsible collaboration, we must structure groupwork carefully, assign manageable tasks, and state our expectations clearly, at least until students have learned to work together. Although teachers can organize workshops several ways, the following suggestions offer a useful place to begin:

1. Divide the class into heterogeneous groups of five to seven students, ensuring that each group is as diverse as possible with respect to gender, race, age, and writing ability. Groups smaller than five sometimes mean that one student alone must arbitrate disagreements; groups larger than seven often develop cliques. Encourage students to get to know group members through risk-free in-class assignments that build trust. Once students seem comfortable talking with one another, keep the groups together for the entire term. If personality conflicts arise, help the groups resolve them instead of shuffling students (and problems) around. Realigning the groups means that students must get to know one another all over again.

3. For a discussion of how writing workshops encourage active learning, see Kenneth A. Bruffee, *Collaborative Learning: Higher Education, Interdependence, and the Authority of Knowledge* (Baltimore: Johns Hopkins University Press, 1993). Useful advice about the roles teachers and students assume in workshop settings is found in Steven Zemelman and Harvey Daniels, "Climate in the Classroom," in *A Community of Writers* (Portsmouth, NH: Heinemann, 1988), pp. 47–68; and James D. Williams, "The Classroom as Workshop," in *Preparing to Teach Writing*, 2d ed. (Mahwah, NJ: Lawrence Erlbaum Associates, 1998), pp. 79–98.

2. Give the groups specific work to do and define it concretely. Begin with brief tasks taking perhaps ten or fifteen minutes. As students become more experienced, workshop tasks can expand to twenty or thirty minutes (workshops lasting longer than half an hour can begin to be unproductive). The first time, for example, students might read the entire paper but examine only the first paragraph in detail, rewriting the introduction together to clarify the writer's promise. Or students might choose a paragraph that looks skimpy, writer and reader helping each other generate additional support. Begin with the concrete words on the page and ask students to apply one or two rewriting strategies at a time. Later on, the groups can focus on whole compositions and more abstract concerns of purpose, audience, and message. Sometimes, it helps to duplicate instructions for workshop activities so that every student has a copy. The Framework for Judging (p. 127) is a useful, flexible list. Early in the term, students might review one another's drafts by responding only to the first two or three sets of questions from the framework. Later on, they might use all of the questions, taking longer to write down and discuss their responses. An important strategy for getting workshops off to a constructive start is focusing on something other than punctuation and grammatical problems. Rewriting involves more than editing, a principle you want to establish early on.

3. Give students a language for discussing their work. In the beginning, they won't know what to ask one another or how to express their impressions of a classmate's draft. So before the workshop gets underway, demonstrate the activity with the whole class, modeling the kinds of issues you want discussed and the talk you expect to hear. Illustrate the task by discussing a student's draft or examples taken from students' previous work. In the early part of the term, it helps to let writers talk first, explaining their intentions and setting the agenda for the kind of help they want. You may want to write some conversation starters on the board so that students can refer to them during groupwork. Here are some examples:

> *Writer:* "The main point I wanted to get across in this paragraph was . . . ."
> "What do you still need to know that I haven't told you?"
> "My biggest worry about this paper is . . . ."
> *Reader:* "The best thing about this paper is . . . ."
> "What part of the paper gave you the most trouble?"
> "As a reader, the part of your paper that most confused me was . . . ."

Workshops early in the term should begin with the writer's explanation of some strategy or problem in the draft. When the writer speaks first, the reader must postpone the impulse to suggest, "You should have done thus and so." Discussions also should begin by noting strengths, using them to improve weak sections of the paper. When writers or readers identify a problem, they should explain *why* it's a problem and *how* to solve it. Otherwise, the workshop deteriorates into fault finding rather than problem solving.

By about the middle of the term, students will have gained confidence in giving and receiving advice and will understand its value in improving the final draft. Now's the time to ensure that advice is rigorous. Continue modeling workshop tasks, perhaps previewing a handout of four to six questions you have prepared. Reverse the turn taking and ask readers to speak first, explaining a problem they see and helping the writer solve it. Writers should be less fragile by this time and need to hear where and why a draft confuses a reader. Workshops should involve more than talk. Students can read a draft and write a paragraph about it before discussing it with the writer. Or they might write responses to questions you have given them on a handout. Talk is useful, but writers can take written responses home with them to consult as they rewrite the draft. If necessary, duplicate sample responses to discuss with the class so that students can improve their written suggestions.

4. Monitor the groups to make sure students use their time productively and phrase comments constructively. Make one relatively quick pass through the class in the first few minutes of an activity to be sure all students understand what they are supposed to do. Students who have no draft should sit slightly apart from the group and write one; excluding them from the activity usually ensures that they will be prepared next time. Once everyone has begun working, spend some time observing each group, standing near the group but able to see most of the class as well. Listen carefully to the kind of talk going on, intervening only when a group seems uncertain about what it's supposed to be doing or is obviously wasting time. When students request "teacher's opinion," avoid giving it. Respond instead with a question that helps the group examine the draft more closely or enables students to arbitrate the issue themselves. In this way, you wean them from seeing you as the only authority and encourage them to become independent critics of their own prose. If you intervene in groupwork too often, you wind up teaching several classes instead of just one and deprive students of opportunities to take responsibility for their own learning. Later in the term, you may decide to observe the groups less frequently, but don't assume that groupwork gives you a "free period." Use the time to read over students' shoulders or to give special help to students who need it.

At the end of a workshop activity, take a few minutes to evaluate or debrief it. Share with the students some of your observations as you monitored their work. You might point out, for example, how one group solved a disagreement about the assignment, or ask a student to read a particularly detailed response to a draft, or praise another student for encouraging quieter members of the group to speak up. Remind students that they are free to accept or reject a classmate's advice but only after seriously considering the reader's perspective. Ask students what kinds of suggestions they found most useful and explain why such comments as "Everything looks fine" offer writers little help. Communicating your assessment of the workshop enables students to adjust their behavior and their language so that next time their responses to classmates' drafts will be even more constructive.

Planned carefully, writing workshops realize the primary objective of a writing course: students and teachers writing, reading, discussing, and improving one another's work. Although students need practice learning how to work together and guidance in evaluating drafts effectively, workshops are one of the best ways to teach students to become independent critics. Many students regard workshops as one of the most helpful features of a writing course. Even teachers who prefer more traditional course designs still find groupwork helpful, especially when scheduled a few days before a paper is due. Then students seem most receptive to constructive comments on drafts and most likely to incorporate specific suggestions in rewriting the paper. Students who typically postpone drafting until the night before an assignment deadline may still write their drafts the night before "workshop day," but they'll also have a few more days to rewrite it prior to the deadline. At first, we must direct their work closely, cutting off escape routes and making rewriting more attractive than calling the first draft "finished." In time, however, rewriting becomes less novel, a more natural stage of composing, a way of insuring that final drafts represent the students' best work.

STUDENT-GENERATED CRITERIA

Rewriting calls attention to the criteria for good writing. All teachers (or their surrogates, the textbooks) spend some time enumerating the qualities of effective papers. The discussion usually remains pretty one-sided though, the teacher like Moses delivering the ten commandments of acceptable English prose. Instead of legislating these stylistic do's and don't's, we can encourage the class to develop its own guidelines. It takes time, and we'll have to pose questions about areas students have overlooked, but in the long run, student-generated criteria have several advantages. First, they allow us to change roles. Instead of acting as lawgivers and rule enforcers, we become advisors, helping students define and attain standards that the class, not the teacher, has established. To be sure, teachers have an obligation to make clear the standards by which student writing will be judged, but unless students can anticipate what constitutes a successful response to an assignment, they will continue to write poorly, in our classes and in other courses. Second, when students develop their own definitions of "good writing," they become better at solving writing problems. Teacher or textbook criteria often limit a student's practical understanding of writing principles. Student-generated criteria express principles of good writing in language students understand, weaning them from the security they seek (and unfortunately, have come to expect) by asking us, "What do you want in this paper?"

The hidden agenda, of course, is that students will develop criteria similar to those we'd use anyway. We communicate our expectations implicitly and explicitly in every class meeting, as we teach, as we explain workshop and in-class activities, as we guide students in discussing their papers with one another. Student-generated criteria merely synthesize class discussion and record generalizations students infer from examining one another's work. Generating criteria for good writing can be as complicated as developing a rubric for each assignment, a process discussed in Chapter 14, or as simple as building a checklist. The checklist reproduced below was not generated all at once. It developed gradually, throughout the course, as students discussed assignments, sample papers, and one another's drafts. From time to time, we ended class discussion or a writing workshop by defining additional principles to add to the list. Although no two classes will develop identical lists, the one below frames its criteria as questions intended to guide rewriting:

Subject, Audience, Purpose

1. What's the most important thing I want to say about my subject?
2. Who am I writing this paper for? What would my reader want to know about the subject? What does my reader already know about it?
3. Why do I think the subject is worth writing about? Will my reader think the paper was worth reading?
4. What verb explains what I'm trying to do in this paper (*tell a story, compare X and Y, describe Z*)?
5. Does my first paragraph answer questions 1–4? If not, why not?

Organization

6. How many specific points did I make about my subject? Did I overlap or repeat any points? Did I leave any points out or add some that aren't relevant to the main idea?
7. How many paragraphs did I use to talk about each point?
8. Why did I talk about them in this order? Should the order be changed?
9. How did I get from one point to the next? What signposts did I give the reader?

Paragraphing (*Ask these questions of every paragraph*)

10. What job is this paragraph supposed to do? How does it relate to the paragraph before and after it?
11. What's the topic idea? Will my reader have trouble finding it?

12. How many sentences did it take to develop the topic idea? Can I substitute better examples, reasons, or details?
13. How well does the paragraph hold together? How many levels of generality does it have? Are the sentences different lengths and types? Do I need transitions? When I read the paragraph out loud, did it flow smoothly?

Sentences (Ask these questions of every sentence)

14. Which sentences in my paper do I like the most? The least?
15. Can my reader "see" what I'm saying? What words could I substitute for *people, things, this/that, aspect,* and so forth?
16. Is this sentence "fat"? (Apply the "Paramedic Method.")
17. Can I combine this sentence with another one?
18. Can I add adjectives and adverbs or find a more lively verb?

Things To Check Last

19. Did I check spelling and punctuation? What kinds of words do I usually misspell? What kinds of punctuation problems did I have in my last paper?
20. How does my paper end? Did I keep the promises I made to my reader at the beginning of the paper?
21. When I read the assignment again, did I miss anything?
22. What do I like best about this paper? What do I need to work on in the next paper?

Students need to view rewriting as more than editing, polishing, or proofreading, as more than correcting flaws in papers we've already graded. Although a draft represents an initial attempt to express a message, most writers don't find its meaning and form until they've reviewed the draft. Students need time to let their compositions grow. They need to examine every level of the discourse, review the decisions they made, and incorporate responses from teachers and other students. They may rewrite the piece several times until they're satisfied that it says what they mean. But so must all writers, even talented ones such as Hemingway, who revised the last page of *Farewell to Arms* thirty-nine times before it suited him. Hearing that, an interviewer asked him, "Was there some technical problem there? What was it that had you stumped?" "Getting the words right," he replied.

part three

TEACHING AS RHETORIC

thirteen

Developing Writing Assignments

A problem well put is half solved.

JOHN DEWEY

TRADITIONAL ASSIGNMENTS

When teachers confront a set of student papers, they begin evaluating them by reading the first word of the first paper in the stack. That's not the best place to begin. Because each composition represents a response to a specific "invitation" to write, the problems in many papers may be the fault, not of the writer, but of the assignment. Before we discuss what evaluating student writing entails, let's first examine assignments, which significantly influence our students' work.

How would you react if an administrator on whom your job depends asked you to respond in writing to the following invitations?

1. "My School"
2. Write a letter to one of your students' parents.
3. Describe the top of your desk.
4. Only ten percent of the students in our department fail their English courses.
5. Assume that you're about to be fired. Defend yourself.

If your job really depended on completing these five assignments, you'd have every right to be angry. You've got very little to go on. You've no idea what criteria will be used to evaluate your responses, and each assignment raises so many questions you'd scarcely know where to begin. What about my school? Am I supposed to describe it, praise it, suggest improvements? What kind of letter am I supposed to write? What, for heaven's sake, has the top of my desk to do with anything? And what's the significance of the percentage in number 4? Does it mean that we're not failing enough students or that we should be proud that so many complete our courses successfully? And how can I defend myself if I don't know why I'm being fired?

Although each assignment raises enough questions to make responding to it an unsavory experience, the five topics are typical of assignments traditionally given students in writing courses.

Group 1

"My Hometown"

"My First Semester of College"

"My Favorite Sport/Teacher/TV Program"

Group 2

Write a friendly letter.

Write a letter applying for a job.

Write a letter to the editor of the school newspaper.

Write a letter to your school principal/mayor/state representative.

Group 3

Describe your bedroom.

Define *freedom*.

Compare Marlow and Kurtz.

Group 4

Jonathan Swift has an unmistakable style.

Studying foreign languages offers excellent preparation for careers in business.

Group 5

Pretend that you are an animal.

Assume that you've wrecked the family car.

Write a composition defending multiple-choice tests.

But surely all of these topics can't be faulty? No, they're not. They all contain at least one feature of carefully designed writing assignments. But each group also omits information that would strengthen a student's response. To evaluate these assignments, let's return briefly to the communication triangle.

DEFINING A RHETORICAL PROBLEM

Before writers can respond to an assignment, they must define for themselves a rhetorical problem. Defining the problem requires, at the least, assessing their relationship to the subject and the reader.

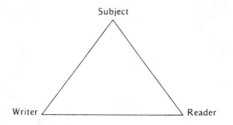

Who am I writing this for and what responses am I trying to effect in my reader? Is my audience predisposed toward reading what I have to say? What do I know about my subject? How do I feel about it? Can I commit myself to addressing it honestly? What angle or point of view can I take in treating the topic? Beyond answering questions like these, writers also juggle other constraints: a deadline for the assignment, concerns about doing well, the demands of a form (letter, essay, report), an aim (persuasive, referential, self-expressive, literary), and a mode (classification, narration, description, evaluation).

Effective writing assignments encourage students to define progressively more complex rhetorical problems. Because students learn to write by writing, our responsibility is to control and vary the rhetorical demands of writing tasks. When we do, we give students practice adjusting relationships among writer, reader, and subject, manipulating more and more complex variables. However, most writing assignments, like those in the five groups, leave too many variables to chance. They don't provide enough information to help students define rich rhetorical problems. Instead, they present students with a "paper-writing problem," a meaningless exercise in jumping hurdles for a grade.

The titles in group one, for example, suggest a broad subject but present no additional information. Consequently, students are likely to produce vague, general compositions addressed to the teacher or to no one in particular. Although the topics encourage students to draw on personal experiences, a strength, are they really worth committing oneself to? When, in real life, are writers required to address such topics? What purpose can students find for responding to the assignment? What constitutes a successful response?

The assignments in group two are better. They specify an audience and a form of discourse, but they explain neither the subject nor the purpose for writing. Group three's assignments spell out modes of discourse and a broad subject but fail to address audience, purpose, and form. If students dared question the teacher, they could legitimately ask why it should matter to anyone what their bedrooms look like. The

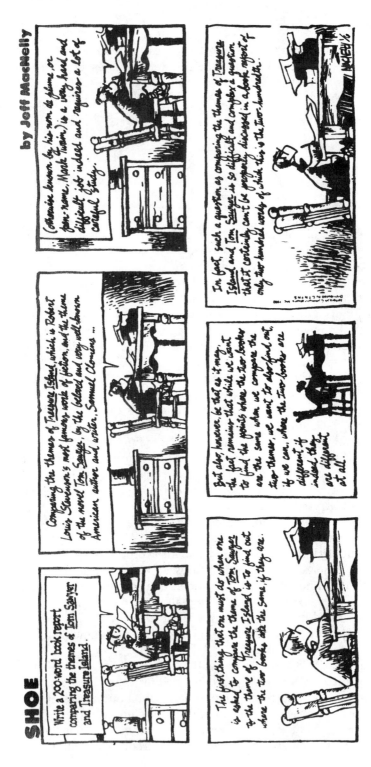

FIGURE 13.1 By permission of Creators Syndicate, Inc.

statements in group four represent conclusions about a topic. They're often prefaced by "Comment on the following statement" or followed by "Do you agree or disagree?" The statements usually restrict the subject and express a point of view; they also may imply a purpose for the assignment, a mode of development, and the kinds of support students can use. However, they do not specify audience (or presume it to be the teacher), and they should phrase more explicitly what aim, mode, and perhaps support is required so that students have a clearer rhetorical context for their response.

The assignments in group five specify a subject—an animal, a car wreck, multiple-choice tests—and suggest a stance to adopt. They encourage role-playing, which sometimes allows students to imagine unfamiliar rhetorical situations. The first assignment—Pretend that you are an animal—suggests a silly role, or at best, one irrelevant to a writing course. Unless it's intended to interest very young writers, the assignment serves no real purpose and gives students no practice with the kinds of writing they encounter in school or adult life. The second assignment—Assume that you've wrecked the family car—makes a good beginning but needs development. It doesn't tell students what to do with the situation they imagine themselves in. What's the purpose of the assignment? Who's the audience? A parent? A police officer? Someone who can repair the car? What form of discourse does the assignment call for? The third assignment—Write a composition defending multiple-choice tests—forces students to adopt a stance on testing that they may not in fact support, consequently insisting that some students write dishonestly. The assignment would be more helpful if it specified an audience, gave students a choice between attacking or defending the tests, and suggested some criteria for constructing an effective argument, such as "Support your position with at least four reasons."

All writing assignments must account for more variables than a phrase or even one sentence can identify.[1] If we omit some of the factors that, in real life, help us define rhetorical contexts, we can expect students to perform poorly. Even if we give students complete freedom in defining some elements of the assignment, in some way we must *account for* (but not necessarily spell out) all of the following variables:

1. The students' interest in and understanding of the subject
2. The purpose or aim of the composition
3. The audience (which needn't always be the teacher)
4. A role for the student to take with respect to the subject and audience

1. Donald M. Murray gives excellent advice on developing writing assignments; he distinguishes between "open" and "closed" assignments in *A Writer Teaches Writing*, 2d ed. (Boston: Houghton Mifflin, 1985), pp. 94–102. See also James D. Williams, "Writing Assignments," in *Preparing to Teach Writing* 2d ed. (Mahwah, NJ: Lawrence Erlbaum Associates, 1998), pp. 242–57.

5. The form of discourse (which needn't always be an essay)
6. Criteria for success.

Assignments also may include due dates and descriptions of what the final presentation should look like. In addition, many assignments offer prewriting help, perhaps furnishing important data or posing a few leading questions (although too many questions may overwhelm students and provoke incoherent, undeveloped responses).

Let's consider the following example to see how it accounts for the six features listed above:

> "Carolina: Preparing for a Lifetime" advertises the university to prospective students. Analyze the brochure to determine whether or not it is generally effective. Then report your findings in a three-page letter addressed to the admissions counselors who wrote the brochure. A successful letter will state clearly whether or not the brochure is generally effective and will support this claim by analyzing relevant evidence such as textual information, pictures, and layout. Drafts are due on Thursday, December 3; the final version is due on Tuesday, December 8.

Are students likely to have some interest in and understanding of the subject? Probably, if they are high school or first-year college students. The students completing this assignment were first-semester college students who had received similar promotional materials from several institutions in the course of applying to college. Having completed orientation and several weeks of classes, these students could be expected to develop a claim about the brochure's general effectiveness. They had sufficient personal experience with university life to judge whether or not the brochure misrepresented the university and contained adequate information for prospective students. Most students found the brochure "generally effective" but offered suggestions for improving it. A few students did not think that it was effective and marshaled evidence to support that claim. The assignment's "whether or not" permits either option and consequently avoids obligating students to take a position that they may not in fact support.

The primary purpose or aim of the assignment is to "analyze this brochure." In a college writing course that stresses analysis and argumentation, this aim would be appropriate. An assignment usually reveals its purpose in one crucial verb, *analyze* in this case, and much of the challenge in drafting effective assignments involves making the purpose-verb clear. When I draft an assignment I often find that I have included several verbs that students could interpret as clues to the assignment's purpose. As I revise the assignment, I try to "clear the field" of these distractions. Keeping an assignment short also allows the purpose-verb to stand out.

Other verbs, especially "to determine" and "report your findings," complicate our sample assignment. The task requires both analysis (examining the elements of the brochure, considering their function and relationship to one another, and evaluating the parts in relation to the whole) and argumentation (proving the claim). Because students must use analysis in the service of argument, the assignment is challenging. It presupposes that students have already practiced simple analysis and written simple arguments. Notice that the verbs in the assignment define the process writers must follow to complete the task successfully. That is, students must first analyze the brochure, then use their analysis to determine its effectiveness, then report their findings in a letter. Organizing the task in this way advises students that forming an opinion about the brochure first, before they have analyzed it carefully, may weaken their letters.

The audience is "the admissions counselors who wrote the brochure," a relatively difficult audience for students to gauge because they may be unfamiliar with the work admissions counselors perform. The assignment requires students not only to reconstruct the counselors' decisions in developing the brochure but also to address a group audience instead of a single individual. The class spent considerable time discussing the audience for this assignment and sent representatives to the admissions office to interview counselors, research that helped students understand how the brochure was used and why it included certain information.

The assignment omits explicit information defining the student's role. Implicitly, however, students must adopt the role of "consumer-critic." They are consumers because they form part of the audience for whom the brochure was intended; critics, because the assignment requires them to judge the brochure's effectiveness, to evaluate it. Both roles are reasonable, real roles that students can imagine for themselves.

The form, "a three-page letter," serves the purposes of this assignment better than an essay would. Essays are not customary means of conveying evaluative information to admissions counselors; essays report findings to English teachers. If we want students to produce meaningful writing, we must design meaningful assignments, tasks that encourage students to use writing to act. An essay response to this assignment encourages writing for a grade. A letter or memorandum, on the other hand, establishes a connection between school-sponsored writing and the world outside school. Outside school, consumers report their opinions about products such as brochures in letters.

Spelling out the "criteria for success" is important for several reasons. As we draft assignments, the criteria help us determine in advance the *most significant* features we expect to find in students' responses. The criteria also help focus class discussion and groupwork and make our expectations unmistakably clear to students. Discussing the demands of an assignment in class is important, but if students miss that class, misunderstand our verbal instructions, or fail to take notes, they are doomed. When the assignment puts this crucial information in writing, students can refer to it when they need to: "A successful letter will state clearly whether or not the brochure is generally effective and will support this claim by analyzing relevant evidence such as textual information, pictures, and layout." A statement such as this need not list all the features we expect to see in an A paper, but it should define the most important ones.

As our discussion of the sample assignment makes clear, writing good instructions is difficult. It requires knowing our students well, anticipating problems, finding words to describe the task, and avoiding whatever clutter may distract students from it. Slapping topics on the blackboard or explaining things as we go takes less time, but if an assignment is to teach composing, we must prepare it as carefully as we do each class meeting. In writing it down, we must decide its function as a teaching tool, assess its relation to other assignments, and plan other kinds of instruction—class discussions and groupwork—to support the assignment. Although writing assignments also must take into account the abilities of students and the progression of the course, the following questions should help you design rich rhetorical problems for students to solve.

A Heuristic for Designing Writing Assignments

1. *What do I want the students to do?* Is it worth doing? Why? What will the assignment tell me about what they've learned? How does it fit my objectives at this point in the course? Does the assignment assess what students can *do* or what they *know*? Am I relating their work to the real world (including academic settings) or only to my class? Does the assignment require specialized knowledge? Does it appeal to the interests and experiences of my students?

2. *How do I want them to do the assignment?* Are students working alone or together? In what ways will they practice prewriting, writing, and rewriting? Are writing, reading, speaking, and listening reinforcing one another? Have I given students enough information to make effective choices about the subject, purpose, form, and mode?

3. *For whom are students writing?* Who is the audience? Do students have enough information to assume a role with respect to the audience? Is the role meaningful?

4. *When will students do the assignment?* How does the assignment relate to what comes before and after it in the course? How much time in and outside of class will students need for pre-writing, writing, and rewriting? To what extent will I guide the students' work? What kinds of help can students constructively offer one another? What deadlines do I want to set for collecting the students' papers (or various stages of the project)?

5. *What will I do with the assignment?* How will I evaluate the work? What constitutes a "successful" response to the assignment? Will other students or the writer have a say in evaluating the paper? What problems did I encounter when I wrote my response to this assignment? How can I improve the assignment?

Beyond developing effective individual assignments, writing teachers also must arrange them in some sequence, a subject we will discuss in more detail in Chapter 15. Because writing teachers don't share a consistent philosophy of teaching or of language learning, the profession has yet to develop a consensus on what the best sequence of assignments might be for any group of writers. Many beginning teachers inherit courses already outlined for them in curriculum guides and course manuals someone else has designed. Experienced teachers may develop their own courses, making altogether independent decisions about what they want students to do or adhering to minimal guidelines developed in consultation with other teachers. Sequencing assignments is difficult because it requires us to answer important questions about what writing is and how people learn. How we answer these questions defines our philosophy of teaching, which in turn shapes the writing courses we teach.

fourteen

Responding to Student Writing

The writing teacher must not be a judge, but a physician. His job is not to punish, but to heal.

DONALD M. MURRAY

THE BASICS AND TESTING

The writing teacher's primary responsibility, Charles Cooper maintains, is to guide students through the composing process.

> To do that the teacher will have to be concerned mainly with the *essence* of compositions, rather than the *accidents* of transcriptions, to use Janet Emig's terms. Unfortunately, just as we're learning what to do about the essences, some people are using the talk about basic skills to revive misplaced concern with the accidents; but surely the *most* basic of all the writing skills are matters of persona, audience, and purpose and the word and sentence adjustments the writer makes as he tries to speak with a certain voice to a special audience on a particular topic. ("Responding to Student Writing," p. 32)

Perhaps no words have generated as much controversy among teachers, parents, and the public as "basics," "minimal competence," and "testing." For most people, each word has psychologically comfortable, positive connotations. Who can oppose what is basic? Surely none of us supports *in*competence. And how many of us mathematically inept English teachers would dispute the numbers that experts attach to tests? As a society we've learned to trust statistics. I.Q. scores reveal how smart we are. SAT and ACT scores determine whether or not we may enter college. "Leading economic indicators" tell us our dollars won't buy what they did ten years ago. Insurance figures predict how we're likely to die. Casualty figures released weekly during the Vietnam war told us we were winning.

With similar illogic, many people believe that we can solve educational problems through legislatively mandated competency tests. Test results presumably will tell us if students learn, teachers teach, and the curriculum is sound. "The effectiveness of minimum competency tests," writes Kenneth Goodman, "depends on the truth of some or all of five propositions:

1. Failure to achieve is due to a lack of school standards.
2. Student failure is largely the result of lack of teacher concern for student success, or teacher mediocrity or both.
3. Solutions for teaching-learning problems are built into current, traditional materials and methods.
4. Test performance is the same as competence; furthermore, existing tests can be used for accurate individual assessment and prediction.
5. If students are required to succeed they will.

None of these propositions, however, is true. ("Minimum Standards: A Moral View," p. 5)

For many educators, going "back to the basics" has become synonymous with going back to the secure good old days, which our selective memories usually recall as having been better than the good old present. In the main, advocates of testing programs are concerned about students, understand the problems teachers face, and want to help solve those problems. Testing students, they believe, will help resolve the literacy crisis.

Many researchers, however, insist that standardized tests aren't valid measures of writing performance. "Although widely used," write Charles Cooper and Lee Odell, "standardized tests measure only editing skills—choosing the best sentence, recognizing correct usage, punctuation, and captialization" (*Evaluating Writing*, p. viii). Writing teachers, confronted with considerable pressure to submit to accountability-through-testing must educate themselves about the uses and abuses of tests.[1] To support teachers and encourage the responsible use of writing tests, the Conference on College Composition and Communication, a constituent organization of the National Council of Teachers of English, has adopted the following Resolution on Testing and Writing:

RESOLVED: that

1. No student shall be given credit for a writing course, placed in a remedial writing course, exempted from a required writing course, or certified for competency without submitting a piece of written discourse.
2. Responsibility for giving credit, exemption, or accreditation shall rest, not with local administrators or state officials, but with the composition faculty in each institution.

---

1. For a comprehensive discussion of issues surrounding assessment, see Edward M. White, *Teaching and Assessing Writing*, 2d ed. (The Jossey-Bass Higher Education Series; San Francisco: Jossey-Bass, 1994).

3. Tests of writing shall be selected and administered under the primary control and supervision of representatives of the composition faculty in each institution.
4. Before multiple choice or so-called objective tests are used, the complexities involved in such testing shall be carefully considered. Most important, these tests shall be examined to determine whether they are appropriate to the intended purpose.
5. Before essay tests are used, the complexities of such tests shall be carefully considered. Most importantly, topics shall be designed with great care. Also, readers of the essay tests shall be trained according to principles of statistically reliable holistic and/or analytic reading.
6. The nature and purpose of the test and the various uses of the results shall be clearly explained to all instructors and students prior to the administration of the test.
7. All possible steps shall be taken to educate the universities and colleges, the public and legislatures that, though composition faculties have principal responsibility for helping students develop writing skills, maintenance of these skills is a responsibility shared by the entire faculty, administration, and the public.
8. The officers and Executive Committee of CCCC shall make testing a major concern in the immediate future in order to provide information and assistance to composition instructors affected by a testing situation.

The impulse to assess competence in writing is not solely an educational issue. Nor is it simply a concern of writing teachers. Increasing economic and political pressures will make testing our students' writing abilities a concern well into the twenty-first century. Although high school teachers are thoroughly familiar with the impulse to "teach to the test," many college teachers have yet to discover how large-scale testing programs affect curriculum, soak up an institution's funding for writing courses, and undermine teachers' authority to assign grades. Whenever possible, teachers should involve themselves in these issues so that students, who are rarely consulted, may demonstrate their writing abilities in ways that are educationally sound and so that teachers in other disciplines must assume greater responsibility for having students write.

DESCRIBING, MEASURING, JUDGING

The papers in Cooper and Odell's *Evaluating Writing: Describing, Measuring, Judging* (1977) provide a comprehensive discussion of techniques for evaluating students' writing. Because writing evaluations have many uses, the editors caution, "It is critical for teachers . . . to know why they are evaluating before they choose measures and procedures" (p. ix). We may evaluate writing for any one of at least eleven reasons:

Administrative

1. Predicting students' grades in English courses.
2. Placing or tracking students or exempting them from English courses.
3. Assigning public letter or number grades to particular pieces of writing and to students' work in an English course.

Instructional

4. Making an initial diagnosis of students' writing problems.
5. Guiding and focusing feedback to student writers as they progress through an English course.

Evaluation and Research

6. Measuring students' growth as writers over a specific time period.
7. Determining the effectiveness of a writing program or a writing teacher.
8. Measuring group differences in writing performance in comparison-group research.
9. Analyzing the performance of a writer chosen for a case study.
10. Describing the writing performance of individuals or groups in developmental studies, either cross-sectional or longitudinal in design.
11. Scoring writing in order to study possible correlates of writing performance.

(Evaluating Writing, p. ix)

This chapter concerns itself principally with the fourth and fifth purposes for evaluating writing. When we diagnose writing problems (item 4 in the list above), we examine students' work descriptively, not to grade it or to respond with comments that students will read, but to determine simply what strengths and weaknesses characterize the paper. "Joan organizes her paper well and knows how to support her main points," we might note, "but her evidence is skimpy, she constructs paragraphs with only two levels of generality, and she consistently misspells words with *ance/ence* and *able/ible* suffixes." Such diagnostic evaluations permit us to design a course of instruction that enhances Joan's development as a writer. For this reason, many teachers treat the first writing assignment diagnostically. It isn't graded; it's mined for information that helps us plan what to teach.

When we respond to student writing (item 5 in the list above) or encourage students to respond to one another's work, we "guide and focus feedback," helping students understand how a reader perceives the writer's message. Sometimes we provide this feedback in conferences;

sometimes we train students to give their classmates good advice. Most of the time, our feedback takes the form of written comments intended to help a student revise a draft or improve a subsequent paper. Writing comments is a form of teaching, a conference on paper. Comments that enhance learning differ from traditional methods of hunting errors and identifying what's wrong with a paper. They also must point out what the student did well, why certain problems undermine effective communication, and how to improve the paper. Comments that teach help students develop effective prewriting, writing, and rewriting strategies. Comments that teach are an open-ended form of evaluation that allows students, guided by responses from the teacher and classmates, to rewrite their drafts or engage the next assignment.

Grading, however, is a closed procedure. Once we assign a grade, we've judged the paper in ways that further revision can't change. Although comments may accompany the grade, most students interpret them not as "feedback" but as a justification for the judgment we've made. From the student's perspective a graded paper is "finished," and additional work won't change either the grade or their feelings about succeeding or failing. Grades represent a necessary form of evaluation, but in this chapter we'll discuss some ways in which grades and our written comments can have a less destructive impact than traditional methods promote.[2]

DIAGNOSTIC READING

The best way to assess students' strengths and weaknesses as writers is to examine carefully samples of their work, ideally two short papers with different discourse aims. Written in class during the first week of the course, these writing samples can tell us what students have already mastered and what areas we need to emphasize. Additional diagnostic evaluations at midterm help us identify improvements students have made since the course began, new problems that emerged as students overcame previous weaknesses, and difficulties that we somehow failed to address and that now need a different approach. At the end of the course, diagnostic evaluations help us determine how students' writing has improved and where the course has failed them.

When we examine a paper diagnostically, we're concerned primarily with describing rather than judging or grading it. Although we inevitably compare it to some mental criteria for effective writing, our primary purpose isn't to determine a letter grade. Rather, we want to know how the students write, what they're having trouble with, and why. To

2. Although experienced teachers seem to have internalized the criteria for A, B, C, D, and F papers, beginning teachers may want a more explicit discussion of grades than they will find in this chapter. I recommend the practical advice William F. Irmscher gives in Chapter 13, "Evaluation," in *Teaching Expository Writing* (New York: Holt, Rinehart and Winston, 1979), pp. 142–78.

demonstrate the procedure, let's examine David's paper, written in forty-five minutes during the second meeting of a first-semester college composition class:

> *Assignment:* Write an essay in which you discuss the way or ways you expect your life to differ from your parents' lives.[3]

> As time changes people's views and outlooks on life change with it. My parents grew up with completely diffrent standards in a completely diffrent time. Because of the time I grew up in, and the time I live in, my life differs greatly from the lives of my parents.
>
> Modern society offers more aid to young people—jobs, school, financial—that my parents could never recieve. Because of this aid my life has been more free than theirs ever was. I have more free time on my hands than they ever did. My parents were, and are, always working to keep and get, the things needed for survival in this life.
>
> Also Because of a higher education than the education of my parents I have diffrent outlooks on life. I have a more well-rounded attitude toward life. I tend to take more things for granted that my parents never would.
>
> We now live in a world of entertainment. My generation has more things in which to occupy their free time that my parents never had.
>
> Because of the time gap separating my parents an I, I have a diffrent lifestyle than they. Lifestyles change with the change of time, and with that so do people's outlook on life.

First we need to look at the assignment. Because it doesn't specify an audience, we shouldn't be surprised to discover that David addresses his composition to his stereotype of the Teacher or to no one in particular. The assignment specifies or implies a mode ("differ" suggests contrast or classification) and a form ("essay"). The topic permits students to draw on personal experience, but it's much too broad. The aim or purpose also may be troublesome because "discuss" can imply "inform," "argue," "explain," and a host of other possibilities. The assignment offers no prewriting help or criteria for success and consequently invites a vague, general response. Given the forty-five-minute time limit, we also can assume that David spent little time prewriting or rewriting the paper.

Indeed, David handled the topic fairly generally. Most of the paragraphs contain only one or two levels of generality. Most of the nouns identify abstractions ("views and outlooks," "modern society," "young people," "well-rounded attitude," "world of entertainment," "lifestyle"). However, David does attempt some classification. He subordinates "jobs,

---

3. The assignment appears among the "Placement Essay Topics" in Mina F. Shaughnessy, *Errors and Expectations: A Guide for the Teacher of Basic Writing* (New York: Oxford University Press, 1977), p. 295.

school, financial" to "aid" in paragraph two and identifies in the three body paragraphs three ways his life differs from his parents'. More "aid" gives him free time and freedom from worry; more education gives him different outlooks on life; a world of entertainment occupies his free time. At the same time, David maintains considerable distance between himself, his subject, and his audience, a stance characteristic of most first papers. Although he probably has quite a bit to say about his life, he might not choose to say it here, certainly not in writing, a more discomfiting medium than speech, and not to a stranger, which is how he must regard his English teacher at the beginning of the term.

Although David hasn't generated enough details to develop the paper effectively, it nevertheless has a structure. He's mastered the five-paragraph formula. The first and last paragraphs repeat the idea that "time gaps" separating two generations create different life-styles and outlooks on life. The three body paragraphs attempt to develop separate subtopics, but the material overlaps, especially when he talks about "free time." David's writing, like that of most first-year students, seems form bound. Form precedes content. David thinks first of the five-paragraph mold and then attempts to find enough material to fill it. He probably needs practice identifying several ways of organizing his work, discovering form *in*, rather than imposing it *on*, the material prewriting generates.

That David stretches himself to find enough to say, a problem prewriting could help him with, also is evident in sentence construction. Students who fear they can't meet a 500-word limit or some self-imposed length requirement often pad their sentences, especially at the end. David does too. The first sentence, for example, might have ended with *change*, but afraid that the paper won't be long enough or that he won't find its message, David adds "with it." Similarly in paragraphs two and three, "in this life" and "toward life" extend sentences that could have closed with *survival* and *attitude* respectively. David writes predominantly simple sentences, but he knows at least one kind of subordination. Four sentences begin with *because*-clauses; the first sentence, with an *as*-clause. He may be avoiding more complex constructions because they'll create additional comma problems; he plays it safe. Risk-free, ungraded sentence-combining exercises might give him greater confidence in varying sentence structures and punctuating them.

Because David writes his way around comma problems, the paper doesn't offer enough evidence to diagnose the logic governing its mispunctuation. Two introductory *because*-clauses are set off; two aren't. The comma in the last sentence correctly separates two independent clauses joined by *and*, but elsewhere, in the first two paragraphs, *and* may govern the misuse of commas. To get at the logic behind these errors, we'd need to discuss the paper with David, asking him why he thinks the misused commas belong there, then pointing out where he's used the comma conventionally and encouraging him to apply what he's done right to the mispunctuated sentences.

A conference with David also might help us understand the logic governing comparisons. David deliberately alternates the conjunction *than* with the relative pronoun *that* to complete comparisons:

That *Constructions*

Subject + Verb + <u>more</u> aid to young people . . . <u>that</u> my parents could (never) recieve.

Subject + Verb + to take <u>more</u> things for granted <u>that</u> my parents (never) would.

Subject + Verb + <u>more</u> things . . . <u>that</u> my parents(never)had.

Than *Constructions*

Clause + Subject + Verb + <u>more</u> free <u>than</u> theirs (ever) was.

Subject + Verb + <u>more</u> free time . . . <u>than</u> they (ever) had.

Also Because of a <u>higher</u> education <u>than</u> the education of my parents.

Subject + Verb + a <u>different</u> life style <u>than</u> they.

In English, we complete comparisons with *than* (or *as*), not *that*. David, however, completes negative comparisons (signaled by *never*) with *that* and positive comparisons (signaled by *ever* or by affirmative phrases and clauses) with *than*. By discussing with him the chart above, we could help him understand two strategies for rewriting the "that constructions": (1) keep *that* but get rid of *more*, or (2) keep *more* but change *that* to *than*.

The paper contains only a few misspellings. *Diffrent* (four times) and *seperating* (once) are logical transcriptions of how most speakers pronounce these words. *An* (for *and*) may not be a "pronunciation spelling" because David spells *and* correctly elsewhere; he probably just left off the *d* as he hurried to finish. In misspelling *receive* as *recieve*, he logically writes "i before e" but forgets (or never confidently learned) "except after c." We might ask him to begin a spelling log, entering these words in one column and their correct spellings in another, so that he can discover which words and sound patterns are likely to give him trouble.[4]

When I analyze a first paper, I make notes about what I've found on a separate sheet kept in each student's folder. Students never see my notes, but I refer to them throughout the term. They help me decide

4. An excellent discussion of types of misspellings and their causes appears in Shaughnessy, Chapter 5.

what writing problems each student should work on and permit me to record a student's progress. Because David can't work on everything at once without becoming frustrated, I would select only one or two areas to emphasize as he rewrites this paper or plans the next one. For David (and doubtless other members of the class), careful prewriting would effect the greatest change in future papers. Writing from an overabundance of material would lengthen paragraphs, help him better support generalizations, and perhaps remove the need to pad sentences. Prewriting also might help him find alternative patterns of arrangement in material, reducing his dependence on the five-paragraph model. In the meantime, he can begin a spelling log and practice ungraded sentence-combining exercises to expand his inventory of subordinate constructions and increase his confidence about using commas.

With practice, you can read a paper diagnostically in two or three minutes. At first it helps to describe the features in detail, but after a while, a few brief notes will remind you of problems the student has overcome, new areas to work on, and questions you need more evidence to answer. Diagnostic readings reveal not only what the student has done but also how and why, allowing you to hypothesize about the causes of writing problems. Merely to identify a paper's errors and attach a letter grade is to ignore considerable evidence that can make your teaching more effective and the student's progress surer.

TEACHING THROUGH COMMENTS

Diagnostic reading is essentially a private response to a composition. We're discussing it with ourselves, explaining its patterns of features and planning a course of instruction for the student. When we write comments, on the other hand, we're communicating with a different audience, the student. As with any communication, purpose governs how we express the message and how our audience is likely to respond. The only appropriate purpose for comments on students' papers is to offer feedback and guide learning. Some comments, however, seem written for other reasons: to damn the paper with faint praise or snide remarks, to prove that the teacher is a superior error hunter, to vent frustration with students, to condemn or disagree with the writer's ideas, to confuse the writer with cryptic correction symbols.[5] Most of us learned

---

5. A revealing study of initial and terminal comments in a sample of 3,000 papers is Robert J. Connors and Andrea A. Lunsford, "Teachers' Rhetorical Comments on Student Papers," *College Composition and Communication* 44 (May 1993), 200–23: "The teachers whose comments we studied seem often to have been trained to judge student writing by rhetorical formulae that are almost as restricting as mechanical formulae. The emphasis still seems to be on finding and pointing out problems and deficits in the individual paper, not on envisioning patterns in student writing habits or prompts that could go beyond such analysis" (p. 218). See also Chris M. Anson, ed., *Writing and Response: Theory, Practice, and Research* (Urbana, IL: NCTE, 1989).

how to comment on papers by first surviving and then imitating the responses of teachers to our own work. Few of us, I suspect, looked forward to getting our papers back (except to learn the grade) and could probably sympathize with the following assessment of the experience:

> Confused and angry, he stared at the red marks on his paper. He had awked again. And he had fragged. He always awked and fragged. On every theme, a couple of awks and a frag or two. And the inevitable puncs and sp's. The cw's didn't bother him anymore. He knew that the teacher preferred words like courage and con-temptible person to guts and fink. The teacher had dismissed guts and fink as slang, telling students never to use slang in their themes. But he liked to write guts and fink; they meant something to him. Besides, they were in the dictionary. So why couldn't he use them when they helped him say what he wanted to say? He rarely got to say what he wanted to say in an English class, and when he did, he always regretted it. But even that didn't bother him much. He really didn't care anymore.
>
> How do you keep from awking, he asked himself. The question amused him for a moment; all questions in English class amused him for a moment. He knew what awk meant; he looked it up once in the handbook in the back of the grammar book as the teacher told him to. But the illustration didn't help him much. He got more awks, and he quit looking in the handbook. He simply decided that he oughtn't awk when he wrote even though he didn't know how to stop awking.
>
> Why not frag now and then, he wondered for almost thirty sec-onds. Writers fragged. Why couldn't he? Writers could do lots of things. Why couldn't he? But he forgot the question almost as quickly as it entered his mind. No sense worrying about it, he told himself. You'll only live to frag again.
>
> Damn, he whispered. He knew it had to be damn. He decided that the teacher didn't have the guts to write damn when she was angry with what he wrote. She just wrote dm in the margin. She told the class it meant dangling modifier, but he was sure it meant damn.
>
> Choppy! He spat the word out to no one in particular. He always got at least one choppy. "Mature thoughts should be written in long, balanced sentences," the teacher said once. He guessed his thoughts weren't balanced. Choppy again. But he didn't care any-more. He'd just chop his way through English class until he never had to write again.
>
> He stared at the encircled *and* at the beginning of one of his sentences. The circle meant nothing at first. Then he remembered the teacher's saying something about never beginning sentences with a conjunction. He didn't know why she said it; writers did it.

But he guessed that since he wasn't a writer he didn't have that privilege.

The rep staggered him. The teacher had drawn a red line from the red rep to the word commitment. He had used it four times. It fit, he thought. You need commitment if you believe in the brotherhood of man, he argued with himself. Why did she write the red rep? He didn't know. But there were so many things he didn't know about writing.

Why do we have to write anyway, he asked himself. He didn't know. No good reason for it, he thought. Just write all the time to show the teacher that you can't write.

Most of the time he didn't know why he was asked to write on a specific topic, and most of the time he didn't like the topic or he didn't know too much about it. He had written on the brotherhood of man four times during the last four years. He had doubts about man's brotherhood to man. People really got shook about it only during National Brotherhood Week, he had written once in a theme. The rest of the year they didn't much care about their fellow man, only about themselves, he had written. The teacher didn't like what he said. That teacher, a man, wrote in the margin: "How can you believe this? I disagree with you. See me after class." He didn't show up. He didn't want another phony lecture on the brotherhood of man.

That wasn't the only time a teacher disagreed with what he wrote. One even sent him to the principal's office for writing about his most embarrassing moment even though she had assigned the topic. She told the principal he was trying to embarrass her. But all he did was write about his most embarrassing moment, just as she had told him to. And it was a gas. Another time a teacher told him to write about how a daffodil feels in spring. He just wrote *chilly* on a piece of paper and handed it in. The teacher was furious. But he didn't care. He didn't give a dm about daffodils in spring. He didn't care much about what he did last summer either, but the teacher seemed to.

He looked for the comment at the end of the theme. Trite. Nothing else; just trite. He usually got a trite. It would probably mean a D on his report card, but he didn't care. It was hard for him not to be trite when he wrote on the brotherhood of man for the fourth time in four years. He used all the clichés. The teacher wanted them, he thought. So he gave them to her. But he was never sure just what the teacher wanted. Some kids said they had figured out just what the teacher wanted. They said they knew what kinds of words, what kinds of thoughts, and what kinds of sentences she liked. They said they had her "psyched out"; that's why they got A's. But he didn't have her psyched out, and he wasn't going to worry about it anymore.

Every week she told the class to write a theme on some topic, and he knew that she picked out the topics because she liked them. Every week—"Write a theme on such and such." Nothing else— just those instructions. So he gave the topic a few minutes' thought and wrote whatever came to mind. He thought in clichés when he tried to write for her. They were safe, he once thought. But maybe not. Trite again.

He wadded up the brotherhood of man and threw it toward the waste basket. Missed. He always missed—everything.

Drop out, fink, he told himself. Why not? He didn't know what was going on. A dropout. He smiled. Frag, he thought. Can't use dropout all alone. He knew it was a frag. At least he had learned something. The bell rang. No more awks, no more frags, no more meaningless red marks on papers. No more writing about daffodils and the brotherhood of man—until next week. (Edward B. Jenkinson and Donald A. Seybold, "Prologue," *Writing as a Process of Discovery*, pp. 3–6)

As this student's plight reveals, comments that simply point out errors or justify a grade tend to ignore the student who reads them. Formative comments, on the other hand, the kind that support learning, praise what has worked well, demonstrate how or why something else didn't, and encourage students to try new strategies. In an essay describing several approaches to formative evaluation, Mary Beaven defines six assumptions on which to base our written responses to students' writing:

1. Growth in writing is a highly individualistic process that occurs slowly, sometimes over a much longer period of time than the six-, ten-, or even fifteen-week periods teachers and researchers usually allow.
2. Through their evaluatory comments and symbols teachers help to create an environment for writing. Establishing a climate of trust, in which students feel free to explore topics of interest to them without fear that their thoughts will be attacked, is essential.
3. Risk taking, trying new behaviors as one writes, and stretching one's use of language and toying with it are important for growth in writing. As writers break out of old, "safe" composing behaviors, they often make *more* mistakes until they become comfortable with new ways of using language. Teachers must encourage and support this kind of risk taking and mistake making.
4. Goal setting is also an important process in the development of students. Goals need to be concrete and within reach, and students need to see evidence of their progress. Teachers, then, should urge students to work toward a limited number of goals at a time.

5. Writing improvement does not occur in isolation because writing is related to speaking, listening, reading, and all other avenues of communication, including the experience of living. Prewriting activities, responding to literature, class discussion, revisions, developing a sensitivity to self and others, experiences both in and out of the English classroom affect growth in writing.

6. Effective formative evaluation depends on our understanding clearly other procedures that encourage growth in writing: diagnosing what students are able to do; arranging for writing often in many modes; discussing usage, syntactical, and rhetorical deficiencies by working with the students' own writing, not by preteaching rules; giving feedback and encouragement; assessing how much growth individuals have shown, without comparing them to one another and without expecting "mastery" of some uniform class standard.

(Adapted from *Evaluating Writing*, pp. 136–38)

Beaven's assumptions are crucial because much research argues against commenting on students' papers—ever. Surveying this research, George Hillocks concludes: "The results of all these studies strongly suggest that teacher comment has little impact on student writing" (*Research on Written Composition*, p. 165). It makes no difference whether the comments are tape-recorded or written; appear in the margins or at the end of the paper; are frequent or infrequent; are positive, negative, or a mixture of both (though students receiving negative criticism wrote less and developed negative attitudes about themselves as writers and about writing). "Indeed, several [studies] show no pre-to-post gains for *any* groups, regardless of the type of comment" (p. 165). In the face of this evidence, writing teachers must consider whether or not they should even invest their time in commenting on students' work. I believe they should, but only under two circumstances: (1) if the comments are focused and (2) if students also have opportunities actively to apply criteria for good writing to their own work. The studies Hillocks surveyed "indicate rather clearly that engaging young writers actively in the use of criteria, applied to their own or to others' writing, results not only in more effective revisions but in superior first drafts" (p. 160).

With these assumptions in mind, let's return to David's paper, not to read it diagnostically this time, but to respond to it as we would if we planned to return it to him. I've reproduced the paper twice so that we can compare the responses of two different teachers.

The first set of comments identifies and corrects errors. In addition to placing symbols and abbreviations in the left margin, the teacher underlines misspellings, circles punctuation problems, and rewrites some of David's prose. Comments at the end of the paper address generally what's wrong with the piece and recommend a few changes

As time changes people's views and outlooks on life change

Sp
Rep.
P

with it. My parents grew up with completely <u>diffrent</u> standards in a completely <u>diffrent</u> time. Because of the time I grew up in, and the time I live in, my life differs greatly from the lives of my parents.

Modern society offers more aid to young people--jobs,

//
Sp

school, financial--that my parents could never <u>recieve</u>. Because *than* *ever* of this aid my life has been more free than theirs ever was. I have more free time on my hands than they ever did. My parents *cliché*

P

were, and are, always working to keep and get the things needed for survival in this life. *b   I have more education than my parents do* Also Because of a higher education than the education of my parents I have diffrent outlooks on life. I have a more well-rounded attitude toward life. I tend to take more things for *cliché*   *cliché* granted that my parents never would.

Not a ¶
awk

We now live in a world of entertainment. My generation has ? more things (in) which to occupy their free time that my parents never had.

Sp
Rep.

Because of the time gap <u>seperating</u> my parents <u>an</u> I, I have a diffrent lif(es)yle than they. Lif(es)yles change with the change of time, and with that so do people's outlook on life.

Avoid clichés and be more specific.
Proofread for spelling and comma problems.

(but notice the commanding tone of the imperative verbs). For several reasons, this traditional scheme fails to teach writing. First, David may not know what the marginal abbreviations refer to. By frustrating trial and error he may have learned that *P* can mean "passive," "punctuation," "pronoun," "poor phrasing," "point?"—take your pick. *Awk* and its not-so-distant cousin *?* communicate "the teacher didn't like what I said here for some reason." David must puzzle out the reason, guess *why* the phrasing is awkward, and predict as best he can *how* to rewrite it.

Second, the comments don't help David become an independent judge of his own prose. Finding his mistakes underlined again and again, or circled, or corrected, he can easily conclude that he has no responsibility

As time changes people's views and outlooks on life change

Beginning a paper is tough, isn't it? Notice that the

with it. My parents grew up with completely diffrent standards in

sentences in this paragraph repeat one idea three times. Can

a completely diffrent time! Because of the time I grew up in, and

you tell us instead why you think that these differences are

the time I live in, my life differs greatly from the lives of my

interesting?

parents.

Modern society offers more aid to young people--jobs,

school, financial--that my parents could never recieve. Because

of this aid my life has been more free than theirs ever was. I

What do you do with your free time? What do they do?

have more free time on my hands than they ever did. My parents

were, and are, always working to keep and get the things needed

for survival in this life.

Also Because of a higher education than the education of my

parents I have diffrent outlooks on life. I have a more well-

Can you give specific examples of these differences?

rounded attitude toward life. I tend to take more things for

granted that my parents never would.

We now live in a world of entertainment. My generation has

more things in which to occupy their free time that my parents

never had.

Because of the time gap seperating my parents an I, I have a

diffrent lifestyle than they. Lifestyles change with the change

of time, and with that so do people's outlook on life.

You have a strong sense of how to organize your paper by dividing a topic into three subtopics. Do you have the feeling that you're trying to develop too many big ideas for such a short paper? Let me suggest that you pick the one subtopic that interests you most and explore it in greater detail in your next draft.

Suppose, for example, that you wanted to develop the ideas in the second paragraph. How could you help your readers understand that your life "has been more free than theirs ever was"? How could you show us this difference? Can you think of examples and details that illustrate how much free time your parents and you have and what you and they do with it? Before writing your next draft, spend at least 30 minutes jotting down notes that might explain or support what you want to say about one of your subtopics. Please log the spelling problems in your journal and bring it to your conference next week. If you can't account for all of the check marks, I'll be glad to help.

for finding problems he's previously overlooked. The teacher, he believes, will find his mistakes for him. Then, because teachers *always* discover a few errors, he can dismiss the corrections in an effort to protect himself from criticism. Such circular reasoning, which the teacher abets, won't make him a self-sufficient editor.

Third, the comments presuppose that David knew more than in fact he did. They assume that his errors result from carelessness or failure to apply the rules. Perhaps the teacher believes that David overlooked mistakes, didn't proofread his paper, or worse, defied conventions repeatedly discussed in class. David, however, didn't intend to do poorly; he probably wanted to please his teacher and earn a good grade. Except for mistakes prompted by haste, students write errors because they don't know that they *are* writing errors.

Finally, because most of the comments address problems at the level of the word, David is likely to conclude that writing well is largely a matter of "getting the words right." In failing to comment on broader concerns, the teacher promotes the view that purpose, audience, and what a writer wants to say matter very little. The teacher remains an editor, not an "aid-itor," refusing to *respond* to the piece in ways a reader would.

In *Errors and Expectations: A Guide for the Teacher of Basic Writing* (1977), Mina Shaughnessy maintains, "The errors students make . . . no matter how peculiar they may sound to a teacher, are the result not of carelessness or irrationality but of *thinking*" (p. 105). She bases this conclusion on a study of 4,000 essays written between 1970 and 1974 by students entering City College in New York, which had just opened its doors to large numbers of basic writers. She describes and classifies the problems she finds, devoting chapters of her book to problems of handwriting and punctuation; derailed syntax; common errors of tense, inflection, and agreement; spelling errors; vocabulary problems; and errors beyond the level of the sentence. She supports her discussion with copious examples from student papers.

Shaughnessy reads the unique genre called "student writing" in ways that explain how and why errors appear. "Once he grants students the intelligence and will they need to master what is being taught," she argues, "the teacher begins to look at his students' difficulties in a more fruitful way: he begins to search in what students write and say for clues to their reasoning and their purposes, and in what *he* does for gaps and misjudgments" (p. 292). Although errors may appear to us unconventional ways of using language, they are logical; they reflect unique rules and hypotheses students devise to attempt communication. Errors also are regular; they occur in deliberate, often ingenious patterns.

Instead of isolating mistakes in line after line of a student's work, Shaughnessy encourages us to examine the paper systematically for *patterns* of error, reconstructing the student's unique grammar and formulating hypotheses to explain why or how the patterns developed.

What a student does right also may explain the pattern, especially when errors seem partially under control or result from mislearning or misapplying some textbook pronouncement. Whenever our own logic, the logic of the fluent writer, prevents us from discovering the rationale behind a pattern of errors, we must seek an explanation for it by discussing the evidence with the student.[6]

As the second teacher, I responded to David's paper differently. Notice that I didn't mark everything. That doesn't mean I overlooked problems; instead, I chose to address only a few manageable ones. Because David can't work on everything at once, he needs some help defining priorities. Some teachers may feel irresponsible in not marking every mistake, but with practice those pangs of guilt will diminish. Or we can redirect them by helping students log their own errors, signaled by checks in the margin. The purpose of our comments, remember, isn't to compete with other teachers in an error-hunting contest but to guide students' learning. Just as a class meeting organizes discussion around one or two topics, so too limiting the scope of our comments makes learning more efficient.

Second, the comments don't label problems; rather, they emphasize how and why communication fails. My assessment of David's paper is that it doesn't say much. It *asserts* that David's lifestyle differs from his parents' but gives slim evidence to support his claim. The assignment is partly to blame, but even so, David might have developed specific examples to illustrate these differences in lifestyles. My endnote directs him to explore one of the broad areas that he has touched on and develop it further. I could have suggested that he elaborate on all three of his subtopics—jobs, school, financial—but I'm not sure that David could have done that. The subtopics seem to me to represent a rote three-part division of his subject that David can't sustain; "financial" morphs into "entertainment" in paragraph four. Because simple skills precede complex ones, I'd like to know if David can generate sufficiently elaborated evidence for one subtopic before advising him to support all three. The questions create a kind of dialogue between David and me. In answering them, David must reread what he's written, eventually learning to ask similar questions of subsequent drafts. If the comments balance praise and criticism, David is more likely to read them and understand what strategies seem to have worked well. To keep lines of communication open, students can submit their own questions or comments about what concerns them, letting us know how carefully they are evaluating their work and what kinds of suggestions might help most.

Some teachers would find even the second endnote on David's paper too prescriptive. They would prefer a more conversational response that focuses primarily on the issues David raises. Such a style of commenting

6. Beyond Shaughnessy's work, teachers will find helpful Elaine O. Lees, "Evaluating Student Writing," *College Composition and Communication* 30 (December 1979), 370–74; and David Bartholomae, "The Study of Error," *College Composition and Communication* 31 (October 1980), 253–69.

establishes between the teacher and student a written dialogue about the text, a provisional discussion that responds to the writer's message and also encourages the student to explore additional possibilities in the piece. The focus is not so much on the writer, who is assumed to be interested in improving and engaged in the subject, but rather on the writing, which presents ideas worth exploring. Conversational commentary would avoid spelling out specific revision strategies but instead would draw David back into his essay to examine his decisions and the possibilities for exploring his topic further. Richard Straub, in "Teacher Response as Conversation: More than Casual Talk, an Exploration," describes the method this way:

> Teachers who make their comments part of a larger conversation with the student do not view the text as an anonymous artifact; they view the text as a meeting place for writers and readers, a "public social reality," a means for intersubjective dialogue. Their comments say, here's how I understand what you are saying, here's what I'm thinking about it, and here's what you might consider if you want me to meet you somewhere further along in this discussion. (p. 392)

Though I prefer to give students explicit suggestions for improving a draft, Straub and the teachers whose comments he discusses assign a high priority to the student's message. Regardless of the method used, all comments on students' papers, whether given orally or in writing, should respond in some constructive way to what the writer is saying.

Finally, in view of the research Hillocks surveyed, comments belong on students' drafts, not on final versions. If comments are to have any effect, students need opportunities to incorporate them. Commenting on drafts encourages and guides further revision. It also ensures that comments remain focused on the work-in-progress, not on the grade a student's work eventually receives.

Responding to papers in ways that enhance learning is as time-consuming as locating errors, more so until the procedure becomes comfortable and each student's problems more familiar. Although we obviously can't approach every paper in the same way, the following procedure offers some suggestions for planning written comments much as we prepare classes: (1) assess what the student needs to learn (steps 1–2), (2) plan what to teach and how (steps 3–4), (3) conduct the lesson (steps 5–10), and (4) keep notes to evaluate learning and plan future lessons (step 11).

Teaching through Comments

1. Read the paper through without marking on it. Appreciate its message. Identify several elements that seem effective.
2. Identify one or two problems. In deciding what to teach this time, view the paper descriptively, not to judge it, but to discover what the text reveals about decisions the writer

made. You may want to ask yourself the following questions:

a. Was the student committed to the assignment?

b. What did the student intend to do? What was the purpose for writing?

c. How did the writer define the audience for the piece?

d. How thoroughly did the student probe the subject?

e. How are paragraphs arranged?

f. What are the most frequent types of sentences?

g. What patterns of errors in spelling, punctuation, grammar, and usage does the paper contain? In what contexts do the errors appear? What makes them similar?

Examining scratch notes and earlier drafts also helps reconstruct how the student created the final draft.

3. Formulate tentative hypotheses to explain the problem you want to focus on. You can assume that there's a logic to what appears on the page, even if it isn't your logic. Try to define that logic so that your comments can turn it around or modify it. For example, "I disliked the story because it's ending confused me" assumes (logically but unconventionally) that 's marks the possessive pronoun just as it does most nouns. Students who put commas in front of every *and* may be misapplying the rule for punctuating series or conjoining independent clauses; they need to learn that a "series" of two coordinated subjects or verbs doesn't need the comma. Merely labeling the error "misplaced comma" doesn't teach students *why* and *how* your logic and theirs differ.

4. Examine what the student has done well. Can this evidence help the student solve a problem elsewhere in the paper? How can the student's strengths be used to repair weaknesses?

5. Now you are ready to begin commenting on the paper. You have examined the evidence, decided what you want to teach, and identified specific examples of the problem (and perhaps its solution) on which to base your lesson.

6. Questions can call attention to troublespots, but avoid questions that prompt simple "yes" or "no" answers. Preface questions with *why, how,* or *what* so that students must reexamine the paper and become conscious critics of their own prose ("How often have you used this kind of sentence in this paragraph?"). Avoid imperatives ("Proofread more carefully"), which identify problems but don't help students learn *how* to solve them.

7. Avoid labeling problems *unless* you also give students a way of overcoming them. If something is "unclear" or "awkward," let students know the source of your confusion ("Do you mean . . . or . . . ?"). Refer to other sections of the paper that illustrate a strategy worth repeating ("You're using abstract

words here; why not give me another example as you did in paragraph 2?"). Eschew, when you can, Latinate grammatical terms, abbreviations, and private symbols. They may be clear to you—after all, you've marked hundreds of papers with them—but they might mystify the student.

8. Make praise work toward improvements. Students need to know how a reader responds to their work, but they're rarely fooled by token praise. Avoid "good" or "I like this" unless you add a noun ("Good sentence variety here") or *because* ("I like these details because they help me see Uncle Max"). Remember to commend students for progress they've made.

9. Avoid doing the student's work. Rewriting an occasional sentence can give students a model to imitate, *if* you make it clear what principle the model illustrates. Circled or underlined words (and most marginal symbols) simply locate and label errors; the student probably didn't "see" the problem and needs practice proofreading and editing. A better strategy for handling surface errors might be to place a check in the margin next to the line in which a misspelled word or punctuation problem occurs. Then ask the student to examine the entire line, locate the problem, and determine how to eliminate it. Students who can't find the error on their own should feel free to ask you what the check means. Students may log these errors and their corrections in their journals so that they develop a sense of what they're overlooking. Logs can be discussed briefly in conference to identify patterns in the errors and work out strategies for anticipating them in future papers.

10. Write out a careful endnote to summarize your comments and to establish a goal for the next draft. Endnotes can follow a simple formula:

   a. Devote at least one full sentence to commending what you can legitimately praise; avoid undercutting the praise with *but* ("I like your introduction, *but* the paper is disorganized)."

   b. Identify one or two problems and explain why they make understanding the piece difficult.

   c. Set a goal for the student to work toward in the next draft.

   d. Suggest specific strategies for reaching the goal ("In your next draft, do this: . . . .").

   Traditional endnotes address a paper's weaknesses, but if you want to see the strengths repeated, praise them when you find them. Silence tells students nothing. Traditional endnotes also omit goals and offer few explicit suggestions for reaching them. Including goals and strategies gives the endnote a teaching function, helps redirect a writer's energies, and reduces the amount of trial-and-error learning students must go through to improve their writing. Subsequent papers are more likely to show improvement if you explicitly define what you think needs work and how to go about it. Your suggestions also will encourage students to see connections between what they discuss in class and what they practice in their assignments, between problems they've encountered in one draft and solutions worth trying in the next.

Setting goals and offering specific solutions to writing problems can be difficult at first, especially if you don't know what to suggest to address the problem you see. But with practice, you'll find yourself developing a repertoire of goals and strategies to adapt to individual papers. State each goal positively, perhaps mentioning problems in previous papers that now have been solved or pointing to specific strengths in this paper. Instead of writing "This paper shows little thought," write "In planning your next paper, spend fifteen minutes freewriting; then fill a page with notes on your subject and decide how to group them under three or four headings." Not, "Your sentences are hopeless"; rather, "You've made considerable progress in organizing the whole essay. Now it's time to work on sentences. Read this draft aloud to hear where sentences could be combined or made less wordy. Your ideas will come across more forcefully if you avoid passive voice verbs and sentences that begin with *There are* and *It is.*" Phrase the goal in language that encourages students to experiment and take risks. Avoid prescribing additional goals until students have reached those you've already given them.

11. Write yourself a note to chart the student's progress, a reminder you can keep in the student's folder. Describe briefly what areas no longer seem to be problems, what problems you addressed this time, and what needs attention later on. If this draft enabled you to teach a principle of paragraphing, remind yourself to evaluate the next paper in light of the paragraph-goal you set. If you also noticed sentence problems this time around, a note will remind you to set a sentence-goal when paragraphs begin to look stronger.

At first reading these eleven steps seem cumbersome, but after some practice, the procedure saves time. Writing teachers expect to spend many hours commenting on papers. We do this work conscientiously because we believe that students will read what we've written and will profit from our advice. Too often, however, they don't, and consequently, we resent having devoted so much energy to an apparently pointless task. One advantage of the procedure described above is that students *will* read what we've written. They'll expect us to say "bad" things, but they'll discover that we've said "good" things about their work too. They'll read about their weaknesses as they search for comments praising the paper. Second, the procedure offers specific help with weaknesses, especially in the goal-setting endnote. If the endnote explains *how* to tackle a problem, students will attempt the strategy we've suggested at least once. If we then praise the attempt, or even notice that the writer tried something new, he or she may try it again. Focused feedback, not diffuse comments, makes learning efficient. Third, the procedure saves us time because it focuses on only one or two problems. With practice, we can develop a mental repertoire of endnotes addressing specific problems. Although the long endnote on page 236 may appear to have taken considerable time to write, it didn't. I would like my students to think so, but I drew on a stock endnote I've used many times, simply modifying it to fit the particular paper I was commenting on.

SELF-EVALUATION

Students also must have a role in evaluating their work. They should respond to their own writing and that of other classmates for several reasons. Good writers are proficient in addressing varied audiences. Students develop this proficiency not only by writing for others but also by gaining responses to their work from audiences other than the teacher. Furthermore, because composing is highly idiosyncratic, students learn new strategies for solving writing problems by explaining their decisions to other students and hearing how they have negotiated the demands of a similar assignment. As students become progressively more independent and self-confident, their responses to one another's work become more incisive. They learn constructive criticism, close reading, and collaboration.

Writing workshops, discussed in Chapter 12, offer one way of encouraging students to respond to one another's writing. Self-evaluation encourages students to assess their own compositions. As Mary Beaven suggests, "Self-evaluation strengthens students' editing abilities, giving them control over decisions that affect their own writing growth as they learn to trust their own criteria of good writing" (*Evaluating Writing*, p. 153). Self-evaluation typically requires students to answer questions designed to elicit information about their work. Students submit their answers when they turn in a draft or final version. Although self-evaluation questions should change with each assignment to reflect the work students are doing, Beaven (p. 143) offers the following questions as a starting point:

1. How much time did you spend on this paper?
2. (After the first evaluation) What did you try to improve, or experiment with, on this paper? How successful were you? If you have questions about what you were trying to do, what are they?
3. What are the strengths of your paper? Place a squiggly line beside those passages you feel are very good.

4. What are the weaknesses, if any, of your paper? Place an X beside passages you would like your teacher to correct or revise. Place an X over any punctuation, spelling, usage, etc., where you need help or clarification.
5. What one thing will you do to improve your next piece of writing? Or what kind of experimentation in writing would you like to try? If you would like some specific information related to what you want to do, write down your questions.
6. (Optional) What grade would you give yourself on this composition? Justify it.

Self-evaluation benefits teachers as well as students. The answers to self-evaluation questions tell us what concerns students. As they become more aware of what they wanted to do and where a paper fails to realize their intentions, we can offer help, acting less like a judge and more like an experienced, trusted advisor. We discover how students perceive the composing process, what sorts of risks they're taking, and when to encourage and applaud growth. Self-evaluation realizes an important goal in a writing course: to help students become self-sufficient writers. As Beaven urges, students must have opportunities to decide for themselves "what they are going to learn, how to go about that learning process, and how to evaluate their own progress" (p. 147). Beaven recommends that students evaluate their own papers from the beginning of the course. Initially, we can comment on the quality of their assessment, modifying the goals they've set for themselves or suggesting alternatives when students seem headed in unprofitable directions. Later in the course, as students gain confidence in recognizing the qualities of good writing, we can give them more responsibility for evaluating, even grading, their work.

If answering a long list of questions begins to bore students, teachers can shift to other methods of self-evaluation. Some teachers, for example, ask students to write a paragraph or two describing the major strengths and weaknesses of a draft or final paper. These notes also might explain how students defined their purpose and audience or comment on organizational and stylistic goals that received special attention. Many teachers find these statements surprisingly perceptive and extremely useful in composing their own responses to students' work. They encourage an ongoing dialogue about writing between teacher and student.

ATOMISTIC EVALUATION

Measures of writing performance can be grouped into two categories: atomistic and holistic measures. Atomistic measures evaluate some part of the composing process, or certain features of the written product, or a skill presumed to correlate with writing ability. When teachers or administrators place students into writing courses on the basis of a vocabulary test such as the Verbal portion of the Scholastic Aptitude Test (SAT), they assume that a knowledge of words correlates with skills needed to write well. For some students it does; for others it doesn't. Students may score well on vocabulary tests yet produce ineffective compositions; they may score poorly on the test and write well. One reason is that composing involves much more than skill with words.

Editing, mechanics, and usage tests also are atomistic measures. They reveal whether or not students recognize conventions of edited American English. But because composing requires the ability to generate discourse, not merely to analyze it, editing tests can tell us only about some of the skills students use when they write. Tests of syntactic maturity are atomistic too. They enable us to evaluate the length and complexity of sentences and reveal what types of coordination and subordination students achieve in their writing.[7] This information is useful in planning instruction that enlarges students' repertoire of syntactic options. Nevertheless, because they focus primarily on the ability to construct sentences, such tests assess only one of many skills important to composing.

Atomistic measures aren't "bad" tools for evaluating student performance. They measure what they were designed to measure. Because they evaluate some activities required in composing or assess particular features in the product, they isolate problems we can help students overcome. They're misused when we mistake the part for the whole, when we ask atomistic measures to tell us everything we need to know about our students' writing ability. Writing assessments are invalid when procedures intended to evaluate only one aspect of composing are presumed to indicate "writing ability."

HOLISTIC EVALUATION

Holistic measures assume that all the features of a composition or all the skills that comprise writing ability are related, interdependent. When we grade papers holistically, we assert that their rhetorical effectiveness lies in the combination of features at every level of the discourse, that the whole is greater than the sum of its parts. Charles Cooper describes the procedure this way:

> Holistic evaluation of writing is a guided procedure for sorting or ranking written pieces. The rater takes a piece of writing and either (1) matches it with another piece in a graded series of pieces or (2) scores it for the prominence of certain features important to that kind of writing or (3) assigns it a letter or number grade. The placing, scoring, or grading occurs quickly, impressionistically, after the rater has practiced the procedure with other raters. The rater does not make corrections or revisions

---

7. For a description of the procedure developed by Kellogg W. Hunt, see his "A Synopsis of Clause-to-Sentence Length Factors," *English Journal* 54 (April 1965), 300, 305–09; and Kellogg W. Hunt, "Early Blooming and Late Blooming Syntactic Structures," in *Evaluating Writing*, pp. 91–104.

in the paper. Holistic evaluation is usually guided by a holistic scoring guide that describes each feature and identifies high, middle, and low quality levels for each feature. (*Evaluating Writing*, p. 3)

As most teachers know, if six of us were to assign individual numbers or letter grades to the same paper, all of us might evaluate it differently. How then does holistic, "impressionistic" scoring represent an improvement over traditional methods? First of all, holistic scoring is a group activity that requires readers to agree beforehand on the criteria that will determine the ranking of papers. The readers agree to match their impressions of any particular paper to preselected model papers, a scoring guide, or a list of features that define each rank.[8] Second, before readers begin scoring the papers, they practice the procedure, using sample papers written on the same topics by the same kinds of students as those whose work they will score later. The practice session allows raters to "calibrate" themselves to the models, scoring guide, or list of features. When raters consistently agree on what rankings the sample papers should have, the actual scoring can begin. During the scoring session, each student's paper is read at least twice, by two different raters, and assigned a number or letter ranking. When raters disagree on a score, the paper is read by a third reader or given to a panel that determines the score. Because raters don't stop to mark the paper, to correct or revise the student's work, they can score a large number of papers in a short time, "spending no more than two minutes on each paper" (p. 3). And because they have practiced matching each paper against predetermined criteria, they "can achieve a scoring reliability as high as .90 for individual writers" (p. 3).

Holistic evaluation assumes, first, that written discourse communicates a complete message to an audience for a particular purpose. Consequently, "holistic evaluation by a human respondent gets closer to what is essential in such a communication than frequency counts [of errors or of word or sentence elements] do" (p. 3). Rather than single out a few features in the piece, as atomistic measures require, holistic scores recognize all the decisions students make in writing the paper.

Second, holistic measures are flexible. Working together, English teachers can define criteria consistent with a particular course or writing program. Designing and trying out the procedure requires careful work,

8. For a description of holistic scoring using sample student papers as models, see Edward M. White, *Assigning, Responding, Evaluating: A Writing Teacher's Guide*, 3d ed. (New York: St. Martin's Press, 1999). Primary Trait Scoring, developed to score the essays for the National Assessment of Educational Progress, uses an elaborate scoring guide, described by Richard Lloyd-Jones, "Primary Trait Scoring," in *Evaluating Writing*, pp. 33–66. The best known "analytic scale" appears in Paul B. Diederich, *Measuring Growth in English* (Urbana, IL: NCTE, 1974). The prominent features of a piece of writing receive weighted numerical values, "ideas" and "organization" receiving greater weight than "handwriting" and "spelling." Diederich also constructs an attractive argument for involving the entire English faculty in evaluating writing performance so that bias doesn't unduly affect students' final grades.

but once the scale is in place, readers can score large numbers of papers quickly and reliably. Because raters make no comments on the papers, holistic evaluations provide no feedback for students; that is, the scores serve an administrative, not an instructional, purpose and usually help teachers make decisions about placement or final grades.

Third, holistic evaluation removes much of the subjective static that unavoidably interferes with placement and grading decisions. Although we all try to evaluate our students' work objectively, our judgments are always influenced to some degree by factors that have nothing to do with writing. Students who misbehave in class, whose socioeconomic or racial backgrounds differ from ours, whose handwriting is poor, whose past performance has already branded them as D or F students, or whose papers happen to be near the bottom of the stack may receive lower grades than their actual writing ability warrants. However, when papers are coded so that students' names don't appear, when at least two teachers must agree on the score, when all of us in the writing program participate, judgments become considerably more objective and consistent. Furthermore, in developing specific, uniform criteria to guide our scoring, we must discuss, as a faculty, what constitutes "good writing" and how the school's composition program develops the writing abilities of its students. Such questions lie at the center of all writing instruction, and working out the answers together improves both the program and our teaching.

What works for teachers works for students too. Teachers who are themselves trained in holistic scoring can teach their students to score one another's work. They give students the responsibility for assigning grades. The teacher's training is crucial; without it, teachers undermine the procedure, give responsibility with one hand while taking it away with another, and promote irresponsible grading practices. Once trained, however, teachers can help students develop a scoring guide for each assignment, explicitly defining with the class what constitutes a successful response to the assignment. The scoring guide, developed early in the students' work on an assignment, functions to clarify what the assignment requires and may serve as a revision checklist when students discuss their drafts with classmates. When students turn in their final papers, they omit their names and identify the paper with a number the teacher has assigned or with the last four digits of their social security number.

Having collected the papers, the teacher reads them quickly (without marking them), selecting two or three sample papers that meet the criteria for scores at different points in the scale established by the scoring guide. These sample papers become models discussed with the class during the practice session. During the practice session, which must be held on the same day that students score one another's papers, the students review the scoring guide again and then rate the models. The teacher discusses the ratings with the class, allowing students to "calibrate" themselves to the scoring guide. When students reach consensus on what rankings the models should have, the actual scoring begins.

During the scoring session, each student's paper receives two readings, by two different students who assign it a score that most closely matches the criteria defined by the scoring guide. To make two readings of each student's work possible, teachers may swap papers across groups (if the class is divided into permanent workshop groups) or they may require students to submit two copies of the final draft. When student raters disagree on a score by more than one point, as sometimes happens, the teacher acts as the third reader to resolve the conflict. If necessary, the teacher can convert the scores into letter grades by fiat or by discussing with the class the range of scores an assignment receives.

Because very young children can reliably score one another's work, older students, some of whom will be teachers themselves in a few years, can certainly manage the responsibility. Those who will raise the most static about the procedure tend to be students who have made good grades by learning over the years to "please the teacher." If the teacher no longer gives the grades, these students must adjust their usual definitions of success to "please the reader," an audience of classmates. Students trained to use holistic scoring rapidly learn what it means to write for a reader because they tend to see much more writing than they would in a teacher-graded class. They also become confident about how to improve their own work and offer better advice to classmates about their drafts. Letting students score one another's compositions realizes a teacher's conviction that students can learn to recognize good writing, in their own work and in the work of others, and can take active responsibility for their own learning. Teachers who share this conviction can release their control over grades and teach students to assess one another's writing carefully.

HANDLING THE PAPER LOAD

Both theory and practice suggest that students should write more than they do, in English classes and in other disciplines. But the size of our classes and other demands on our time work against us. Our students' work deserves a thoughtful response, but thoughtful responses take time. How can we keep up with the paper load? The question is one that both experienced and inexperienced teachers ask. Fortunately, those who ask it most have developed some of the best answers.

High school teachers, who usually teach 130 to 150 students a day, know many ways to keep students writing while simultaneously encouraging constructive responses from an interested reader.[9] They understand two important principles: the "reader" need not always be the teacher, and the writing need not always receive *written* responses.

9. See the collection of practical essays compiled by the NCTE Committee on Classroom Practices in Teaching English, *How to Handle the Paper Load* (Urbana, IL: NCTE, 1979).

We sometimes underestimate the value of ungraded writing assignments. Freewritings, journal entries, sentence-combining problems, and brief paragraphs can give students almost daily writing practice. They may serve several purposes: to summarize the main points of class discussion, to react to a reading assignment, to work out possibilities for future papers. We don't have to respond to these writings as we do to drafts or finished papers. Students can simply add them to their folders for review later, or they can exchange papers for a five-minute response from classmates. Or, we can collect them, skim them, and assign them a daily grade or write a few words at the top of the page. Or, we may respond orally in class by asking a few students to read their work aloud.

On longer, graded assignments, we can use other methods to save time without diminishing the quality of instruction. Many teachers find conference teaching successful. Student–teacher conferences can occur at any time during composing and offer teachers an excellent way to provide feedback when it is most useful, during planning, drafting, or rewriting. Conferences are most effective when teachers listen carefully and allow students to set the agenda. Students should begin the conference, perhaps by reading and commenting on a draft or by explaining what pleases and puzzles them most about the project they are working on. The teacher then responds to the comments, addressing the student's agenda first before raising other issues. The student ends the conference by reacting to the teacher's suggestions and summarizing what strategies will shape the next draft.

Another way to handle the paper load involves asking students to build portfolios of multiple drafts and final versions of several assignments.[10] Portfolios are collections of students' work assembled over time. They originated in fine arts departments, where students customarily select their best paintings, photographs, or drawings to submit for a grade. Although portfolios are relatively new to writing programs, they have several functions. Some institutions now use portfolios of high school writing to determine a student's placement in college writing courses. Other schools have substituted portfolios for competency exams, replacing a one-time test with writing completed in several disciplines throughout the first three years of college. The most common use of writing portfolios is the class portfolio, a collection of work students submit at the end of a single writing course.

Class portfolios permit teachers to assign a great deal of writing. Students keep all of their drafts and final versions in a folder, bring it

10. For a discussion of portfolios and their uses, see *Portfolios: Process and Product,* ed. Pat Belanoff and Marcia Dickson (Portsmouth, NH: Boynton/Cook, 1991); *New Directions in Portfolio Assessment: Reflective Practice, Critical Theory, and Large-Scale Scoring,* ed. Laurel Black, Donald A. Daiker, Jeffrey Sommers, and Gail Stygall (Portsmouth, NH: Boynton/ Cook, 1994); and Kathleen Blake Yancey and Irwin Weiser, eds. *Situating Portfolios: Four Perspectives* (Logan: Utah State University Press, 1997).

to class and conferences, and produce an impressive quantity of work. At the end of the term (and sometimes also at midterm), students revise some of these writings yet again and submit the portfolio for a grade. Most teachers who use portfolios define some of the work that must be in the folder, let students choose the rest, and ask them to write a self-evaluation that comments on the entire collection. For example, the teacher might require four papers: a persuasive essay, an analysis of an academic text, any paper the student wishes to include, and a letter describing the contents of the portfolio and chronicling the student's development as a writer. For one of these assignments, perhaps the "student's choice," all drafts and scratchwork must accompany the final draft.

Throughout the term, students work on these assignments, just as they would in a traditional class. Teachers may write comments on drafts and discuss them in conference. Classmates also can offer feedback in writing workshops. If midterm grades are necessary, students may submit two pieces from their portfolios-in-progress at that time for grading. But they also may revise the papers again before the completed portfolio is due.

Regardless of what goes into the portfolio, teachers must define in advance what they expect it to include and how they will evaluate it. Individual pieces of writing do not receive grades; instead, teachers read the entire portfolio holistically, assigning a single comprehensive grade for all of the work. For this reason, they must develop a scoring guide in advance of receiving the portfolios, a difficult task because the portfolio comprises, by design, a diversity of writing. Although individual teachers can develop their own scoring guide independently, most teachers define the nature of the portfolio and the criteria used to judge it collaboratively. They reach consensus about what all of their students' portfolios will contain, develop a common scoring guide, and organize themselves into a review panel to evaluate one another's students' portfolios.

Portfolios demand a great deal of reading time at the end of the term and raise questions about reliably scoring such a diverse body of work; nevertheless, they have clear advantages. A carefully designed scoring guide can increase reliability, and because readers assess the portfolio as a whole, not individual papers, evaluating portfolios takes less time than grading and commenting on final drafts. Moreover, portfolios remain the best way of evaluating students' growth in writing over time. When drafts and scratchwork are included, they can document the composing process, especially rewriting. Portfolios also demonstrate to students that writing is process. Most students take greater pride and pleasure in preparing their portfolios than they do in writing individual papers for the teacher to grade. Plagiarism is virtually unheard of; while it may be tempting to cheat on one assignment, a portfolio contains so much material that must be genuine that students will find it difficult to copy someone else's work. Teachers also find their collaboration in a portfolio project rewarding. In defining the portfolio's contents and devising the standards by which it will be judged, teachers must articulate the goals of their writing courses, a conversation that reinforces convictions about the best practices for teaching writing. Portfolio projects encourage teachers to support one another in setting standards and designing courses, decisions that foster collegiality and give teachers ownership of their work.

All of these methods—in addition to class discussions of students' papers, self-evaluations, and peer responses—encourage students to write frequently, to have their work read by a variety of audiences, and to share the authority for evaluating writing. Teachers unwilling to share that authority face at least two unpleasant consequences. They feel obligated to mark too many papers (or to assign too little writing), and worse, they prevent their students from learning what the standards for effective writing are. Sharing responsibility for the paper load not only keeps us sane; it's also good teaching.

fifteen

Designing Writing Courses

For however many models for imitation he may give them from authors they are reading, it will still be found that fuller nourishment is provided by the living voice, as we call it, more especially when it proceeds from the teacher himself, who, if his pupils are rightly instructed, should be the object of their affection and their respect.

MARCUS FABIUS QUINTILIANUS

TEACHING AS RHETORIC

No two writing courses are exactly alike. Even if we begin a new term with the same textbook and course outline, by the second week of class we'll discover reasons to change our original plans. Just as writers confront unique possibilities in every act of composing, writing teachers discover with each group of students different ways to engage the process of teaching. The purpose of this chapter is to explore the dimensions of that process and to construct an extended definition of teaching-as-rhetoric.

Teaching, like writing, occurs in a rhetorical context: somebody says something to someone else for a purpose. We can even substitute terms in the communication triangle to diagram these rhetorical elements.

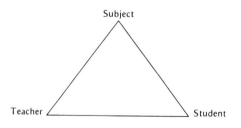

We need to define the terms *teacher*, *student*, and *subject* broadly though. Students can be the teacher, helping one another or assuming responsibility for their own learning. Conversely, the paid professional responsible for the class may learn a great deal about composing from students. The subject of a writing course also can vary. In some classrooms, where students and the teacher write, read, and discuss their writings, the subject is composing. In other classes, perhaps not properly called writing courses at all, grammar, literature, or a textbook become the subject.

As in writing, teaching brings teacher, student, and subject together in a social context that changes from one class meeting to the next. Teaching also expresses itself in several forms of discourse—lectures, class discussion, conferences, groupwork, comments on students' papers—all characterized by different aims and rhetorical strategies. When we explain a principle of writing, the aim is referential; when we praise student performance, the aim is persuasive; when we share our compositions with students, the aim may be self-expressive, referential, or persuasive.

Teaching is a complicated rhetorical act, a process of communication that requires us constantly to realign our relationship to our students and the subject matter. How we teach is shaped by whom and what we teach. To some extent we also define how we behave as teachers in light of our previous experiences as students. We emulate teachers whose classrooms we enjoyed and avoid the habits of those who most displeased us. By continually planning, executing, and revising our teaching performance, we eventually develop a style that best expresses our teaching self.

Because writing teachers know a great deal about communication, we should all expect to be superb teachers. But we need as much training as any group of teachers for at least two reasons. First, knowing *about* teaching does not always translate into *being* an effective teacher, any more than knowing about writing makes students effective writers. Transforming what we know, our competence for teaching, into effective performance requires practice and guided feedback. Conscientious teachers learn not only from reading and talking about their craft but also from the experience of teaching. We collect student evaluations to learn how our audience perceives us. We periodically invite experienced teachers to observe our classes because direct observation in realistic settings can help us understand the complex interactions that occur between teacher and students. Effective teachers continually seek to improve both what they know and what they do.

Second, our past experiences as students may offer us little guidance. Many of us exempted college writing courses. Those of us who didn't may have taken writing courses quite different from those influenced by current theories and practices. The field has changed so rapidly that many principles of writing instruction used today were unfamiliar as recently as ten years ago. Furthermore, most of our experiences as students occurred in courses fundamentally different from writing courses. Literature courses, for example, principally concern themselves with decoding texts, not creating them. Their primary goal is to make students intelligent readers not writers, consumers of language instead of producers. Because writing courses put students and teachers on the creating end of language, they require different strategies. Neither lecture nor discussion will serve writing teachers as effectively as it does teachers of literature or other content courses.

Teaching, like composing, is a process of communication characterized by rhetorical choices. It requires planning, execution, and review. Planning, analogous to prewriting, involves making decisions about the design of the course and each class meeting. In developing a course syllabus and lesson plans we preteach the course, setting down on paper what we *intend* to do in any given class. Executing the plan, actually conducting the class, is analogous to drafting. It entails doing what we set out to do but making adjustments, sometimes from one moment to the next, if our audience or subject matter require them. Like essays, each class has a beginning, middle, and end, and some of the same rhetorical principles that shape written discourse also make a teacher's oral performance effective. Review, analogous to rewriting, involves assessing how well the actual teaching performance realizes our intention. If we know what to look for, this assessment helps us revise our teaching. A useful way of reviewing our performance, absent a live observer, is to videotape a class and replay the tape when we have time to analyze it. Some suggestions about what to watch for conclude this chapter.

GENERAL PRINCIPLES OF COURSE DESIGN

All writing courses share a common goal: giving students enough guided practice in composing that they become more fluent, effective writers at the end of the course than they were at the beginning. To attain this goal we make pedagogical decisions based on what we know about how students learn to write. Our assumptions about composing, in turn, depend on theories, research, and classroom practices that experience has validated as "workable." Unfortunately, if we're not thoroughly knowledgeable about theories, research, and practice, the whole pyramid can topple. Throughout our careers as teachers, we'll confront questions we can't answer, and if we haven't had time to read and assimilate the theories and research that could reveal the answers, we must look to those who have.

We can find some answers to questions about teaching writing in "Teaching Composition: A Position Statement," developed in 1974 and revised in 1984 by the NCTE Commission on Composition. Because it provides an important foundation for designing courses, the position paper is reprinted below in its entirety.

> I. *The Act of Writing.* Writing is a powerful instrument of thought. In the act of composing, writers learn about themselves and their world and communicate their insights to others. Writing confers the power to grow personally and to effect change in the world.

The act of writing is accomplished through a process in which the writer imagines the audience, sets goals, develops ideas, produces notes, drafts, and a revised text, and edits to meet the audience's expectations. As the process unfolds, the writer may turn to any one of these activities at any time. We can teach students to write more effectively by encouraging them to make full use of the many activities that comprise the act of writing, not by focusing only on the final written product and its strengths and weaknesses.

II. *The Purposes for Writing*. In composing, the writer uses language to help an audience understand something the writer knows about the world. The specific purposes for writing vary widely, from discovering the writer's own feelings, to persuading others to a course of action, recreating experience imaginatively, reporting the results of observation, and more.

Writing assignments should reflect this range of purposes. Students writers should have the opportunity to define and pursue writing aims that are important to them. Student writers should also have the opportunity to use writing as an instrument of thought and learning across the curriculum and in the world beyond school.

III. *The Scenes for Writing*. In the classroom where writing is especially valued, students should be guided through the writing process; encouraged to write for themselves and for other students, as well as for the teacher; and urged to make use of writing as a mode of learning, as well as a means of reporting on what has been learned. The classroom where writing is especially valued should be a place where students will develop the full range of their composing powers. This classroom can also be the scene for learning in many academic areas, not only English.

Because frequent writing assignments and frequent individual attention from the teacher are essential to the writing classroom, writing classes should not be larger than twenty students.

Teachers in all academic areas who have not been trained to teach writing may need help in transforming their classrooms into scenes for writing. The writing teacher should provide leadership in explaining the importance of this transformation and in supplying resources to help bring it about.

IV. *The Teachers of Writing*. Writing teachers should themselves be writers. Through experiencing the struggles and joys of writing, teachers learn that their students will need guidance and support throughout the writing process, not merely comments on the written product. Furthermore, writing teachers who write know that effective comments do not focus on pointing out errors, but go on to the more productive task of encouraging revision, which will help student writers to develop their ideas and to achieve greater clarity and honesty.

Writing teachers should be familiar with the current state of our knowledge about composition. They should know about the nature of the composing process; the relationship between reading and writing; the functions of writing in the world of work; the value of the classical rhetorical tradition; and more. Writing teachers should use this knowledge in their teaching, contribute to it in their scholarly activities, and participate in the professional organizations that are important sources of this knowledge.

The knowledgeable writing teacher can more persuasively lead colleagues in other academic areas to increased attention to writing in their classes. The knowledgeable teacher can also work more effectively with parents and administrators to promote good writing instruction.

V. *The Means of Writing Instruction.* Students learn to write by writing. Guidance in the writing process and discussion of the students' own work should be the central means of writing instruction. Students should be encouraged to comment on each other's writing, as well as receiving frequent, prompt, individualized attention from the teacher. Reading what others have written, speaking about one's responses to their writing, and listening to the responses of others are important activities in the writing classroom. Textbooks and other instructional resources should be of secondary importance.

The evaluation of students' progress in writing should begin with the students' own written work. Writing ability cannot be adequately assessed by tests and other formal evaluation alone. Students should be given the opportunity to demonstrate their writing ability in work aimed at various purposes. Students should also be encouraged to develop the critical ability to evaluate their own work, so that they can become effective, independent writers in the world beyond school.

We have yet to reach some of these goals. For example, most of us teach more than twenty students per class and devote too much attention to essay writing. If some of these principles sound idealistic and others lie outside our control, the goals nevertheless are worth working toward.

For the most part, the position paper suggests practices we can implement now, without waiting for the system to change. If writing practice should be a major emphasis of the course, we can reduce substantially the amount of time spent talking about textbooks, assigned readings, and workbook exercises so that students have more time to write and discuss their papers. If audience is important, we can design assignments that address varied audiences, promote group activities that give students a greater sense of readers' expectations, and compose carefully our written responses to students' work. If assigning grades rarely encourages and improves writing, we can devise more positive methods of providing feedback: written comments, conferences, groupwork, self-evaluation. As we plan what we intend to teach and how to go about it, the position statement provides general guidelines for writing curricula and teaching practices.

COURSE MODELS

Although the position statement implies, generally, that sound writing courses offer students guided practice in composing, it doesn't specify a particular curriculum. That is because writing teachers and researchers believe that we can reach these goals by several routes. Like essays, writing courses need structure, a purposeful shape that relates parts to the whole, but there may be many ways to achieve this coherence. One way to classify writing courses is to examine what element of the communication triangle receives primary focus.

What-centered courses, perhaps the most common, emphasize a subject matter. To this group belong courses in writing about films or literature or essays. Typically, students see a film or discuss a reading assignment and then write a theme about it. Courses emphasizing linguistic forms also are what-centered; the sequence of instruction begins with words and progresses through sentences to paragraphs to outlines to whole essays (or vice versa, moving from essays "down" to diction). Courses treating rhetorical "modes" (typically, description, narration, exposition, and persuasion) can be what-centered *if* the primary activity involves reading, discussing, and imitating essays or paragraphs illustrative of each mode. Occasionally, what-centered courses treat in some systematic progression several forms of discourse: essays, letters, term papers, syllogisms, dialogues, advertisements, poems.

What-centered courses focus primarily on Moffett's "it," on principles, forms, or models. They are content courses that, regardless of the "it" under study, usually emphasize style. The stylistic content may derive from the study of literature, model essays, grammar, or principles in a handbook, but the approach to this material is usually the same. The teacher explains the content, presents several models or examples of it, and gives students opportunities to analyze and imitate the models. Lecture and teacher-led discussion predominate most class periods. When students write, they usually write essays. The approach assumes that, by imitation, students will internalize the forms and stylistic principles they have studied and begin to use them on their own. Although this approach has a revered history, going all the way back to classical imitation and the *Progymnasmata* of Hermogenes and Aphthonius, it has disadvantages. Forms practiced by rote or imitation may not become internalized, especially if the teacher explains only what the form is but not *how* to reproduce it. Because what-centered courses focus primarily on content and the teacher's expertise in expounding it, many composition specialists prefer other models that are more student-centered.

How-centered courses avoid overemphasizing any one element of the communication triangle, but instead focus on the process whereby writers balance all three: the writer's persona, the subject, and the reader. Process-centered courses belong to this category. They assume that if students understand the composing process and become conscious of their behavior as writers, they'll be better able to control those practices. Although the class may spend time discussing student papers and specific prewriting, writing, or rewriting strategies, the course places primary emphasis on students' actually writing. Whereas the focus of what-centered courses can be expressed as nouns—modes, essays, research papers, literature—process-centered courses are characterized by verbs: talking, listening, reading, planning, researching, drafting, revising, collaborating. The teacher writes too and shares that writing with the class.

Process-centered courses can easily assume some other focus, especially if teachers feel guilty for not being the dominant figure in the classroom. We turn process-centered courses into what-centered courses every time we're tempted to interrupt students engaged in writing with an explanation of some subject matter. Or, if we "explain" prewriting strategies during the first few weeks and never refer to them again, we've made prewriting a subject matter, a body of information to learn about rather than an activity to practice. The same fate attends sentence combining or diagramming levels of generality in paragraphs and sentences when these exercises assume too much prominence. Then a useful strategy for manipulating sentences becomes an end in itself, not a means of helping writers plan, draft, and revise their own work.

Process-centered courses also tend to be student- or *who*-centered. But because who-centered courses don't always focus on students, we should take a closer look at what is essentially a third approach to teaching. We've all taken courses in which the significant "who" is the teacher. In fact, we deliberately seek out such a mentor as an undergraduate or graduate student because the professor's research, area of specialization, or teaching style appeals to us. While teacher-centered courses have value, they do not make effective writing courses. When lectures or teacher-controlled discussions predominate, the course shunts students to the side. An outside observer, evaluating the visible, outward evidence of the teacher's energetic performance, might conclude that the students in this class are learning to write, that the teacher is earning her salary. But the students probably aren't learning to write, primarily because they're not doing any writing. They're just sitting there.

When students become the significant "who," the observer views quite a different scene. Several groups of students discuss one another's drafts. Other students work alone, writing at their desks. One student consults a shelf of handbooks and dictionaries; another sits beside the teacher having a conference. Although the teacher *appears* to be working with only one student, in fact he's planned, coordinated, and managed activities for every student in his class, lessons that actively involve all students in writing. In a student-centered course (as in a process-centered course), teachers individualize instruction as much as class size permits. Textbooks, if used at all, serve as resources or reference works. Teachers spend little time lecturing and most of their time guiding students' practice.

ACTIVE AND COLLABORATIVE LEARNING

Most writing teachers and researchers express a clear preference for writing courses that are how- instead of what-centered and student-instead of teacher-centered. Such courses most consistently realize the goals defined in the position statement appearing earlier in this chapter. However, not all process-centered courses are alike. In recent years, at least two models for process-centered courses have emerged. They differ with respect to what we mean by *process*.

The older model assumes that the composing process is highly individual, that writing is a matter of a person's making sense of the self and the world. The process under study in this model is the unique composing process of an individual writer. The model assumes that becoming a confident writer is a matter of self-reflective practice, the student actively and repeatedly engaging the process. The teacher's role is to help individual students become self-conscious of their behavior as writers. The teacher gives students frequent opportunities to practice prewriting, writing, and rewriting and intervenes regularly both to praise effective strategies and to redirect inefficient effort. Because the emphasis is on the self, assignments often call for self-expressive writing, personal reactions to texts, and writing from personal experience. In this model, writers must work through the prewriting stage pretty much on their own, first discovering what they themselves honestly think and feel about a subject. Freewriting and keeping journals, for instance, help writers make sense of their experiences and find truths to tell. Prewriting and drafting are individual, not group activities. The teacher and classmates can offer useful advice later, as writers revise their drafts for a reader, so this model makes generous use of draft workshops and student-teacher conferences. *Authentic voices, truth telling*, and *honest language* are the watchwords.

Teachers such as Ken Macrorie, Peter Elbow, and Donald Murray have written numerous helpful books outlining this process-centered approach. William Coles also employs the model in *The Plural "I,"* a dramatic narrative of a first-year composition class at Case Institute of Technology. Each of the book's thirty sections comprises a writing assignment, a classroom dialogue generated by the assignment, and whenever necessary, Coles' commentary. "Though the real subject of our assignments was going to be language—what it is, how it functions, why it is important—for their nominal subject I decided on the concepts of amateurism and professionalism."[1] Coles' course has both a subject matter (language) and a theme (amateurism and professionalism). The assignments also appear to invite the study of traditional rhetorical modes: description, definition, cause-effect, comparison-contrast, narration. On the surface, these elements in Coles' course make it seem what-centered. Below the surface, however, the course focuses on the process of using language and on students as language users. Coles views language "as the means by which all of us run orders through chaos thereby

---

1. William E. Coles, Jr., *The Plural "I": The Teaching of Writing* (New York: Holt, Rinehart and Winston, 1978), p. 6. Teaching and learning is the nominal subject of the thirty assignments in Coles' *Teaching Composing: A Guide to Teaching Writing as a Self-Creating Process* (Rochelle Park, NJ: Hayden, 1974).

giving ourselves the identities we have"[2]; a *professional*, then, is "someone able to use the language of his system to grow as a person" (*The Plural "I,"* p. 213). Coles' students come to learn that language has the power to shape "the plural I," the writer's many selves. As readers of Coles' book, we observe his discussions with students about their papers and come to understand how teaching sounds and feels. We also discover that, in Coles' view, "what we are up to as teachers of writing is to enable students to develop voices or styles of their own, the kind of control of language . . . that will enable them to shape and control, rather than to be shaped and controlled, by their environments."[3]

Coles' emphasis on developing individual voices and controlling environments is characteristic of the first type of process-centered teaching. A more recent model looks at process differently. Although it too stresses practice with prewriting, drafting, and rewriting, it rejects the view that writers are isolated individuals. Contrary to Coles, this second model insists that writers are always "shaped and controlled by their environments." To portray writers as solitary individuals is to divorce them from the social context in which language always operates. Language is a form of social interaction, a process of shaping our environment even as it shapes us. We write to make meaning, but we also write to make a difference.

The process under study in this second model, then, is not the composing proces of the individual writer but of the writer as a member of a discourse community.[4] The model assumes that writers are always members of several communities, each using writing in special ways. Students become effective writers by practicing these special strategies and conventions. College students, for example, must master new forms and purposes for writing if they are to do well in their courses. Analyzing and then practicing these forms are the principle activities in most writing-across-the-curriculum courses. In this second process-centered model, student writing is rarely a self-expressive, psychological exercise. Instead, assignments spell out fully contextualized real-world (including the academic world) tasks. They usually call for referential and persuasive writing because informing and persuading members of a discourse community is a significant function of literacy in real life. The teacher's role is to build a community of writers who encourage one another to

2. William E. Coles, Jr., "The Teaching of Writing as an Invitation to Becoming," paper presented at the Institute on Writing, Iowa City, Iowa, May 1979, p. 1.

3. William E. Coles, Jr., "Teaching the Teaching of Composition: Style for the Sake of Style for the Sake of Style," paper presented at the Institute on Writing, Iowa City, Iowa, May 1979, p. 1.

4. For descriptions of courses that take this second approach to process-centered teaching, see David Bartholomae and Anthony Petrosky, *Facts, Artifacts and Counterfacts: Theory and Method for a Reading and Writing Course* (Portsmouth, NH: Boynton/Cook, 1986); and "Unhappy Consciousness in First-Year English: How to Figure Things Out for Yourself," in *Writing as Social Action*, ed. Marilyn M. Cooper and Michael Holzman (Portsmouth, NH: Boynton/Cook, 1989), pp. 28–60.

use writing to make meaning and effect change. Because many students have learned to be individual competitors, the teacher deliberately fosters collaboration so that student must help one another learn and may share in the group's achievements. In this model, students are always members of a stable writing group, working together for the entire term so that they develop trust in one another, accept responsibility for one another's successes and failures, and come to appreciate the diverse abilities they bring to the community. Because the emphasis is on the group, not the self, every class meeting may involve group activities, not only responding to drafts but also talking out plans for writing projects and sometimes writing collaborative group projects. Teachers may give students responsibility for devising their own assignments, assigning one another research and writing tasks, setting appropriate deadlines, and revising drafts together. *Collaboration, community,* and *responsibility* are the watchwords.

Regardless of which process-centered model appeals to you, we are fortunate to have choices in designing our writing courses. The model we choose depends on our perception of what writers do, what we believe the process entails, and how we think students learn. Answering those questions may take a professional lifetime, but provisional answers will define our philosophy of teaching writing—for the time being.

PRELIMINARY DECISIONS

Before we can design a writing course, or any other course for that matter, we must determine, at least provisionally, who our students are and what our goals will be. Regardless of the model we adopt, knowing something about our students is crucial. If you are teaching for the first time, your best option is to talk with more experienced teachers, including administrators who oversee the courses assigned to you. Although they may at first describe your students in terms of test scores or grades, ask questions that will reveal more about their academic abilities and interests. Borrow some sample papers to get a clearer sense of your students' strengths and weaknesses as writers. Consider too their backgrounds. Find out what you can about their age, gender, ethnicity, and socioeconomic class, the communities they come from, and the sorts of life experiences they are likely to have had. This information may help you determine what kinds of reading and writing they may already be familiar with. Your colleagues teaching other subjects can fill you in on the assignments they give, which may suggest comparable tasks for your class. Your purpose in collecting all this information is not to stereotype your students but to understand, in a preliminary way, the abilities and interests they likely will bring to your class.

As you inquire about your students, you also may discover essential support services for them. Library orientation programs, guidance or career centers, writing centers, and computer labs can offer valuable help to your entire class. Individual students may need supplemental instruction with teachers especially trained to assist with reading problems, learning disabilities, physical and emotional challenges, or language difficulties characteristic of nonnative speakers of English. These specialists can advise you when a student may need additional help and how you can best work with the support staff to ensure the student's progress.

After discovering all you can about your students, consider your goals for the course. What do you want your students to know and be able to do? In many schools the goals for its writing courses will be set forth in policy statements, teacher's guides, or other administrative documents. Even so, try to put them in your own language so that you can explain them to yourself and your students. If necessary, develop additional goals that reflect your priorities and philosophy. Keep them simple, reasonably concrete, and limited to five to ten statements that capture the essential aims of your course. Goals statements are highly contextual, deriving from the particular needs of students, from complex institutional assumptions about the importance of writing in a particular school, and from shared understandings about what it means to be a competent writer. For this reason, the following goals may not be relevant to your situation, but they illustrate how such statements might be phrased:[5]

> To give students practice writing for various audiences and rhetorical purposes.
>
> To increase students' confidence in planning, drafting, and revising short papers.
>
> To familiarize students with research methods by requiring some form of research for each assignment.
>
> To encourage students to give and receive effective advice for improving a piece of writing.
>
> To help students gain proficiency in their use of standard edited English.
>
> To assist students in preparing and delivering a five-minute oral presentation.

Goals in hand, you are ready to take the next step in designing your course: developing a sequence of writing assignments. The writing assignments are the essential backbone of your course. They define the work you and your students will do and determine whatever readings and class activities will support it. The temptation to select a textbook at this point will be great, but resist it until you have roughed out your own assignments. Textbooks should support, not drive, a writing course.

---

5. Though controversial, the goals outlined by the National Council of Teachers of English and the International Reading Association merit every writing teacher's consideration; see *Standards for the English Language Arts* (Urbana, IL: NCTE, 1996).

Design your assignments first, based on your goals, and rest assured that any number of composition textbooks, handbooks, and anthologies can be made to suit your purposes. Some textbooks are worth mining for assignment ideas, but you probably will have to elaborate on the "Suggestions for Writing" that you find in them. Ideas for assignments also may be found by consulting fellow teachers, online sites, and departmental idea files. If the program you are teaching in specifies the nature and sequence of assignments, more than likely you must still fill in some details. Although you may need to revise your assignments later, drafting them now, in a form that you might hand out to students, will help you clarify what you want them to accomplish.

Most teachers consider, almost simultaneously with drafting assignments, their order or sequence. The possibilities are numerous.[6] Generally speaking, assignments should build on rhetorical skills that students have previously practiced. This means that students might address close, familiar audiences before writing for more remote, unfamiliar, or mass audiences. It may also mean breaking complex tasks into a series of smaller subtasks. Summarizing an essay, for example, may help students subsequently analyze it. Analyzing letters to the editor can precede students' composing their own letters. Designing questions for an interview, then taking notes during the interview, then writing up the interview to share with group members may help students pool their interview research to use for a longer project. The assignment discussed in Chapter 13, "Analyze the brochure to determine whether or not it is generally effective," uses analysis in the service of argument. It assumes that students have practiced analyzing short documents, have some experience evaluating texts and graphics, perhaps have created their own brochures, and have constructed simple arguments.

Not all of the subskills you identify in a task need to be practiced in separate, graded assignments, though they could be. Ungraded "trial runs" and various prewriting activities could serve just as well. As you sequence your assignments, you can make notes about the skills students will need to complete them successfully. Such notes can be invaluable as you plan each class period because they will suggest other activities that support students' work on each assignment. Be cautious about judging some assignments as "easier" than others. Ask yourself, "What does *easier* mean in this context?" Narration and description, for example, often regarded as rhetorically less difficult than exposition or argumentation, can in fact be quite challenging, depending on the nature of the assignment and students' familiarity with these aims of discourse. A

6. In addition to Bartholomae and Petrosky's *Facts, Artifacts and Counterfacts: Theory and Method for a Reading and Writing Course* and Coles' *Teaching Composing: A Guide to Teaching Writing as a Self-Creating Process* and *The Plural "I": The Teaching of Writing,* see James Moffett, *Active Voice: A Writing Program across the Curriculum* (Portsmouth, NH: Boynton/Cook, 1992); and Mike Rose, "Remedial Writing Courses: A Critique and a Proposal," *College English* 45 (February 1983), 109–28.

more dependable strategy is to examine carefully the verbs in your assignments to determine what the task requires and what subskills may need to be practiced beforehand.

COURSE OUTLINES

To this point, we've made several important decisions. We've chosen a model for our writing course, collected important information about our prospective students, established the goals for the course, and designed and sequenced several writing assignments.

As in planning an essay, we've determined the course's outer shape. Now let's examine how to hold the inner parts together, how to discover the relationships among "paragraphs" or units of the course. Most teachers work out these relationships by developing a course outline prior to the first day's class meeting. For college courses the outline, usually called a *syllabus*, lists the major "events" and provides a one-page meeting-by-meeting schedule of topics and due dates for writing projects and reading assignments. In public schools, the terms *curriculum guide* and *lesson plans* denote written documents that outline the course. The curriculum guide, developed by the entire English faculty or mandated by the school's administrators, offers a broad outline of the course (or a series of courses), defines course goals, and recommends classroom activities, readings, and writing assignments. Teachers adapt the general curriculum guide to the needs of a particular group of students by breaking it out into daily or weekly lesson plans. Whereas lesson plans and curriculum guides provide road maps for the teacher, syllabuses are intended primarily as information for students.

According to Joseph P. Ryan, the syllabus has both an informative and a pedagogical function.[7] It informs students, teachers, and administrators about the course. Administrators view the syllabus as evidence of our expertise. Prospective students can use the information to decide if they're interested in learning what the course teaches; students already enrolled can determine what the course requires and what it offers in return. Other teachers can use the syllabus to acquaint themselves with our interests or to guide their own teaching, especially if they're planning for the first time a course we've taught often. If called on to teach the course in our absence, they can use the syllabus to plan their presentation. Once the course begins, Ryan maintains, the syllabus serves an important pedagogical function:

> Students in the course use the syllabus to determine what it is they are to learn (course content), in what sense they are to learn it (behavioral

7. The following paragraph paraphrases "The Function and Format of a Course Syllabus," unpublished faculty development material written by Joseph P. Ryan, University of South Carolina at Columbia. Ryan also developed the "Checklist for a Course Syllabus," which I have modified to incorporate information unique to writing courses.

objectives), when the material will be taught (schedule), how it will be taught (instructional procedures), when they will be required to demonstrate their learning (exam dates), and exactly how their learning will be assessed (evaluation) and their grade determined. ("The Function and Format of a Course Syllabus," p. 1)

Because the syllabus serves as a teaching tool, we need to design it carefully, each time incorporating improvements based on previous experiences with the course. Although syllabuses generally include information given in the following checklist, some items may not be appropriate for every writing course. Consider the list not as a series of fixed regulations for composing syllabuses but as a general set of guidelines. Some teachers compile most of the information into a "course policies statement," appending to it a one- or two-page course schedule (section VII in the checklist).

Checklist for a Course Syllabus

I. Descriptive Information
   A. Course number, title, and catalogue description
   B. Credit awarded for the course
   C. Statement of prerequisites (if any)
   D. Intended audience for the course
   E. Instructor's name, office location, office hours, office telephone number, and e-mail address
II. Specifications of Course Goals and Content
   A. Course goals—the syllabus should state specifically the purposes of the course and what it teaches students to *do* (e.g., "To give students practice writing for various audiences and rhetorical purposes").
   B. Course content—the syllabus should list specific terms, principles, and procedures covered throughout the course; if the syllabus lists only general topics or "events," explain in a separate section how the course moves from one topic to the next, how the parts create a coherent whole.
III. Reading Assignments
   A. Full bibliographical citations for all required texts and supplementary readings (when used)
   B. Specific page references keyed to particular course goals and content
   C. Dates by which time students should have read the assignment
IV. Writing Assignments
   A. The number of writing assignments
   B. Brief descriptions of each assignment
   C. Due dates for assignments

    D. Statement of the instructor's policy on revising papers

    E. Statement of instructor's policy on accepting late papers

    F. Requirements for special writing activities such as journals, terms papers, portfolios

    G. If important, a statement of the instructor's preferences about the format for papers (margins, kind of paper to use, turning in all drafts, and so on)

  V. Description of Instructional Procedures—the syllabus should identify how much emphasis the course gives to lectures, discussion, conferences, in-class writing, group-work, student presentations, field trips, guest speakers, and so on.

  VI. Course Requirements

    A. Academic requirements—the syllabus should specify all required work (with due dates) and explain how it will be evaluated.

    B. Administrative requirements—the syllabus should explain the instructor's policies on class attendance and participation, on granting incompletes, on missing or late assignments.

  VII. Course Schedule—the syllabus should provide a meeting-by-meeting calendar of events or, at the least, list dates for all assignments.

  VIII. Evaluation and Grading of Students—the syllabus should specify which activities and assignments will determine the student's grade, what criteria will determine if required work is satisfactory, and what formula translates the instructor's assessment of the student's work into a letter grade.

LESSON PLANS

Lesson plans guide teachers in managing classtime effectively. Most teachers draft weekly lesson plans before the course begins. Then, during the course, we break the week's work into smaller units as we prepare each day's class. Developing the plan in too much detail beforehand may lock us and our students into a course of instruction that may not reflect the needs or interests of the class. "Staying on schedule" assumes greater importance than supporting the diverse rates of development among our students. On the other hand, postponing work on lesson plans until the first day of class leaves us without a thoughtful blueprint and forces us to design the course hastily, extemporaneously, or not at all. As a result, the course will seem fragmented and incoherent, frustrating for teacher and students alike. Unlike a syllabus, which follows certain conventions because it is a public document, lesson plans can have whatever format works best for us. In time, we develop our own requirements for the information we include. The suggestions given here offer one model that you can modify according to how much teaching experience you've had and what kind of writing course you're teaching.

Most weekly lesson plans resemble informal outlines. The plan should answer the following questions: What do I want my students to do this week? How will I enable them to do it? How will I know if students have done the work well? The first question helps me determine goals for the week's work. The second question lets me develop specific assignments and class activities to help students reach the goals. The third question requires me to decide how I'll evaluate my students' progress as well as my own teaching. If I conclude that a particular teaching objective wasn't met, I can adjust next week's lesson plan to allow for more practice or to review work that gave students more trouble than I'd anticipated. Evaluating the weekly lesson plan may simply mean reviewing mentally on Friday what happened in class and jotting down a few notes to suggest how I might have done it better. From time to time I also ask students what they enjoyed most about the week's work, when I belabored a point they already felt confident about, and what they want help with next week. When the course has ended, these weekly assessments, viewed cumulatively, suggest revisions I can make to improve the course.

A weekly lesson plan, drafted before the course begins, might look like this:

Week 1 (Three Class Meetings)

Topics:	Introduction to the course.
	The writing process.
	Diagnostic paper.
Objectives:	To introduce students to the work of the course and to one another.
	To discuss our practices as writers.
	To discuss what writing entails and define terms: *communication triangle, persona, prewriting, writing, rewriting, purpose, audience.*
	To complete an ungraded diagnostic paper in class.
	To diagnose each student's strengths and weaknesses (writing profiles are for my own information) and select sample papers to discuss in class next week.
Readings:	Chapter 1, "Planning the Paper," in the textbook.
Writing Assignments:	Diagnostic paper (in class—Day 3).
Class Activities:	Students interview and introduce one another (Day 1).
	Discuss policy statement and course schedule (Day 1).
	Discuss writing habits (Day 1).
	Define rhetorical terms (Day 1).
	Groupwork to plan diagnostic paper (Day 2).
	In-class prewriting (Day 2).

	In-class writing (diagnostic paper on Day 3).
Evaluation:	Review rhetorical terms on Day 2 to be sure definitions were clear.

Observe groupwork (Day 2) to find out if directions were adequate and if groups need advice on working together.

Examine notes and freewritings written on Day 2 (and submitted together with the diagnostic paper) to determine what kind of reassurance and help students need with prewriting strategies.

Ask students what was the most and least troublesome part of the diagnostic assignment (Day 3).

Experienced teachers might manage the entire week's classes guided only by the weekly lesson plan. I can't do it and, like most teachers, find it necessary to prepare each class the day before I teach it. I usually overprepare, mapping out the day's work in such detail that I can still help students reach their destination via detours. The process is analogous to developing a block plan to organize an essay or devising an open-ended script for a one-hour play in which I never know what some of the student-actors will do or say. As I draft lesson plans, I try to observe a few rules about using class time. Because I believe that writing classes should be workshops, I plan first what the students will do, not what I will do. If students need time to discuss their plans for a writing project with one another, I will develop instructions for groupwork first. Second, I try to keep things moving, changing class activities about every ten or fifteen minutes. Even attentive, engaged adults begin to be restless after doing the same thing for more than twenty minutes. Finally, I expand my weekly plan in several ways: by developing objectives for each class, by listing questions to guide discussion, by apportioning class time to make sure everything gets done on schedule, by writing out instructions for groupwork, by devising "stand-by" activities in case we finish the planned work before the period ends, by writing out assignments for formal writing projects. Then, the lesson plan for Day 2 might look like this:

Day 2 (Sixty-Minute Period)

Objectives:	To review rhetorical concepts and terms discussed on Day 1, especially *persona, audience, purpose,* and *prewriting.*
	To plan the diagnostic paper by giving students experience with listing, groupwork, and freewriting.
Reading (10 minutes):	Discuss Chapter 1, "Planning the Paper."

Why is a plan or blueprint important to a carpenter? To a writer? What strategies does the textbook suggest for planning a piece of writing? In what ways do those strategies help writers make decisions about persona, audience, purpose? Which strategies have you used before? Do you use planning strategies the textbook didn't mention?

Listing (10 minutes):	Think about a significant writing project you completed recently; write what it was at the top of a sheet of paper ("term paper," "college application essay"). Draw a line down the center of the paper; at the top of one column write "Easy"; at the top of the other column write "Difficult." In ten minutes, list as many words and phrases as you can to describe what was easy and difficult about completing the project. You'll use this information in your first paper.
Groupwork (25 minutes):	Have students probe the subject of their diagnostic paper, what makes writing easy and difficult for them.

1. Ask students to work in pairs with someone they don't know.
2. Explain the procedure (3–4 below), writing these questions on the board to guide the group's talk.
   a. What makes writing easy for you? Why?
   b. What makes writing difficult for you? Why?
3. As one student in each pair responds to question 2a, the other records words and phrases that capture the impression. Then, students should reverse roles. Both students should respond to question 2a before repeating the talking-notetaking procedure for question 2b. Allow fifteen minutes for this step.
4. Have students swap notes, returning them to the person who originally spoke the words and phrases. Give students five minutes to review the notes and add details.
5. If we get off schedule, reduce step 4 to three minutes and cut the time for reviewing the freewriting (below) to three minutes.

Freewriting (10 minutes):	After students review the notes, ask them to complete a five-minute freewriting. Explain the procedure: "Write whatever comes to your mind. Don't worry about punctuation, spelling, or complete sentences; just keep writing whatever ideas occur to you. If you don't know where to start begin with 'What makes writing difficult for me?' If you get stuck, just write 'difficult' as often as you need to until you get another idea." After five minutes, ask students to stop writing. Give them five minutes to read their freewritings and circle words and phrases that especially appeal to them.
Wrap-up (5 minutes):	Did they worry about spelling during the freewriting exercise? Did they get at least one good idea?

Hand out the diagnostic assignment; explain that the papers will be written in class next time. Assign another five-minute freewriting as homework. Remind students to bring to the next class both freewritings and the notes from the groupwork. They can use these materials in writing the diagnostic paper and will turn them in on Day 3. I'll review their work but won't grade it. Encourage students to continue planning the paper by adding to the notes.

Assignment for Diagnostic Paper
Write a two-page essay for your classmates and me in
which you explain what makes writing easy and difficult
for you. Give at least two examples to help us understand
specifically what you like most and least about writing
in school. You may use your notes and freewritings. The
purpose of your essay is to give us information that will
help us help you become a better writer. Your essay will
not receive a grade.

The daily plan may seem excessively rigid, almost too detailed. No
class is quite so willing to follow our plan to the minute. Indeed, experienced teachers might write out only the assignment and a few brief
phrases to remind themselves of what to do. But the value of a lesson
plan lies in its preparation, not its execution. Drafting the plan helps us
visualize our performance, to preteach the class. If we're confident about
what we intend to do, we'll feel secure about deviating from the plan
when we need to. For example, if students begin discussing the textbook
enthusiastically, we can let discussion continue for another five minutes,
knowing that the class will still have enough time for groupwork and
freewriting. Adjusting the plan during class can enhance rather than
subvert learning if we know precisely what our objectives are. Instead
of representing attempts to save the period from disaster, on-the-spot
revisions permit students to reach the original goal by a different route.

Although the class syllabus and our lesson plans can be quite detailed,
they also must be flexible. Like prewriting, designing a syllabus and
lesson plans represent a crucial first step, a way of defining the outer
shape of the course and the relationships among its inner parts. But as
in composing, the act of teaching may reveal new messages or different
dimensions of our student audience that hadn't occurred to us before.
If we're willing to let the course grow, our experiences in the classroom
will reshape the original outline and permit us to discover new meaning
in what we teach.

THE TEACHING PERFORMANCE

Effective teachers, like effective public speakers, engage their audiences.
We can all remember teachers whose enthusiasm and energy made
attending class enjoyable. Although the work was difficult, we didn't
mind; we respected and liked the teacher. But we've also endured boring
classes conducted by a frozen, unsmiling figure seated behind a desk,
eyes glued to yellowed lecture notes. We had trouble concentrating on
what was being said; we saved those homework assignments for last,
trying to work up enough enthusiasm to do them all. Despite what the
boring teacher knew, we thought to ourselves, it doesn't come across.

Teachers can sense when a class runs amuck, when teaching a particular group of students day after day makes us contemplate some other
profession. Our natural response is to assume that the class is especially

"slow," or lazy, or a lost cause. But nine times out of ten, we can do something about the problem. We don't have to wait for a new group of students. A bad class may offer an excellent opportunity to evaluate our performance.[8] It gives us a valid reason for asking someone whose advice we trust to observe what's going on, to make notes describing how we interact with students, and to suggest solutions to teaching problems. Alternately, we can videotape the class, studying in private the enormous amounts of information a camera reveals about our interactions with students.

The discussion that follows offers suggestions for evaluating our teaching performance. The word *performance* may suggest cheap theatrical tricks, comedy routines, razzle-dazzle, but we're not talking here about performances that substitute entertainment for education. Instead, we'll examine how teachers effectively use verbal and nonverbal codes to reinforce instruction and enhance learning—to get the message across. If we can't all become accomplished actors in the classroom, we can nevertheless learn a few simple techniques for using the props, blocking the scenes, and commanding the dialogue that dresses our message to advantage and holds the attention of our media-sophisticated students.

Most of us feel uncomfortable in the presence of an observer or videotape camera. We believe that our students' performance as well as our own will change, becoming to some extent "artificial." That's partly true, but our discomfort stems primarily from a natural reluctance to be evaluated, to be judged and perhaps found inferior. Although the procedure outlined below could be used to discuss a class with an outside observer, it's designed primarily for examining the evidence a videotape provides. One advantage of videotaping a class is that no one else needs to see the performance. The technician who operates the equipment probably tapes so many classes that ours becomes indistinguishable from the others. Although we doubtless sense the camera's presence and even play to it for the first few minutes, our actions don't change as drastically as we feel they do. After a few minutes, as we become preoccupied with what we're saying and how our students respond, the camera assumes less prominence. When videotaping a class, however, make sure that the camera captures the entire room and records both the teacher's and the students' performance.

---

8. Michael C. Flanigan, "Observing Teaching: Discovering and Developing the Individual's Style," *Journal of the Council of Writing Program Administrators* 3 (Winter 1979), 17–24, describes an observation program that focuses "on teachers' needs, not on evaluating teachers for administrative purposes":

> First, the observer gathers information about the objectives, concerns, and style of the teacher. Second, the observer describes in detail what went on in the teacher's class. And third, the observer connects what the teacher says she or he wants to achieve with what the observer saw and heard in class (p. 18).

Most of the information in this section of Chapter 15 derives from descriptions of over 300 writing classes I have observed using Flanigan's procedure.

A second advantage of videotaping a class is that we can review it days or weeks later, long after our recollections of the class have faded. We can play back sections to examine what prompted a lively discussion or an unproductive silence. Because the act of teaching requires enormous concentration, we may not be able to see everything the camera does. We can't teach well and evaluate what's happening at the same time. A videotape preserves the moment for later, when we are free to concentrate on what we're seeing.

A third advantage is that we can destroy the tape if it might be used against us. Videotaping, as described here, has a *diagnostic* purpose. It's a means of self-evaluation. Videotapes should never be used without our consent to *judge* teaching effectiveness or influence hiring decisions. If we wish to invite someone to view the tape with us, fine, but our purpose should be to describe what we do, to identify strengths and weaknesses, and to improve teaching and learning by setting goals for ourselves.

Most people's initial response to seeing themselves on videotape is similar to hearing their voice on a tape recorder. Especially if someone is present to witness our reaction, we become self-conscious, embarrassed—but fascinated nevertheless. We rarely turn the tape off. The response is perfectly natural—give in to it—but, if possible, view the tape alone the first time so that you won't feel obliged to react for the benefit of someone else in the room. Once the newness of what you're seeing wears off, you can stop watching what you look like and begin studying other elements of the total picture more objectively.

What "elements" should you study? What can the tape tell you? Begin by looking at the areas discussed on the following pages. Use the questions and suggestions under each heading to review what you do. Each set of questions implies solutions to problems encountered by beginning as well as experienced teachers. You may want to view the tape several times, each time concentrating on a different area. Watch for *patterns* in your behavior or the students' responses. And remember that every teaching performance reveals both strengths and weaknesses. Applaud yourself for the strengths and select only one or two weaknesses to work on between now and the time you videotape another class.

1. *Previewing.* Before you view the tape, go back over the lesson plan for that day. Recall what you intended to do. All in all, do you think you achieved your purpose? In what ways was this class typical of your teaching? Untypical? Can you recall particular moments when you thought you were teaching well? When students seemed especially engaged? Those sections of the tape should get close scrutiny.

2. *Seating Patterns.* Draft a seating chart. As you view the tape, notice the roles different students take in conversation. Some will initiate discussion; some will talk only after other students have first taken a turn; some may not have said anything. Notice where each kind of student-talker sits. As a rule, students who talk most sit near the front to the

middle of the class, where they have direct eye contact with the teacher. Students who feel left out (or wish to exclude themselves) may sit in the back of the class or on the extreme left and right sides. Now, notice how you interact with each kind of student-talker. In what ways do you establish opportunities for students to participate? How much of the talk is student-to-teacher conversation? Do you draw reluctant students into the conversation by moving toward them, by establishing eye contact with them, by calling on them? How often do you redirect a student's question to another student for an answer? Which students can you depend on to summarize discussion, make connections, or introduce new lines of thought? How do you defer students who volunteer all the time?

3. *Organization*. Examine the structure of the day's lesson and points of transition between activities. Do students have a clear sense of where you are taking them as you move through the period? Do you begin the class with an explicit statement of what will be done that day? Do you explain briefly how today's class relates to the previous class meeting? Writing a *brief* outline on the board, a few words or phrases describing the day's work, can help students see connections between activities. The outline also informs students how much you intend to do and consequently encourages them to observe the time limits you've set for each activity. Do you announce specific transitions from one section of the lesson to the next and explain how the activities relate to one another? Do you take a few minutes at the end of class to summarize (or let students summarize) the day's work? Do you introduce briefly what will happen the next time the class meets? Does the class have an ending, or does it just disintegrate as students collect their books and scramble for the door? How successfully did you budget your time? If you ran out of time, where and why did you depart from the lesson plan? Was the detour unavoidable? Constructive? Do you need to revise future lesson plans to include an optional activity (if you had time left over) or an activity you can cut (if you ran short of time)?

4. *Methods*. In addition to teacher-talk, how often did you use other resources and techniques during the class period?

	Frequently	Occasionally	Never
Brief conferences with students			
Student-to-teacher discussion			
Student-to-student discussion			
Groupwork			
In-class writing			
In-class reading			
Work with professional texts			
Work with student papers			
Student-led presentations			
Handouts			

	Frequently	Occasionally	Never
Blackboard			
Overhead projector			
Tape recorder			
Other resources			

5. *Pacing.* Pacing refers to the "tempo" a teacher creates by varying class activities. It's perhaps the most difficult element to control in teaching, but it's also extremely important. Because students approach the course with varied levels of enthusiasm, some are easily motivated; others, easily bored. If the pace is too slow, even interested students become inattentive; if it's too fast, students will feel lost and frustrated. As you watch the tape, notice the students' body language. Are several students shifting position impatiently? Have usually attentive students broken eye contact with you to stare somewhere else or to doodle in their notebooks? Are they staring at you but asleep behind the eyebrows? Are they looking at one another, carrying on silent eye-to-eye conversations? When you detect an unmistakable lack of attention, make a note of what was going on at that point and where you were standing or sitting. Then rewind the tape and play it back. You may discover that you didn't vary your talk or your position frequently enough. You may have been monopolizing the conversation. Because young adults have an attention span of only ten to fifteen minutes, they'll lose interest in what's happening unless *something* changes every fifteen minutes. Pacing is a matter of controlling those changes, and effective teachers develop a "sense" of when to make a change. Although a change of pace must occur frequently, it needn't be dramatic. Here are some suggestions:

    a. *Change your position.* Stand up, sit down, walk up a side aisle or into a "hole" in the seating pattern.

    b. *Change activities.* Shift from teacher-talk to work at the blackboard to groupwork to in-class writing to discussing student papers to work with an overhead projector. If you've been doing all the work, let students do something.

    c. *Change topics.* Move from discussing a reading assignment to discussing a student's paper to discussing how to plan the next assignment.

    d. *Change the kind of talk you are doing.* If you've been asking undirected questions addressed to the entire class, shift to directed questions, calling on specific students by name. If you've been discussing *what* a writer says, talk about *how* or *why* the piece is effective; then move students away from the piece altogether, asking them which strategies might be useful in their own writing. Discussions of abstract principles can yield to concrete applications of those principles and vice versa. Switch from cognitive questions, which elicit facts, to affective questions, which elicit feelings.

6. *Questioning Strategies*. What kinds of questions do you ask? How often do questions begin with *who, what, when, where, why,* and *how*? Are you asking too many questions that require simple "yes" or "no" answers and consequently truncate discussion? Good questions are short, contain one topic, and avoid undefined terms. Although every teacher phrases questions poorly from time to time, we usually sense students' confusion by watching their faces and body language. Rephrasing the question generally produces a response. Some teachers, however, phrase questions in ways that persistently undermine discussion. They develop a pattern of composing questions that students find difficult to answer, not because they aren't prepared but because they can't figure out what the question means. The pattern is relatively easy to revise if you know what the problem is.

One type of discussion stopper is the question that contains undefined terms: "How does the conclusion *reiterate* the introduction?" "What is the *chain of causality* here?" Rephrasing these questions to define technical terminology will solve the problem: "Does the conclusion *reiterate or repeat* the introduction?"

Another pattern involves unclear pronoun references: "If *that* is a valid example, would you accept *that* as true?" "How does *this* develop your idea?" "*That*'s right. *That*'s connected to the effect before *that* one. What's *that*?" Because we know what we're thinking of when we phrase questions, they may be clear to us but not to students. *That, this,* and *it* can be confusing unless the context makes the reference clear. Teachers can revise this pattern by placing nouns after the confusing pronoun—"that example," "this paragraph," "this way of handling the introduction"—or by substituting nouns for pronouns.

A third pattern illustrates what happens when teachers persistently ask questions without "prewriting" them mentally beforehand. The questions pile up, as in these examples: "OK, what kind of definition of rhetoric are we dealing with here and how does it tie in and what audience do you suppose the writer had in mind?" "Do we understand the essay and is there a meaning here and I had the feeling that something happened so how would you explain the ending?" Confronted with so many options, students will say nothing; at best, they'll attempt to answer only the last question in the series. A better strategy would be to break the questions apart, getting at issues one at a time.

The "what about" or "how about" question almost always prompts silence. "How 'bout the introduction?" establishes a broad topic for discussion, but it doesn't define where the conversation is headed. Instead of risking a wrong answer, students will wait for the teacher to stake out the territory more clearly before entering the discussion.

Some questions aren't really questions at all but statements intended to express a teacher's authority in the classroom. For example, "Any questions?" typically occurs at transitional points in a class and announces that the teacher is ready to move on to the next topic or activity.

Students will ask a question at this point only if they really need to. Usually, they'll say nothing because they too are willing to move on. "Any questions?" really means, "Let's go on to the next item on the agenda."

Unfortunately, some teachers use questions to mask their own insecurities or to criticize students. The following types of questions not only subvert discussion but also are pedagogically inappropriate. The point-less question—"We still have a few minutes, so I might as well ask you what the textbook says about topic sentences"—is obviously a filler, unimportant to the teacher and consequently also to the students. The loaded question—"Doesn't Frank's opening paragraph develop too much material?"—obviously requires a "yes" answer. End of discussion. The intimidating question—"We've discussed this strategy before; does anyone need it explained *again*?"—requires students to admit ignorance. Using loaded questions to trap students into giving incorrect answers is pedagogically unsound; students may fall into the trap once, but they may never respond to another question.

Isolated examples of the questioning strategies discussed here needn't concern you. A consistent pattern should. It means that the way you phrase questions is limiting students' participation in the conversation.

Notice too if you're giving students enough time to respond. Teachers who feel especially uncomfortable with the silence following a question often answer it themselves or pose another just as a student is leaning forward, beginning to raise a hand, or dropping a jaw to speak. See if you can discover similar body language as you view the tape. Remember that students need more time to respond than you might think. You already have a range of responses in mind as you utter the question. Students, on the other hand, have to hear your question, comprehend it, think it through, develop something to say, and indicate that they want a turn in the discussion. Silence doesn't *necessarily* mean that you've asked a poor question.

If a student's response is weak or inaccurate, what do you do? If you help students articulate their questions and answers precisely, you're teaching them to suit their responses to a specific audience, reinforcing principles that operate in speech as well as writing. If a student's response is confusing or off the topic, if it contains vague terms, encourage the speaker to clarify the communication.

In addition to examining how students respond to your questions, look at how you respond to theirs. What do you say when a student asks a question you can't answer? Do you bluff an answer, become excessively apologetic, or do you simply say that you don't know and will find out? When students ask questions you can reasonably expect other students to answer, do you redirect the question? Questions not only help you to teach new material but also to reinforce what you've already taught. For example, if Sally had trouble understanding *thesis statement*, a directed question later in the discussion might ask her to define the term in her own words, to find the thesis statement in a student's paper, or to summarize the discussion.

Finally, the videotape will reveal who does most of the talking and how many students participate in discussion. In an average writing class, teachers talk as much as 70 to 80 percent of the time. That percentage is much too high if we believe that writing classes should be student-centered. We can reduce it in at least two ways. First, we can limit teacher-led discussion, giving over more classtime to groupwork and writing. Second, when whole-class discussion is appropriate, we can involve more students by calling on them. As you view the tape, how often do you call on individual students? How often do you invite responses from anyone who wants to respond? Some teachers object to calling on students because they think it embarrasses them. Teachers who hold this philosophy can expect the same few students to participate in discussion, while the majority of the class listens.

Other teachers, myself among them, call on individuals by name because it signals the expectation that every class requires every student's active participation. Calling on students has several advantages. It's a teacher's best method of assessing what individual students know and what they may be confused about. It encourages students to take turns in the conversation and to share the space a discussion occupies in class. It also invites into the conversation students whose culture teaches them not to speak until spoken to or who are silent out of courtesy, not out of shyness or a failure to prepare for class.

We are not "picking on students" or embarrassing them simply by calling on them; we signal those negative attitudes by other means, generally facial expressions, tone of voice, or stance. Teachers can avoid embarrassing students by putting the student's name at the beginning of a question: "Tony, why does Sara need examples in the second paragraph?" Hearing his name, Tony has a fair opportunity to hear the question and begin framing his answer. Generously rewarding students who have responded to a question when called on also will mitigate any embarrassment. Teachers develop a range of terms to reward answers: "nope," "maybe," "OK," "yes," "good point," "absolutely," "excellent." They reserve stronger rewards for students who respond when called on, who deal well with difficult problems, or who need increased confidence.

7. *Directions*. Because effective writing classes involve students frequently in prewriting, writing, and rewriting, giving good directions is crucial. What does the videotape tell you about when and how you direct student's work? Most teachers explain what a task involves and how to do it, but effective directions require additional information. Good directions answer the following questions for students: What do you want me to do? How should I do it? How much time do I have? Why am I doing it? How will I know if I've done it well? Revealing how long an activity should take lets students budget their time. Explain-

ing the purpose or goal helps students understand why the task is important. Describing how you will hold students accountable for their work encourages them to do it well. Teachers sometimes express this need for accountability by saying, "We'll discuss your work in class" or "I'll collect it" or "You'll share the results with members of your group." Directions for in-class activities should form a concise paragraph, spoken before an activity begins but after students have received handouts or assembled necessary papers and books. Avoid smearing directions through the first few minutes of the activity. If necessary, break the task apart into discrete steps, explaining each step with a new set of complete directions.

After you've given the directions and students have begun their work, monitor the activity. First, walk down the aisles to ensure that everyone understands what to do and has the necessary materials. Postpone conversations with individual students until you've made a complete pass through the room; otherwise, a three-minute talk with one student may prevent you from discovering (until too late) that several students in the back of the class have misunderstood your directions. After this initial walk through the class, return to the front of the room and scan the class for a minute or so, then walk around again, stopping at several places in the room to watch students work. Your purpose during this phase of the activity is twofold. You want to evaluate students' performance throughout the activity, and you want to be accessible if they have difficulty.

Although you may feel silly just standing there, avoid the temptation to interrupt the work. Students may need your help less than you think they do; give them the opportunity to work through difficulties on their own. A teacher's mere presence offers sufficient incentive to keep students working, and if students have questions, they'll ask them. If a student's question is irrelevant to the task at hand, defer it until the activity is over. If students are discussing drafts in groups, don't allow them to drag you into the conversation. Unless students are unmistakably headed in the wrong direction, you need not intervene. Instead, read over students' shoulders, eavesdrop on group discussions, watch, and listen. The evidence you collect now will help you discuss the strengths and weaknesses of the students' performance after the activity has ended.

8. *Routine Matters.* How do you handle routine procedures such as taking attendance and collecting or distributing papers? Are administrative chores consuming too much time? Taking roll, for example, needn't consume the first five minutes of class. Take roll later in the period, while students are writing or engaged in some group activity. Or take roll immediately after class by recalling which seats were vacant or by looking through assignments collected that day to determine whose papers are missing. Returning papers is best done at the end of class so that students can discuss with you after class any questions they may

have about your comments. Handing out papers at the beginning of class means that some students will pay more attention to your comments or the grade than to the lesson. Distributing handouts during class takes concentration; avoid continuing a discussion or giving directions until everyone has a copy of the material.

9. *Personal Qualities.* When you've viewed the videotape to assess each of the preceding areas, examine it again, this time to focus on the impression your voice, appearance, and mannerisms may be giving your students. Without meaning to, beginning teachers sometimes undermine their performance by communicating that they're afraid of their students or lack confidence in themselves as teachers. Even if you do feel that way, your students don't need to know it. By acting confidently you may begin to convince yourself that you are a competent, capable teacher.

Pay attention to the quality of your voice. Do you speak energetically or in timid, barely audible tones? A normal speaking voice tends to be less effective in a classroom than it is in one-to-one conversation. A teaching voice must vary pitch to a greater extent, must project itself across a greater distance to the back of a classroom, must overemphasize slightly (but not too much) words you want to stress, and must avoid annoyingly repetitious fillers ("uh," "ya know," "for sure," "ya see"). A teaching voice should feel as if you're exaggerating your normal conversational tone.

Second, notice how you use your eyes. Confident teachers establish eye contact with their students and *rarely* break it. You may need to glance at a paper or toward the board, but reestablish eye contact as soon as you can. A gaze fixed on notes, the back wall, the floor, or only one or two students makes it appear as if you have excluded the rest of the class, the audience for your discourse.

Third, observe your stance and patterns of movement. Do you consistently hide behind the security of the desk or podium? Move out into the room, carrying with you whatever open book or paper you need so that you won't have to dive back behind the desk to retrieve a page number. Do you stand with your back to the class as you write on the board? Stand with your right or left side toward the class so that you can maintain eye contact and let students see what you're writing. Do you define your "territory" to extend only to the first row of seats, or do you occasionally move into the first few rows and up side aisles? Staying in one place for longer than ten minutes can slow the pace of the class. Walking nervously is distracting, so light somewhere for a few minutes, then move again. Leaning carelessly against a chair, the wall, or a window ledge expresses a nonchalance your students may interpret as an excuse to treat their own work cavalierly. To "see" these problems requires viewing the tape dispassionately, adopting the students' angle of vision and interpreting nonverbal messages as the class might perceive them.

sixteen

Teaching Writing with Computers

It is easy to forget that whether it consists of energized particles on a screen or ink embedded in paper or lines gouged into clay tablets, writing itself is always first and foremost a technology, a way of engineering materials in order to accomplish an end.

DENNIS BARON

Writing teachers understand that students must develop an ability to communicate, to read and write well if they are to grow as individuals, participate in society, and find success in and beyond school. But teachers also are learning that writing instruction often requires more than helping students learn how to compose printed essays. In an age when books, articles, essays, e-mail, instant messages, and Web pages are all primary forms of communication, writing teachers must help students gain mastery of both print and electronic media. In practice, print and electronic messages and documents are better seen as intertwined than as separate forms of communication. Few people write any more without the use of a computer, and most of the research writers do is facilitated by electronic databases and networks. Similarly, almost no electronic communication is possible unless the participants are adept at reading and writing alphabetic text. Most writing today requires that students apply both language and technology skills as they arrange ideas to communicate successfully.

This chapter provides an overview of important intersections between computers and writing instruction, considering ways that each informs the other. The chapter also explains why teachers might want to use computers in their instruction. It demonstrates that many computer activities can help students learn successful writing habits, such as developing compositions through a process that evolves over time and considering the dimensions of a rhetorical situation. Finally, the chapter looks specifically at common computer technologies, offering practical advice for incorporating them into the writing class.

HOW HAVE COMPUTERS BEEN USED TO TEACH WRITING?

Internet hype and the turn-of-the-century fervor attending dot-com stock offerings might lead us to believe that teaching with technologies is a recent development. In fact, computers have been an important component of writing instruction since personal computers were introduced in the early 1980s. Initial uses of microcomputers in writing instruction often emphasized tutorials and drills that assisted students in recognizing sentence errors and fixing grammar problems. Soon, however, teachers recognized the potential of word processors to enhance a writer's ability to draft and revise documents freely. Early studies revealed that writers tended to produce and revise more text using word processors. Still, computers provided no easy fix for writing problems. Reflecting on studies of word processing, Gail Hawisher and Cynthia Selfe conclude that "a writer's or student's particular habits and strategies for composing take precedence over the influence of computers" ("Reflections on Computers and Composition Studies," p. 7). Today, word processors have become so indispensable that teachers seldom ask whether they are good for writing, focusing instead on strategies that make the best use of the technology.

Later developments in technology-assisted instruction added a social dimension by using local area networks (LANs) to promote collaboration among students. Unlike the Internet, which connects computers all over the globe, local networks tie together machines on a small scale—all of the computers in a classroom, for instance. Collaborative writing software, such as the Daedalus Integrated Writing Environment, capitalized on local networks, allowing students to send and receive electronic mail, hold synchronous or "real-time" conversations,[1] and share texts. Writing teachers who began using network writing software were quickly impressed with its potential for emphasizing writing as a social act.

Though computers initially were used to tutor individual students in recognizing grammar problems or to help them draft and revise texts, by the late 1980s new possibilities arose for facilitating collaborative prewriting, reviewing, and revising. Additionally, teachers found that

1. Electronic messaging systems fall into two groups, synchronous and asynchronous. Like a phone call, synchronous messages are exchanged instantaneously with little or no time lapse between the sending and receiving of a message. Common synchronous messaging systems are Internet chat programs and instant messaging systems. Asynchronous messages, like notes posted to a bulletin board, are exchanged over a longer period of time. Messages are sent or posted to a common forum, and participants can read through them at their convenience. Common asynchronous messaging systems are e-mail and Internet discussion forums. Teachers can capitalize on the strengths of each kind of messaging system as they incorporate them into their teaching.

the computer introduced new class dynamics that were both productive and challenging. Some found that the roles of teacher and student tended to shift during electronic interactions. A teacher's voice might be de-emphasized on the network, providing opportunities for more student-centered class activities. Others saw that networked interactions could incorporate marginalized voices into communication activities. Students who for a variety of reasons might hesitate to participate in traditional activities were able to engage more readily in electronic writing.[2]

While some teachers were exploring developments in networked communication, others were investigating the emerging possibilities of multimedia composition. In the early 1990s, writers were using software programs to compose projects that incorporated images, sounds, and even video clips. These compositions also provided links that readers could click on to move between materials. These projects diverged from earlier forms of writing. A printed text is generally read from beginning to end in a linear fashion, but these electronic compositions were more associative, combining any number of reading possibilities into a fluid "hypertext."[3]

The latest efforts to use computers to teach writing combine the possibilities of multimedia and hypertext with the benefits that come from using networked computers. This combination began with the maturation of the World Wide Web in the first half of the 1990s and the resulting growth of the Internet. Today, collaboration and communications technologies on the Web provide numerous possibilities for students working on print projects or wishing to explore new forms of writing. Making the best use of these possibilities requires applying what we know about writing and learning as we incorporate technology into our teaching. Let's look more closely at how some of the latest technologies can be used for writing instruction.

WHY USE COMPUTERS?

For teachers who are comfortable experimenting with computers, the prospect of incorporating information technologies into their writing classes may be refreshing and liberating. For others, however, retooling their teaching to include computers can be confusing, distracting, even

2. These shifts and developments are not unaccompanied by challenges and concerns. Teachers are still developing strategies for managing student-centered classes to best effect. Additionally, early observations about the ability of electronic networks to overcome communications barriers have been criticized as too simplistic. For a discussion of the complexities of electronic communications environments, see Marilyn M. Cooper, "Postmodern Possibilities in Electronic Conversations," in *Passions, Pedagogies, and Twenty-First-Century Technologies*, ed. Gail E. Hawisher and Cynthia L. Selfe (Logan: Utah State University Press, 1999), pp. 140–60.
3. For more on the history and nature of hypertext, see George P. Landow, *Hypertext 2.0: The Convergence of Contemporary Critical Theory and Technology* (Baltimore: Johns Hopkins University Press, 1997).

disconcerting. Still, whether we know our way around computers or have spent most of our lives trying to avoid them, at some point writing teachers must deal with the ever-present integration of communications technologies into school, work, and society. Johndan Johnson-Eilola is only one of many contemporary scholars who have observed that "there is a profound cultural shift here which, as educators, we cannot simply reject but must work with and beyond, using powerful methods for constructing new literacies and ways of living" ("Living on the Surface," p. 188). Johnson-Eilola suggests that, as communications technologies increasingly influence our personal and professional interactions, we have a responsibility to investigate their implications and devise strategies for teaching these new literacies.

Keeping up with change in and of itself is hardly a good reason to use computers in teaching. But as the historical sketch at the beginning of this chapter suggests, computers can be incorporated into writing instruction in a variety of useful ways, ranging from methods that make teaching more efficient to strategies that provide fundamental benefits to writers. Let's examine some of these advantages in more detail.

1. *Computers can facilitate class management and simplify logistics.* Technologies as basic as e-mail can go a long way toward orchestrating class activities simply and efficiently. E-mail allows teachers to send timely reminders about class activities or to communicate quickly with students who need answers to simple questions. Web courseware and other software facilitate record-keeping and the posting of assignments. Computer networks are especially helpful in permitting teachers to duplicate and distribute papers, to set up peer-review activities, and to reduce the steps involved in turning in assignments. Since conducting a successful writing class involves a tremendous amount of work already, it makes good sense to rely on computer technologies whenever they can simplify things.

2. *Computers can provide timely and unique access to information.* Though online resources obviously have their drawbacks, computers are invaluable in helping writers locate and retrieve resources for their projects. Making sure that students are comfortable with keyword searches, for instance, will enable them to conduct research successfully whether online or in the library. Showing students how to use sources from the World Wide Web critically will provide them unprecedented access to government reports, studies, statistics, articles, news, and other up-to-the-minute information. Teaching students to find and join electronic conversations will link them with individuals who can provide expertise for and interested feedback on writing projects.

3. *Computers can allow students to practice writing and test ideas.* Computers offer numerous ways for writers to explore topics in low-threat environments. Computers lend themselves to prewriting activities because the evolving text can be changed quickly or incorporated into more formal documents at a later time. Freewriting is easily accom-

plished using word processors or e-mail messages. Many teachers also use electronic messaging systems such as discussion forums or class chat software to provide spaces for writing practice. These activities enable students to develop their ideas through an exchange of messages with a potential reader. Students see that their views matter and that alternative perspectives deserve attention. Though less formal than essay assignments, these computer-based activities can make composing an enjoyable, integral part of a writing class.

4. *Computers can help students engage a variety of rhetorical situations.* Computers encourage students to write with a purpose within a given rhetorical situation for a concrete audience. E-mail, for instance, requires authors to consider exactly who the audience for a given composition might be. The recipient of the message might be an individual or a group of people. Teachers can complicate this understanding of audience by pointing out the problematic nature of electronic messages, noting that even messages addressed to an individual exist within a larger context of networks and may be open to public scrutiny. Online communication provides concrete examples students can refer to as they learn to negotiate the complexities of communicating in any situation.

5. *Computers can help students view writing as a process.* Beginning writers don't always appreciate the ways that successful compositions evolve over time. Computers make this concept evident, showcasing the process of drafting and revising. Logistically, computers make working with multiple drafts possible, allowing students to revise without having to retype entire documents. Technically, computers provide tools that emphasize writing as a process. The advanced features of word processors, for example, enable students to "track changes" made in a document. These changes will be indicated in colored text in the original document, helping writers see where they have made substantive revisions and where they have only scratched the surface.

6. *Computers can help students provide feedback and see writing as a social act.* Anyone familiar with e-mail or other forms of electronic messaging knows that writers can receive nearly instantaneous feedback on their ideas. Similarly, writers who participate in electronic conversations soon come to understand that their messages don't exist in a vacuum. A poorly conceived posting to an e-mail discussion list, for instance, is likely to be challenged quickly by other members of the group. Many teachers also find that assigning Web compositions gives students opportunities to write for real audiences. Knowing that a Web researcher or even a casual surfer may consult these compositions at any time prompts students to consider carefully the impact their writing decisions can have on a potential audience.

7. *Computers can facilitate collaborative work and student-centered learning.* From simple e-mail to network meeting software, computers offer a wealth of technologies that enable collaborators to work together, drawing upon one another's strengths and expertise as they develop projects.

Computer-assisted assignments also can shift class activity toward students. Either by working through tasks at their own pace or by assisting classmates as they learn new technologies, students can enjoy a new sense of responsibility and accomplishment in what they are learning.

8. *Computers can extend the boundaries of the class geographically and temporally.* Computer technologies allow teachers to open their classes to new people and experiences, bringing the world in through the classroom door. From asking students to interact with international online communities to inviting scholars, artists, and other experts to visit the class electronically, writing teachers can easily extend the boundaries of the typical classroom. Furthermore, when using computers, students and teachers often notice shifts in the ways that work gets accomplished in and out of class. Students find themselves participating in course discussions and other activities online long after the class period has ended. Teachers realize that learning can take place in rewarding ways both inside and outside the classroom.

Key to all of these (and other) reasons for using computers to teach writing is the phrase "computers can." Computers won't automatically produce learning. Instead, when used judiciously in the service of well-founded instructional goals, technology presents students with opportunities to practice strategies and habits likely to improve their writing. Like pencils, paper, tape recorders, even chalkboards, computers can provide tremendous benefits for teachers and students. But like all technologies, computers work best when they support the goals students and teachers have established for their work together.

GENERAL GUIDELINES FOR TEACHING WITH COMPUTERS

Probably the most important principle to keep in mind when using instructional technology is that even teachers need to be learners from time to time. Allow yourself opportunities to experiment with various technologies, and don't be discouraged when the results aren't always what you expect. Like learning to paint, sing, juggle, even write or teach, becoming adept at using computers is a process involving both failures and successes. You can make the process go more smoothly by keeping the following strategies in mind.

When learning to teach with technology, take small bites. Upon seeing the fully developed electronic materials of an experienced teacher, you may be tempted to try it all or to begin with the most advanced technologies. That's not necessary. As you teach with computers, you will soon realize two things: (1) assignments and class activities quickly can become more involved and complicated than you anticipated, and (2) even the most basic of computer technologies can be an incredibly powerful teaching tool. You could easily spend an entire term showing your students how to use the advanced features of word processors to their fullest effect. This one strategy alone emphasizes the importance of prewriting, drafting, feedback, and revising, while easing yourself and your students into computer-assisted instruction. Similar first steps might involve using basic e-mail exchanges, electronic conversations, courseware, or online research, strategies discussed later in this chapter.

In addition to learning to teach with computers one step at a time, try to work within the constraints of the resources available at your school. Because circumstances will vary widely from school to school, a necessary first step is to investigate the resources available to you. You also should establish and nurture a healthy relationship with your school's technical support people. Some schools hire computer support personnel who can provide technical assistance and information about available resources. Some schools also pay instructional technology consultants who can help you plan and carry out teaching activities. It's always possible to extend the computer-assisted possibilities at your school by tapping into other resources, including those discussed in the sections that follow, but you will have a much easier time if you begin working with the people and technologies available close to home.

Investigate ahead of time any computer-assisted activities that you want your class to undertake. You don't need to master every aspect of a technology that you wish to use, but be sure to find out what kind of logistical information you and your students will need to get started. For instance, does your school require that every student have a user account and password before logging on to a computer? If so, you would want to find out how they can obtain such accounts and then how they would use them to log on to the machines before sending your students to a computer lab to do research on the Web. You also might check on the availability of lab attendants or seek out a person students could contact if they run into problems. Your main concern is to ensure that whatever tasks you assign can be carried out without unnecessary complication.

In addition to investigating tasks ahead of time, provide your students with clear instructions that will help them avoid potential pitfalls. If you are working with students directly in a computer lab or classroom, you may be able to talk them through the steps involved in a given task. However, if you are sending students out on their own, give them a simple handout that details each step of their task. Instructions for many tasks may already be available from support staff, or you may be able to arrange for a consultant to help you and your students get started. As you investigate logistics, also keep in mind that technologies tend to change quickly. Unless you have recently mapped out the steps involved, double check the logistics before initiating assignments.

Even if you have planned an assignment carefully and provided detailed guidelines for your students, tasks that rely on advanced technologies can sometimes run into unforeseen problems. Perhaps a server hosting a Web page you had planned to use is offline. The school may be experiencing network problems. A virus may have struck your computer lab the morning of class. To best handle these contingencies, experienced computer teachers have developed two techniques, the "workaround" and Plan B. The workaround assumes that there is more than one way to accomplish a given computer task. If, for instance, your class Web page containing links to hate-speech Web sites is unavailable, you might ask your students to use a search engine to find the same sites on their own. Similarly, there may be times when you need to fall back on or quickly develop a substitute activity, a Plan B. A freewriting exercise that you had planned to conduct using e-mail might just as easily be carried out using pen and paper. Instead of doing online research, students might conduct impromptu interviews of classmates. Before giving up, consider a workaround that accomplishes the task at hand, but also be ready to adopt Plan B, which will fulfill your instructional goals but by a different route.

As you plan your class, consider ways that technology might influence how you conduct each activity. Can you capitalize on the student-centered dynamics that attend using technology in a classroom situation? As students begin using computers in class, some are likely to work through simple tasks easily, while others will struggle or run into problems. If you try to help every student individually, you will quickly find yourself spread too thin. Instead, consider distributing the technical problem-solving among students. If some students fall behind, find out who has already completed the task, then ask them to assist students who are having trouble. Deputizing students in this way encourages a sense of confidence in those who are able to help and builds skills that carry over to other kinds of collaborative work.

Similarly, for work both inside and outside of class, consider forming collaborative groups that allow students with a range of expertise to help one another develop their technical skills. Some teachers survey students at the beginning of the term to assess their technical strengths and use this information to establish collaborative groups (you can learn more about surveying students' technical skills from the Information Technology Skills Assessment and Tutorial at http://sites.unc.edu/~itsat). Pay attention, though, as you and your students work together with computer technologies. Some students who are already computer savvy may take over the technical aspects of a project. To avoid this problem and ensure that everyone learns necessary skills, consider asking group members to rotate roles as they work on projects or stipulate that all students must become familiar with the technical dimensions of projects. Warn students about and guard yourself against the tendency to "take over the mouse" when helping someone learn to use computers.

Finally, let's look more closely at a few potential problems that teachers using technology sometimes encounter. Even the most recent studies still indicate that access to computers is inequitable. Access varies widely by socioeconomic class, with the poorest students having the most limited access. Wide disparities in computer access exist among schools as well, again with underfunded schools having the worst access. As a teacher, access issues will impact you directly, determining what kinds of activities you can undertake. Indirectly, however, access issues also will affect you. The differing backgrounds of your students may influence their comfort levels and abilities to work with technology. Your students may not have equal access to technology at home or within the school, or the computers available to you may not support all the activities you are planning. Older computers, for example, may not support a courseware package you want to use. To address these concerns, teachers must be diligent about access issues. Find out if the school's or community's computers are readily available to students who don't have their own PCs. Be sure that the capacities of your students' computers are up to the tasks you assign. Finally, discuss access issues openly with your students and with other teachers and administrators as well. Such discussions remind people that information technologies are not yet equitably available to others, a necessary step toward solving the problem (for more information on access issues, see Closing the Digital Divide at http://www.digitaldivide.gov).

Teachers who work with technology also confront copyright issues. What drives most network activity is the ease of reproducing electronic resources. However, as teachers take advantage of an easy mechanism for distributing materials, they find few clear guidelines for when it is appropriate to do so. Although computers can make reproducing materials easy, the copyright protections given to any work generally apply online and off. The best strategy when reproducing any resource is first to obtain permission and then to give appropriate credit. For teachers, however, the procedures for using materials are complicated by the fair-use provision of United States copyright law, which allows limited reproduction of materials for educational purposes. The fair-use provision enables teachers to use certain materials without securing permission—for example, photocopying a magazine ad in the morning to show in class that afternoon. Online, teachers can rely on the fair-use provision as well. However, because reproducing materials electronically may make them available to a wide audience, extra care may be required. While spontaneously circulating a printed magazine ad in class might fall under the fair-use provision of United States copyright law, posting the same ad to the Web may not. It may be necessary to assign passwords to certain online materials to prevent unauthorized readers from accessing them. Keep in mind, however, that even if you password protect materials placed online, you may be infringing on the copyright owner's rights if doing so devalues the material. Scanning a complete short story or poem, for example, and placing it online for your students to read instead of asking them to buy the work at a fair price would be an infringement. Again, obtaining permission is the surest way to use materials appropriately. Another way to avoid copyright problems is to use materials available online but in the public domain, meaning that the owners have either released their copyright claims or that those claims have expired. In general you can use these materials in any way you wish (for more information on copyright concerns, see the information at http://fairuse.stanford.edu).

Finally, some teachers find themselves increasingly concerned with issues of academic honesty when students work with online materials. Many of these concerns are well founded. Some Web sites specialize in reselling school papers; students wishing to cut corners can easily download these essays to submit as their own. Some teachers address this possibility by going online themselves and locating the paper in question. In some ways the ability to track down borrowed papers electronically levels the playing field for teachers who previously had no access to papers kept in private files. Other teachers, however, find that the best way to avoid problems with online (indeed with any kind of) plagiarism is to build into assignment sequences steps that demonstrate the student's writing process. Asking students to e-mail the class preliminary thoughts about paper topics, then assigning an annotated bibliography early in the project, and finally requiring a draft will make it difficult for students to fabricate papers at the last minute. Attending to the process will go a long way toward ensuring that students are doing their own work (for information on handling Internet plagiarism, see the resources at http://www.plagiarized.com/index.shtml).

Having covered some of the general strategies for teaching with computers, let's examine some specific options. The following pages will not explain everything you need to know about using a particular technology—you'll want to investigate the resources and logistics at your own school—but they will sketch possibilities, helping you imagine how you might use various computer-assisted activities in your teaching. The sections that follow also point to some of the potential pitfalls related to teaching with particular technologies. As you read, avoid thinking that you need to be completely familiar with an option before deciding to use it. Consider any work that you plan to do with technology as the beginning of a process through which you and your students together learn how computers can support writing instruction.

WORD PROCESSORS

Even teachers who are skeptical of some of the latest technical advances usually will admit that the computer-based word processor is of great value in enabling writers to draft and revise their work. Still, most writers and even many writing teachers aren't aware of the advanced features of word processors and the best strategies for using them. Figure 16.1 illustrates one of the most powerful aspects of modern word processors.

Most word processors offer review tools, including an "insert comment" feature that allows readers to comment on a paper. Using the

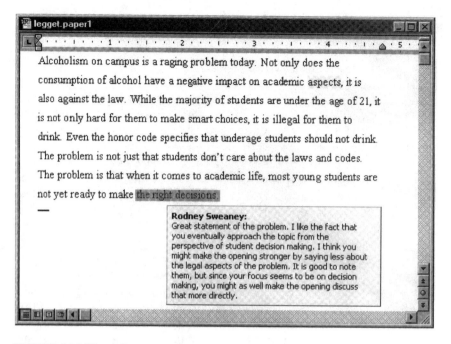

FIGURE 16.1 Word Processor Comments

insert-comment feature a reviewer named Rodney Sweaney has commented on the paper in Figure 16.1. Rodney's comments are indicated
with highlighting. When the paper's author selects a highlighted phrase,
Rodney's comment will appear in a pop-up window, as seen in the
figure. Highlighted comments offer a nonintrusive way of giving authors
feedback. You can use the feature for your own readings of students'
drafts or as part of the writing workshops that you conduct with students.

Another powerful feature of most word processors is the ability to
track changes made to a document as it is revised. Figure 16.2 shows
how the paper commented on above was revised. By activating the
"track changes" feature of the word processor, the writer is able to revise
a draft without losing any of the original material. The word processor
displays new text by underlining it and shows deleted material as
strike-through text. Here we see that the writer has taken the feedback
shown in the previous figure to heart, reworking the paper at the suggestion of the reviewer. The track-changes feature allows students and
teachers to see and appreciate the differences between substantive and
surface-level rewriting. Later, writers can decide to accept or reject each
change, giving them further opportunities to reflect on the revision
process.

As you explore the advanced features of word processors, you will no

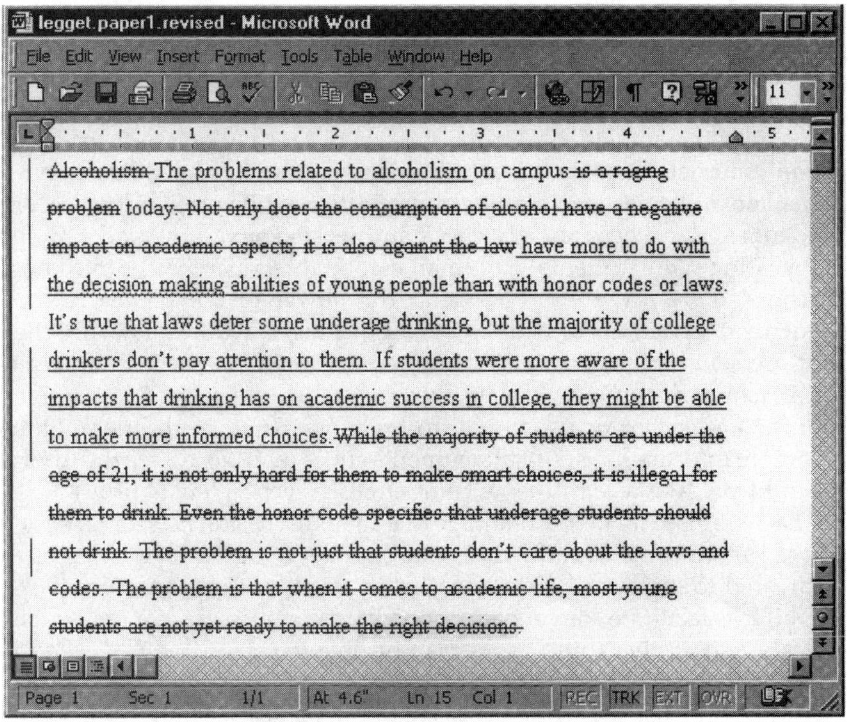

FIGURE 16.2 Tracking Changes in a Word Processor

doubt find other ways of using them to help students develop successful writing habits (for additional ideas, see http://www.emunix.emich.edu/ ~krause/Tips/word.html and http://cal.bemidji.msus.edu/English/ Morgan/Docs/TenTech niques.html). For example, you might explore spelling and grammar/style checkers with your students. By experimenting with these options, writers can modify the ways that the computer interacts with their compositions. Grammar and spelling checkers can be turned on or off. Style checkers can be switched to Casual, Standard, Formal, and Technical settings, to name a few. Grammar/style checkers can be told to flag specific problem areas for writers, such as passive sentences, possessives, and subject-verb agreement. Reflecting on these word-processing features from a writer's perspective can reveal their potential benefits and hazards. Similar exercises can help students explore a word processor's outline feature and its document templates and wizards.[4]

4. For more information on the advanced features of word processors visit the online documentation for Microsoft Word at http://microsoft.com/education/tutorial/class room/o2k/word.asp and for Corel WordPerfect at http://www.corel.com/products/wordperfect/cwp7/tipsandtricks/index.htm.

E-MAIL

E-mail offers another simple way to integrate computers into a writing class. Many students already have e-mail accounts, and those who don't can quickly obtain one from either the school's technology services office or an Internet portal site such as Yahoo! (http://www.yahoo.com). E-mail obviously can facilitate communication with your students. Most students and teachers already check and receive e-mail regularly. Communicating with students via e-mail can be integrated easily into most teachers' daily activities. To extend the power of e-mail, teach your students to attach documents to e-mail messages. Attachments are files that are sent along with an e-mail message from one user to another. By attaching documents to their messages students can submit assignments to a teacher or use e-mail to exchange drafts with one another (for more information about attachments and e-mail basics, see the tutorials at http://www.learnthenet.com/english/section/email.html).

Teachers also can take advantage of e-mail discussion lists, or listservs. These lists compile the addresses of a number of subscribers. Messages addressed to the e-mail discussion list are sent to all of the subscribers. E-mail lists facilitate conversation and allow members to share messages quickly and easily. Your school may be able to establish a class list for you, or you can set one up easily at http://groups.yahoo.com. Setting up an e-mail list for your class enables you to post reminders and other messages concerning class business. A class e-mail list, however, provides even more benefit to students as a space for sharing ideas and holding conversations about writing projects. E-mail has been characterized as a hybrid between spoken and written conversation. By participating regularly in e-mail discussions, students enjoy an opportunity to practice a unique kind of communication and develop skills that will benefit all of their writing.[5] E-mail conversations, like other forms of asynchronous online discussions, will prove more valuable to your students if you keep some strategies in mind while integrating them into your teaching.

Treat the e-mail discussion as a student-centered space. Some teachers take an active part in the conversations that evolve on a class e-mail list. Others maintain a hands-off policy. Regardless of your level of engagement, don't feel as if you must channel the discussion at all times. Some teachers designate weekly student moderators who post initial discussion messages and take a leadership role in the conversation. Most experienced teachers also allow electronic conversations to have a social dimension. When any group comes together, whether for work or play, members invariably spend some of their time cementing the social bonds

---

5. For a discussion of the rhetoric of e-mail, see Gail E. Hawisher and Charles Moran, "The Rhetorics and Languages of Electronic Mail," in *Page to Screen: Taking Literacy into the Electronic Era*, ed. Ilana Snyder and Michael Joyce (London: Routledge, 1998), pp. 80–101.

that will enable them to function successfully as a unit. Don't be surprised if some of the exchanges that take place on a class e-mail list engage in a bit of friendly banter or drift off topic occasionally. A healthy class e-mail list can accommodate such exchanges as long as they don't overwhelm the list's ability to facilitate more serious conversation.

Prepare also for occasional conflicts. Ideally a class e-mail list will provide a space where students can openly express their views. While the resulting differences of opinion may at times be disconcerting, allowing them to play out can go a long way toward teaching students the importance of supporting their claims with evidence and accommodating alternative points of view. Because electronic exchanges lack the social cues available in face-to-face conversations, debates may become especially charged, and members may occasionally post messages lacking substance or attacking individuals ("flames"). Still, as long as list members try to clarify misunderstandings and avoid personalizing their debates, a heated exchange can be more productive than a series of complimentary messages. Again, the key is to ensure that conflicts don't overshadow the healthy exchange of ideas. Many teachers discuss potential problems with their students and develop guidelines for appropriate decorum, or netiquette, for the class e-mail list (for more information on netiquette, see CompSite's resources at http://www.abacon.com/compsite/conversation/netiquette.html). In most cases, teachers can pave the way for productive exchanges by alerting students early on to the tendency of some electronic conversations to become heated and by establishing some ground rules for when they do.

Experienced teachers also develop a strategy for promoting participation in electronic conversations. A common mistake when first incorporating electronic discussions into a course is assuming that the conversations will evolve of their own accord. Though class e-mail discussions can prove fascinating, busy students can't be expected to devote themselves to them without some kind of motivation. Some teachers grade each student's postings to ensure that every member of the list contributes. This practice, however, can stifle the spontaneity of conversations by requiring postings that feel like formal compositions. A good compromise requires motivating students to participate without stifling them with the knowledge that their every word is being evaluated. Some teachers assign a certain number of postings per week but don't grade the messages themselves. Others ask students to submit at selected intervals during the semester a portfolio of messages that is graded. The portfolio can contain messages that best represent a student's contributions to class conversations.

Related to the need to promote participation in e-mail exchanges is an obligation to treat electronic activities as essential components of a course. Teachers who require students to read and post extensive electronic messages every other day must account for that activity in the weekly class workload. As you integrate conversational activities into your teaching, remember that they can involve significant work. Use them to further your goals for the course, not simply to keep students busy. You might ask students to devote one week's conversation to paper topics as a way of generating ideas for an upcoming assignment. You could ask students to post summaries of relevant readings as the class embarks on coordinated research projects. Or you might scale back e-mail exchanges during times of intensive drafting and review. The key is to avoid tacking activities on top of a preexisting design for your course; instead, use the technology to support your instructional goals.

Finally, you may want to use e-mail to promote collaboration and conversation with groups and individuals outside your class. Tens of thousands of international e-mail discussion lists treat countless topics in every discipline. These discussion lists—as well as the newsgroups and Web forums discussed below—can afford you and your students instant access to expertise and provide a unique look at the ways that issues are debated in a field. These groups also can serve as a sounding board, allowing students to pose queries and test ideas with live audiences. When participating in an international e-mail discussion, you and your students must respect the rhetorical dynamics of an established, knowledgeable community. A good strategy is to begin merely as a reader of the group's messages, analyzing the kinds of conversations that take place but not posting any messages. "Lurking" in this way allows potential new members of the discussion to assess the audience for any messages that they eventually post. Teachers also should warn students that posting messages to an online community represents a serious act of communication. Asking the group to answer simple homework questions or jumping into a conversation unprepared is likely to have negative results. Students can gain tremendously from joining online debates, but they must do so judiciously (you can find strategies for successfully participating in e-mail conversations as well as resources for locating discussion lists by consulting CompSite's e-mail resources at http://www.abacon.com/compsite/conversation/lists.html).

Before asking your students to participate in an online community, you can develop a better sense of how they operate by joining one yourself. Consider the e-mail discussion lists related to teaching and sponsored by the National Council of Teachers of English (NCTE). NCTE's NewTeach discussion list is geared toward mentoring beginning teachers. NCTE-Talk is a high-traffic list devoted to virtually every aspect of language arts teaching (you can find out more about NewTeach, NCTE-Talk, and a number of other teaching-related lists at http://www.ncte.org/lists/). The TechRhet e-mail list is devoted to issues of teaching writing using computers (go to http://groups.yahoo.com/group/TechRhet).

NEWSGROUPS AND WEB FORUMS

Newsgroups can be thought of as electronic equivalents of bulletin boards. Unlike e-mail discussion lists that deliver mail to individual e-mail accounts, newsgroups provide a central server where participants post messages relating to the group's topic. Like e-mail, newsgroups are asynchronous; messages are stored for a generous period of time on a server, and participants can read and respond to them at any time. Tens of thousands of newsgroups cover topics ranging from technical advice, to professional problems, to the bizarre eating habits of marsupials. The key feature of newsgroups is their ability to bring together people from diverse backgrounds who share a common interest in a topic. Assignments and activities that make use of newsgroups require the same strategies that you might use when asking students to participate in an international e-mail discussion list. Newsgroups, however, offer the advantage of providing a ready collection of messages that you and your students can analyze. A good initial strategy for using newsgroups is to ask students to analyze a "thread" of conversation (a series of messages generated in response to a specific question or posting) or to assess the audience of a specific newsgroup. Web sites such as Google (http://groups.google.com), which archives newsgroup messages, make an excellent starting point for working with international electronic conversations (for examples of how newsgroups can support the teaching of writing, see the online workshop at http://sites.unc.edu/ngworkshop).

Web discussion forums, like newsgroups, collect posted messages over time on a central server. Web forums, however, display the messages on easily accessible Web pages. Web discussion forums are generally used for two purposes. First, like newsgroups, Web forums permit discussing topics with interested parties around the world. Second, like a class e-mail list, Web forums enable students and teachers to conduct course business and hold class discussions (you can locate Web forums relating to international topics and learn more about using them in your classes by consulting CompSite's Web forum information at http://www.aba con.com/compsite/conversation/forums.html). Many teachers use Web forums in class because they offer the benefits of class e-mail discussion lists, while providing an easy way to access and store student messages. The strategies discussed above for integrating e-mail discussions into your classes also apply to using Web forums in your teaching.

SYNCHRONOUS COMMUNICATION

Telephone or face-to-face conversations allow us to respond directly to what another party says. If we are unsure about someone's meaning or we disagree with a key point, we can ask for clarification or raise an objection, intervening in the conversation immediately. Computers also allow this kind of synchronous exchange through the use of instant messaging systems, chat programs, and online collaborative environments. With computers, however, usually these synchronous discussions take place in writing, not orally. Participants compose their comments by typing them on a computer keyboard, producing texts that are a kind of hybrid between speaking and writing. Teachers who use synchronous communication in their writing classes report that students are better able to explore topics freely in the quickly evolving spontaneous exchanges that take place. Others suggest that students benefit from the fact that the discussions require participants to compose their thoughts in writing. Still others believe that computer-based, real-time conversations can have a democratizing effect on classroom discourse. Students who might remain quiet in face-to-face situations tend to contribute more in an environment where participants are judged on the quality of the writing they produce rather than on gender, ethnicity, or some other factor.

For all of these reasons, numerous teachers have incorporated synchronous discussions into their writing courses. Many writing teachers devote class time to such discussions, asking students in the same room to log on and "talk" with one another via computers. The first few moments of a synchronous exchange may involve playful experimentation as students become familiar with the fluid environment and find their real-time voices. Allowing time for writers to become comfortable participating in real-time discussions, however, will enable a class to overcome initial awkwardness. With practice, students will engage in dynamic exchanges that reveal many facets of a topic and that encourage written analysis and argumentation on a regular basis.

Of course, synchronous conversations are not without their difficulties and limitations. The playful bantering that tends to characterize the exchanges can overshadow the productive exploration of ideas. Similarly, as with most forms of electronic discourse that lack physical cues, written real-time exchanges are prone to misunderstanding and can become heated. Again, developing with your students guidelines for synchronous decorum is a good idea. Most teachers also take a more active role in real-time discussions than they might on a class e-mail list or discussion forum. Synchronous conversations are almost always more productive when a teacher or other moderator seeds them with an initial message that provides several potential avenues through which discussion can develop. Many teachers also take on a channeling role during the conversations, acknowledging messages that make intelligent points and asking for clarification or elaboration when necessary.

Another difficulty for some participants is that the pace of real-time exchanges promotes messages that skim the surface of issues instead of exploring them in depth. This complaint probably represents a valid observation about the nature of all real-time conversations. Teachers experienced with using synchronous environments have learned to work with them on their own terms, in ways consistent with their goals. They advise students not to bog down trying to digest every message that scrolls down the screen. Instead participants should focus on the "threads" of a conversation that interest them and that will be most useful. Because real-time conversations touch briefly on numerous facets of an argument or topic, teachers may assign them during the early stages of a writing project. Like freewriting or brainstorming activities, synchronous discussions can be developed later into more formal compositions. Finally, seasoned teachers make transcripts of synchronous conversations, asking students to review them later to catch up on messages they may have missed and to reflect more deeply on the ideas brought to light during the conversation.

When it comes to incorporating real-time discussions into your class, you are likely to have several options. All of your students will need access to a computer with a network connection. If you teach in a computer classroom or have access to a computer lab, you may be able to use collaborative software on a local network to conduct whole-class synchronous discussions easily. If not, other real-time options are available on the Internet. The simplest of these are likely to be Web-based chat programs available at your school. Often incorporated into a courseware package, chat options also can be found on Web sites such as Yahoo! (http://groups.yahoo.com). A surprising number of students are familiar with instant messaging systems such as America Online's Instant Messenger. You are more likely to use instant messaging to communicate one-on-one with students—to answer questions during virtual office hours, for instance—than to discuss issues with an entire class.

Teachers with more experience using computers also conduct real-time activities in virtual online environments called MOOs.[6] Several kinds of virtual environments exist on the Internet, but MOOs predominate in educational contexts. MOOs provide a more fully developed environment than typical chat software does because users are able to compose text that describes virtual spaces and objects. For instance, after logging on to the Lingua MOO, users see the following textual description: "Welcome to the Courtyard of LinguaMOO. Several Benches sit beneath large shade trees that line the walkways between buildings" (*Lingua MOO,* opening screen). By typing simple commands users can interact with objects within the courtyard or move to other spaces within the MOO. Users can also hold conversations with one another. Teachers who use MOOs will often construct spaces of their own—virtual classrooms or coffee shops, for instance—where they can hold meetings and host real-time discussions. Because MOOs require some training for participants, you will need to plan in advance how best to use this technology with your class. Fortunately, the educational MOO community is quite helpful and willing to advise new teachers (for more information about MOOs, see CompSite's information at http://www.abacon.com/compsite/conversation/moos.html).

6. *MOO* stands for "MUD Object Oriented." The initialism *MUD* denotes certain online environments called "Multiple User Dimensions" that allow several people to meet electronically. "Object Oriented" refers to the object-oriented programming used in software that creates these online environments.

COURSEWARE

Courseware—sometimes known as "class-management software"—refers to a collection of Web-based tools designed for education. Because most courseware relies on the Web for its interface, it is generally easy to learn and can be accessed from any recent computer that has an Internet connection. Numerous courseware packages are available; some of the most common are CourseInfo, WebCT, and TopClass. Generally they all provide three kinds of tools: communications systems such as e-mail, discussion forums, and chat tools; collaboration options such as file sharing and group-facilitation spaces; and class management tools such as gradebooks and activity-tracking features.

Let's look at some of the courseware features that are most useful for writing classes. Keep in mind that the particular package that you use may have different names for these technologies, but generally, they perform similar functions.

- *Announcement features* let teachers post regular messages to the class. Announcements are composed directly into a form provided by the courseware package for quick posting. Such daily announcements let teachers highlight important tasks and offer them the flexibility to adjust their teaching plans as the course evolves. Students who regularly use courseware develop the habit of checking the latest announcements to see if any important deadlines are approaching or if assignments have changed.

- *Assignment options* provide a space for posting formal assignments. Often the courseware allows teachers to upload prewritten files—an assignment created with a word processor, for example—as well as offering a form for composing assignments online. Posting assignments electronically saves paper, but over time, it also creates an easily accessible archive of assignments for students who must or who prefer to consult them outside of class.

- *Document spaces* allow teachers to post files that students can view online. Teachers customarily use this feature to provide essays and other materials that they want students to read. Articles and other texts, images, even video or sound files can be posted to a class document space. Of course, you will need to address copyright issues associated with disseminating such materials electronically.

- *File-sharing systems* differ from assignment and document spaces by allowing students to upload and download materials to the class space. Asking students to share files can be one of the most powerful ways to use a courseware package in your writing class. Any activities centered around drafting and revising compositions can benefit from the efficiency of online file sharing. When you integrate the word processing activities discussed earlier in this chapter with file-sharing systems, students will be able to read, review, and respond to one another's drafts productively.

- *Group spaces* promote collaborative work. Most advanced courseware systems allow teachers to create separate file-sharing and communications spaces for small groups within a larger class. Group spaces afford collaborators an opportunity to share ideas and develop projects in relative privacy. Teachers have access to the group's materials and can observe or participate in small-group activities, but other members of the class will be excluded. Teachers also can adapt the group-creation feature of most courseware to suit particular needs, splitting a class in half, for instance, to make chat sessions more manageable.

- *Whiteboards* provide a shared space where class members can sketch, type, paste images, and sometimes demonstrate Web pages. Some courseware also integrates a chat function into the whiteboard system, allowing participants to hold discussions as they work together to develop projects. Though whiteboards offer great promise in promoting collaboration, they can be difficult to use. In general, groups larger than six or seven students will find interacting with whiteboards unwieldy.

The courseware available at your school probably comes with instructions. Manuals and other documents will explain each feature, and additional resources may offer advice about how to use the package effectively. If your school does not provide a courseware solution, you can rely on options freely available on the Internet (see http://sites.unc.edu/tools for more information). Because courseware is designed for use in a variety of disciplines, it contains some features that aren't likely to provide obvious benefits for writing classes. As with any technology, spend some time experimenting with the courseware available to you, but be prepared to adapt or drop features that don't meet your needs.

THE WORLD WIDE WEB

Teachers use the World Wide Web in two ways, as a teaching resource and as a multimedia composition platform. Without knowing much about computers at all, teachers can tap into the Web's electronic storehouses of teaching materials and information. Finding assignment ideas, teaching advice, and raw materials to use in class requires knowing only a few simple online search strategies. As a resource for students, the Web promotes the development of research skills such as finding, managing, and evaluating online information. Such skills increasingly are crucial to academic and professional success. With a little bit of experimentation, however, writing teachers and their students can create their own Web compositions. The technical steps required to create pages for the Web are relatively simple. With a little guidance, writers can begin building sites that allow them to publish for a real audience, exploring in the process the rhetorical decisions involved in composing documents that can contain links, text, images, and multimedia.

Let's go over some basic information about using the Web as a resource. The Internet, a vast system of computer networks, shares files and facilitates communication by using what are known as "protocols." E-mail, for instance, is often shared using the "post office protocol." The Web connects Internet servers across the globe by means of the hypertext transfer protocol, the "http" you see at the beginning of a Web address. Each Web server retains a unique address or domain name, http:// www.unc.edu for example. Files that reside on this Web server are identified by an Internet address consisting of the domain name of the server and information about the file itself. This unique address is called a URL (uniform resource locator). So, a URL such as http://www.unc. edu/news.html indicates a file called "news.html" located on a Web server at the domain "www.unc.edu."

You probably are already familiar with moving around on the Web, but teachers and students who browse the Web need to learn something about how it is organized. When browsing the Web, we can move from an organization's Web site, to an online business, to materials for a composition course, to a government database, and beyond. When clicking and following links, however, we can become lulled into the sense that we are moving through a seamless collection of documents. Sophisticated Web readers maintain an awareness of where the files they are looking at are located, which person or organization is responsible for them, and how they are connected to other documents. More like detectives than casual readers, Web researchers know that each file on the Web offers clues about its authorship and the best ways to approach it (you can learn more about Web URLs from the online tutorials at http:// milton.mse.jhu.edu:8001/research/education/url.html).

Understanding the nature and location of files on the Web is only the first step in learning to read Web materials critically. Because almost anyone with an Internet account can publish on the Web, the quality and variety of Web materials varies tremendously. As you and your students conduct research online, take every opportunity to emphasize the need for critical judgment. To assess the strengths and weaknesses of a source, readers should evaluate the authors or entities producing materials, the possible purposes motivating their creation, their internal logic, the rhetorical strategies they use, the types of evidence they employ, their correctness, and their sophistication. One way to introduce students to Web evaluation is to ask them to discuss the pros and cons of print and online resources. For instance, print resources may benefit from going through a review process as they make their way to publication. Online resources, on the other hand, may benefit from the currency that comes with immediate dissemination. Teachers who stress Web evaluation skills not only help students use electronic materials appropriately but also sharpen the ability to approach all resources critically (for more information on evaluating Internet sources, see CompSite's resources at http://www.abacon.com/compsite/resources/evalcentral. html).

Finally, you and your students should become efficient at finding information on the Web. To do so requires using Web search engines and constructing queries based on keywords. Search engines (sometimes called "Internet directories") provide databases that store information about Web files. Most search engines also provide collections of Web links organized by subject. Currently, the most powerful search engines are Google (http://google.com) and AltaVista (http://altavista.com), but keep in mind that search engines often arise or evolve quickly on the Internet (for the latest information on search engines check SearchEngineWatch at http://searchenginewatch.com). For researchers the essential feature of search engines are the databases because they can be searched using keywords. A researcher submits a query or list of keywords to the database, which then returns a listing of any files that contain those keywords. Of course, keyword searches can be more complex. For example, researchers can combine search terms either to broaden or limit the results of a query. They also can exclude search terms to refine a search, construct queries that look for particular phrases, and employ a number of other sophisticated techniques to locate online information. Since Internet searching (and the majority of library research) relies heavily on constructing and submitting successful queries to databases, teachers owe it to their students to explore with them the intricacies of constructing effective keyword searches (for more information on Internet searching and keyword queries, see the Finding Information on the Internet Tutorial at http://www.lib.berkeley.edu/Teaching Lib/Guides/Internet/FindInfo.html).

For teachers, the Web provides many resources directly relevant to our work in the classroom. As you learn to locate and use Web materials, you will no doubt find sites that offer assignments, advice, classroom materials, and other resources that are just right for you and your students. Here are a few sites to get you started:

- Colorado State University's Resources for Writers and Teachers (http://writing.colostate.edu/tools.htm)
  This site offers writing tutorials and guides as well as links to writing and teaching resources on the Internet.

- NCTE's Teaching Ideas Site
  (http://www.ncte.org/teach)
  Sponsored by NCTE, this site offers teaching ideas related to literature, journalism, technology, writing, and more.

- The Studio for Instructional Technology and English Studies' Teaching Pages
  (http://sites.unc.edu/teaching)
  This page features links to reading resources for writing teachers and to collections of assignments.
- CompSite's Teaching Tools Page
  (http://www.abacon.com/compsite/instructors)
  Sponsored by Allyn and Bacon Publishers, this site contains links to readings and resources, assignment collections, class sites, and other useful advice for teachers.
- The World Lecture Hall's English/Writing/Rhetoric Class Links
  (http://wnt.cc.utexas.edu/~ccdv543/wlh/report2.cfm?Descri ptorID=33)
  The University of Texas sponsors this page containing links to Web class sites for hundreds of composition courses.

While many teachers and students rely on the Web's ability to deliver resources, others use the Web as a writing space for creating their own electronic compositions. Although some Web sites are incredibly sophisticated, most can be created with surprising ease, even by beginning computer users. In fact, most pages today are composed using Web authoring programs that operate much like a word processor. Underlying this simplicity is a formatting language called "hypertext markup language" (HTML), which tells Web browsers how to display the information on the page. As authors gain experience, they come to learn more about the underlying complexities of Web pages, but a writing class can begin composing them knowing little or nothing about HTML.

Of course, Web authors do need to wrestle with what might be unfamiliar rhetorical concerns. Since Web projects often depend on creating links between documents, authors must act as information architects, developing ideas into "chunks" that can be arranged in multiple ways. Web authors also compose in the context of ready-made resources that can be incorporated into their work. So, in addition to presenting their own information about an issue or topic, Web authors collect, categorize, annotate, and organize online resources created by others. Furthermore, Web compositions, much more than printed essays, involve authors in a process of document design. They must consider emphasis, the use of colors, grouping, and layout as they decide how the Web page will look (for more information on Web composition, see ProjectCool at http://www.projectcool.com).

To get a sense of some of these design concerns, let's examine briefly the sample Web page in Figure 16.3. The image shows the opening screen of a Web page devoted to the problem of alcohol consumption on a college campus. The layout of this page reflects a number of decisions about how the document is designed. Document design relies on

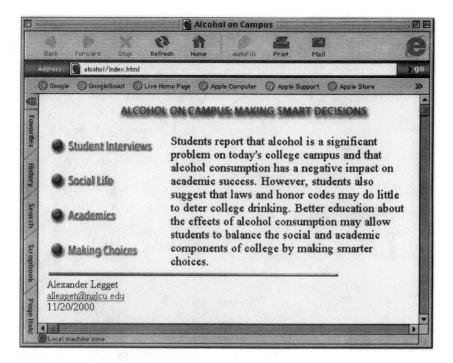

FIGURE 16.3 Sample Web Page

such concepts as grouping (organizing and presenting related materials similarly), emphasis (guiding a reader toward significant information), and layout (placing information effectively on the page). Examining the Web page shown in Figure 16.3 reveals some of these design strategies at work. The ample use of white space foregrounds the menu of links on the left-hand side and controls the flow of information. The small bullets marking each line of links provide emphasis and help guide the reader's eye toward them. The bullets and links are grouped and presented in a uniform font to help readers remain oriented to their function.

Also of interest is the relationship between the design elements and the text presented on this opening page. Some researchers believe that Web readers prefer to skim pages initially, gathering a quick sense of the information they provide. Then, readers decide either to devote more attention to the site or to move on to a new site. Accordingly, Web authors should compose an opening page that provides a sensible overview of a project in language carefully distilled to offer essential information. The page shown in Figure 16.3 uses design to give quick clues about the site's structure as well as access to its major components. It also complements these features with an introduction that uses words economically to describe the project.

We still have much to learn about how people read on the Web. Most likely we will discover that several modes of reading Web pages are possible and that successful Web authors are effective rhetoricians, thoughtfully addressing the concerns of their audience and composing with a clear sense of purpose. Because the Web provides wildly new rhetorical situations, it also affords excellent opportunities not only to experiment with new kinds of composing but also to practice writing strategies that we know to be successful in any rhetorical context.

Afterword

Donald Murray, a writer and teacher I greatly admire, once wrote, "The teacher of writing, first of all, must be a person for whom the student wants to write." To be a person requires both honesty and courage. To be honest with students is to acknowledge that writing courses belong to them, not to us. Their ideas, their voices shape the course and become its content. To be honest with ourselves is to recognize that we too are writers and, like our students, wrestle with the difficult process of creating meaning through language. A writing course then is also our opportunity to write, to share with students our voice and our wars with words.

But viewing writing courses this way also takes courage. Although the academic tradition expects us to profess a subject with authority, our first responsibility is to listen with understanding to our students' voices. Our function, first and foremost, is not to tell them what to say or how to express it but to help them find their own meanings and styles. To listen, then, is to profess that student voices matter, matter more in fact than our own.

It also takes courage to admit that we cannot be authorities, in the usual sense, transmitting a body of knowledge to students. Although age, experience, and training distance us from younger writers, we need not concern ourselves with bridging the gap, with teaching students what we know. Instead we must use our training and knowledge to help them discover their own world, their own ways of sharing it with others in writing. To be a person is much more difficult than being an authority, or a phony, or a mass of sympathies. Yet if we want our students to write well, we must understand what is truly basic to composing—a person communicating with another person.

Some Important Dates in the History of Composition and Rhetoric

The Classical Period

Corax of Syracuse	fl. 460 BCE
Gorgias of Leotini	fl. 420 BCE
Socrates	470?–399 BCE
Lysias	444?–380? BCE
Isocrates	436–338 BCE
Plato	427–347 BCE
Gorgias	c. 387–385 BCE
Phaedrus	c. 370 BCE
Aristotle	384–322 BCE
Rhetorica	c. 335 BCE
Demosthenes	384–322 BCE
Theophrastus	c. 370–285 BCE
Rhetorica ad Alexandrum	c. 340 BCE
On Style	317–307 BCE
Dionysius Thrax, Greek grammar	c. 100 BCE
Cicero	106–43 BCE
De Inventione	86 BCE
De Oratore	55 BCE
Brutus	46 BCE
Orator	46 BCE
Topica	44 BCE
Rhetorica ad Herennium	c. 86–82 BCE
Seneca the Elder	c. 60 BCE–41 CE
Suasoriae	c. 37 BCE–41 CE
Controversiae	c. 37 BCE–41 CE
Quintilian	35–100 CE
Institutio Oratoria	c. 94–95 CE
Longinus, *On the Sublime*	c. 40 CE
Hermagoras	fl. c. 150 CE
Hermogenes, *Progymnasmata*	150 CE

The Middle Ages

Donatus	fl. 333
Augustine of Hippo	354–430
De Doctrina Christiana	396–427
Aphthonius, *Progymnasmata*	c. 400
Martianus Capella, *De Nuptiis Philologiae et Mercurii*	c. 410–439
Priscian	fl. 500
Boethius	c. 475–525
Cassiodorus, *Institutiones Divinarum et Tararum*	c. 551–562
Isidore of Seville, *Etymologiae*	c. 600
Bede	673?–735
Alcuin	735?–804
Beowulf manuscript written	c. 1000
Battle of Hastings	1066
First Crusade	1096–1099
Averroes, commentaries on Aristotle	1126–1198
John of Salisbury, *Metalogicon*	1159
Matthew of Vendome, *Ars Versificatoria*	c. 1170
Alain of Lille, *De Arte Praedicatoria*	c. 1199
Geoffrey of Vinsauf, *Poetria Nova*	c. 1208–1213
John of Garland, *Parisiana Poetria*	c. 1220
Thomas Aquinas	1225–1274
Dante	1265–1321
English displaced French in courts and schools of England	1300–1400
Robert of Basevorn, *Forma Praedicandi*	1322
Chaucer	c. 1340–1400
George Trebizond, *Five Books of Rhetoric*	1433
Wordlists published; beginning of English lexicography	c. 1440
Gutenberg Bible	1456

The Renaissance

Desiderius Erasmus	1466?–1536
De Duplici Copia Verborum ac Rerum	1512
Juan Luis Vives	1492–1540
Martin Luther posts *Ninety-Five Theses*	1517
Philip Melanchthon, *Elementorum Rhetorices*	1519
Leonard Cox, *The Arte or Crafte of Rhetoryke*	1530
Leonard Johannes Susenbrotus, *Epitome Troporum ac Schematum*	1540
Peter Ramus, *Dialecticae*	1543
Omer Talon, *Rhetorica*	1548
Thomas Wilson, *The Rule of Reason*	1551
The Arte of Rhetorique	1553
Reign of Queen Elizabeth I	1558–1603

Richard Rainolde, *The Foundacion of Rhetorike*	1563
William Shakespeare	1564–1616
First known graphite pencil	1565
Gabriel Harvey, *Ciceronium vel Oratio post Reditum*	1577
Henry Peacham, *The Garden of Eloquence*	1577
Angel Day, *The English Secretary*	1586
George Puttenham, *The Arte of English Poesie*	1589

The Seventeenth Century

America

Jamestown settled	1607
Slavery introduced into Virginia	1619
Pilgrims land at Plymouth	1620
Harvard College founded	1636
First printing press in America	1639
Bay Psalm Book, first book printed in America	1640
Roger Williams, *Key into the Language of America* for the Narragansett Indians	1643
John Eliot translated the Bible into an Algonquian Indian language	1663
New England Primer	c. 1683
Publick Occurrences, first American newspaper	1690
Salem witchcraft trials	1692

Great Britain and the Continent

Francis Bacon, *The Advancement of Learning*	1605
John Milton	1608–1674
King James translation of the Bible	1611
Thomas Hobbes, *A Brief of the Art of Rhetorique*	1637
John Bulwer, *Chirologia*	1644
Thomas Blount, *The Academie of Eloquence*	1654
John Smith, *The Mysterie of Rhetorique Unvail'd*	1657
The Royal Society founded	1662
John Locke, *Essay concerning Human Understanding*	1690

The Eighteenth Century

America

Boston News Letter, first continuous newspaper	1704
Cotton Mather, *Manuductio ad Ministerium*	1726
George Washington	1732–1799
Thomas Jefferson	1743–1826
Benjamin Franklin, "Proposal for the Education of the Youth of Pennsylvania"	1749
Ebenezer Kinnersley lectured in English at the College of Philadelphia	1753–1773
The Stamp Act	1765

John Witherspoon lectured at the College of New Jersey (later Princeton)	1768–1794
First Continental Congress	1774
Revolutionary War	1775–1783
Declaration of Independence	1776
Articles of Confederation	1777
Noah Webster, *Grammatical Institutes of the English Language*	1783–1785
Constitution ratified	1788
Lindley Murray, *English Grammar, Adapted to the Different Classes of Learners*	1795

Great Britain and the Continent

The Daily Courant, first daily newspaper	1702
Edmund Burke	1729–1797
David Hume, *Essays Moral, Political and Literary*	1741
Johann Wolfgang von Goethe	1749–1832
Samuel Johnson, *A Dictionary of the English Language*	1755
John Lawson, *Lectures concerning Oratory*	1758
John Ward, *A System of Oratory*	1759
Robert Lowth, *The Short Introduction to English Grammar*	1762
Thomas Sheridan, *A Course of Lectures on Elocution*	1762
Henry Home, Lord Kames, *Elements of Criticism*	1762
Adam Smith, *Lectures on Rhetoric and Belles Lettres*	1762–1763
Thomas Gibbons, *Rhetoric*	1767
George Campbell, *The Philosophy of Rhetoric*	1776
Joseph Priestley, *Course of Lectures on Oratory and Criticism*	1777
John Walker, *Elements of Elocution*	1781
Hugh Blair, *Lectures on Rhetoric and Belles Lettres*	1783
French Revolution	1789–1802

The Nineteenth Century

America

Horace Mann	1796–1859
Library of Congress founded	1800
Ralph Waldo Emerson	1803–1882
Nature	1836
"The American Scholar"	1837
"The Poet"	1844
John Quincy Adams, first Boyleston Professor of Rhetoric at Harvard University	1806–1809
Joseph McKean, second Boyleston Professor	1809–1819
War with England	1812–1815
Henry Ward Beecher	1813–1887

Edward Channing, third Boyleston Professor	1819–1851
Lectures	1856
Samuel Hall opened first normal school for elementary teachers	1823
Samuel P. Newman, *A Practical System of Rhetoric*	1827
Noah Webster, *An American Dictionary of the Language*	1828
William McGuffey, *Eclectic Readers*	1836–1857
Envelopes for mail first used	1839
Charles Sanders Peirce, American pragmatism	1839–1914
Adhesive postage stamps first used	1842
Samuel F. B. Morse demonstrated telegraph to Congress	1844
Richard Green Parker, *Aids to English Composition*	1844
William T. Shedd translated Franz Theremin, *Eloquence a Virtue*	1844
Henry N. Day, *Elements of the Art of Rhetoric*	1850
Francis Child, fourth Boyleston Professor	1851–1876
Literacy as qualification for voting in Massachusetts	1857
National Teachers Association founded (later NEA)	1857
Eraser attached to pencil	1858
G. P. Quakenbos, *Advanced Course of Composition and Rhetoric*	1859
John Dewey	1859–1952
The School and Society	1899
Democracy and Education	1916
Civil War	1861–1865
Morrill Act established agricultural colleges	1862
Metal paper fasteners patented	1864
Twenty colleges founded for African Americans	1865–1870
Christopher Latham Sholes invented typewriter	1867
Transcontinental railroad completed	1869
Essay required for Harvard entrance examination	1874
Edwin A. Abbott, *How to Write Clearly*	1874
Tax-supported high schools established	c. 1874
Alonzo Reed and Brainerd Kellogg, *Graded Lessons in English*	1875
American Library Association founded	1876
Adams Sherman Hill, fifth Boyleston Professor	1876–1904
The Principles of Rhetoric and Their Application	1878
Alexander Graham Bell patented the telephone	1878
Modern Language Association founded	1883
Harvard established first-year composition course	1885
John F. Genung, *The Practical Elements of Rhetoric*	1885
Hand-held pencil sharpener	1890
William James, *Principles of Psychology*	1890
Barrett Wendell, *English Composition*	1891

Fred Newton Scott and Joseph Denney,	
Paragraph-Writing	1891
International Copyright Act	1891
Reports by Harvard's Committee on Composition	
and Rhetoric	1892–1897
NEA Committee of Ten included English in high	
school program of study	1894
Paper clip patented	1898
Gertrude Buck, *The Metaphor*, an early doctoral	
dissertation in rhetoric	1899

Great Britain and the Continent

Gilbert Austin, *Chironomia*	1806
Charles Dickens	1812–1870
Battle of Waterloo	1815
Matthew Arnold	1822–1888
Essays in Criticism	1865
Culture and Anarchy	1869
Discourses in America	1885
James Rush, *The Philosophy of the Human Voice*	1827
Slip-in metal pen points manufactured	1828
Richard Whateley, *Elements of Rhetoric*	1828
Thomas DeQuincey, essays on rhetoric, style,	
and language	1828–1876
Reform Bill	1832
Reign of Queen Victoria	1837–1901
Herbert Spencer, "The Philosophy of Style"	1852
Charles Darwin, *Origin of Species*	1859
Alexander Bain, *English Composition and Rhetoric*	1866
John Henry Newman, *An Essay in Aid of a Grammar*	
of Assent	1870
Oxford English Dictionary	1884–1928
Jean Piaget	1896–1980

The Twentieth Century

Kenneth Burke	1897–1993
Counter-Statement	1931
A Grammar of Motives	1945
A Rhetoric of Motives	1950
Edwin Lewis, *Specimens of the Forms of Discourse*	1900
First Nobel Prize for Literature	1901
Edwin C. Wolley, *Handbook of Composition*	1907
Le Baron Russell Briggs, sixth Boyleston Professor	1904–1925
Otto Jespersen, *A Modern English Grammar on*	
Historical Principles	1909–1949
National Council of Teachers of English founded	1911

Speech Communication Association founded	1914
Desk-model office stapler	1914
World War I	1914–1917
James Winans, *Public Speaking*	1915
Jerome Bruner	1915–
On Knowing: Essays for the Left Hand	1962
The Process of Education	1963
Toward a Theory of Instruction	1966
First Pulitzer Prizes awarded	1918
H. L. Mencken, *The American Language*	1919
I. A. Richards and C. K. Ogden, *The Meaning of Meaning*	1923
Linguistic Society of America founded	1924
Charles T. Copeland, seventh Boyleston Professor	1925–1937
Cellophane tape invented	1925
Workbooks introduced into English courses	1926
Charles Woolbert, *The Fundamentals of Speech*	1927
John E. Warriner, *Grammar and English Composition*	1932
Leonard Bloomfield, *Language*	1933
William F. Thrall and Addison Hibbard, *Handbook to Literature*	1936
Association of Teachers of English in Negro Colleges founded (later CLA)	1937
College English Association founded	1938
Cleanth Brooks and Robert Penn Warren, *Understanding Poetry*	1938
World War II	1939–1945
Television broadcasts at New York World's Fair	1939
John C. Hodges, *Harbrace College Handbook*	1941
John Crowe Ransom, *The New Criticism*	1941
Ballpoint pens manufactured	1943
ENIAC computer completed	1945
International Reading Association founded	1947
James McKrimmon, *Writing with a Purpose*	1950
Conference on College Composition and Communication founded	1950
Commercial xerographic copiers available	1950
Korean War	1950–1953
Segregation declared unconstitutional	1954
Noam Chomsky, *Syntactic Structures*	1957
Stephen Toulmin, *The Uses of Argument*	1958
Basic Issues in the Teaching of English	1959
Wayne Booth, *The Rhetoric of Fiction*	1961
Vietnam War	1961–1973
Lev Vygotsky, *Thought and Language*	1962

Richard Braddock, Richard Lloyd-Jones, and Lowell Schoer, *Research in Written Composition*	1963
Albert Kitzhaber, *Themes, Theories, Therapy*	1963
Marshall McLuhan, *Understanding Media*	1964
National Defense Education Act (1958) promoted study of language and composition	1964
Edward P. J. Corbett, *Classical Rhetoric for the Modern Student*	1965
Frank O'Hare, *Sentence Combining: Improving Formal Grammar without Formal Grammar Instruction*	1965
Dartmouth Conference	1966
Webster's Third New International Dictionary	1966
Research in the Teaching of English began publication	1967
Rhetoric Society of America founded	1968
Paulo Freire, *Pedagogy of the Oppressed*	1968
Donald Murray, *A Writer Teaches Writing*	1968
ARPAnet computer network established	1969
Chaim Perelman and L. Olbrechts-Tyteca, *The New Rhetoric*	1969
Janet Emig, *The Composing Processes of Twelfth Graders*	1971
Freshman English News began publication	1972
Wyoming Conference on English	1973
Peter Elbow, *Writing without Teachers*	1973
Students' Right to Their Own Language	1974
Teaching English in the Two-Year College began publication	1974
Writing-across-the-curriculum program established at Carleton College	1974
Bay Area Writing Project established	1974
J. A. Austin, *How to Do Things with Words*	1975
Michel Bakhtin, *The Dialogic Imagination*	1975
Newsweek published "Why Johnny Can't Write"	1975
Council of Writing Program Administrators founded	1976
Gary Tate, *Teaching Composition: Ten Bibliographical Essays*	1976
Michel Foucault, *The Archaeology of Knowledge*	1976
Mina Shaughnessy, *Errors and Expectations: A Guide for the Teacher of Basic Writing*	1977
E. D. Hirsch, Jr., *The Philosophy of Composition*	1977
Personal computers increased in popularity	c. 1977
James Moffett, *Teaching the Universe of Discourse*	1978
Journal of Basic Writing began publication	1978
Journal of Advanced Composition began publication	1980
The Writing Center Journal began publication	1980
Post-It Notes developed	1980

James Kinneavy, *A Theory of Discourse*	1980
Rhetoric Review began publication	1982
Internet created	1983
Written Communication began publication	1984
Center for the Study of Writing and Literacy	1985–1995
George Hillocks, Jr., *Research on Written Composition:*	
New Directions for Teaching	1986
English Coalition Conference	1987
Longman Bibliography of Composition and Rhetoric	1987
Stephen M. North, *The Making of Knowledge in*	
Composition: Portrait of an Emerging Field	1987

A Selected Bibliography

Although the "List of Works Consulted" immediately following cites many helpful books, articles, online resources, and videotapes, this list represents only a few essential resources for writing teachers. If you have not taught writing before or want to make your teaching more effective, these books offer useful places to begin.

Corbett, Edward P. J., Nancy Myers, and Gary Tate, eds. *The Writing Teacher's Sourcebook.* 4th ed. New York: Oxford University Press, 2000.

Dixon, Peter. *Rhetoric.* London: Methuen, 1971.

Elbow, Peter. *Writing without Teachers.* New York: Oxford University Press, 1973.

Hillocks, George, Jr. *Teaching Writing as Reflective Practice.* New York: Teachers College Press, 1995.

Lindemann, Erika, and Gary Tate, eds. *An Introduction to Composition Studies.* New York: Oxford University Press, 1991.

Murray, Donald. *A Writer Teaches Writing.* 2d ed. Boston: Houghton Mifflin, 1985.

Shaughnessy, Mina. *Errors and Expectations: A Guide for the Teacher of Basic Writing.* New York: Oxford University Press, 1977.

Tate, Gary, ed. *Teaching Composition: Twelve Bibliographical Essays.* Fort Worth: Texas Christian University Press, 1987.

White, Edward M. *Teaching and Assessing Writing.* 2d ed. The Jossey-Bass Higher Education Series. San Francisco: Jossey-Bass, 1994.

Williams, James D. *Preparing to Teach Writing.* 2d ed. Mahwah, NJ: Lawrence Erlbaum Associates, 1998.

List of Works Consulted

Abbreviations: CCC—*College Composition and Communication*
CE—*College English*
EJ—*English Journal*
MLA—The Modern Language Association of America
NCTE—National Council of Teachers of English
PMLA—*Publications of the Modern Language Association of America*
RTE—*Research in the Teaching of English*

HISTORY OF RHETORIC AND COMPOSITION

Aristotle. *On Rhetoric: A Theory of Civic Discourse.* Trans. George A. Kennedy. New York: Oxford University Press, 1991.

Bacon, Francis. *Advancement of Learning.* Great Books of the Western World, Vol. 30. Chicago: Encyclopaedia Britannica, 1952.

Bator, Paul. "Aristotelian and Rogerian Rhetoric." *CCC* 31 (December 1980), 427–32.

Berlin, James A. *Rhetoric and Reality: Writing Instruction in American Colleges, 1900–1985.* Studies in Writing and Rhetoric. Carbondale: Southern Illinois University Press, 1987.

———. *Writing Instruction in Nineteenth-Century American Colleges.* Studies in Writing and Rhetoric. Carbondale: Southern Illinois University Press, 1984.

Berthoff, Ann E. "I. A. Richards and the Philosophy of Rhetoric." *Rhetoric Society Quarterly* 10 (Fall 1980), 195–210.

Bizzell, Patricia, and Bruce Herzberg, eds. *The Rhetorical Tradition: Readings from Classical Times to the Present.* Boston: Bedford Books, 1990.

Brereton, John C., ed. *The Origins of Composition Studies in the American College, 1875–1925.* Pittsburgh Series in Composition, Literacy, and Culture. Pittsburgh: University of Pittsburgh Press, 1995.

Brody, Miriam. *Manly Writing: Gender, Rhetoric, and the Rise of Composition.* Carbondale: Southern Illinois University Press, 1993.

Burke, Kenneth. "Rhetoric—Old and New." In *New Rhetorics,* edited by Martin Steinmann, Jr., 60–76. New York: Charles Scribner's Sons, 1967. Reprinted from *Journal of General Education* 5 (April 1951), 203–09.

Campbell, George. *The Philosophy of Rhetoric,* edited by Lloyd F. Bitzer. Carbondale: Southern Illinois University Press, 1963.

Cicero. *De Oratore.* Trans. E. W. Sutton and H. Rackham. In *Readings in Classical Rhetoric,* edited by Thomas W. Benson and Michael H. Prosser, 91–107. Bloomington: Indiana University Press, 1972.

Comprone, Joseph. "Kenneth Burke and the Teaching of Writing." *CCC* 29 (December 1978), 336–40.

Conley, Thomas M. *Rhetoric in the European Tradition*. Chicago: The University of Chicago Press, 1990.

Connors, Robert J. *Composition-Rhetoric: Backgrounds, Theory, and Pedagogy*. Pittsburgh Series in Composition, Literacy, and Culture. Pittsburgh: University of Pittsburgh Press, 1997.

———. "Journals in Composition Studies." *CE* 46 (April 1984), 348–65.

———. "The Rise and Fall of the Modes of Discourse." *CCC* 32 (December 1981), 446–63.

Connors, Robert J., Lisa S. Ede, and Andrea A. Lunsford, eds. *Essays on Classical Rhetoric and Modern Discourse*. Carbondale: Southern Illinois University Press, 1984.

Corbett, Edward P. J. "The Theory and Practice of Imitation in Classical Rhetoric." *CCC* 22 (October 1971), 243–50.

———. "The Usefulness of Classical Rhetoric." *CCC* 14 (October 1963), 62–64.

Crowley, Sharon. *Composition in the University: Historical and Polemical Essays*. Pittsburgh Series in Composition, Literacy, and Culture. Pittsburgh: University of Pittsburgh Press, 1998.

Dixon, Peter. *Rhetoric*. London: Methuen, 1971.

Enos, Theresa, ed. *Encyclopedia of Rhetoric and Composition: Communication from Ancient Times to the Information Age*. New York: Garland, 1995.

Freedman, Aviva, and Ian Pringle, eds. *Reinventing the Rhetorical Tradition*. Conway, AR: L & S Books, 1980.

Fulkerson, Richard. "Composition Theory in the Eighties: Axiological Consensus and Paradigmatic Diversity." *CCC* 41 (December 1990), 409–29.

Gere, Anne Ruggles. *Writing Groups: History, Theory, and Implications*. Studies in Writing and Rhetoric. Carbondale: Southern Illinois University Press, 1987.

Golden, James L., and Edward P. J. Corbett, eds. *The Rhetoric of Blair, Campbell, and Whately*. New York: Holt, Rinehart and Winston, 1968.

Golden, James L., Goodwin F. Berquist, and William E. Coleman. *The Rhetoric of Western Thought*. 2d ed. Dubuque, IA: Kendall Hunt, 1978.

Halloran, Michael. "Rhetoric in the American College Curriculum: The Decline of Public Discourse." *PRE/TEXT* 3 (1982), 245–69.

Harris, Joseph. *A Teaching Subject: Composition since 1966*. Prentice Hall Studies in Writing and Culture. Upper Saddle River, NJ: Prentice Hall, 1997.

Hochmuth, Marie. "Kenneth Burke and the 'New Rhetoric.'" *Quarterly Journal of Speech* 38 (April 1952), 133–44.

Horner, Winifred Bryan, ed. *Historical Rhetoric: An Annotated Bibliography of Selected Sources in English*. Boston: G. K. Hall, 1980.

———. *Nineteenth-Century Scottish Rhetoric: The American Connection*. Carbondale: Southern Illinois University Press, 1993.

———, ed. *The Present State of Scholarship in Historical and Contemporary Rhetoric*. Rev. ed. Columbia: University of Missouri Press, 1990.

Howell, Wilbur S. *Eighteenth-Century British Logic and Rhetoric*. Princeton, NJ: Princeton University Press, 1971.

———. *Logic and Rhetoric in England, 1500–1700*. New York: Russell & Russell, 1961.

Johnson, Nan. *Nineteenth-Century Rhetoric in North America.* Carbondale: Southern Illinois University Press, 1991.

Joseph, Miriam. *Rhetoric in Shakespeare's Time.* New York: Harcourt, Brace and World, 1962.

Kennedy, George A. *Classical Rhetoric and Its Christian and Secular Tradition from Ancient to Modern Times.* Chapel Hill: University of North Carolina Press, 1980.

———. *A New History of Classical Rhetoric.* Princeton, NJ: Princeton University Press, 1972.

Kitzhaber, Albert R. *Rhetoric in American Colleges, 1850–1900.* Ph.D. diss., University of Washington, 1953. SMU Studies in Composition and Rhetoric. Dallas: Southern Methodist University Press, 1990.

———. *Themes, Theories, and Therapy: The Teaching of Writing in College.* New York: McGraw-Hill, 1963.

Knoblauch, C. H., and Lil Brannon. *Rhetorical Traditions and the Teaching of Writing.* Upper Montclair, NJ: Boynton/Cook, 1984.

Lunsford, Andrea A. "Alexander Bain's Contributions to Discourse Theory." *CE* 44 (March 1982), 290–300.

———, ed. *Reclaiming Rhetorica: Women in the Rhetorical Tradition.* Pittsburgh Series in Composition, Literacy, and Culture. Pittsburgh: University of Pittsburgh Press, 1995.

Miller, Susan. *Textual Carnivals: The Politics of Composition.* Carbondale: Southern Illinois University Press, 1991.

Murphy, James J. *Rhetoric in the Middle Ages.* Berkeley: University of California Press, 1974.

———, ed. *The Rhetorical Tradition and Modern Writing.* New York: MLA, 1982.

———, ed. *A Short History of Writing Instruction from Ancient Greece to Twentieth-Century America.* Davis, CA: Hermagoras Press, 1990.

———, ed. *A Synoptic History of Classical Rhetoric.* Davis, CA: Hermagoras Press, 1983.

Ohmann, Richard M. *English in America: A Radical View of the Profession.* New York: Oxford University Press, 1976.

Parker, William Riley. "Where Do English Departments Come From?" *CE* 28 (February 1967), 339–51.

Plato. *The Dialogues of Plato.* Trans. Benjamin Jowett. Great Books of the Western World Vol. 7. Chicago: Encyclopaedia Britannica, 1952.

Quintilian. *The Institutio Oratoria of Quintilian.* 4 vols. Trans. H. E. Butler. Loeb Classical Library. Cambridge, MA: Harvard University Press, 1920–22.

Rudolph, Frederick. *Curriculum: A History of the American Undergraduate Course of Study since 1636.* San Francisco: Jossey-Bass, 1978.

Russell, David R. *Writing in the Academic Disciplines, 1870–1990: A Curricular History.* Carbondale: Southern Illinois University Press, 1991.

Scaglione, Aldo. *The Classical Theory of Composition from Its Origins to the Present: A Historical Survey.* Chapel Hill: University of North Carolina Press, 1972.

Stewart, Donald C. "The Status of Composition and Rhetoric in American Colleges, 1880–1902: An MLA Perspective." *CE* 47 (November 1985), 734–46.

[Stone, George Winchester.] "The Beginning, Development, and Impact of the MLA as a Learned Society: 1883–1958." *PMLA* 73 (December 1958), 23–44.

Tobin, Lad, and Thomas Newkirk, eds. *Taking Stock: The Writing Process Movement in the Nineties.* Portsmouth, NH: Boynton/Cook, 1994.

Weaver, Richard. "Language Is Sermonic." In *The Rhetoric of Western Thought.* 2d ed., edited by James L. Golden, Goodwin F. Berquist, and William E. Coleman, 202–11. Dubuque, IA: Kendall Hunt, 1978.

Winterowd, W. Ross. *Rhetoric: A Synthesis.* New York: Holt, Rinehart and Winston, 1968.

RESEARCH

Beach, Richard, and Lillian S. Bridwell, eds. *New Directions in Composition Research.* New York: Guilford Press, 1984.

Braddock, Richard, Richard Lloyd-Jones, and Lowell Schoer. *Research in Written Composition.* Urbana, IL: NCTE, 1963.

Daiker, Donald A., and Max Morenberg, eds. *The Writing Teacher as Researcher: Essays in the Theory and Practice of Class-Based Research.* Portsmouth, NH: Boynton/Cook, 1990.

Flood, James, Julie Jensen, Diane Lapp, and James R. Squire, eds. *Handbook of Research on Teaching the English Language Arts.* New York: Macmillan, 1991.

Hayes, John R., et al., eds. *Reading Empirical Research Studies: The Rhetoric of Research.* Hillsdale, NJ: Lawrence Erlbaum Associates, 1992.

Heilker, Paul, and Peter Vandenberg, eds. *Keywords in Composition Studies.* Portsmouth, NH: Boynton/Cook, 1996.

Hillocks, George, Jr. *Research on Written Composition: New Directions for Teaching.* Urbana, IL: ERIC Clearinghouse on Reading and Communication Skills and the National Conference on Research in English, 1986.

Jolliffe, David, ed. *Advances in Writing Research, Volume Two: Writing in Academic Disciplines.* Norwood, NJ: Ablex, 1988.

Kirsch, Gesa, and Patricia A. Sullivan, eds. *Methods and Methodology in Composition Research.* Carbondale: Southern Illinois University Press, 1992.

Lauer, Janice M., and J. William Asher. *Composition Research: Empirical Designs.* New York: Oxford University Press, 1988.

McClelland, Ben W., and Timothy R. Donovan, eds. *Perspectives on Research and Scholarship in Composition.* New York: MLA, 1985.

Moran, Michael G., and Martin J. Jacobi, eds. *Research in Basic Writing: A Bibliographic Sourcebook.* Westport, CT: Greenwood Press, 1990.

Moran, Michael G., and Debra Journet, eds. *Research in Technical Communication: A Bibliographic Sourcebook.* Westport, CT: Greenwood Press, 1985.

Moran, Michael G., and Ronald F. Lunsford, eds. *Research in Composition and Rhetoric: A Bibliographic Sourcebook.* Westport, CT: Greenwood Press, 1984.

Mosenthal, Peter, Lynne Tamor, and Sean A. Walmsley, eds. *Research on Writing: Principles and Methods.* New York: Longman, 1983.

North, Stephen M. *The Making of Knowledge in Composition: Portrait of an Emerging Field.* Upper Montclair, NJ: Boynton/Cook, 1987.

Sommers, Nancy I. "The Need for Theory in Composition Research." *CCC* 30 (February 1979), 46–49.

COMPOSING, READING, AND LITERACY

Baratz, Joan C., and Roger W. Shuy, eds. *Teaching Black Children to Read.* Washington, DC: Center for Applied Linguistics, 1969.

Bartholomae, David. "Inventing the University." In *When a Writer Can't Write: Studies in Writer's Block and Other Composing Process Problems*, edited by Mike Rose, 134–65. Perspectives in Writing Research. New York: Guilford Press, 1985.

Bazerman, Charles. *Shaping Written Knowledge.* Madison: University of Wisconsin Press, 1988.

Berthoff, Ann E. "From Problem-Solving to a Theory of Imagination." *CE* 33 (March 1972), 636–49.

Bizzell, Patricia. *Academic Discourse and Critical Consciousness.* Pittsburgh Series in Composition, Literacy, and Culture. Pittsburgh: University of Pittsbrugh Press, 1992.

Booth, Wayne C. "The Rhetorical Stance." *CCC* 14 (October 1963), 139–45.

Britton, James, et al. *The Development of Writing Abilities, 11–18.* Schools Council Research Series. London: Macmillan Education, 1975.

Brodkey, Linda. *Academic Writing as Social Practice.* Philadelphia: Temple University Press, 1987.

Burke, Kenneth. *Counter-Statement.* 3d ed. Berkeley: University of California Press, 1968.

———. *A Grammar of Motives.* Berkeley: University of California Press, 1969.

———. *A Rhetoric of Motives.* Berkeley: University of California Press, 1969.

Chiseri-Strater, Elizabeth. *Academic Literacies: The Public and Private Discourse of University Students.* Portsmouth, NH: Boynton/Cook, 1991.

Christensen, Francis, and Bonniejean Christensen. *Notes toward a New Rhetoric.* 2d ed. New York: Harper & Row, 1978.

Coe, Richard. "Rhetoric 2001." *Freshman English News* 3 (Spring 1974), 1–13.

———. *Toward a Grammar of Passages.* Studies in Writing and Rhetoric. Carbondale: Southern Illinois University Press, 1988.

Comprone, Joseph. "Recent Research in Reading and Its Implications for the College Composition Curriculum." *Rhetoric Review* 1 (January 1983), 122–37.

Cooper, Charles, and Anthony R. Petrosky. "A Psycholinguistic View of the Fluent Reading Process." *Journal of Reading* 19 (December 1976), 184–207.

Cooper, Marilyn. "The Ecology of Writing." *CE* 48 (April 1986), 364–75.

Cooper, Marilyn M., and Michael Holzman. *Writing as Social Action.* Portsmouth, NH: Boynton/Cook, 1989.

Cowley, Malcolm, ed. *Writers at Work.* New York: Viking, 1958.

D'Angelo, Frank. *A Conceptual Theory of Rhetoric.* Boston: Little, Brown, 1975.

———. "A Generative Rhetoric of the Essay." *CCC* 25 (December 1974), 388–96.

Dillon, George L. *Constructing Texts: Elements of a Theory of Composition and Style*. Bloomington: Indiana University Press, 1981.

Donelson, K. L. "Variables Distinguishing between Effective and Ineffective Writers in the Tenth Grade." *Journal of Experimental Education* 35 (Summer 1967), 37–41.

Ede, Lisa, and Andrea Lunsford. "Audience Addressed/Audience Invoked: The Role of Audience in Composition Theory and Pedagogy." *CCC* 35 (May 1984), 155–71.

———. *Singular Texts/Plural Authors: Perspectives on Collaborative Writing*. Carbondale: Southern Illinois University Press, 1990.

Emig, Janet. *The Composing Processes of Twelfth Graders*. NCTE Research Report No. 13. Urbana, IL: NCTE, 1971.

———. "Hand, Eye, Brain: Some 'Basics' in the Writing Process." In *Research on Composing: Points of Departure*, edited by Charles R. Cooper and Lee Odell, 59–71. Urbana, IL: NCTE, 1978.

Fahnestock, Jeanne, and Marie Secor. "Teaching Argument: A Theory of Types." *CCC* 34 (February 1983), 20–33.

Flower, Linda. *The Construction of Negotiated Meaning: A Social Cognitive Theory of Writing*. Carbondale: Southern Illinois University Press, 1994.

Flower, Linda S., and John R. Hayes. "A Cognitive Process Theory of Writing." *CCC* 32 (December 1981), 367–87.

———. "The Dynamics of Composing: Making Plans and Juggling Constraints." In *Cognitive Processes in Writing*, edited by Lee W. Gregg and Erwin R. Steinberg, 31–50. Hillsdale, NJ: Lawrence Erlbaum Associates, 1980.

———. "Problem-Solving Strategies and the Writing Process." *CE* 39 (December 1977), 449–61.

Flynn, Elizabeth A. "Composing as a Woman. " *CCC* 39 (December 1988), 423–35.

Frederiksen, C., M. Whiteman, and J. Dominic, eds. *Writing: The Nature, Development and Teaching of Written Communication*. 2 vols. Hillsdale, NJ: Lawrence Erlbaum Associates, 1981.

Gregg, Lee W., and Erwin R. Steinberg, eds. *Cognitive Processes in Writing*. Hillsdale, NJ: Lawrence Erlbaum Associates, 1980.

Harris, Joseph. "The Idea of Community in the Study of Writing." *CCC* 40 (February 1989), 11–23.

Hayes, John R., and Linda S. Flower. "Identifying the Organization of Writing Processes." In *Cognitive Processes in Writing*, edited by Lee W. Gregg and Erwin R. Steinberg, 3–30. Hillsdale, NJ: Lawrence Erlbaum Associates, 1980.

Heath, Shirley Brice. *Ways with Words: Language, Life, and Work in Communities and Classrooms*. New York: Cambridge University Press, 1983.

Hirsch, E. D., Jr. *The Philosophy of Composition*. Chicago: University of Chicago Press, 1977.

Kinneavy, James L. "A Pluralistic Synthesis of Four Contemporary Models for Teaching Composition." In *Reinventing the Rhetorical Tradition*, edited by Aviva Freedman and Ian Pringle, 37–52. Conway, AR: L & S Books, 1980.

———. *A Theory of Discourse*. New York: W. W. Norton, 1980.

Kintgen, Eugene R., Barry M. Kroll, and Mike Rose, eds. *Perspectives on Literacy*. Carbondale: Southern Illinois University Press, 1988.

Kirsch, Gesa. *Women Writing in the Academy: Audience, Authority, and Transformation*. Studies in Writing and Rhetoric. Carbondale: Southern Illinois University Press, 1993.

Knoblauch, C. H., and Lil Brannon. *Critical Teaching and the Idea of Literacy*. Portsmouth, NH: Boynton/Cook, 1993.

Kolers, Paul A. "Experiments in Reading." *Scientific American* 227 (July 1972), 84–91.

Kroll, Barry M., and Robert J. Vann, eds. *Exploring Speaking-Writing Relationships*. Urbana, IL: NCTE, 1981.

Lamb, Catherine E. "Beyond Argument in Feminist Composition." *CCC* 42 (February 1991), 11–14.

Larson, Richard L. "Problem-Solving, Composing, and Liberal Education." *CE* 33 (March 1972), 628–35.

Lauer, Janice M. "Invention in Contemporary Rhetoric: Heuristic Procedures." Ph.D. diss., University of Michigan, 1967.

LeFevre, Karen Burke. *Invention as a Social Act*. Studies in Writing and Rhetoric. Carbondale: Southern Illinois University Press, 1987.

Luke, Allan. "Literacies as Social Practices." *English Education* 23 (October 1991), 131–47.

Miller, Susan. "What Does It Mean to Be Able to Write? The Question of Writing in the Discourses of Literature and Composition." *CE* 45 (March 1983), 219–35.

Moffett, James. "I, You, and It." *CCC* 16 (December 1965), 243–56.

———. *Teaching the Universe of Discourse*. Portsmouth, NH: Boynton/Cook, 1983.

Murray, Donald M. "Internal Revision: A Process of Discovery." In *Research on Composing: Points of Departure*, edited by Charles Cooper and Lee Odell, 85–103. Urbana, IL: NCTE, 1978.

Ong, Walter J. "Literacy and Orality in Our Times." *ADE Bulletin* 58 (September 1978), 1–7.

———. "The Writer's Audience Is Always a Fiction." *PMLA* 90 (January 1975), 9–21.

Perl, Sondra. "The Composing Processes of Unskilled College Writers." *RTE* 13 (December 1979), 317–36.

Pianko, Sharon. "A Description of the Composing Processes of College Freshman Writers." *RTE* 13 (February 1979), 5–22.

Rafoth, Bennett A., and Donald L. Rubin, eds. *The Social Construction of Written Communication*. Writing Research: Multidisciplinary Inquiries into the Nature of Writing. Norwood, NJ: Ablex, 1988.

Reither, James A. "Writing and Knowing: Toward Redefining the Writing Process." *CE* 47 (October 1985), 620–28.

Rohman, D. Gordon. "Pre-Writing: The Stage of Discovery in the Writing Process." *CCC* 16 (May 1965), 106–12.

Rose, Mike. *Writer's Block: The Cognitive Dimension*. Studies in Writing and Rhetoric. Carbondale: Southern Illinois University Press, 1984.

———, ed. *When a Writer Can't Write: Studies in Writer's Block and Other Composing Process Problems*. Perspectives in Writing Research. New York: Guilford Press, 1985.

Salvatori, Mariolina. "Reading and Writing a Text: Correlations between Reading and Writing." *CE* 45 (November 1983), 657–66.

Sommers, Nancy I. "Revision Strategies of Student Writers and Experienced Writers." *CCC* 31 (December 1980), 378–88.

Villanueva, Victor, Jr., ed. *Cross-Talk in Comp Theory: A Reader*. Urbana, IL: NCTE, 1997.

Wallace, Karl R. "*Topoi* and the Problem of Invention." *The Quarterly Journal of Speech* 58 (December 1972), 387–95.

Winterowd, W. Ross, ed. *Contemporary Rhetoric: A Conceptual Background with Readings*. New York: Harcourt Brace Jovanovich, 1975.

Witte, Stephen P. "Topical Structure and Revision: An Exploratory Study." *CCC* 34 (October 1983), 313–41.

Witte, Stephen, and Lester Faigley. "Coherence, Cohesion, and Writing Quality." *CCC* 32 (May 1981), 189–204.

Woodson, Linda. *A Handbook of Modern Rhetorical Terms*. Urbana, IL: NCTE, 1979.

Writers Writing (three documentary films about the writing process). Produced by Learning Designs and WNET/Thirteen, 1985. Distributed by the Encyclopaedia Britannica Educational Corporation, Chicago.

LANGUAGE AND LINGUISTICS

Baron, Dennis E. *Declining Grammar and Other Essays on the English Vocabulary*. Urbana, IL: NCTE, 1989.

———. *Grammar and Good Taste: Reforming the American Language*. New Haven, CT: Yale University Press, 1982.

Baugh, Albert C., and Thomas Cable. *A History of the English Language*. 4th ed. Englewood Cliffs, NJ: Prentice Hall, 1993.

Becker, Alton L. "A Tagmemic Approach to Paragraph Analysis." *CCC* 16 (December 1965), 237–42.

Bloomfield, Leonard. *Language*. New York: Henry Holt, 1933.

Braddock, Richard. "The Frequency and Placement of Topic Sentences in Expository Prose." *RTE 8* (Winter 1974), 287–302.

Britton, James. *Language and Learning*. 2d ed. Portsmouth, NH: Boynton/ Cook, 1993.

Brown, Roger. *A First Language: The Early Stages*. Cambridge, MA: Harvard University Press, 1973.

Bruffee, Kenneth A. "Social Construction, Language, and the Authority of Knowledge: A Bibliographical Essay." *CE* 48 (December 1986), 773–90.

Cazden, Courtney B. *Child Language and Education*. New York: Holt, Rinehart and Winston, 1972.

———. *Classroom Discourse: The Language of Teaching and Learning*. Portsmouth, NH: Boynton/Cook, 1988.

Chase, Stuart. "How Language Shapes Our Thoughts." In *Speaking of Words*, edited by James MacKillop and Donna Cross, 29–33. New York: Holt, Rinehart and Winston, 1978.

Chomsky, Noam. *Language and Mind*. Cambridge, MA: MIT Press, 1972.

———. *Syntactic Structures*. The Hague: Mouton, 1957.

Conference on College Composition and Communication. "Students' Right to Their Own Language." *CCC* 25 (Special Fall Issue 1974).

Creswell, Thomas J. *Usage in Dictionaries and Dictionaries of Usage*. Publication of the American Dialect Society, Numbers 63–64. University: University of Alabama Press, 1975.

DeBeaugrande, Robert. "Linguistic Theory and Composition." *CCC* 29 (May 1978), 134–40.

Elgin, Suzette Haden. *A Primer of Transformational Grammar: For the Rank Beginner.* Urbana, IL: NCTE, 1975.

Faigley, Lester L. "Generative Rhetoric as a Way of Increasing Syntactic Fluency." *CCC* 30 (May 1979), 176–81.

Farr, Marcia, and Harvey Daniels. *Language Diversity and Writing Instruction.* New York: ERIC Clearinghouse on Urban Education and the Institute for Urban and Minority Education; Urbana, IL: ERIC Clearinghouse on Reading and Communication Skills and NCTE, 1986.

Francis, W. Nelson. "Revolution in Grammar." *Quarterly Journal of Speech* 40 (October 1954), 299–312.

———. *The Structure of American English.* New York: Ronald Press, 1958.

Gelb, I. J. *A Study of Writing.* Rev. ed. Chicago: University of Chicago Press, 1963.

Gibson, Walker. *Tough, Sweet and Stuffy.* Bloomington: Indiana University Press, 1966.

Gilyard, Keith. *Voices of the Self: A Study of Language Competence.* Detroit: Wayne State University Press, 1991.

Gunderson, Doris V., ed. *Language and Reading.* Washington, DC: Center for Applied Linguistics, 1970.

Halliday, M. A. K., and Ruqaiya Hasan. *Cohesion in English.* English Language Series No. 9. London: Longman, 1976.

Harris, Zellig S. *Discourse Analysis Reprints.* Papers on Formal Linguistics No. 2. The Hague: Mouton, 1963.

Hartwell, Patrick. "Grammar, Grammars, and the Teaching of Grammar." *CE* 47 (February 1985), 105–27.

Herndon, Jeanne. *A Survey of Modern Grammars.* 2d ed. New York: Holt, Rinehart and Winston, 1976.

Hockett, Charles F. *A Course in Modern Linguistics.* New York: Macmillan, 1958.

Hunt, Kellogg W. *Grammatical Structures Written at Three Grade Levels.* NCTE Research Report No. 3. Urbana, IL: NCTE, 1965.

———. "A Synopsis of Clause-to-Sentence Length Factors." *EJ* 54 (April 1965), 300, 305–09.

Hunter, Susan, and Ray Wallace, eds. *The Place of Grammar in Writing Instruction: Past, Present, Future.* Portsmouth, NH: Boynton/Cook, 1995.

Jakobson, Roman. "Linguistics and Poetics." In *Style in Language,* edited by Thomas Sebeok, 350–77. Cambridge, MA: MIT Press, 1960.

Joos, Martin. *The Five Clocks.* New York: Harcourt, Brace and World, 1961.

Karrfalt, David H. "The Generation of Paragraphs and Larger Units." *CCC* 19 (October 1968), 211–17.

Kline, Charles R., Jr., and W. Dean Memering. "Formal Fragments: The English Minor Sentence." *RTE* 11 (Fall 1977), 97–110.

Lanham, Richard. *Style: An Anti-Textbook.* New Haven, CT: Yale University Press, 1974.

Lehmann, Winfred. *Historical Linguistics: An Introduction.* New York: Holt, Rinehart and Winston, 1962.

Malmstrom, Jean. "Linguistic Atlas Findings Versus Textbook Pronouncements on Current American Usage." *EJ* 48 (April 1959), 191–98.

McDavid, Raven I. "American English: A Bibliographic Essay." *American Studies International* 17 (Winter 1979), 3–45.

Meade, Richard A. "Who Can Learn Grammar?" *EJ* 50 (February 1961), 87–92.

Meade, Richard A., and W. Geiger Ellis. "Paragraph Development in the Modern Age of Rhetoric." *EJ* 59 (February 1970), 219–26.

Nystrand, Martin, ed. *Language as a Way of Knowing: A Book of Readings.* Symposium Series 8. Toronto: Ontario Institute for Studies in Education, 1977.

Pitkin, Willis L. "Discourse Blocs." *CCC* 20 (May 1969), 138–48.

Pooley, Robert C. *The Teaching of English Usage.* 2d ed. Urbana, IL: NCTE, 1974.

Pyles, Thomas. *The Origins and Development of the English Language.* 3d ed. New York: Harcourt Brace Jovanovich, 1982.

Rodgers, Paul C. "A Discourse-Centered Rhetoric of the Paragraph." *CCC* 17 (February 1966), 2–11.

The Sentence and the Paragraph. Urbana, IL: NCTE, 1963, 1965, and 1966.

Smitherman, Geneva. *Talkin' and Testifyin'.* Boston: Houghton Mifflin, 1977.

Stern, Arthur A. "When Is a Paragraph?" *CCC* 27 (October 1976), 253–57.

Weaver, Constance. *Grammar for Teachers: Perspectives and Definitions.* Urbana, IL: NCTE, 1979.

Whorf, Benjamin Lee. *Language, Thought and Reality,* edited by John B. Carroll. Cambridge, MA: MIT Press, 1967.

Williams, James D. "Rule-Governed Approaches to Language and Composition." *Written Communication* 10 (October 1993), 542–68.

Womack, Thurston. "Teachers' Attitudes toward Current Usage." *EJ* 48 (April 1959), 186–90.

COGNITION AND HUMAN DEVELOPMENT

Adams, James L. *Conceptual Blockbusting: A Pleasurable Guide to Better Problem Solving.* San Francisco: W. H. Freeman, 1974.

Beard, Ruth M. *An Outline of Piaget's Developmental Psychology for Students and Teachers.* Students Library of Education. London: Routledge and Kegan Paul, 1969.

Berger, Kathleen Stassen. *The Developing Person Through the Life Span.* New York: Worth, 1998.

Bruner, Jerome. *On Knowing: Essays for the Left Hand.* Cambridge, MA: The Belknap Press, 1962.

Dewey, John. *Experience and Education.* New York: Macmillan, 1938.

Flower, Linda. "Cognition, Context, and Theory Building." *CCC* 40 (October 1989), 282–311.

———. "Writer-Based Prose: A Cognitive Basis for Problems in Writing." *CE* 41 (September 1979), 19–37.

Flower, Linda S., and John R. Hayes. "The Cognition of Discovery: Defining a Rhetorical Problem." *CCC* 31 (February 1980), 21–32.

Gregory, R. L. *The Intelligent Eye.* New York: McGraw-Hill, 1970.

Haswell, Richard H. *Gaining Ground in College Writing: Tales of Development and Interpretation.* SMU Studies in Composition and Rhetoric. Dallas: Southern Methodist University Press, 1991.

Hays, Janice N. "Intellectual Parenting and a Developmental Feminist Pedagogy of Writing." In *Feminine Principles and Women's Experience in American Composition and Rhetoric,* edited by Louise Wetherbee Phelps and Janet Emig, 153–90. Pittsburgh Series in Composition, Literacy, and Culture. Pittsburgh: University of Pittsburgh Press, 1995.

———. "Models of Intellectual Development and Writing: A Response to Myra Kogen et al." *Journal of Basic Writing* 6 (1987), 11–27.

Kohlberg, Lawrence. *The Philosophy of Moral Development.* New York: HarperCollins, 1984.

Lefrancois, Guy R. *Of Children: An Introduction to Child Development.* 8th ed. Belmont, CA: Wadsworth, 1995.

Magolda, Marcia B. Baxter. *Knowing and Reasoning in College: Gender-Related Patterns in Students' Intellectual Development.* San Francisco: Jossey-Bass, 1992.

Perry, William, Jr. *Forms of Intellectual and Ethical Development in the College Years: A Scheme.* New York: Holt, Rinehart and Winston, 1968.

Ryle, Gilbert. *The Concept of Mind.* New York: Barnes & Noble, 1949.

Vygotsky, Lev. *Thought and Language.* Trans. Alex Kozulin. Cambridge, MA: MIT Press, 1962.

TEACHING AND LEARNING

Anderson, Daniel. *CompSite* (an online resource for composition teachers maintained by Allyn and Bacon). http://www.abacon.com/compsite (accessed 10 July 2000).

Anson, Chris M., Joan Graham, David A. Jolliffe, Nancy S. Shapiro, and Carolyn H. Smith. *Scenarios for Teaching Writing: Contexts for Discussion and Reflective Practice.* Urbana, IL: NCTE in cooperation with Alliance for Undergraduate Education, 1993.

Applebee, Arthur N. *Writing in the Secondary School: English and the Content Areas.* NCTE Research Report No. 21. Urbana, IL: NCTE, 1981.

Atwell, Nancie. *In the Middle: Writing, Reading, and Learning with Adolescents.* 2d ed. Portsmouth, NH: Boynton/Cook, 1998.

Bartholomae, David. "Teaching Basic Writing: An Alternative to Basic Skills." *Journal of Basic Writing* 2 (Spring/Summer 1979), 85–109.

Berlin, James A. "Rhetoric and Ideology in the Writing Class." *CE* 50 (September 1988), 477–94.

Berlin, James A., and Michael Vivion, eds. *Cultural Studies in the English Classroom.* Portsmouth, NH: Boynton/Cook, 1993.

Berthoff, Ann E., ed. *Reclaiming the Imagination: Philosophical Perspectives for Writers and Teachers of Writing.* Upper Montclair, NJ: Boynton/Cook, 1984.

———. *The Sense of Learning.* Portsmouth, NH: Boynton/Cook, 1990.

Bizzell, Patricia, and Bruce Herzberg. *The Bedford Bibliography for Teachers of Writing.* 4th ed. Boston: Bedford Books, 1996. http://www.bedfordstmartins.com/bb/contents.html (accessed 10 July 2000).

Black, Laurel. *Between Talk and Teaching: Reconsidering the Writing Conference.* Logan: Utah State University Press, 1998.

Bleich, David. *Know and Tell: A Writing Pedagogy of Disclosure, Genre, and Membership.* Portsmouth, NH: Boynton/Cook, 1998.

Boley, Tommy J. "A Heuristic for Persuasion." *CCC* 30 (May 1979), 187–91.

Bruffee, Kenneth A. "The Brooklyn Plan: Attaining Intellectual Growth through Peer-Group Tutoring," *Liberal Education* 64 (December 1978), 447–68.

———. "Collaborative Learning and the 'Conversation of Mankind.'" *CE* 46 (November 1984), 635–52.

———. *Collaborative Learning: Higher Education, Interdependence, and the Authority of Knowledge.* Baltimore: Johns Hopkins University Press, 1993.

Bullock, Richard, and John Trimbur, eds. *The Politics of Writing Instruction: Postsecondary.* Portsmouth, NH: Boynton/Cook, 1991.

Caywood, Cynthia L., and Gillian R. Overing, eds. *Teaching Writing: Pedagogy, Gender, and Equity.* Albany: State University of New York Press, 1987.

Coles, William E. "The Teaching of Writing as an Invitation to Becoming." Paper presented at the Institute on Writing. Iowa City, IA. May 1979.

———. "Teaching the Teaching of Composition: Style for the Sake of Style for the Sake of Style." Paper presented at the Institute on Writing. Iowa City, IA. May 1979.

Connors, Robert, and Cheryl Glenn. *The New St. Martin's Guide to Teaching Writing.* Boston: Bedford/St. Martin's, 1999.

Cooper, Charles R. "An Outline for Writing Sentence-Combining Problems." *EJ* 62 (January 1983), 96–102, 108.

Corbett, Edward P. J., Nancy Myers, and Gary Tate, eds. *The Writing Teacher's Sourcebook.* 4th ed. New York: Oxford University Press, 2000.

Daiker, Donald A., Andrew Kerek, and Max Morenberg, eds. *Sentence Combining and the Teaching of Writing.* Conway, AR: L & S Books, 1979.

Dethier, Brock. *The Composition Instructor's Survival Guide.* Portsmouth, NH: Boynton/Cook, 1999.

Dieterich, Daniel, ed. *Teaching about Doublespeak.* Urbana, IL: NCTE, 1976.

Donovan, Timothy R., and Ben W. McClelland, eds. *Eight Approaches to Teaching Composition.* Urbana, IL: NCTE, 1980.

Eble, Kenneth. *The Craft of Teaching: A Guide to Mastering the Professor's Art.* 2d ed. San Francisco: Jossey-Bass, 1988.

"English/Writing/Rhetoric." *The World Lecture Hall* (a collection of links to Web sites for a variety of writing courses). http://wnt.cc.utexas.edu/~ccdv543/wlh/report2.cfm?DescriptorID=33 (accessed 20 July 2000).

Enos, Theresa, ed. *A Sourcebook for Basic Writing Teachers.* New York: Random House, 1986.

Fahnestock, Jeanne, and Marie Secor. "Teaching Argument: A Theory of Types." *CCC* 34 (February 1983), 20–30.

Foster, David. *A Primer for Writing Teachers: Theories, Theorists, Issues, Problems.* 2d ed. Portsmouth, NH: Boynton/Cook, 1993.

Freire, Paulo. *Pedagogy of the Oppressed.* Trans. Myra Bergman Ramos. New York: Seabury, 1968.

Fulkerson, Richard. *Teaching the Argument in Writing*. Urbana, IL: NCTE, 1996.

Garrison, Roger. "One-to-One: Tutorial Instruction in Freshman Composition." *New Directions for Community Colleges* 2 (Spring 1974), 55–84.

Gebhardt, Richard C. "Imagination and Discipline in the Writing Class." *EJ* 66 (December 1977), 26–32.

Graves, Richard, ed. *Writing, Teaching, Learning: A Sourcebook*. Portsmouth, NH: Boynton/Cook, 1999.

Hairston, Maxine. "Diversity, Ideology, and Teaching Writing." *CCC* 43 (May 1992), 179–93.

———. "Using Carl Rogers' Communication Theories in the Composition Classroom." *Rhetoric Review* 1 (September 1982), 50–55.

Hamilton-Wieler, Sharon. *Collaborative Writing Workshop* (a videocassette offering advice on establishing a collaborative writing classroom). Produced by Indiana University at Indianapolis, 1990. Distributed by NCTE, Urbana, IL.

Harris, Muriel. *Teaching One-to-One: The Writing Conference*. Urbana, IL: NCTE, 1986.

Hartwell, Patrick. "Teaching Arrangement: A Pedagogy." *CE* 40 (January 1979), 548–54.

Hashimoto, Irvin Y. *Thirteen Weeks: A Guide to Teaching College Writing*. Portsmouth, NH: Boynton/Cook, 1991.

Healy, Mary K., and Ken Macrorie. *Writing across the Curriculum Workshops* (three videocassettes focusing on writing-to-learn, research, and revising for teachers from various disciplines). Produced in 1986 and distributed by Boynton/Cook, Portsmouth, NH.

Hiatt, Mary P. "Students at Bay: The Myth of the Student Conference." *CCC* 26 (February 1975), 38–41.

Hillocks, George, Jr. *Teaching Writing as Reflective Practice*. New York: Teachers College Press, 1995.

Holt, John. "How Teachers Make Children Hate Reading." In *The Norton Reader*. 6th ed., edited by Arthur M. Eastman, 224–32. New York: W. W. Norton, 1984. Reprinted from *Redbook* (November 1967).

Irmscher, William. *Teaching Expository Writing*. New York: Holt, Rinehart and Winston, 1979.

Kneupper, Charles. "Teaching Argument: An Introduction to the Toulmin Model." *CCC* 29 (October 1978), 237–41.

Larson, Richard L. "Discovery through Questioning: A Plan for Teaching Rhetorical Invention." *CE* 30 (November 1968), 126–34.

Lowman, Joseph. *Mastering the Techniques of Teaching*. 2d ed. San Francisco: Jossey-Bass, 1995.

Lunsford, Andrea A. "What We Know—and Don't Know—about Remedial Writing." *CCC* 29 (February 1978), 47–52.

Lynn, Steven. "Reading the Writing Process: Toward a Theory of Current Pedagogies." *CE* 49 (December 1987), 902–10.

Macrorie, Ken. *Twenty Teachers*. New York: Oxford University Press, 1984.

———. *Uptaught*. Rochelle Park, NJ: Hayden, 1970.

Malinowitz, Harriet. *Textual Orientations: Lesbian and Gay Students and the Making of Discourse Communities*. Portsmouth, NH: Boynton/Cook, 1994.

Mann, Richard D., et al. *The College Classroom: Conflict, Change, and Learning.* New York: Wiley, 1970.

McCracken, Nancy Mellin, and Bruce C. Appleby, eds. *Gender Issues in the Teaching of English.* Portsmouth, NH: Boynton/Cook, 1992.

Mellon, John C. *Transformational Sentence-Combining: A Method for Enhancing the Development of Syntactic Fluency in English Composition.* NCTE Research Report No. 10. Champaign, IL: NCTE, 1967.

Moffett, James. *Coming on Center: Essays in English Education.* 2d ed. Portsmouth, NH: Boynton/Cook, 1988.

Moffett, James, and Betty Jane Wagner. *Student-Centered Language Arts and Reading: A Handbook for Teachers.* 4th ed. Portsmouth, NH: Boynton/Cook, 1991.

Murray, Donald M. *Learning by Teaching: Selected Articles on Writing and Teaching.* Portsmouth, NH: Boynton/Cook, 1982.

———. "The Listening Eye: Reflections on the Writing Conference." *CE* 41 (September 1979), 13–18.

———. *A Writer Teaches Writing.* 2d ed. Boston: Houghton Mifflin, 1985.

NCTE Commission on Composition. "Teaching Composition: A Position Statement." *CE* 46 (October 1984), 612–14.

NCTE and the International Reading Association. *Standards for the English Language Arts.* Urbana, IL: NCTE, 1996.

Newkirk, Thomas, ed. *Nuts and Bolts: A Practical Guide to Teaching College Composition.* Portsmouth, NH: Boynton/Cook, 1993.

O'Hare, Frank. *Sentence Combining: Improving Student Writing without Formal Grammar Instruction.* NCTE Research Report No. 15. Urbana, IL: NCTE, 1973.

Odell, Lee, ed. *Theory and Practice in the Teaching of Writing: Rethinking the Discipline.* Carbondale: Southern Illinois University Press, 1993.

Purdue University's Online Writing Lab (a site offering information about teaching writing and a collection of writing-related handouts). http://owl.english.purdue.edu (accessed 10 July 2000).

Race in the Classroom: A Multiplicity of Experience (a videocassette depicting five classroom vignettes in which race or culture become factors in teaching and learning). Produced by the Derek Bok Center, Harvard University, 1992. Distributed by Anker Publishing Company, Bolton, MA.

"Resources for Writers and Teachers." *The Writing Center at Colorado State University* (a collection of tutorials, writing guides, and links to writing and teaching resources). http://writing.colostate.edu/tools.htm (accessed 17 January 2001).

Rose, Mike. *Lives on the Boundary: The Struggles and Achievements of America's Underprepared.* New York: Free Press, 1989.

Ryan, Joseph P. "The Function and Format of a Course Syllabus." Unpublished faculty development material. University of South Carolina. Columbia, Fall 1978.

Severino, Carol, Juan C. Guerra, and Johnnella E. Butler, eds. *Writing in Multicultural Settings.* Research and Scholarship in Composition. New York: MLA, 1997.

Shaughnessy, Mina. "Diving In: An Introduction to Basic Writing." *CCC* 27 (October 1976), 234–39.

————. *Errors and Expectations: A Guide for the Teacher of Basic Writing.* New York: Oxford University Press, 1977.

Simmons, Jo An McGuire. "The One-to-One Method of Teaching Composition." *CCC* 35 (May 1984), 222–29.

Smagorinsky, Peter. *Standards in Practice, Grades 9–12.* Urbana, IL: NCTE, 1996.

Stewart, Donald C. "Composition Textbooks and the Assault on the Tradition." *CCC* 29 (May 1978), 171–76.

Stock, Patricia L., ed. *fforum: Essays on Theory and Practice in the Teaching of Writing.* Upper Montclair, NJ: Boynton/Cook, 1983.

Student Writing Groups: Demonstrating the Process (a videocassette illustrating a method whereby students read and respond to one another's writing). Produced in 1988 and distributed by Wordshop Productions, Inc. Tacoma, WA.

Tarvers, Josephine Koster. *Teaching in Progress: Theories, Practices, and Scenarios.* 2d ed. New York: Longman, 1998.

Tate, Gary, ed. *Teaching Composition: Twelve Bibliographical Essays.* Fort Worth: Texas Christian University Press, 1987.

Tchudi, Stephen, and Susan Tchudi. *The English/Language Arts Handbook: Classroom Strategies for Teachers.* 2d ed. Portsmouth, NH: Boynton/Cook, 1991.

Teaching Critical Thinking (seven videocassettes on teaching critical thinking through class discussion, course content, assignments, writing, reading, and collaborative activities). Produced by the Critical Literacy Project, Oakton Community College TV Service, 1993. Distributed by PBS Adult Learning Service, Alexandria, VA.

Tufts University's Teaching Reference Site (a clearinghouse with links to information about course design, instructional technology, and professional development). http://ase.tufts.edu/cte/pages/resource.htm (accessed 10 July 2000).

Walvoord, Barbara Fassler. *Helping Students Write Well: A Guide for Teachers in All Disciplines.* New York: MLA, 1982.

Williams, James D. *Preparing to Teach Writing: Research, Theory, and Practice.* 2d ed. Mahwah, NJ: Lawrence Erlbaum Associates, 1998.

Witte, Stephen P. Review of *Sentence Combining and the Teaching of Writing,* ed. Donald Daiker, Andrew Kerek, and Max Morenberg (Conway, AR: L & S Books, 1979). *CCC* 31 (December 1980), 433–37.

Yancey, Kathleen Blake, ed. *Voices on Voice.* Urbana, IL: NCTE, 1994.

Zemelman, Steven, and Harvey Daniels. *A Community of Writers.* Portsmouth, NH: Heinemann, 1988.

Zoellner, Robert. "A Behavioral Approach to Writing." *CE* 30 (January 1969), 267–320.

TEACHER PREPARATION

Bridges, Charles W., ed. *Training the New Teacher of College Composition.* Urbana, IL: NCTE, 1986.

Conference on College Composition and Communication. Task Force on the Preparation of Teachers of Writing. "Position Statement on the

Preparation and Professional Development of Teachers of Writing."
    CCC 33 (December 1982), 446–49.

Flanigan, Michael C. *Strategies in College Teaching* (four videocassettes
    designed to help faculty and graduate students improve their
    teaching). Produced by Indiana University Television, Bloomington,
    IN, 1976.

Gere, Anne Ruggles. "Teaching Writing Teachers: A Review." *CE* 47 (January
    1985), 58–65.

The Learning Space (a clearinghouse for information about professional
    development, grants, and other resources for teachers). http://
    www.learningspace.org (accessed 10 July 2000).

The Modern Language Association of America (the home page of a
    professional organization serving college teachers of English and
    foreign languages). http://www.mla.org (accessed 10 July 2000).

National Council for Teachers of English (the home page of a professional
    organization serving English teachers, providing links to teaching
    ideas, discussion lists, and other resources useful to teachers).
    http://www.ncte.org (accessed 20 July 2000).

The National Writing Project (a site providing professional development
    information and instructional resources primarily for secondary
    teachers of English language arts). http://www.writingproject.org
    (accessed 15 January 2001).

A Process-Centered Composition Program (a series of nine videocassettes used to
    train composition teachers). Produced by Indiana University
    Television, 1976. Distributed by Indiana University Instructional
    Support Services, Bloomington.

Smagorinsky, Peter, and Melissa E. Whiting. *How English Teachers Get Taught:
    Methods of Teaching the Methods Class.* Urbana, IL: NCTE, 1995.

CURRICULUM AND ACADEMIC PROGRAMS

Anson, Chris M., John E. Schwiebert, and Michael M. Williamson. *Writing
    across the Curriculum: An Annotated Bibliography.* Westport, CT:
    Greenwood Press, 1993.

Bartholomae, David, and Anthony Petrosky, eds. *Facts, Artifacts and
    Counterfacts: Theory and Method for a Reading and Writing Course.*
    Portsmouth, NH: Boynton/Cook, 1986.

Bazerman, Charles, and David R. Russell, eds. *Landmark Essays on Writing
    across the Curriculum.* Davis, CA: Hermagoras Press, 1994.

Coles, William E. *The Plural "I": The Teaching of Writing.* New York: Holt,
    Rinehart and Winston, 1978.

———. *Teaching Composing: A Guide to Teaching Writing as a Self-Creating
    Process.* Rochelle Park, NJ: Hayden, 1974.

Fulwiler, Toby. "How Well Does Writing across the Curriculum Work?" *CE*
    46 (February 1984), 113–25.

Fulwiler, Toby, and Art Young, eds. *Language Connections: Writing and Reading
    across the Curriculum.* Urbana, IL: NCTE, 1978.

———, eds. *Programs That Work: Models and Methods for Writing across the
    Curriculum.* Portsmouth, NH: Boynton/Cook, 1989.

Harkin, Patricia, and John Schilb, eds. *Contending with Words: Composition and Rhetoric in a Postmodern Age.* New York: MLA, 1991.

Huff, Roland, and Charles R. Kline, Jr. *The Contemporary Writing Curriculum: Rehearsing, Composing, and Valuing.* New York: Teachers College, Columbia University, 1987.

Jenkinson, Edward B., and Donald A. Seybold. *Writing as a Process of Discovery: Some Structured Theme Assignments for Grades Five through Twelve.* Bloomington: Indiana University Press, 1970.

Kinneavy, James L. "Writing across the Curriculum." In *Profession 83,* 13–20. New York: MLA, 1983.

Klaus, Carl H., and Nancy Jones. *Courses for Change in Writing.* Upper Montclair, NJ: Boynton/Cook, 1984.

Lindemann, Erika. "Three Views of English 101." *CE 57* (March 1995), 287–302.

Lunsford, Andrea A. "An Historical, Descriptive, and Evaluative Study of Remedial English in American Colleges and Universities." Ph.D. diss., The Ohio State University, 1977.

Moffett, James. *Active Voice: A Writing Program across the Curriculum.* 2d ed. Portsmouth, NH: Boynton/Cook, 1992.

Neel, Jasper P. *Options for the Teaching of English: Freshman Composition.* New York: MLA, 1978.

Olson, Gary A., ed. *Writing Centers: Theory and Administration.* Urbana, IL: NCTE, 1984.

Rose, Mike. "Remedial Writing Courses: A Critique and a Proposal." *CE 45* (February 1983), 109–28.

Young, Art, and Toby Fulwiler, eds. *Writing across the Disciplines: Research into Practice.* Upper Montclair, NJ: Boynton/Cook, 1986.

TECHNOLOGY

AltaVista (an Internet search engine that searches the entire text of Web documents). http://www.altavista.com (accessed 20 July 2000).

Anderson, Daniel. *Teaching Literature Online: A Guide to Teaching with Technology in the Literature Classroom.* New York: Longman, 1999.

Anderson, Daniel, Bret Benjamin, and Bill Paredes-Holt. *Connections: A Guide to Online Writing.* Boston: Allyn and Bacon, 1998.

Anderson, Daniel, Chris Busiel, Bret Benjamin, and Bill Paredes-Holt. *Teaching Online: Internet Research, Conversation, and Composition.* 2d ed. New York: HarperCollins, 1998.

Barker, Joe. *Finding Information on the Internet* (a guide to locating information using Web search engines). Mod. 18 July 2000. http://www.lib.berkeley.edu/TeachingLib/Guides/Internet/FindInfo.html (accessed 20 July 2000).

Baron, Dennis. "From Pencils to Pixels: The Stages of Literacy Technologies." In *Passions, Pedagogies and Twenty-First-Century Technologies,* edited by Gail E. Hawisher and Cynthia L. Selfe, 15–33. Logan: Utah State University Press, 1999.

Bolter, Jay David. *Writing Space: The Computer, Hypertext, and the History of Writing.* Hillsdale, NJ: Lawrence Erlbaum Associates, 1991.

Cooper, Marilyn M. "Postmodern Possibilities in Electronic Conversations." In *Passions, Pedagogies and Twenty-First-Century Technologies,* edited by Gail E. Hawisher and Cynthia L. Selfe, 140–60. Logan: Utah State University Press, 1999.

Copyright and Fair Use (a Web site providing guidance for instructors concerned about copyright issues). http://fairuse.stanford.edu (accessed 20 July 2000).

Corel Corporation. "WordPerfect 7 Tips and Tricks." *Corel Products* (a Web site providing online documentation and tips for using the WordPerfect word processor). http://www.corel.com/products/wordperfect/cwp7/tipsandt ricks/index.htm (accessed 20 July 2000).

Google (a Web search engine that sorts resources based on the number of Internet sites linked to them, resulting in searches that return relevant and well-received resources). http://www.google.com (accessed 20 July 2000).

Google's Usenet Archives (a searchable archive of newsgroup messages useful for investigating online communities). http://groups.google.com (accessed 20 March 2001).

GSC Online. *The Instructor's Guide to Internet Plagiarism* (a Web site offering information and online tools for locating and handling Internet plagiarism). http://www.plagiarized.com/index.shtml (accessed 20 July 2000).

"Harness E-mail." *Learn The Net* (a Web site offering introductory information and resources for learning about e-mail). http://www.learnthenet.com/english/section/email.html (accessed 20 July 2000).

Hawisher, Gail E., and Charles Moran. "The Rhetorics and Languages of E-mail." In *Page to Screen: Taking Literacy into the Electronic Era,* edited by Ilana Snyder and Michael Joyce, 80–101. London: Routledge, 1998.

Hawisher, Gail E., and Cynthia L. Selfe, eds. *Evolving Perspectives on Computers and Composition Studies.* Urbana, IL: NCTE, 1991.

———, eds. *Passions, Pedagogies, and Twenty-First-Century Technologies.* Logan: Utah State University Press, 1999.

———. "Reflections of Computers and Composition Studies." In *Page to Screen: Taking Literacy into the Electronic Era,* edited by Ilana Snyder and Michael Joyce, 3–19. London: Routledge, 1998.

Haynes, Cynthia, and Jan Rune Holmevik. *Lingua Moo* (the home page of an educational MOO that also provides information about and access to MOO software and other resources). http://lingua.utdallas.edu (accessed 15 July 2000).

Johnson-Eilola, Johndan. "Living on the Surface: Learning in the Age of Global Communication Networks." In *Page to Screen: Taking Literacy into the Electronic Era,* edited by Ilana Snyder and Michael Joyce, 185–210. London: Routledge, 1998.

Krause, Steve. "Word Processing Ideas." *Computer Teaching Tips: Simple Ideas for Teaching Writing and Reading in Computer Labs* (a Web page providing exercises that use word processors to teach writing skills, with links to pages suggesting other ways to use technology to support writing instruction). Mod. 1 April 2000. http://www.emunix.emich.edu/~krause/Tips/word.html (accessed 20 July 2000).

Landow, George P. *Hypertext 2.0: The Convergence of Contemporary Critical Theory and Technology.* Baltimore: Johns Hopkins University Press, 1997.

Microsoft Corporation. "Word 2000." *Microsoft in Education* (a Web site offering online documentation and suggestions for using the features of the Microsoft Word word processor). http://microsoft.com/education/tutorial/classroom/o2k/word.asp (accessed 20 July 2000).

Morgan, M. C. "Hands Off: Ten Techniques for Tutoring on Word Processors" (exercises for using word processors to teach writing as well as detailed explanations of issues involved in peer tutoring). http://cal.bemidji.msus.edu/English/Morgan/Docs/TenTechniques.html (accessed 20 July 2000).

Petroski, Henry. *The Evolution of Useful Things.* New York: Alfred A. Knopf, 1992.

ProjectCool (a Web site that offers a starting point for learning about Web composition and that treats basics to advanced design techniques). http://www.projectcool.com (accessed 20 July 2000).

SearchEngineWatch (a Web site offering strategies for successful online searches, explanations covering the logistics of keyword searches, and links to the latest search engines). http://www.searchenginewatch.com (accessed 20 July 2000).

Selfe, Cynthia L. *Technology and Literacy in the Twenty-First Century: The Importance of Paying Attention.* Studies in Writing and Rhetoric. Carbondale: Southern Illinois University Press, 1999.

Selfe, Cynthia L., and Susan Hilligoss, eds. *Literacy and Computers: The Complications of Teaching and Learning with Technology.* Research and Scholarship in Composition. New York: MLA, 1994.

Taylor, Todd, and Janice Walker. *The Columbia Guide to Online Style.* New York: Columbia University Press, 1998.

Taylor, Todd W., and Irene Ward, eds. *Literacy Theory in the Age of the Internet.* New York: Columbia University Press, 1998.

Technology and Rhetoric E-Mail Discussion Group (the home page of an online community devoted to discussing issues of teaching writing using technology). http://www.groups.yahoo.com/group/TechRhet (accessed 20 March 2001).

The Alliance for Computers and Writing (a site providing support for writing teachers seeking to incorporate technology into their teaching). http://english.ttu.edu/acw (accessed 10 July 2000).

The Studio for Instructional Technology and English Studies (a Web site for teachers at the University of North Carolina at Chapel Hill that offers assignment ideas, links to teaching materials, class sites, and other resources). http://sites.unc.edu (accessed 20 July 2000).

United States Department of Commerce. *Closing the Digital Divide* (a comprehensive Web site providing government information and links to additional resources discussing access to technology). http://www.digitaldivide.gov (accessed 20 July 2000).

Yahoo! (an Internet search engine that provides collections of resources organized by topic and additional services such as free e-mail accounts). http://yahoo.com (accessed 20 July 2000).

Yahoo! (a Web site allowing instructors to create e-mail discussion lists and other tools for collaborative work). http://groups.yahoo.com (accessed 20 March 2001).

PROFESSIONAL ISSUES

Conference on College Composition and Communication. "Statement of Principles and Standards for the Postsecondary Teaching of Writing." *CCC* 40 (October 1989), 329–36.

Elbow, Peter. *What Is English?* New York: MLA; Urbana, IL: NCTE, 1990.

Hairston, Maxine. "Breaking Our Bonds and Affirming Our Connections." *CCC* 36 (October 1985), 272–82.

Hook, J. N. *A Long Way Together: A Personal View of NCTE's First Sixty-Seven Years.* Urbana, IL: NCTE, 1979.

Lloyd-Jones, Richard, and Andrea A. Lunsford, eds. *The English Coalition Conference: Democracy through Language.* Urbana, IL: NCTE, 1989.

ASSESSMENT

Anderson, Daniel. *The Information Technology Skills Assessment and Tutorial* (a Web site providing tools for teachers wishing to assess their students' technology skills). http://sites.unc.edu/~itsat (accessed 20 July 2000).

Anson, Chris M., ed. *Writing and Response: Theory, Practice, and Research.* Urbana, IL: NCTE, 1989.

Bain, Robert A. "Reading Student Papers." *CCC* 25 (October 1974), 307–09.

Bartholomae, David. "The Study of Error." *CCC* 31 (October 1980), 253–69.

Beaven, Mary H. "Individualized Goal Setting, Self-Evaluation, and Peer Evaluation." In *Evaluating Writing: Describing, Measuring, Judging,* edited by Charles R. Cooper and Lee Odell, 135–56. Urbana, IL: NCTE, 1977.

Belanoff, Pat, and Marcia Dickson, eds. *Portfolios: Process and Product.* Portsmouth, NH: Boynton/Cook, 1991.

Black, Laurel, Donald A. Daiker, Jeffrey Sommers, and Gail Stygall, eds. *New Directions in Portfolio Assessment: Reflective Practice, Critical Theory, and Large-Scale Scoring.* Portsmouth, NH: Boynton/Cook, 1994.

Conference on College Composition and Communication. Committee on Teaching and Its Evaluation. "Evaluating Instruction in Composition: Approaches and Instruments." *CCC* 33 (May 1982), 213–29.

Conference on College Composition and Communication. "Resolution on Testing and Writing." Denver, Colorado. 1 April 1978.

Connors, Robert J., and Andrea A. Lunsford. "Teachers' Rhetorical Comments on Student Papers." *CCC* 44 (May 1993), 200–23.

Cooper, Charles R. "Responding to Student Writing." In *The Writing Processes of Students,* edited by Walter T. Petty and Patrick J. Finn, 31–39. Buffalo: State University of New York, 1975.

Cooper, Charles R., and Lee Odell, eds. *Evaluating Writing: Describing, Measuring, Judging.* Urbana, IL: NCTE, 1977.

———, eds. *Evaluating Writing: The Role of Teachers' Knowledge about Text, Learning, and Culture.* Urbana, IL: NCTE, 1998.

Diederich, Paul B. *Measuring Growth in English.* Urbana, IL: NCTE, 1974.

Elbow, Peter, and Pat Belanoff. *Sharing and Responding.* 3d ed. Boston: McGraw-Hill, 2000.

Flanigan, Michael C. "Observing Teaching: Discovering and Developing the Individual's Style." *Journal of the Council of Writing Program Administrators* 3 (Winter 1979), 17–24.

Freedman, Sarah Warshauer. *Response to Student Writing.* NCTE Research Report No. 23. Urbana, IL: NCTE, 1987.

Goodman, Kenneth. "Minimum Standards: A Moral View." In *Minimum Competency Standards: Three Points of View*, 3–5. N.P.: International Reading Association, 1978.

Hake, Rosemary L., and Joseph M. Williams. "Style and Its Consequences: Do as I Do, Not as I Say." *CE* 43 (September 1981), 433–51.

Horvath, Brooke. "The Components of Written Response: A Practical Synthesis of Current Views." *Rhetoric Review* 2 (January 1984), 136–56.

Knoblauch, C. H., and Lil Brannon. "Teacher Commentary on Student Writing: The State of the Art." *Freshman English News* 10 (Fall 1981), 1–4.

Kroll, Barry M., and John C. Shafer. "Error-Analysis and the Teaching of Composition." *CCC* 29 (October 1978), 242–48.

Larson, Richard L. *Evaluation of Teaching College English.* Urbana, IL: NCTE, 1970.

Lawson, Bruce, Susan Sterr Ryan, and W. Ross Winterowd, eds. *Encountering Student Texts: Interpretive Issues in Reading Student Writing.* Urbana, IL: NCTE, 1989.

Lees, Elaine O. "Evaluating Student Writing," *CCC* 30 (December 1979), 370–74.

NCTE Committee on Classroom Practices in Teaching English. *Classroom Practices in Teaching English 1979–1980: How to Handle the Paper Load.* Urbana, IL: NCTE, 1979.

NCTE Task Force on Measurement and Evaluation in the Study of English. *Common Sense and Testing in English.* Urbana, IL: NCTE, 1975.

Sommers, Nancy I. "Responding to Student Writing." *CCC* 32 (May 1982), 148–56.

Straub, Richard. "Teacher Response as Conversation: More than Casual Talk, an Exploration." *Rhetoric Review* 14 (1996), 374–98.

Straub, Richard, and Ronald F. Lunsford. *Twelve Readers Reading: Responding to College Student Writing.* Cresskill, NJ: Hampton, 1995.

Tchudi, Stephen, ed. *Alternatives to Grading Student Writing.* Urbana, IL: NCTE, 1997.

White, Edward M. *Assigning, Responding, Evaluating: A Writing Teacher's Guide.* 3d ed. Boston: Bedford/St. Martin's, 1999.

———. *Teaching and Assessing Writing.* 2d ed. The Jossey-Bass Higher Education Series. San Francisco: Jossey-Bass, 1994.

White, Edward M., William D. Lutz, and Sandra Kamusikiri, eds. *Assessment of Writing: Politics, Policies, Practices.* Research and Scholarship in Composition. New York: MLA, 1996.

Wiener, Harvey S. "Collaborative Learning in the Classroom: A Guide to Evaluation." *CE* 48 (January 1986), 52–61.

Witte, Stephen, and Lester Faigley. *Evaluating College Writing Programs.* Studies in Writing and Rhetoric. Carbondale: Southern Illinois University Press, 1983.

Yancey, Kathleen Blake, and Irwin Weiser, eds. *Situating Portfolios: Four Perspectives.* Logan: Utah State University Press, 1997.

TEXTBOOKS

Bain, Alexander. *English Composition and Rhetoric.* Enlarged ed. 2 vols. New York: American Book Company, n.d.

Baker, Sheridan. *The Practical Stylist.* 8th ed. New York: Addison-Wesley, 1998.

Beale, Walter, Karen Meyers, and Laurie White. *Stylistic Options: The Sentence and the Paragraph.* Glenview, IL: Scott, Foresman, 1982.

Burt, Forrest, ed. *The Effective Writer: A Freshman English Manual.* Boston: American Press, 1978.

Coe, Richard. *Process, Form, and Substance: A Rhetoric for Advanced Writers.* 2d ed. Englewood Cliffs, NJ: Prentice Hall, 1990.

Corbett, Edward P. J. *The Little Rhetoric and Handbook.* 2d ed. Glenview, IL: Scott, Foresman, 1982.

Corbett, Edward P. J., and Robert Connors. *Classical Rhetoric for the Modern Student.* 4th ed. New York: Oxford University Press, 1999.

D'Angelo, Frank. *Process and Thought in Composition.* 3d ed. Boston: Little, Brown, 1985.

Elbow, Peter. *Writing with Power: Techniques for Mastering the Writing Process.* New York: Oxford University Press, 1981.

———. *Writing without Teachers.* New York: Oxford University Press, 1973.

Hacker, Diana, and Betty Renshaw. *Writing with a Voice.* Boston: Little, Brown, 1985.

Hall, Donald, and Sven Birkerts. *Writing Well.* 9th ed. New York: Addison-Wesley, 1997.

Irmscher, William. *The Holt Guide to English.* Alternate ed. New York: Holt, Rinehart and Winston, 1985.

Lanham, Richard. *Revising Prose.* 4th ed. Boston: Allyn and Bacon, 2000.

———. *The Revising Prose Videotape* (a videocassette illustrating the revision process presented in Lanham's *Revising Prose).* Produced by the UCLA Office of Instructional Development, 1981. Distributed by Rhetorica, Inc., Los Angeles.

Macrorie, Ken. *The I-Search Paper.* Portsmouth, NH: Boynton/Cook, 1988.

———. *Telling Writing.* 4th ed. Upper Montclair, NJ: Boynton/Cook, 1985.

Mahaney, William E. *Workbook of Current English.* 2d ed. Glenview, IL: Scott, Foresman, 1981.

Morenberg, Max, Jeffrey Sommers, Donald Daiker, and Andrew Kerek. *The Writer's Options: Lessons in Style and Arrangement.* 6th ed. New York: Addison-Wesley Longman, 1999.

Neeld, Elizabeth Cowan. *Writing*. 3d ed. Glenview, IL: Scott, Foresman/Little, Brown, 1990.

Strong, William. *Sentence Combining and Paragraph Building*. New York: Random House, 1981.

Weathers, Winston, and Otis Winchester. *The New Strategy of Style*. 2d ed. New York: McGraw-Hill, 1978.

Whissen, Thomas. *A Way with Words*. New York: Oxford University Press, 1982.

Williams, Joseph P. *Style: Ten Lessons in Clarity and Grace*. 6th ed. New York: Addison-Wesley, 1999.

Williston, Glenn R. *Understanding the Main Idea, Middle Level*. Providence, RI: Jamestown Publishers, 1976.

Winterowd, W. Ross. *The Contemporary Writer: A Practical Rhetoric*. 2d ed. New York: Harcourt Brace Jovanovich, 1981.

Woods, William F. "Composition Textbooks and Pedagogical Theory, 1960–80." *CE* 43 (April 1981), 393–409.

Young, Richard E., Alton L. Becker, and Kenneth L. Pike. *Rhetoric: Discovery and Change*. New York: Harcourt, Brace and World, 1970.

Zinsser, William. *On Writing Well*. 6th ed. New York: HarperCollins, 1998.

Index